Outside *in the* Teaching Machine

Outside *in the* Teaching Machine

GAYATRI CHAKRAVORTY SPIVAK

Routledge•New York and London

Published in 1993 by

Published in Great Britain by

Routledge
29 West 35 Street
New York, NY 10001

Routledge
11 New Fetter Lane
London EC4P 4EE

The author gratefully acknowledges the permission of the journals and publishers that
follow to print here these essays in their revised form. *d i f f e r e n c e s,* a journal
of feminist cultural studies, for "In a word. *Interview*" (with Ellen Rooney), from vol.
1, no. 2 (summer 1989); SUNY Press, Albany, for "More on Power/Knowledge,"
from Thomas E. Wartenberg, ed., *Rethinking Power,* 1992; Polity Press, for
"Poststructuralism, Marginality, Postcoloniality and Value," from Peter Collier
and Helga Geyer-Ryan, eds., *Literary Theory Today,* 1990, and "The Politics of
Translation," from Michele Barrett and Anne Phillips, eds., *Destabilizing Theory:
Contemporary Feminist Debates,* 1992; *Cultural Critique,* for "Woman in Difference:
Mahasweta Devi's 'Douloti the Bountiful'," from no. XIV, winter 1989–90; *The Cardozo
Law Review,* for "Not Virgin Enough to Say That [S]he Occupies the Place of the
Other," from vol. XIII, no. iv (December 1991); The Dunlop Art Gallery, Regina,
Canada, for "Inscriptions: of Truth to Size," from the exhibition catalogue for
Inscription by Jamelie Hassan, 1990; *Public Culture,* for "Reading *The Satanic Verses*"
from vol. 2, no. 1 (Fall 1989); *Critical Quarterly,* for "In Praise of *Sammy and Rosie
Get Laid*" from no. 31.2 (Summer 1989); *Yale Journal of Law and the Humanities,* for
"Constitutions and Culture Studies," from vol. 2, no. 1 (Winter 1990); and *New
Literary History,* for "The Making of Americans, the Teaching of English, and the
Future of Culture Studies," from vol. XXI, no. iv, Autumn, 1990.

Printed in the United States of America on acid-free paper.

Library of Congress Cataloging-in-Publication Data

Spivak, Gayatri Chakravorty.
    Outside in the teaching machine / by Gayatri Chakravorty Spivak.
      p.   cm.
    Includes bibliographical references.
    ISBN 0-415-90488-9 (Cloth)—ISBN 0-415-90489-7 (Paper)
    1. Feminist literary criticism. 2. Women and literature.
I. Title.
PN98.W64S65   1993
809'.89287—dc20   93-13881
                                          CIP

PARES CHANDRA CHAKRAVORTY

Table of Contents

Foreword

In the last five years, we have seen an explosion of marginality studies in college and university teaching in the United States. In one way or another, all the pieces included in this book are part of that struggle. The lead piece, "In a Word," shows the shift in my work from a "strategic use of essentialism" to considerations of institutional agency that accompanied the explosion. Indeed, I was not aware of my strategic use of essentialism. I knew it in response to Elizabeth Grosz, a woman who cared enough to interview me.[1] And its revision also came as a response, to Ellen Rooney, a woman with whom I march in step. These essays, then, may be seen as interconnected attempts ("essays" in the old sense) at thinking through the shift from (anti-) essentialism to agency. I have preserved the fact that bits of them float into each other's boundaries. Five of the pieces were presented and published in a British context, one is on Canadian subject matter, but my own position as a U.S. academic seems clear to them. Such a caution emerges out of my conviction that, as the margin or "outside" enters an institution or teaching machine, what *kind* of teaching machine it enters will determine its contours. Therefore the struggle continues, in different ways, after the infiltration.

The joker in the pack is "Limits and Openings of Marx in Derrida." I am a feminist much marked by Derrida's work. This fact has drawn peculiar responses. Janet Todd has described me as "an early apologist for Derrida" in *Feminist Literary History*.[2] Deborah Mitchell has recently remarked: Spivak "has published the authoritative translation of Derrida's *On* [sic] *Grammatology*. But the rest of her oeuvre is considered less impressive."[3] Yet, as Russell Berman has noted: "Spivak's position is one that the deconstructive establishment has attempted to marginalize."[4] "Limits and Openings," spoken in a shorter version at the first ten-day Derrida symposium at Cérisy-la-Salle in 1980, reflected a Marxist outsider's impatience in the bosom of that establishment, European style. Further development of that (always respectful) impatience will be found in "Identity as Wound and the Tearing of Time: Djebar and Derrida," in *Identity Talk,* forthcoming with Routledge.

I have arranged the essays in loose groupings. Two essays focus on Foucault. I have long held that in the arena of decolonization proper, the call to a complete boycott of so-called Western male theories is class-interested and dangerous. For me, the agenda has been to stake out the theories' limits, constructively to use them. Three essays focus on Derrida. As I have repeatedly acknowledged, all my work is a forcing of deconstruction(s) into "an impure, contaminating, negotiated, bastard and violent . . . filiation . . ."[5] Those three pieces work out the limits of that enterprise. The rest relates to the responsibility of the academic/intellectual/artistic hybrid. The final section is resolutely U.S. I hope it will seem merely predictable to my readers if I close with the brief statement that these days my thoughts turn more and more to the (im)possibility of Culture Studies.

New York   Gayatri Chakravorty Spivak
February 1993

1

In a Word: *Interview*

Ellen Rooney   *To undertake to place contemporary debates on essentialism in "context" is perhaps already to take sides in the controversy those debates have engendered. In some lexicons, at least, context is an anti-essentialist slogan; to contextualize is to expose the history of what might otherwise seem outside history, natural and thus universal, that is, the essence.*

As an idiom, "in a word" signals a moment of compressed and magically adequate expression. To summarize a matter "in a word" is to locate or hit upon its proper form, to capture its essential quality, and thus to say all that need be said. The problem of essentialism can be thought, in this way, as a problem of form, which is to say, a problem of reading. Context would thus emerge as a synonym for reading, in that to read is to demarcate a context. Essentialism appears as a certain resistance to reading, an emphasis on the constraints of form, the limits at which a particular form so compels us as to "stipulate" an analysis.

In "Rape and the Rise of the Novel," Frances Ferguson glosses stipulation as "trying to put a limit to ambiguity by defining the understanding of a term or a situation" (109); to put it in a word, perhaps. She argues that the "intense formality of the law of rape seems designed to substitute the reliability of invariable formulae for the manipulable terms of psychological states" (95); these "invariable formulae" ("rape," in a word) serve to foreclose the question of consent and to define rape in terms compatible with phallocentrism. For the law and for some feminists as well, the victim's "body is thus converted into evidence, having become [a] text" (91). But while the body is formally legible, individual psychological states, specifically concerning consent and its absence, go unread. In a phallocentric context, this "intense formality" functions to exclude the victims entirely from the definition of rape; for example, "for ancient Hebrew law, the act of sex carries with it the inevitability of consent. For Brownmiller and Dworkin, it carries with it the impossibility of consent."

1

The significance of form is thus stipulated in advance, an effect of the morphology of the body. Context is swallowed whole, and women, as subjects, disappear with it, absorbed entirely into their bodies.[1]

The body is of course essentialism's great text: to read in its form the essence of Woman is certainly one of phallocentrism's strategies; to insist that the body too is materially woven into social (con)texts is anti-essentialism's reply. But feminism's persistent return to the body is only in part a rejoinder to the resilience of anti-feminism's essentialism. Caught between those who simply "read off" the body and those who take its ineluctable power to be a fragmentary social relation is the feminist who speaks "as a woman."

Feminisms return to the problem of essentialism—despite their shared distaste for the mystifications of Woman—because it remains difficult to engage in feminist analysis and politics if not "as a woman." Within every feminist reading practice, for example, essentialism appears as a problem both of the text and of the critic who reads "as a woman." Elizabeth Spelman calls this phrase the "Trojan horse of feminist ethnocentrism," inevitably dissembling the differences among women (x). The body can figure here as a trump card, seeming literally to embody the womanness of woman, obscuring the fact that "only at times will the body impose itself or be arranged as that of a woman or a man."[2] *We seem to desire that what unites us (as feminists) preexist our desire to be joined; something that stands outside our own alliances may authorize them and empower us to speak not simply as feminists but as women, not least against women whose political work is elsewhere. In the U.S., this is an old dream of "nonpartisanship" at the heart of politics, as well as what Donna Haraway calls "the feminist dream of a common language . . . a perfectly faithful naming of experience." In a word.*[3]

Yet simply to label this political dream of women essentialism is to layer another political refusal over the rifts among us. The word essentialism can also work to conceal political divisions among women, insofar as it represents them as purely theoretical, questions of enlightenment. Political failures, if it be a failure not to unite all women under a single banner, are read as wholly intellectual failures—easily corrected. The original evasion is repeated; political difference is reduced to a matter of bad form, in a word, to essentialism.

In reading the body, to find "woman"; in "women," to secure feminism; to capture in a word the essence of a thing: essentialism is a dream of the end of politics among women, of a formal resolution to the discontinuity between women and feminisms. Antiessentialism may mimic this formalism, even as it seeks to diagnose it. Gayatri Spivak suggests—by

*turning repeatedly to the question of the word: which word to choose?
to what end?—another reading.*

ER   As you know, some current discussions of the topic of essentialism
have resulted in calls for a new willingness to take the "risk of essentialism," and these calls include citations from some of your most recent
remarks. I'm thinking here of Alice Jardine's comment in *Men in Feminism*
that "one of the most thought-provoking statements of recent date by a
feminist theorist [is] Gayatri Spivak's suggestion (echoing Heath) that
women today may *have* to take 'the risk of essence' in order to think
really differently,"[4] or of Bruce Robbins's interview with Edward Said,
where Robbins asks: "One idea that has been much repeated in conversa-
tions about intellectuals and their relation to collectivity, especially among
feminists, is the necessity to accept 'the risk of essence,' a phrase associated
with Gayatri Spivak and Stephen Heath. Does it seem at all generalizable
or useful in the case of the Palestinians?"[5]

You've examined the question of essentialism throughout your work,
and you've said a number of different things about it, at times warning
against defining women in terms of woman's putative essence and stress-
ing the possibility that essentialism may be a trap, and, at other times,
most recently in working on the text of the Subaltern Studies Group,
talking about the "*strategic* use of a positivist essentialism in a scrupulously visible political interest." I'd like to talk about the necessary risks
of taking what may seem to be essentialist positions; about how we can
signal the difference between a strategic and a substantive or a real
essentialism; about the possibility of mobilizing people to do political
work without invoking some irreducible essentialism; ultimately, how we
can determine when our essentializing strategies have become traps, as
opposed to having strategic and necessary positive effects?[6]

GS   Strategy works through a persistent (de)constructive critique of
the theoretical. "Strategy" is an embattled concept-metaphor and unlike
"theory," its antecedents are not disinterested and universal. "Usually,
an artifice or trick designed to outwit or surprise the enemy" (*Oxford
English Dictionary*).

The critical moment does not come only at a certain stage when one
sees one's effort succeeding. It is not only in that moment of euphoria
that we begin to decide that we had been strategic all along. The strategic
use of an essence as a mobilizing slogan or masterword like *woman* or
worker or the name of a nation is, ideally, self-conscious for all mobilized.
This is the impossible risk of a lasting strategy. Can there be such a thing?
At any rate, the critique of the "fetish-character" (so to speak) of the

masterword has to be persistent all along the way, even when it seems that to remind oneself of it is counterproductive. Otherwise the strategy freezes into something like what you call an essentialist position, when the situation that calls forth the strategy is seemingly resolved. The Subaltern Studies Group started working as a countermovement within South Asian history as written even by politically correct historians trying, among other things, to fabricate a national identity in decolonization: a different structural position from someone working from within the U.S. university. If one is considering strategy, one has to look at where the group—the person, the persons, or the movement—is situated when one makes claims for or against essentialism. A strategy suits a situation; a strategy is not a theory. And if one is considering "positivism," one might take into account the importance of positivism in the discipline of history in the nineteenth century.[7]

Within mainstream U.S. feminism the good insistence that "the personal is political" often transformed itself into something like "*only* the personal is political." The strategic use of essentialism can turn into an alibi for proselytizing academic essentialisms. The emphasis then inevitably falls on being able to speak from one's own ground, rather than matching the trick to the situation, that the word strategy implies. Given the collaboration between techniques of knowledge and structures of enablement, better I think to look for the bigger problem: that strategies are taught as if they were theories, good for all cases. One has to be careful to see that they do not misfire for people who do not resemble us and do not share the situation of prominent U.S. universities and colleges.

ER   Could I ask one further thing? When you spoke just then about noting our own essentialism, that sounded to me as if it were a reassertion of the need for the critique of essentialism. I think your description of the way in which your remark has been taken up in discourses that are produced from sites of influence and power is absolutely true. And the marking of the critical moment—what you call the strategic moment—is erased. What's reasserted then is actually the need for a kind of naïveté in the assertion of personal identity.

GS   Identity is a very different word from essence. We "write" a running biography with life-language rather than only word-language in order to "be." Call this identity! Deconstruction, whatever it may be, is not most valuably an exposure of error, certainly not other people's error, other people's essentialism. The most serious critique in deconstruction is the critique of things that are extremely useful, things without which we cannot live on, take chances; like our running self-identikit. That should be the approach to how we are essentialists.

A young man who knew Nietzsche better than he knew anything else thought that I was claiming that Derrida was "a poor man's Nietzsche." Isn't that the way many people read Derrida? If you knew Heidegger best, he would seem to be a poor man's Heidegger; if you knew Plato best, he would seem to be a poor man's Plato, and if a feminist, a rich woman's feminist? Perhaps what I'm saying here is that Derrida is a poor man's Althusser. In Althusser's naively powerful essay, "Marxism and Humanism," he writes that merely knowing an ideology does not dissipate its effect.[8] One of Derrida's most scandalous contributions is to begin with what is very familiar in many radical positions and to take it with the utmost seriousness, with literal seriousness, so that it questions the position (de)constructively as the wholly intimate other. One is left with the useful yet semimournful position of the unavoidable usefulness of something that is dangerous. Those might be the lineaments of the deconstructive critique of essence.

I have, then, reconsidered my cry for a strategic use of essentialism. In a personalist culture, even among people within the humanities, who are generally wordsmiths, it's the idea of a *strategy* that has been forgotten. The strategic has been taken as a point of self-differentiation from the poor essentialists. So long as the critique of essentialism is understood not as an exposure of error, our own or others', but as an acknowledgment of the dangerousness of something one cannot not use. I would stand by it as one stand among many. The critique of essentialism should not be seen as being critical in the colloquial, Anglo-American sense of being adversely inclined, but as a critique in the robust European philosophical sense.

ER   Could we pick up on the reference that you have made to deconstruction and talk about what you have called "the greatest gift of deconstruction: to question the authority of the investigating subject without paralyzing him, persistently transforming conditions of impossibility into possibility."[9] I think that one of the things that's most striking about your arguments about essentialism and about your work generally is the way you both assert the importance of positionality and refuse to essentialize it. How much would you say that your general thinking about essentialism is shaped by your conceptualization and your own practice of self-positioning or self-identification? What kind of relationship is there between the broad project to deconstruct—in the very precise sense that you were just invoking—identity, not to refuse identity but to deconstruct identity (a project you've participated in) and your own frequent concern to identify yourself, to position yourself, to refuse what you have pointed to most recently in "Can the Subaltern Speak?" as a tendency on the part of supposed critics of essentialism to make their own positions transparent and unproblematic?

GS   Assuming that there is such a thing as *the* story of a life (about which more later), it would sound rather different from all the other tellings about oneself that one engaged in. I believe that the way to save oneself from either objective, disinterested positioning or the attitude of there being no author (and these two opposed positions legitimize each other), or yet *the* story of one's life, is to "recognize" oneself as also an instantiation of historical and psychosexual narratives that one can piece together, however fragmentarily, in order to do deontological work in the humanities. When one represents oneself in such a way, it becomes, curiously enough, a deidentification of oneself, a claiming of an identity from a text that comes from somewhere else. I can compare this to the Derridean insight about the mother tongue that I discuss in Chapter Three: a mother tongue is something that has a history before we are born. We are inserted into it; it has the possibility of being activated by what can be colloquially called motives. Therefore, although it's unmotivated it's not capricious. We are inserted into it, and, without intent, we "make it our own." We intend within it; we critique intentions within it; we play with it through signification as well as reference; and then we leave it, as much without intent, for the use of others after our deaths. To an extent, the way in which one conceives of oneself as representative or as an example of something is this awareness that what is one's own, one's identity, what is proper to one, is also a biography, and has a history. That history is unmotivated but not capricious and is larger in outline than we are. This is different from the idea of talking about oneself. I have come to feel this more fully through the writings of Assia Djebar, the Algerian novelist. In *Anti-Oedipus,* Deleuze and Guattari talk about the way in which a socius is produced and then becomes a "miraculating" agency operating like a quasi cause.[10] The example they use is Capital, but in fact, culture, ethnos, sexuality, all of these things become miraculating agencies as if by a miracle one speaks as an agent of a culture or an agent of a sex or an agent of an ethnos et cetera . . . . A body without organs (necessary postsupposition of any sphere of agency?), has inscribed on its recording surface this miraculating agency, which seems like a quasi cause. What your re-cognize, or graph (a second time, something supposedly having *preexisted*) as representing, what your self represents, is that kind of a miraculating agency, a history, a culture, a position, an institutional position. But, via that persistent critique that I was talking about, you may be aware that this is miraculating you as you speak, rather than that you are speaking in unmediated identity. Of *course* that awareness is always beside, before, after the point, but that's life. The essence of life. These are uses of essence which you cannot go around. You are written into these uses of essence. This is the strategy by which history plays you, your language plays you, whatever the miraculating agency might be speaks you. It's not a question of choosing the strategy. You are, to an extent, distanced from it with humility and respect when you "build for difference."

ER   Yes, and given what you have said in response both to that question and another, I'd like actually to skip to some things I thought we would talk about later, namely, why has antiessentialism been so powerful in the way you were just referring to, as a kind of term of abuse, and how important are the questions of the disciplines, the institutional constraints of the U.S. academy, and the interventions of cross- or counterdisciplinary discourses like women's studies or area studies? What is the purchase the essentialism debate has on the academy? How does its inflection differ from discipline to discipline? Is antiessentialism an effect of anti-disciplinary or cross-disciplinary work? Within feminism and within some other discourses, essentialism seems to be a kind of blind spot that won't go away. It hasn't, by and large, been historicized or related to the history of high philosophical essentialisms, but has been invoked to distance and disallow certain kinds of discourses. Why hasn't the response to that been a kind of philosophical essentialism that fights back, that resists this abuse, and the ahistorical and in some ways not very informed use of the word essentialism?

GS   And why there hasn't been a philosophical essentialism?

ER   In response, yes.

GS   Because essentialism is a loose-tongued phrase, not a philosophical school. It is used by nonphilosophers simply to mean all kinds of things when they don't know what other word to use. In disciplinary philosophy, Hilary Putnam, Nelson Goodman, et al. seem to be coping with the problem of the irreducibility of the mediation of the real without influencing the "essentialism debate." And they don't sound like poststructuralist feminists. In fact, when the question of essences is philosophically considered it doesn't seem very sexy. For example, nonfoundationalist ethics, which from the analytic ground cannot proceed very far: let us say, the work of a Thomas Nagel, or the more interesting work of a Bernard Williams. Nonfoundationalist moral philosophy doesn't look a bit like antiessentialism outside of philosophy. The question of antiessentialism and essentialism is not a philosophical question as such. Is essentialism a code word for a feeling for the empirical, sometimes? Even as antiessentialism is sometimes no more than an emphasis on the social? Why is the thought of the social free of essences? To worry about such distinctions too much might keep us from infiltrating the knowledge venture of imperialism, which was absolutely spectacular and which still holds institutional power—the establishment of anthropology, comparative literature, comparative philology, comparative religion, world history, et cetera: Eurocentric crossculturalism, and that's what we are, in fact, looking at, watered down and diluted in the house of a so-called interdisciplinary antiessentialism in the humanities and the social sciences. If these still dominate the techniques of knowledge, round about them is the operation of the structures of enablement, often tedious institutional skirmishes. If one establishes an interdisciplinary space which does not engage with this most important arena (a silent, unemphatic arena) of warring power in the disciplines themselves, where the people who don't publish much, who don't teach very well, engage day after day, with distribution requirements, let us say; if one doesn't budge them and consolidate ways of gathering the empirical, antiessentialism versus essentialism can prove a red herring.

ER   Your invocations of the knowledge venture and the philosophical discussion of the irreducibility of the essences reminds me of a passage from "A Literary Representation of the Subaltern," which speaks, I think, to the relationship between essentialism and the production of knowledge. It's one of your takes on the argument that "only a native can know the scene" and you say:

> The position that only the subaltern can know the subaltern, only women can know women, and so on, cannot be held as a theoretical presupposition either, for it predicates the possibility of knowledge on identity. Whatever the political necessity for holding the position, and whatever the advisability of attempting to "identify" (with) the other as subject in order to know her, knowledge is made possible and is sustained by irreducible difference, not identity. What is known is always in excess of knowledge. Knowledge is never adequate to its object. The theoretical model of the ideal knower in the embattled position we are discussing is that of the person identical with her predicament. This is actually the figure of the impossibility and non-necessity of knowledge. Here the relationship between the practical—need for claiming subaltern identity—and the theoretical—no program of knowledge production can presuppose identity, as origin—is, once again, of an "interruption" that persistently brings each term to crisis.[11]

This passage touches upon a number of issues I'd like to talk about: the first is deconstruction and what it's taught us about identity and difference, the proper and reading and their relationship to the production of knowledge. How would you say your interest in deconstruction has fed your thinking about essentialism? What's the importance of deconstruction in dismantling essentialism? How are essentialism and antiessentialism related in Derrida's text?

GS   In terms of the first bit that you read, there is the further problem of "clinging to marginality." The trend speed in post-Fordist capitalism is superfast, and it is a truism to point out that tertiary education in the United States is run like the general economy, nearly 4,000 degree-granting institutions, impossible telematic contact. Unless you have worked within other systems with equally intelligent colleagues and students, you don't realize how much some of the dogma on antiessentialism has been picked up by this political and economic structure. In the last decade, some of the "clinging to marginality" is being fabricated so that the upwardly mobile, benevolent student (the college is an institution of upward mobility; it would be ridiculous to deny that), the *so-called* marginal student, claiming validation, is being taught (because we don't have the sense of strategy that I was speaking of, what was good in strategy has now become a slogan, and we don't look at the years passing, the situation changing) speaking for oneself, which is then, in fact, working precisely to contain the ones whom this person is supposed to represent. In other words, the miraculation is working as if it truly is a miracle, an academic miracle. Mariah speaks for Lucy as *Lucy* is taught in a too-benevolent class:

> "I was looking forward to telling you that I have Indian blood, that the reason I'm so good at catching fish and hunting birds and roasting corn and doing all sorts of things is that I have Indian blood. But now, I don't know why, I feel I shouldn't tell you that. I feel you will take it the wrong way."
>
> This really surprised me. What way should I take this? Wrong way? Right way? What could she mean? To look at her, there was nothing remotely like an Indian about her. Why claim a thing like that? I myself had Indian blood in me. The Carib Indians were good sailors, but I don't like the sea; I only like to look at it. To me my grandmother is only a grandmother, not an Indian. My grandmother is alive; the Indians she comes from are all dead. If someone could get away with it, I am sure they would put my grandmother in a museum, as an example of something now extinct in nature, one of a handful still alive.

In fact, one of the museums to which Mariah had taken me devoted a whole section to people, all dead, who were more or less related to my grandmother.

Mariah says, "I have Indian blood in me," and underneath everything I could swear she says it as if she were announcing her possession of a trophy. How do you get to be the sort of victor who can claim to be the vanquished also?[12]

Why should deconstruction "dismantle" essentialism? Deconstruction considers that the subject always tends toward centering and looks at the mechanism of centering among randomness; it doesn't say there *is* something called the decentered subject. When I say this, one rejoinder I often hear is: "Well, you just centered the subject in Derrida."[13] To think about the danger of what *is* useful, is not to think that the dangerous thing doesn't exist. The former is the lesson of deconstruction for me. Thus does deconstruction teach me about the impossibility of antiessentialism. It teaches me something about essentialisms being among the conditions of the production of doing, knowing, being, but does not give me a clue to the real. The real in deconstruction is neither essentialist nor antiessentialist. It invites us to think through the counterintuitive position that there might be essences and there might not be essences. A "poor man's" agnosticism, all right? "Poor man's" there means to take literally, trivially, what is implicit in the radical moment. Deconstruction is not an essence. It is not a school of thought; it is a way of rereading. Deconstruction itself can lead to an essentialism. *Enlightened Absence* is an example, I think, of essentialist, humanist, deconstructivist feminism.[14] I think it can certainly become a viewpoint in deconstruction, a description of what it is to be feminine, how the antiessential feminine is the essence of the feminine.

ER   Moving in the other direction, off the same passage, and this is related to what you were saying earlier about how one talks about oneself: can you talk about your own history, or the trajectory of your own work, your earliest intellectual and political history, and its impact on your thinking about essentialism? Is your recent work and its partial focus on the problem of essentialism a reinscription of earlier concerns, concerns that perhaps predate your work on Derrida?

GS   One of the lessons learned early for a child in a colonial context, who comes from a background which has the full share of the ambivalence toward the culture of imperialism, is related to the fact that the native language operated very strongly in my part of India. Linguistic subnationalist essentialism informed the public and the private. In school, however, most of my teachers were tribal Christians. A caste Hindu child, secure within her native language, hegemonic Calcutta Bengali, being taught by tribal Christians, who were converted to Christianity from "below," from "outside" the recognized religions of India. They were not Christianized, they *became* Christians. I still cannot think about my school days without an immense sense of gratitude to my parents for having thought to send me to such a school rather than to a more fashionable "Western" school or a less fashionable "native" school. In a situation like that, one begins to realize without realizing the extraordinary plurality of the source of enlightenment; in the very long haul, the general sources of our enlightenment were our race enemies. On the other hand, my direct teachers, who were not coreligionist, who were castewise lower, even outcastes, and yet my teachers, respected teachers, were Christians. Yet Christianity was also the religion of the hardly departed rulers. The sense of what a division there is in one's own making came early.

After independence, the idea of internationalism was under fire from the national party. The lines between socialist internationalism and the fabrication of national identity were finessed by the left in the era of the Third International. Forty years later, thirty years later, graphing one's bio, if one is asked why there is some sympathy for that word that I don't like—antiessentialism—in one's make-up, those are the things that one still thinks of. This indeed is the "experience" of the planned emergence into postcoloniality by a middle-class child in that part of India. The word *experience* is for me as mysterious as the mother tongue, something one is inserted in, self-representation, for example, antimiraculation. . . . That experience makes the strongest bond and also produces the greatest impatience with antiessentialism as a battle cry.

ER   Your reference to the left suggests another way of asking a question similar to the one I asked about deconstruction, a question about Marxism. That is, how has your interest in and your work on Marx influenced your thinking about essentialism? How does that Marxist tradition of antiessentialism fit into your own practice and thinking? Could you talk about a dynamic of essentialism and antiessentialism within Marxism?

GS   In Marx it is the slow discovery of the importance of the question of value that has opened up a lot of things for me. In Marx there is a strong sense that all ontopolitical commitments (just as in our neck of the woods, all ontocultural commitments), that is to say, ontological commitments to political beings, historical agents, should be seen as negotiable, in terms of the coding of value.

I would draw your attention most strongly to, let's say, "The Trinity Formula" in *Capital,* volume 3, where Marx is mocking the idea that

there is anything—in your own terms—essential about specific class formations.[15] And then also the final unfinished chapter on class. Unfortunately, the "Englishing" of Marx obliterated the trace of the counterintuitive nature of Marx's exhortation to his implied reader—the worker.
The worker has to be counter-intuitive in order to realize that he is the
agent rather than the victim of Capital. The entire idea of agency is
structurally negotiable.

The negotiability of commitment and the elusiveness of value are not
popular ideas among Marxists. Marx calls the value-form "contentless
and simple" (*inhaltlos und einfach*). The English translation is "slight in
content."[16] There is a difference. Value is contentless yet not pure form.
Marx is talking about something that cannot appear but must be presupposed to grasp the mechanics of the production of the world. It's the
possibility of the possibility of mediation as it were, which establishes
exchange, its appropriation and extraction as surplus and so on. This way
of understanding Marx's project would not underestimate the importance
of class, but would not see it as a trafficking in ineluctable essences.

ER   Could we move, then, to the relationship between the current
and growing interest in materials from the so-called "third world" and
essentialism? Is there a perception of a strategically essentialist moment
that's located "out there" in the "third world," perhaps in the form of
liberation struggles, which is related to the renewed interest, specifically
among U.S. critics and scholars, in essentialism and in that—that benevolent, as you have called it, but problematic—desire for translations of
"third world" texts and the production of new forms of knowledge about
a "third world" which is also often rendered monolithically, both within
feminism and outside of feminism? How much of the difficulty that
academics in the U.S. have avoiding certain essentialist traps has to do
with the displacement of questions of race and ethnicity into this monolithic and safely distanced "third world" and the consequent effacement
of imperialism as such?

GS   It works both ways. You displace it into the third world, but, on
the other hand, you again reconstruct the third world as people of color
and marginalized people *in* the United States. These migrant communities
become more real than the "original" cultures, to the great irritation of
the activists as well as the intellectual elites in the "original" cultures, for
different kinds of reason. The concept of "decolonization" begins to
combat only internal colonization in the first world. Between two texts
like Frobel Folker's *The New International Division of Labour* and Nigel
Harris's *The End of the Third World*, there is a decade.[17] And then
read Chakravarthi Raghavan's *Recolonization*—published last year, but

already out of date with the break up of the U.S.S.R.[18] Plans for a very definite new economic program, after the Second World War and the accompanying change in global outlines, have now been scrapped. To use that as a culturalist description seems rather shabby. If the "third world" is used as a mobilizing slogan for the developing nations, that's fine, but that is rather different from essentialism. That is in response to specific policies of exploitation. In the arenas where this language is seriously used, each country comes asserting its difference. They really do know it's strategic. That is a strategy that changes moment to moment, and they in fact come asserting their differences as they use the mobilized unity to do some specific thing. I think one might keep that as a reminder.

On the ground of cultural politics as well, the third world and, today, the ruins of the second world are postcolonial worlds only in a highly diversified way. Consider, for example, the idea that magical realism is the paradigmatic style of the third world. What is the hidden ethical, political agenda behind claiming that a style practiced most spectacularly by some writers in that part of the third world which relates most intimately to the United States, namely Latin America (just as India used to relate to Britain), is paradigmatic of a space which is trying to cope with the problem of narrativizing decolonization? In Latin American space, one of the things that cannot be narrativized is decolonization, as the Ariel-Caliban debate and today's intimate involvement with the U.S. have clearly articulated for us.[19]

One might, then, look at the larger third world as diversely postcolonial, making catachrestic claims. . . . Political claims are not to ethnicity, that's ministries of culture. The political claims over which battles are being fought are to nationhood, sovereignty, citizenship, secularism. Those claims are catachrestic claims in the sense that the so-called adequate narratives of the concept-metaphors were supposedly not written in the spaces that have decolonized themselves, but rather in the spaces of the colonizers. There the question of essences becomes the question of regulative political concepts. I don't think about essentialism or anti-essentialism when I look at what's going on in the third world and now the new second. I see either block unity, highly strategic in the strictest political sense, or these catachrestic claims negotiating questions like national language, nationhood, citizenship. Ethnicity and religion are negotiable signifiers in these fast-moving articulations. The question of essence is one of the players on this catachrestic chessboard.

One could look at it another way, as well. Capital is antiessentializing because it is the abstract as such. The essence of nations, cultures, et cetera, are deployed by capital*isms* for the political management of capital. The "politics of overdetermination" is the newest Anglo-U.S.-E.E.C. twist in that management, offering the idea of an antiessentialist multiplicity of agents. "The agent" cannot "be" overdetermined, you know. In order to consolidate the abstraction of agency overdetermination must *effectively* operate as condensation. These admirers of psychoanalysis trivialize it by equating it with deliberate psychodrama as a blueprint for social justice: traffic in antiessentialist essences.

ER   I take the force of your point, that when you think about the third world, especially politically, the problem of essentialism doesn't arise. But in what you have written, for example, about the Subaltern Studies Group, their practice, and their pursuit of an essential category or definition. . .

GS   . . . subaltern consciousness . . .

ER   . . . you describe a certain kind of project: they produce, in the process that you unpack, an antiessentialist encounter with radical textuality, I think that is the way you put it.

GS   Yes.

ER   That was part of what my question was directed at, the way in which your work on that group's work has gotten, at least in some ways, articulated in terms of the debate around essentialism and antiessentialism.

GS   Initially, my intervention made some members uncomfortable. I think I turned out to be more . . . well, I will use your word, antiessentialist . . .

ER   . . . in quotation marks . . .

GS   . . . than they had figured. They are, however, a volatile and singularly unmalicious group, so these differences are getting ironed out on both sides. I have a lot to learn from them. I do not monumentalize them. They are not a group of "third world" historians who are just wonderful and correctly strategically essentialist, et cetera. I think some of them had more invested in the subaltern consciousness than I had thought when I was welcomed in the group. But these are the breaks for a persistent critique. Most deconstructivists think the position too vulgar; most Marxists too elitist, too much in love with Parisian fads; many feminists, mainstream feminists, are beginning to feel that the position is somehow antifeminist. Outside in every machine! Perhaps for the Subaltern Studies Group, I am, occasionally, too much of a U.S. antiessentialist! I *am* one of the subalternists; I don't work *on* them. But they taught me to ask questions that I hadn't thought of myself. I'm against their grain as I am against the grain of the antiessentialist. But they taught me to ask questions that I hadn't thought of myself.

ER You have made several references to the problem of theory, whether it's Marxists accusing you of being too attached . . .

GS Not accusing—thinking of me.

ER Thinking of you . . .

GS I'm not so important that people are accusing me. . . . One of the subalternists did indeed accuse me of various things, but I've written about that in my book.

ER (laughing) Okay . . .

GS But that's an exception—no, when they think of me they think . . .

ER (laughter)

GS If my name comes up, let's put it that way . . .

ER (laughing) Okay . . . in any case, there is one reading of essentialism in the U.S. context that suggests that it tends to be empirical, that it's a kind of a practical rather than a theorized essentialism, or that it's essentialism by default. I wonder what you think of that reading, and that would return me to an earlier question about the absence of a kind of a philosophical rejoinder to antiessentialism. We've already talked about that, but I wonder if you think it's possible at present to construct a kind of self-consciously theorized essentialism, or if there would be any point in even trying to do that. There are, of course, discourses perhaps in the biological or the genetic sciences that seem to be seeking to isolate universal or essential human traits. Is the reductiveness that tends to characterize those kinds of moves a primary strategy of essentialism? Do those kinds of reductions go against the grain or against the disciplinary prejudices and investments of literary and philosophical discourse and thus disable a substantive theoretical essentialism in the debate?

GS Now, sociobiology, cognitive studies, artificial intelligence, which take something as the ground, they are exaggerated cases of most such discourses, hmm?

ER Right.

GS These things become politically offensive, a way, precisely, of differentiating oppressive behavior. I have no problem there; I'm against that. And I don't particularly want to wait to theorize essentialism in order to say that; I really do believe in undermining the vanguardism of theory. I don't want a theory of essences. We have enough of those. We have nothing but the practice of essences. When I said strategy, I meant strategy. I don't even think I'm capable of thinking theory in that sense. With essences, at least I feel that they're so useful that they can become dangerous. With theory, I feel that, for the moment, for me, at least, it's best to keep it at a distance, see it as the practice of its production. Even so, I must ask why essentialism is confused sometimes with the empirical. Why do people make this terminological confusion? Earlier, in my school-teacherly voice, I said that this confusion is a way of not wanting to infiltrate the disciplines, the vested interests, the real problems. Instead, one says that the careful construction of an object of investigation in a field is essentialism. This has something like a relationship with confusing essentialism with the empirical. All we really want to claim is that there is no feminine essence; there's no essential class subject; the general subject of essence is not a good basis for investigation. This is rather different from being antiempirical.

We could base our ontological commitments on various forms of coding. It is, to me, spectacular that someone like Gayle Rubin, coming from a Freudian/Lévi-Straussian structuralist humanism should in fact get into the idea of value as coded in sex-gender systems.[20] Whether we declare ourselves as essentialists or antiessentialists, if we realize that our ontological commitments are dependent on various forms of coding, we can presuppose a variety of general catachrestic names as a grounding. Richard Rorty speaking about the nominalism in poststructuralism is right on target there.[21] What he does with it is something else. Assuming one's ontological commitment as susceptible to an examination of value coding and then to presuppose a catachrestic name in order to ground our project and our investigation allows us to be thoroughly empirical without necessarily being blind essentialists. Ultimately, if you will forgive me for saying so, a lot of self-consciously antiessentialist writing seems to be a bit useless and boring. It's often very derivative, resembling other and better models that are not as scared of essences. It seems to me that to be empirical in this way would be a much greater challenge, require much harder work, would make people read different things, primary texts of active social work. If you're reading development economics you sometimes don't read Cixous's latest thing. To confuse empirical work with the pursuit of essences is, in itself, something that should be examined, and I don't see any need for a substantive theory of essentialism.

ER   We've been talking about feminism all along, but to address it very directly, how would you say feminism, as such, which is already problematic ... (laughs) ... *feminisms!* ... how have feminisms influenced your thinking about essentialism? Did feminism or women's studies put essentialism on the agenda in the U.S. academy? And what would you say—you just now mentioned Cixous—about the way essentialism and antiessentialism are intertwined in the practice of feminist theory and women's studies, in the U.S. or in France, in the work of the antifeminist feminists like Cixous or Kristeva?

GS   I think in general women's studies philosophy is humanist. There is a piece by Jean Grimshaw in the current *Radical Philosophy* on Mary Daly's humanism.[22] Of course, Mary Daly is not representative of U.S. feminism, but I think some lessons can be learned there about the essential-ist or antiessentialist debate.

When I began to write as a feminist, the idea of differences being unjustly made and unjustly not recognized needed the presupposition that what was self-same or identical was an essence. It was okay as a strategic presupposition; it certainly allowed me to learn and teach. But it does seem that like most strategies, for me at least, it has served its purpose, and at this point I can't go on beating that horse anymore. And as I say, my feminism now takes a distance from that debate.

As you know, feminism means something else in France. I really don't have much to do with it because that's very situation-specific. I like reading Irigaray, but I read her within the general tradition of French experimental writing, foregrounding rhetoric. It is only if she is read as the pure theoretical prose of truth—whatever that might be—that she may seem essentialist when she talks about women. Broadly, Kojèvian French intellectuals read Hegel and Marx with an eye to rhetoric. We know Derrida has to be read that way. Why do we become essentialist readers when we read someone like Irigaray?

I'm repelled by Kristeva's politics: what seems to me to be her reliance on the sort of banal historical narrative to produce "women's time"; what seems to me Christianizing psychoanalysis; what seems to me to be her sort of ferocious Western Europeanism; and what seems to me to be her long-standing implicit positivism: naturalizing of the chora, naturalizing of the presemiotic. I'm so put off by this that I can't read her seriously anymore, so it is more my problem. I mean, I'm not generous and catholic enough to learn from her anymore. I find Cixous much more risk-taking.

I think the kind of antiessentialism that I like these days is in the work of Kalpana Bardhan.[23] If you read her, you probably wouldn't see what I was talking about. One has to learn how to honor empirical work. Bardhan talks about how stratified the idea of women is in a place like India. In Bardhan's work (she's a development economist), you begin to see how impossible it is to focus, even within endogamous or exogamous marriage lines, on something called a space out of which you will define and articulate something called a woman. She even diversifies the radicals who can join in their struggle. She diversifies the people who study them. . . . In that kind of work which is not against essentialism but which completely pluralizes the grid, it is my task as a reader, as it is with deconstruction, to read and run with it somewhere else. It is my task as a reader to see where in that grid there are spaces where, in fact, "woman" oozes away. Essences, it seems to me, are just a kind of content. All content is not essence. Why be so nervous about it? Why not demote the word "essence," because without a minimalizable essence, an essence as *ce qui reste,* an essence as what remains, there is no exchange. Difference articulates these negotiable essences. There is no time for essence/anti-essence. There is so much work to be done.

ER Yes, but it seems to me that the reason that can't be done across the board is teaching. I always have to "do" essentialism/antiessentialism with my students because in the first flush of feminist thought they become the most energetic essentialists, or personalists, perhaps. And that's, of course, a quite different thing from a research program or the kinds of books that one wants to write, but in my experience that's part of the reason that the question won't go away. It's a kind of initial question, politically and intellectually, when students discover the possibility of a feminist discourse.

GS Rather than make it a central issue, work it into the method of your teaching so that the class becomes an example of the minimalizing of essences, the impossibility of essences; rather than talk about it constantly, make the class a proof of this new position. If we're talking strategy, you know as well as I do that teaching is a question of strategy. That is perhaps the only place where people like us actually get any experience in strategy. In that context, it seems to me that one can make a strategy of taking away from them the authority of their marginality, the centrality of their marginality, through the strategy of careful teaching, so that they come to prove that that authority will not take them very far because the world is a large place. Others are many. The self is enclosed; the concrete is fabricated. One can do it *in* teaching rather than talk about it *ad infinitum* because they're not ready to take sides.

ER There has been, at least in literary studies, a kind of consensus that feminist critics have done exactly what you describe, taken a very small sample and then generalized about a "feminine aesthetic" or a "women's tradition"—produced ahistorical misrepresentation of things as feminine, feminine, you know, the Feminine, with a capital "F." Insofar as this criticism has been generally accepted, there's a kind of consensus in favor of pursuing specificity, multiplying differences. Is there a way in which multiplication can become pluralism? What are the consequences of that?

GS The real problem, one of the reasons why it becomes pluralism, is that we live in a country which has pluralism—the pluralism of repressive tolerance—as the best of its political credo. Most of us are not interested in changing our social relations, and pluralism is the best we can do. Cultural Studies into multiculturalism.

Once we have established the story of the straight, white, Judeo-Christian, heterosexual man of property as the ethical universal, we must not replicate the same trajectory. We have limits; we cannot even learn many languages. This idea of a global fun-fair is a lousy teaching idea. One of the first things to do is to think through the limits of one's power. One must ruthlessly undermine the story of the ethical universal, the hero. But the alternative is not constantly to evoke multiplicity; the alternative is to know and to teach the student the awareness that this is a limited sample because of one's own inclinations and capacities to learn enough to take a larger sample. And this kind of work should be a collective enterprise. Other people will do some other work. This is how I think one should proceed, rather than make each student into a ground of multiplicity. That leads to pluralism. I ask the U.S. student: "What do you think is the inscription that allows *you* to think the world without any preparation? What sort of coding has produced *this* subject?" I think it's hard for students to know this, but we have a responsibility to make this lesson palliative rather than destructive. This is not a paralyzing thing to teach. In fact, when a student is told that responsibility means proceeding from an awareness of the limits of one's power, the student understands it quite differently from being told, "Look, you can't do all of this." I will share with you what I have learned about knowing, that these are the limitations of what I undertake, looking to others to teach me. I think that's what one should do rather than invoke multiplicity.

ER   How is the problem of the subject related to the relationship between essentialism and the efforts to theorize the body, or bodies, as someone pointed out to me when I showed him this question? What kind of problem is this? Can we theorize our bodies without essentializing them as the body? Is our confusion about how to theorize bodies the root of the problem of essentialism? Insofar as there is another factor that keeps the question of essentialism kind of bubbling, I think it has to do with that fact that, at least in the U.S., the effort to biologize gender is not over in the general culture, political culture, for example, the front page of the *New York Times* a few weeks ago explaining why at certain times of the month we can't find our cars because of our . . .

GS   Really?

ER   . . . hormones raging. Yes.

GS   I didn't see that. It gives me an answer to my question!

ER   (laughs) How is your own effort to address bodies in some of your work part of your thinking about essentialism? And how do race and class actually enter in here, as well as the more obvious gender?

GS The body, like all other things, cannot be thought, as such. I take the extreme ecological view that the body as such has no possible outline. As body it is a repetition of nature. It is in the rupture with Nature when it is a signifier of immediacy for the staging of the self. As a text, the inside of the body (imbricated with the outside) is mysterious and unreadable except by way of thinking of the systematicity of the body, value coding of the body. It is through the *significance* of my body and others' bodies that cultures become gendered, economicopolitic, selved, substantive.

ER This is also is a question that's not in here, per se, because when I looked again at that not very well formulated question about the unconscious and death, I realized that there is no question about psychoanalysis anywhere in here.

GS That's okay.

ER (laughs) Okay?

GS Yah!

ER (laughing) These are my last questions that didn't fit elsewhere. Is it possible to speak of a nonessential essence? Would that be a kind of gloss on strategic essentialism?

GS I don't think so.

ER No?

GS I mean one might just as well speak about an essential nonessence. It's possible to speak of everything. But an essence, if it's minimalizable, is also cross-hatched. Death as such can only be thought via essence or rupture of essence, that mother-tongue analogy that I gave earlier. . . . I cannot approach death as such. Death may be the catachresis that is indistinguishable from essence. May be.

ER I've already asked about deconstruction as a kind of questioning of essences or of the relation between the essential and the antiessential, and as I look back I want to ask you about de Man as opposed . . . I was about to say as opposed to Derrida, but not necessarily as opposed to Derrida, but in his specificity as someone who can be of help.

GS When I knew de Man, he was a phenomenologist, marked by people like Lévi-Strauss, Merleau-Ponty, Poulet. Deconstruction was a thing that appealed to him greatly later and he ran (or ambled off) with it in another direction. How can I call Lévi-Strauss a phenomenologist? Not within the bounds of an interview. De Man was also "interested" in a whole slew of German thinkers who inflected his understanding of deconstruction as a cousin of Romantic Irony. I see his work as lapidary and strong in its very limits. I don't believe he ever gave away his control in the writing. He talked *about* giving up his control, but he never really gave away his control in the way that Derrida constantly tries. De Man even writes about it in the introduction to *The Rhetoric of Romanticism*.[24] From de Man I learned the extreme importance of an absolutely literal-minded reading: To follow the logic of the rhetoric—the tropology—wherever it might lead.

ER   You spoke earlier, several times, about other words that might be used rather than antiessentialist, and although I didn't know you were going to say that, as I was thinking about talking with you, I did fix on certain terms in your work, like "interruption," or "transactional," or "discontinuous." I don't mean that you were thinking of this when you made the earlier remarks, but are these perhaps other words that can serve the strategic, have strategic effects?

GS   The thinking of essences as what remains, the minimalizable, something with which we negotiate in the strategy of teaching in the broadest possible sense, without talking *about* the debate constantly does interrupt the teaching of cultural or literary *substance,* brings it to crisis.

"Transaction": now a transaction can be a transaction between essences, so it is not necessarily antiessentialist. Let's put that aside for a moment, we're running out of time. "Discontinuity," then. Radical discontinuity cannot appear, like pure difference; remember, essences cannot appear either. (There's not much *theoretical* difference between pure essence and pure difference.) Discontinuity must traffic in minimal continua. We go back to *ce qui reste,* fragments of essences to reckon with. That's where writing like Bardhan's is so interesting. Fragments of essences to reckon with rather than preserving myself from essences. If you see this as an antiessentialist project, I start running the other way again.

ER   (laughter).

This is the whole business about strategy, asking what regulates your diagnosis, why do you want me with you, what claims me, what is claiming me?

ER   Can we talk, just because of the very last things that you've said, about the question of audience? When I thought about these questions, I also thought about my own work. I've been writing about pluralism. What I have been calling pluralism is partially what you were just referring to as corporatism. It's an essentialism that doesn't have to do so much with the object of study as with one's audience. The pluralist assumes not just her own transparency—in fact she may articulate her positionality—but the transparency and therefore the unity of one's audience. That's where essence resides, or is expressed, that is what pluralism doesn't acknowledge. Perhaps this isn't what you meant by anticorporatism. . . . I guess what I'm asking is for you to say a little bit more about it. What I see as the pluralist moment is the moment when one doesn't acknowledge—and I've learned this from you, at least I think I have learned it from you—the exclusions that fragment one's audience.

GS   Yes. When one takes the representative position—the homeopathic deconstruction of identity by identity—one is aware that outside of that representation of oneself in the middle of one stream, there are areas that are completely inaccessible to one. When I said "building for difference," the sense of audience is already assuming that the future is simply a future present. The most radical challenge of deconstruction is that notion of thought being a blank part of the text given over to a future that is not just a future present but always a future anterior. It never will be, but always will have been; that is the most practical assurance in view of which one works on, indefinitely outside in the teaching machine. The audience is not an essence, the audience is a blank. An audience can be constituted by people I cannot even imagine, affected by this little unimportant trivial piece of work, which is not just direct teaching and writing. That displaces the question of audience as essence or fragmented or exclusivist or anything. Derrida calls this a responsibility to the trace of the other, I think. . . . It's something that one must remind oneself of all the time. That is why what I cannot imagine stands guard over everything that I must/can do, think, live.

Yet, in the narrow sense, when an audience is responsible, responding, invited, in other words, to coinvestigate, then positionality is shared with it. Audience and investigator: it's not just a binary opposition when an audience really is an audience. It now seems to me that many of the changes I've made in my position are because the audience has become a coinvestigator and I have realized what it is to have an audience. An audience is part of one. An audience shows one something. That may indeed be the transaction. It's a responsibility to the other taking on faces. It is not deessentializing, but attempting to deconstruct the binary opposition between investigator and audience.

Radically, then, one works not for a future present, but imagining the blank certitude of the future anterior. And the audience *is* the unimaginable; less radically in the second session, as it were, in the logical sphere, where one begins to imagine the audience responding, responsible, and invited to be coinvestigator, one starts owning the right to have one's invitation accepted, given that the invitation is, like all letters, open letters intercepted and that people turn up in other places for other occasions with that invitation, so that we begin to deconstruct that binary opposition bit by bit.[25] I don't see that particularly as deessentializing. It's something else. But yes, I think the question you've asked is very important.

ER   As you were answering it . . . you used the word "future"; after I had finished these questions, at the very end, I realized there was no question about history, either as a potentially essentializing discourse or as a potentially antiessentializing discourse. Actually, now these questions, with the words essentializing and antiessentializing . . .

GS   See what happens?

ER   . . . larded in so thickly, are no longer the right questions, having said that, what would you say about history?

GS   I'll give you a very short answer. It depends on your view of history as negotiable determinant or fact.

ER   Thank you.

GS   Thank you.

2

More on Power/Knowledge

What is the relationship between critical and dogmatic philosophies of action? By "critical" I mean a philosophy that is aware of the limits of knowing. By "dogmatic" I mean a philosophy that advances coherent general principles without sufficient interest in empirical details. Kant's warning, that the Jacobins had mistaken a critical for a dogmatic philosophy and had thus brought in terror, has served generations of humanist liberals as the inevitable critique of revolutionary politics. Its latest vindication seems to be the situation of international communism. It can certainly be advanced that one of the many scripts spelling out the vicissitudes of the diversified field of the first waves of global Marxism is the consequence of the realist compromises of reading a speculative morphology as an adequate blueprint for social justice: to treat a critical philosophy as a dogmatic.

Who is the ethical subject of humanism? The misadventures of international communism might teach us something about the violent consequences of imposing the most fragile part of Marx, the predictive Eurocentric scenario, upon large parts of the globe not historically centered in Europe.

It is to ignore the role of capitalism in these scripts to read them simply as various triumphs of liberal democracy. It might be more pertinent to ask now: What is it to use a critical philosophy critically? What is it to use it ethically? Who can do so? This essay will attempt to consider these questions with reference to the word "power" in the famous opening of "Method" in the *History of Sexuality*, volume one.[1] I will suggest (a) that it might be useful to give the proper names of Foucault and Derrida *in* to each other, although such a move would not be endorsed by either; and (b) that the current critical possibility for Foucault's ethics of the care of the self cannot be understood from within liberal humanism, or through calls for alternatives that remind us that they are appropriate only to liberal democracies and/or postindustrial societies of the North Atlantic model.[2]

Reading Foucault and Derrida Together

The lines of alignment and separation between these two proper names were first drawn by academic circumstance and have been redrawn authoritatively since Foucault's death by the magisterial voice of Edward W. Said, by the trivializing voice of Richard Rorty, the judicious voice of David Couzens Hoy, and others.[3] A learned anthology has been compiled on feminism and Foucault.[4] The rising tide of antideconstructionism among individual-rights U.S. feminism has been clinched in, among other texts, the chapter called "Politics and/or Deconstruction" in Zillah R. Eisenstein's new book, *The Female Body and the Law*.[5] The slash between these two proper names, that "emerged out of a strange revolutionary concatenation of Parisian aesthetic and political currents which for about thirty years produced such a concentration of brilliant work as we are not likely to see again for generations," marks a certain *non*alignment: critique, denunciation, nonresponse, uneasy peace in acknowledgment of political work, and, after one's death, a formal tribute by the other.[6] To speak of that impossible double name—Derrida/Foucault—is not to be able to speak *for* it, to give you anything *in* that name. But perhaps one might yet be able to give in *to* both, however asymmetrically.

Let us enter the task at hand by way of the "ism" of names—"nominalism"—and open up once again that famous sentence, written to be repeated: "One needs to be a nominalist, no doubt: power, it is not an institution, and it is not a structure; it is not a certain strength [*puissance*] that some are endowed with; it is the name that one lends [*prêter*] to a complex strategical situation in a particular society."[7] This provisional "naming" by the theorist is not simply to code within a given system. "This multiplicity of force relations can be *coded* . . . either in the form of 'war' or in the form of 'politics.' " The field of possible codings can be, in principle, indefinitely enlarged. The nominalism is a methodological necessity. One needs a name for this thing whose "mechanism [can be used] as a grid of intelligibility of the social order." It is called "power" because that is the closest one can get to it. This sort of proximate naming can be called catachrestic.

Much of U.S. Foucauldianism as well as U.S. anti-Foucauldianism—Said's and Sheldon Wolin's readings come to mind—spring out of a lack of sympathy for Foucault's nominalism.[8] We cannot, however, dismiss these readings as mere misunderstandings. For no other name but "power" could have been attributed to this complex situation. In Chapter Six I will discuss in greater detail that nominalism must bear the responsibility of paleonymy, for names are in the history of the language.

Foucault's nominalism has been noticed by critics. David Hoy meticulously establishes the advantages gained by Foucault over his critics by his use of what Hoy calls "pragmatic nominalism."[9] Yet even in this sympathetic account a general, naturalized referent for the word "power" is tacitly presupposed, and, indeed, attributed to Foucault. This reference is taken for granted, for example, in such important corrective sentences as: "[Foucault's] analytics of power is not intended to tell us what power really is, but only where to look." It is as if, although Foucault's interests are not realist, he has an ontological commitment to a thing named "power." Hoy's impressive attempt, from within the North Atlantic philosophical tradition, to seize the very alienness of the French thinker, trembles on the brink of subject-metaphors: "Foucault thinks of power as *intentionality* without a subject. . . . " and, to explain Foucault's odd thinking of resistance: "to program a computer for chess, presumably *one* must include some considerations about counter-attacks."[10]

These traces of naturalized or merely systemic notions of power, present also in Irene Diamond's good interactive take on Foucault, are what I am calling the consequences of paleonymy. The word "power" points toward what we call the empirical in the history of the language. Poststructuralist nominalism cannot afford to ignore the empirical implications of a particular name.[11]

Such consequences of paleonymy are neither true to Foucault's idea of power nor untrue to them. They are functions of any subject's relationship to language. They become acutely problematic within those strategies of knowledge—that *savoir*—which demands of us that academic learning—*connaissance*—should establish the claims proper to each author in the realm of the roots and ramifications of ideas.[12] I am stating the problem, not solving or denying it. Since the phrase "subject's relationship to language" might have a psychoanalytic ring to it, let me recall my description of the mother tongue in Chapter One.

A mother tongue is a language with a history—in that sense it is "instituted"—before our birth and after our death, where patterns that can be filled with anyone's "motivation" have laid themselves down. In this sense it is " 'unmotivated' but not capricious."[13] We learn it in a "natural" way and fill it once and for all with our own "intentions" and thus make it "our own" for the span of our life and then leave it, without intent—as unmotivated and uncapricious as we found it (without intent) when it found us—for its other users. As Derrida writes, "The 'unmotivatedness' of the sign requires a synthesis in which the completely other is announced as such—without any simplicity, any identity, any resemblance or continuity—within what is not it."

Reading Foucault's nominalism by way of Derrida, I can see that although there is a "need" (Foucault's word) to be a nominalist, the nominalist still falls prey to the very problems that one seeks to avoid. This is marked by the "power is not" statements in the Foucault passage I began with. But the nominalist falls prey to them only *in a certain way*. This is not to "fail," this is the new making-visible of a "success" that does not conceal or bracket problems. Thus reading Foucault slashed in Derrida, let me further propose that the bestowal of the name power upon a complex situation produces power "in the general sense." The traces of the empirical entailed by the word in the history of the language give the so-called narrow senses of power. The relationship between the general and narrow senses spans the active articulation of deconstruction in a considerable variety of ways. As I and many others have noted, writing, trace, differance, woman, origin, parergon, gift—and now, in Derrida's latest phase—such more resonant words as justice, democracy, friendship are cracked and barred in their operation by this two-sense divide. As is Derrida's habit, he does not develop a systematic description of this mode of operation. (There is, after all, no useful definition of deconstruction anywhere in Derrida's work.)

I will not go into the practical reason for this habit of elusiveness. All we need to note here is that the relationship between the two senses is never clear-cut. One bleeds into the other at all times. The relationship is certainly not that between the potential and the actual. In fact, the relationship between undecidability and the obligation and risk of deciding is something like the *rapport sans rapport* between the general and the narrow senses. But, and this seems to me important, this curious relationship between the narrow and the general senses is what makes for the necessary lack of fit between discourse and example, the necessary crisis between theory and practice, that marks deconstruction. If we remember that such a misfit between theory and practice is the main complaint brought by nearly everyone against Foucault—indeed, it is thematized by Foucault himself as putting discourse theory aside in his later phase—we can see how Derrida's speculations about the general and the narrow allow us neither to look for an exact fit between theory and practice in Foucault, nor to ignore or transform the boldest bits of his theoretical writings about power. There is certainly no doubt that Foucault would have resented this way of saving his text, and it seems idle to repeat that the status of the author's resentment is not definitive, though certainly worth accounting for, in both Foucault and Derrida. As long as it is not merely an exercise in diagnostic psychobiography, I should, just as certainly, be interested in such an account.[14]

Nor am I substituting an excuse for an accusation. Indeed, this double gesture in Derrida is the affirmative duplicity (opening up toward plurality) that allows him to claim, most noticeably in *Limited Inc* but in fact in every text, that practice *norms* theory—that deconstruction, strictly speaking, is impossible though obligatory and so on. I have myself argued this as the originary "mistake"—not to be derived from some potential correctness—that inaugurates deconstruction. Foucault is not *in* Derrida, but Foucault slashed with Derrida prevents him from being turned into a merely pragmatic nominalist, or a folk hero for American feminism.

"Power" in the general sense is therefore not only a name, but a catachresis. Like all names it is a misfit. To use *this* name to describe a generality inaccessible to intended description, is necessarily to work with the risk that the word "is wrested from its *proper* meaning," that it is being applied "to a thing which it does not *properly* denote" (*OED*). We cannot find a proper place—it must be effaced as it is disclosed.

It is this critical relationship between the general and the narrow that unsympathetic strong readers such as Habermas and Rorty are unable to grasp. Thus Rorty accuses Foucault's second sense of power of "a certain vacuity": "We liberal reformers [!] think that a certain ambiguity between two uses of the word 'power' vitiates Foucault's work: one which is in fact a pejorative term and the other which treats it as a neutral or descriptive term."[15] In his essay on Derrida, Habermas thinks that the asymmetrical negotiation between the narrow and the general which is the lesson of deconstruction is simply a collapsing of distinctions.[16] Quite predictably, then, Rorty decides that Foucault "refuses to separate the public and the private sphere."[17] Pushing the new pragmatism to its extreme consequences in order to give Foucault an easy out he says that the philosophy of Foucault's final phase should simply claim the same rights of autonomy and privacy as poetry rather than fuss with ethics. "Poetry," "rhetoric," et cetera are small words for these pragmatists and communicationists.[18] They cannot therefore grasp *this* particular rethinking of the dogmatic-critical divide. Indeed, Rorty sees the critical impulse as "a distraction from the history of concrete social engineering."[19]

Foucault's and Derrida's attention to the relationship between the dogmatic and the critical is in the wake of the *early* Heidegger, a course from which Heidegger himself swerved away into a more dogmatic enterprise, following the implications of a sense of poetry and language that are different from Foucault's: that a detailed analysis of the aesthetic element in the conduct of life may lead to a critical appraisal of the postenlighten-ment conception of the ethical person as merely public.

> For me Heidegger has always been the essential philosopher. . . . My entire philosophical development was determined by my reading of Heidegger. . . . I think it is important to have a small number of authors with whom one thinks, with whom one works, but about whom one does not write.[20]

If for Foucault, the dialogue with Heidegger is tacit, for Derrida the rememoration of Heidegger is interminable:

> more than ever, the vigilant but open reading of Heidegger remains in my eyes one of the indispensable conditions, one of them but not the least, for trying to comprehend better and to tell better why, with so many others, I have always condemned Nazism, in the horror of what, in Heidegger precisely, and so many others, in Germany or elsewhere, has ever been able to give in to it. No *immediate presentation* [a phrase in a Heideggerian recanting statement of 1942] for thought could also mean: less ease in armed declarations and morality lessons, less haste toward platforms [*tribunes*] and tribunal [*tribunaux*], even if it were to respond to acts of violence, rhetorical or other.[21]

For both Foucault and Derrida, in different ways, the ontico-ontological difference is a thinking through of the uses and limits of a critical philoso-phy. Their catachrestic nominalism may be trying to touch the ontic with the thought that there is a subindividual (or random, for Derrida) space even under, or below, or before . . . (the grasp begins to falter here, but how can philosophers who will not admit that actual ethical practice is affected, indeed constituted by this, understand why it is worth trying?) the "pre-ontological Being as [Dasein's] ontically constitutive state . . . [where] Dasein *tacitly* understands and interprets something like Being."[22] What-ever the generalizing presuppositions necessary for a systematic statement or knowledge of ethics, these are the conditions within which ethics are *performed,* by subjects constituted in different ways.

I will write further about this resistance to understanding as an episte-mic clash. But let us now turn back to Foucault's text. The condition of possibility of power is the condition of possibility of a viewpoint that renders intelligible its exercise. Robert Hurley has not done us a favor by changing the first "rendering intelligible" into "understanding," while preserving "grid of intelligibility of the *social* order." Here is the sentence: "La condition de possibilité du pouvoir, en tout cas le point de vue qui permet de rendre intelligible son exercice . . . C'est le socle mouvant des rapports de force qui induisent sans cesse, par leur inegalité, des états de pouvoir."[23] "The condition of possibility of power, at least of the point of view that allows its exercise to be made intelligible . . . is the *moving base* of force relations that, by their inequality, incessantly *induce* states of power."

In this passage Foucault *might* be speaking of the point of view of the analysis of power as intelligible rather than the point of view of power. This too can be made to resonate with Derrida. According to Derrida, even the decision that makes the trace of the other in the origin intelligible as writing in the general sense (rather than the usual practice of ignoring the instituted trace to declare a simple origin) cannot be *finally* endorsed.[24] In our Foucauldian passage, the condition of possibility of power's intelligibility is itself such a catachrestic concept-metaphor—"a moving base"—*un socle mouvant*. The metaphor in *induire* or induce, out of inequalities or differences in the magnitudes of force—not the organic "engender" as in the English (generate might have been better)—may be both logical and electrical.[25] In both cases, this moving base of *force* fields clearly takes "power" quite away from the *visée* (or aimed) character of intentionality. The condition of possibility of power (or power as intelligible in its exercise)—"this moving base"—is therefore unmotivated, though not capricious. Its "origin," thus heavily framed, is in "difference," inequalities in force relations. To read this only as "our experience of power," or "institutional power" (as most people—like Walter J. Ong—read "writing" as "systems of graphic marks") is the productive and risky burden of paleonymy that must be persistently resisted as it enables practice.[26] "Force" is the subindividual name of "power," not the place where the "idea" of power becomes "hollow" or "ambiguous."[27]

Why should the burden of paleonymy be resisted? Because if not, the enthusiasm of the Foucauldian can *come* to resemble the flip side of a concern for "our social infrastructure" in the interest of "quality of life, peace of mind, and the economic future."[28] This of course is precisely the element in Foucault that a Rorty would admire. And the resemblance emerges when Hoy, after emphasizing the important point that power in Foucault is productive as well as repressive, then divides the necessary results into thoroughly valorized "positive" and "negative" effects.[29] (I am encouraged by the possibility of giving these adjectives an electrical charge.) From this it follows, for Hoy, that "the exercise of power will invariably meet with resistance, which is the manifestation of freedom."[30]

Resistance can indeed be powerfully and persuasively coded in the form of the manifestation of freedom, but there is no getting around the fact that by privileging that particular coding, we are isolating a crucial narrow sense and cutting off the tremendous, unmotivated monitory force of the general.

Speaking to an interlocutor who would clearly incline to such patterns of privilege, Foucault puts the case firmly yet tactfully:

> Every power relationship implies, at least *in potentia* [and this is a "more rational" name on the chain of power-names—*puissance* in French], a strategy of struggle, in which two forces [a "less rational" name on the same chain] are not superimposed. . . . a relationship of confrontation reaches its term, its final moment . . . when stable mechanisms replace the free play of antagonistic reactions.[31]

Force is the name of the subindividual preontic substance traced with irreducible struggle-structures in the general sense that enables *and* limits confrontation. *Reading* (rather than merely quoting) Foucault, one notices the importance of the parentheses around "(and the victory of one of the two adversaries)," that fits into the ellipsis in the passage I have cited above. To trivialize this into mere functionalism would, *mutatis mutandis*, put the entire materialist tradition out of court, a consummation which Rorty *et al.* would not find implausible.

I am in agreement here with the feminist philosopher Jana Sawicki when she writes, I believe in another kind of response to a similar exigency:

> Rather than seek to legitimate feminist psychoanalytic theory, a Foucauldian looks for its dangers, its normalizing tendencies, how it might hinder research or serve as an instrument of domination despite the intentions of its creators. Whether it serves to dominate or to liberate is irrelevant to judging its truth.[32]

What does this peculiar moving base of a differentiated force field look like? And how does the field polarize? Let us turn the page of *The Will to Knowledge*, where Foucault finds it possible "to advance a few propositions." Here the distinction between the force field on the one hand and its coming into play as power relations on the other is unmistakable if you are on that track: "It is to be supposed that the multiple relations of force that form themselves and play in the apparatuses of production. . . . serve as support to the broad effects of cleavage running through the social body as a whole." "The rationality of power"—one might have said intelligibility—"is that of often explicit tactics which . . . find their support and their condition *elsewhere*, finally delineate [*dessi-*

nent] aggregative apparatuses [*dispositifs d'ensemble*]."[33] "Perhaps," writed Foucault, "we need to go one step further . . . and decipher power mechanisms in terms of a strategy *immanent* to the relationships of force." As indicated above, this "*need* of decipherment," of the individual to calculate that the subindividual has immanent laws of motion, should not be redrawn into the postindividualist register of a determinist functionalism, although perhaps the dominant Anglo-U.S. episteme can hardly avoid doing so.

The electrical metaphor is particularly strong in a nearly untranslatable sentence trying to catch the origin of resistance: "Les résistances . . . sont l'autre terme, dans les relations de pouvoir; elles s'y inscrivent comme irreductible vis-à-vis." Surely the choice of "vis-à-vis"—a casual description of being placed facing something—over the motivated words "confrontation" or "opposition" is to be noticed here.[34] Mark also the curious comma between "term" and "in the relations of power." Surely this is to distinguish between "the *strategic* field of power relations" and the merely inductive force field, which is its support. Resistances are the other term— certainly in the sense of terminal—in the field of power relations, that are inscribed there as irreducibly facing. How Foucault's language is bending here to ward us off from the freedom-talk of "the philosopher-functionary of the democratic state!"[35]

On the very next page Foucault cautions, under the title "Rule of Immanence," that the force field cannot be naturalized and constituted as an object of investigation. One must start from the "local foci" of power/knowledge.

If this sounds too much like the provisional beginnings celebrated everywhere in deconstruction, starting with "The Discourse on Method" in *Of Grammatology*, let me assure you that, even for a reader like me, Foucault *is* not Derrida, nor Derrida Foucault. I cannot find anywhere in Foucault the thought of a founding violence. To quote Marx where one shouldn't, Foucault always remains within the realm of necessity (even in the clinamen to his last phase) whereas Derrida makes for the realm of freedom, only to fall on his face (C3,959). I would not choose between the two.

Indeed, Derrida's initial critique had been in terms of Foucault's ignoring of the violence that founds philosophy. If forced into the thematic by way of which I am reading the two together, the objection might be arranged this way:

In his earliest phase, Foucault makes the ontico-ontological difference workable too quickly, too easily. Madness, "naming" the ontic, becomes the self-consolidating other of Foucault's text, "producing" the ontological by being excluded. Continuing our somewhat forced reading, this Foucault is seen by Derrida as containing madness within the ontico-ontological difference and legitimizing Descartes's reversed position, where, instead of the inarticulate and proximate, it is the "intelligible [that is] irreducible to all . . . sensory or imaginative . . . analysis."[36] What Foucault is thought to overlook is madness as radical alterity, which must be "extinguished" after the necessary invocation of an undivided origin where madness and the cogito are indistinguishable.[37] Foucault is as much written as writing by this tacit extinction, philosophy's hyperbole (rather than *hubris*—Foucault's word).

> Everything can be reduced to a determined historical totality except the hyperbolical project. Now, this project belongs to the narration narrating itself and not to the narration narrated by Foucault. . . . The menacing powers of madness [thus remain] the adverse origin of philosophy.[38]

This is not to obliterate the difference between philosophers. The different ways in which radical alterity is denied and negotiated maps out one history of philosophy even as it historicizes philosophy: "The historicity proper to philosophy is located and constituted in the transition, the dialogue between hyperbole and the finite structure . . ."[39]

We must start, then, from the local foci of power/knowledge—*pouvoir/savoir*.

It is a pity that there is no word in English corresponding to *pouvoir* as there is "knowing" for *savoir*. *Pouvoir* is of course "power." But there is also a sense of "can-do"-ness in "*pouvoir*," if only because, in its various conjugations, it is the commonest way of saying "can" in the French language. If power/knowledge is seen as the only translation of "*pouvoir/savoir*," it monumentalizes Foucault unnecessarily. The French language possesses quite a number of these doublets. In their different ways, "laissez-faire" and "vouloir-dire" are perhaps best known to us. The trick is to get some of the homely verbiness of *savoir* in *savoir-faire*, *savoir-vivre* into *pouvoir*, and you might come up with something like this: if the lines of making sense of something are laid down in a certain way, then you are able to do only those things with that something which are possible within and by the arrangement of those lines. *Pouvoir-savoir*—being able to do something—only as you are able to make sense of it. This everyday sense of that doublet seems to me indispensable to a crucial aspect of Foucault's work.[40]

Power as productive rather than merely repressive resolves itself in a certain way if you don't forget the ordinary sense of *pouvoir/savoir*. Repression is then seen as a species of production. There is no need to valorize repression as negative and production as positive. (Incidentally, this is a much "truer" view of things than most theories of ideology will produce. The notion of "interpellation" is too deeply imbricated with psychoanalysis's involvement with the laws of motion of the mind). Let us consider a homely example that has some importance for bicultural women, women who grow up as daughters of new immigrants, women who ride the hyphen of "ethnic"-American into a different "mother tongue." We are, of course, speaking of a level still above the impersonality of the force field.[41]

Suppose the *savoir* or knowing of (exogamous) marriage in a culture for a woman is: a passing from her father's protection to her husband's in order to produce women and men to perpetuate this circuit; and finally to pass under her son's protection. In terms of this *savoir,* the woman *can* (*peut* in the French, from *pouvoir*) preserve "the stability of marriage" and be loving and loved without being sexy. Suppose on the other hand, exogamous marriage is known as the fulfillment of various kinds of interactive and creative emotive potentials in the woman. In terms of this *savoir,* the woman *can* (*peut*) seek fulfillment elsewhere if, as individually intending subject, she feels her fulfillment thwarted. Both situations are productive—of the stability of marriage on the one hand and of the perceived freedom of women's fulfillment on the other. There is, of course, felt pain involved in both. But, quite apart from that, there are terminals of resistance inscribed *under* the level of the tactics, sometimes explicit, with which these women fill their lives. If this seems a little opaque, let me invite you to think of the terminals of resistance as possibilities for reflexes of mind and activity, as an athlete has reflexes of the body to call upon. And changes in *pouvoir/savoir* can make visible the repressive elements in both situations, even through "disciplinary" means (through the Women's Studies component of the Culture Studies collective for example) of woman's freedom on the one hand, or of woman's right to a special role in the propagation of society on the other.[42]

One must not stop here, of course. The homely tactics of everyday *pouvoir/savoir,* the stuff of women's lives, lead, not only to the governmentality of dress codes and work habits, guilt feelings and guilt trips, but also to the delineation of the great aggregative apparatuses of power/knowledge which deploy the family as a repressive issue, day care as an alibi, and reproductive rights as a moral melodrama in national elections and policy.

Foucault insisted upon the difference between *savoir* and *connaissance,* as he did between *pouvoir* and *puissance,* the latter seen as lodged in the State or the Institution. He never wrote an *Archéologie du pouvoir.* The reasons have been aptly thematized as a change of heart, the changing times and the like. Yet it is also true that, at the time of its writing, Foucault perceived the *Archaeology of Knowledge (savoir)* as a theoretical consolidation of all that had come before.[43]

There may be another theoretical "reason" for the absence of an archaeology of power. The differential substance of *savoir* is discourse, with its irreducible connections to language. Thus *its* archaeology can be written. The differential substance of power is force, which does not have an irreducible connection to language. It is not even necessarily structured like a language, just as a magnetic field (which is symbolizable) is not necessarily structured like a language. Writing its archaeology would entail a first step: writing *pouvoir* in terms of *savoir.* Foucault himself sometimes put this entailment somewhat more polemically, especially in his later interviews—as a turning away from mere language.

The homology I am about to draw, then, is, strictly speaking, an imperfect homology. It is between, on the one hand, *puissance, pouvoir, force* and, on the other, *connaissance, savoir, énoncé.* I repeat, it is an imperfect homology, but can serve as a guide to the status of *pouvoir/ savoir.*

Again, English cannot quite match Foucault's distinction between *énoncé* and *énonciation.* There is of course the authority of the translations of *énoncé* in linguistics and semiotics—utterance, statement, et cetera. There is no reason to reject these translations. Yet it cannot be denied that there is, in French, a sense of the utter*ed,* the stat*ed,* in the simple word *énoncé.*

There can be no doubt at all that the *énoncé* as "the atom of discourse" is a catachresis. I believe this word has broken under the burden of paleonymy. This is what one camp of Foucault criticism would call the *failure* of archaeology.

All through the middle section of *The Archaeology of Knowledge* Foucault tries to be precise about the *énoncé* even as he warns us of all the things that we might think it is because of its various meanings in the history of language. I think it is finally more effective that the distinction between force and power is kept, by contrast, elusive. The immense effort to distinguish between the *énoncé* and discourse is impressive in its elegance, not its usefulness. If the element of the archive emerges at the end of these acrobatics as something like the field of power relations, the analogue of the force field is that "lacunary [*lacunaire*] and shredded [*déchiquetée*] ... enunciative field," that no-place, where bits of the stated, not units, but functions, cut across structures, and are rare.

Perhaps because it is *about savoir, The Archaeology of Knowledge* indicates the gap between practice and theory in its own rhetorical strategy. By this I do not mean the self-conscious imaginary dialogue at the end, but rather the placing of the "Definition of the *Énoncé*" in the middle. The peculiarly abdicatory series of gestures toward the beginning of the section are noteworthy:

> I took care [*je me suis gardé*] not to give a preliminary definition of the *énoncé*. I did not try to construct one as I advanced in order to justify the naïveté of my starting point. ... I wonder whether I have not changed orientation on the way; if I have not substituted another research for my first horizon; whether ... I was still speaking of *énoncés*. ... Have I not varied the ... word discourse as I shifted my analysis or its point of application, to the extent that I lost sight of the *éconcé* itself?[44]

It is by no means certain how these questions should be answered. To my mind, the paragraph marks that misfit between practice (the analysis practiced so far in the book) and theory of which I spoke in the beginning. The word "definition" itself becomes a catachresis here, for, by Foucault's own rhetoric, it may not be a definition that has been or can be used.

Pouvoir/savoir, then, is catachrestic in the way that all names of processes not anchored in the intending subject must be: lines of knowing constituting ways of doing and not doing, the lines themselves irregular clinamens from subindividual atomic systems—fields of force, archives of utterance. Inducing them is that moving field of shredded *énoncés* or differential forces that cannot be constructed as objects of investigation. Ahead of them, making their rationality fully visible, are the great apparatuses of *puissance/connaissance*. Between the first and the second there is the misfit of the general and the narrow senses. Between the last two is the misfit that describes examples that seem not to be faithful to the theorist's argument. If read by way of the deconstructive theorizing of practice, this does not summon up excuse or accusation. This is how theory brings practice to crisis, and practice norms theory, and deviations constitute a forever precarious norm; everything opened and menaced by the risk of paleonymy. Thus I give the name of Foucault in to Derrida.

An Ethics Inaccessible to Liberalism

As I hope I have made clear, there is in both writers a concern with the preontological ontic level of the everydayness of the being.[45] It is at this level that Derrida brings differance into the self-proximity of the ontic—everyday "identity" differed-deferred from itself by randomness and chance.[46] Foucault's concern with this level is already apparent in his early interest in Binswanger's "existential analysis."[47] This is not the place to construct an itinerary of that interest. I should like to give merely a sense of that itinerary by proposing a sentence imitating one Foucault wrote himself. Here is Foucault, writing on "mental illness" in 1954: "Illness is the *psychological truth* of health, to the very extent that it is its *human contradiction*."[48] Now consider this: "*Pouvoir-savoir* is the onto-phenomenological truth of ethics, to the very extent that it is its contradiction in subjecting."

Giving the proper names of Foucault and Derrida in to each other, then, and with the benefit of three decades of work by both philosophers after Derrida's initial criticism of Foucault, I would discover in "madness" the catachrestic name given by the early Foucault to that ontic dimension of Being which eludes Reason's ontology. I would suggest that, in *Madness and Unreason,* his first "real" book, where Foucault takes, by his own well-known account, a serious swerve away from the history of madness to the archaeology of silence, the history and the philosophy (the dogmatic and the critical, loosely, if you like) have not yet brought each other to the crisis that this new politics of practice must assiduously cultivate. Foucault is himself so brilliantly involved in the construction of the name of "madness" that, at this stage, he merely "betrays" his own catachrestic use of it. Put another way, he is himself at once using the inaccessibility of madness (as "truth of Being") as a catachresis for the *ontic*—perhaps through his on-the-job training with Heideggerian existential analysis—and is sufficiently dazzled by the paleonymic promise to make an onto*logical* commitment to madness, to want to speak it in critical speech. I could reread the summing-up of the book in the Introduction to *The Archaeology of Knowledge* in this spirit.[49]

It is not surprising that readers have generally focused on the spectacular account of the definition and exclusion of madness rather than its definitive, intimate, inaccessible, ontic place. For in this early work there is an overriding tendency to shuttle between madness as a primordial ontic space and an ontologically displaced physicomoral condition. Yet the emphasis is certainly on "the essential unknowability of madness."[50] Because this emphasis may easily be restated as "an attempt to grasp a form of human existence entirely other than our own," it is just as certainly appropriate to notice that Derrida's chief critique is the insistence that "madness is within thought."

Within these frames, both Derrida and Foucault are interested in the production of "truth." Deconstruction is not exposure of error. Logocentrism is not a pathology. Deconstruction is "justice," says Derrida. And Foucault: "My objective . . . has been to create a history of the different modes of objectification which transform human beings into subjects." Derrida, too, always rusing on the track of the ruses of the subject centering itself in the act, in decision, in thought, in affirmation, with no hope of closure.

And yet the slash must be honored.

Derrida's tending of ontic "knowing" has become more and more rhetorical since the publication of *Glas* in 1974.[51] If I am right in thinking that the relationship between "folie" and "connaissance" in *Folie et déraison* is homologous to the relationship between self-proximate ontic "knowing" and ontological knowledge, it seems appropriate that no *ethical* position can develop to bridge so absolute a divide.[52] The archaeology of knowledge (rather than silence) may be seen as a method that would make the divide a clinamen.[53] The articulation of *pouvoir savoir* secures the first stage of the clinamen that makes it accessible to a sense of being. The next step, since the unquestioned transparent ethical subject—the white male heterosexual Christian man of property—has now been questioned into specificity and visibility, is to measure the plurality of ethics by researching the ways in which the subject "subjects" itself through "ability to know" (*pouvoir-savoir*). This is what it might mean to say: "Thus it is not power, but the subject, which is the general theme of my research."[54]

I am suggesting, then, that this line of ethical inquiry proceeds from the challenge of the robust Heideggerian notion of ontico-ontological difference, understood as implying ontico-ethical proximity, and *not* neutralized, as by Heidegger himself, by way of *Dichtung* or *Lichtung*.[55]

This immense project was not realized by Foucault. He established one point: that the constitution of the modern "Western" subject may be through the *pouvoir-savoir* of sexuality (even this would of course be ignored by masculist ethical philosophers); but not all subjecting is done that way. In fourth century B.C. Greece it was done through the use of pleasure in the care of the self. I am incapable of judging if Foucault was right about Greece in that period. The point here is that he follows the implications of the limits of existential analysis to come to *this* way of beginning ethical investigations. Undoubtedly this sort of stage-talk on my part is to impose a continuity. But this imposition becomes strategically necessary when, from a point of view where philosophy is seen as a private enterprise, where a complete break between philosophy and "citizenship" (necessarily of the postimperialist or neocolonialist "liberal" state) is taken as normal—from such a point of view, Foucault seems to be pushing for the poet's desire for autonomy as a general ethical *goal*.[56]

The point of my strategic and heuristic use of continuism is to emphasize that, if the ethical subject is *not* taken to be without historical, cultural, linguistic limits, then a study of its constitution(s) is the place to begin ethical investigations. As André Glucksmann writes: any ontico-ethical thinking must take into account or "make appear the dissymetries, the disequilibriums, the aporias, the impossibilities, which are precisely the objects of all commitment."[57]

Derrida too tends to the ontic, but differently, risking his disciplinary practice through the rhetoric of the everyday. His ethical concerns tend more toward a responsibility to the trace of the other than a consideration of the care of the self.[58] For Derrida, Levinas's ethics of absolute alterity has written itself upon and under the ontico-ontological difference.[59] And the being in and out of this difference has been textured by the effort to see man—the major actor—as varieties of other.[60] Foucault's last phase takes him into ground-level ethical codes of gendering.

Remember those "fee boardschool shirkers" in *Finnegans Wake,* "Will, Conn and Otto, to tell them overagait, Vol, Pov and Dev?"[61] Will, can and ought to—*vouloir, pouvoir,* and *devoir* (the ethical) under scrutiny. Derrida watches out for the one who justifies practice by theory or theory by practice, compromised by both. And Foucault says, in one of his last interviews:

> One did not suggest what people ought to be, what they ought to do, what they ought to think and believe. It was a matter rather of showing how social mechanisms up to now have been able to work . . . and then, starting from there, one left to the people themselves, knowing all the above, the possibility of self-determination and the choice of their own existence. . . .
>
> Q[uestion]: Isn't it basically a question of a new genealogy of morals?
>
> M F[oucault]: If not for the solemnity of the title and the imposing marks that Nietzsche left on it, I would say yes.[62]

On this generalized retrospective register, "morals" and "ethics" can be allowed to be interchangeable. We all know that other exchange, barely a year before this: "Q[uestion]: Would it be fair to say that you're not doing the genealogy of morals, because you think the moral codes are relatively stable, but what you're doing is a genealogy of ethics? A[nswer]: Yes, I'm writing a genealogy of ethics."

At this point, what we see most poignantly illustrated is the anxiety of the academic interlocutors: tell us, you *must* be doing this? And the answer comes back, yes, yes.

This essay might seem to be yet another entry in the debate over whether Foucault was from beginning to end an "archaeologist," or if he abandoned "archaeology" as a dead end to take up "genealogy." I seem to have taken the position that there is an asymmetrical homology between *énoncé-savoir-connaissance* and *force-pouvoir-puissance* that has something like a relationship with subindividual-ontic-ontological. Inscribed into the field of the ethical, this homology gives us a hint of how seriously Foucault pursued the track of a *critical* philosophy that was not content to assume its modernist Eurocentric *dogmatic* burden. Reading this way, one is struck by the specificity of Foucault's self-avowed clinamen—away from the "historical" to what in Heideggerian terminology one might call the "historial": ". . . farther and farther away from the chronological outline I had first decided on . . . to [the] analy[sis] of the flesh.[63]" There is a tone of humility in beginning with other civilizations' *souci de soi*— starting with the nearest "other," Greek antiquity—rather than the arrogance of a desire for individual autonomy.

Although I came to be struck by this through my reading of Derrida, I have indicated that this is a different project from the possibility of the ethical "within" alterity and randomness implied by Derrida's work. And indeed there is here a different kind of difference that one might dwell on for a moment.

Foucault's final focusing on the relationship to the self in the experience of the flesh is a practical ontology. Transformed into reflex, such a practical ontology comes to contaminate the ontic but, kept as code, it straddles the ontico-ontological difference in a way that full-dress moral philosophies will, indeed can, never do: "the care of the flesh is ethically prior [*éthiquement premier*] in the measure that the relationship to the self is ontologically prior."[64] This is *pouvoir-savoir* at ground level, "the working of thought upon itself . . . as critical activity," not at degree zero.[65] This is "the soil that can nourish," this "the general form of problemization."[66] Habermas and others have thought this to be a swerve away from the subindividual level that was the most unusual aspect of Foucault's archaeogenealogy. (It is characteristic of Habermas's general epistemic block to this kind of thinking that he calls the subindividual "*supra*subjective.")[67] In actual fact, Foucault makes it clear that, although in search of the role of the ontic in the constitution of the ethical, he is now impelled to focus on another band of the discontinuous spectrum of *pouvoir savoir*—he is not repudiating the articulation of the subindividual level: "I will call subjectivization the procedure by which one obtains the constitution of a subject, or more precisely, of a subjectivity which is of course *only one of the given possibilities of organization of a self-consciousness.*"[68] Here indeed is the consequence of that earlier position that we could only deduce: "*pouvoir-savoir* is the onto-phenomenological truth of ethics, to the very extent that it is its contradiction in subjecting" (see page 22).

In embracing this consequence, Foucault does indeed move away from the *mode* of the critique of humanism that Derrida inhabits, even as, in renouncing mere chronological inquiry and only the particular forms of the technologies of power and strategies of knowledge, he comes closer to the younger philosopher. In this new mode, he soberly tabulates the ingredients of the ethical habit, rather than running and floating with thought tangled in rhetoric, as does Derrida, at the other extreme. In a way, "it is [indeed] clear how far one is from an analysis in terms of deconstruction," as Foucault says right at the end.[69] But the terrain is, in another and related way, nearer. Foucault is no longer tripping up the programs of emancipation (mostly juridico-legal and political), but tracking the "practice of freedom." It is indeed clear how far he is from a Derrida who has put the *praxis* of freedom to the test by the *technè* of each act of writing. Foucault, in his final serene mood, can write: "Liberty is the ontological condition of ethics. But ethics is the deliberate [*réfléchie*] form taken by liberty."[70] The relationship between condition of (im)possibility and practice in Derrida would lead, in my understanding and formulation, to the more gymnastic "persistent critique of what one cannot not want."[71]

It is of course the archaeology/genealogy debate that still exercises readers of Foucault in France as well as in the United States. In the context of the United States, my position would seem to resemble that of Gary Gutting (who says all is archaeology) rather than that held by Dreyfus and Rabinow (who say archaeology was dropped).[72]

However that may be, I would like to suggest that the U.S. approach to Foucault, on either side of the debate, is generally within the same side of a clash of epistemes. Both Gutting on the one hand and Dreyfus and Rabinow on the other like Foucault and want to save him for philosophy. But if an *episteme* can be taken, loosely, to be one level of social *pouvoir savoir,* then these colleagues seem to inhabit a rather different one from Foucault's. It is as if, assembled at a race where the point is to stay on a bicycle at as slow a speed as possible—see how close you can get to *pouvoir-savoir* degree zero in order to think ethics in its "real" problems—

these colleagues would murmur, you can use these machines to get places fast too, you know! It is my belief that nobody who thinks of rhetoric as "befogg[ing] by the tortuous opacities of his prose and dazzl[ing] by the seeming gratuitousness of his audacious claims," can fall into the episteme or mind-set within which Foucault labored.[73]

In order to answer the question "do his writings, beneath all the fire-works and attendant billows of smoke, in fact express a position of sufficient clarity, plausibility, and interest to merit sustained attention?" every challenging thought must be made blunt by Gutting so that influences can be charted, continuities established, exam questions answered.

Dreyfus and Rabinow approach Foucault with grace and sympathy. Yet they too flatten him out and understand his "progress" as rejecting less good for more good alternatives and solutions. Their entire book is plotted on this assumption and never more so than in the interviews at the end, where one feels the tension of making Foucault fit for the consumption of American students and colleagues, to regularize him, normalize him, disciplinarize him. The desperation of the following exchange, tucked at the end of the book, is telling:

> Q. Do you think that the Greeks offer an attractive and plausible alternative?
> A. No! I am not looking for an alternative. . . . You see, what I want to do is not the history of solutions, and that's the reason why I don't accept the word "alternative."[74]

About Rorty's lack of epistemic consonance with Foucault I have already written. Paul Bové has written perceptively about a comparable lack in Charles Taylor.[75]

Roy Boyne's good reading of the relationship between Foucault and Derrida does not finally avoid this epistemically coded tendency to read the critical as altogether dogmatic. As a result he both hopes and regrets more. On the one hand, he sees in the two philosophers a certain "post-existentialist despair."[76] Given Derrida's open early warning that grammatology cannot be a positive science, he somewhat reinvents the wheel by asking and answering in the negative the question: "Is there a positive practice that can emerge from such dark 'realism'?"[77] In fact this "realism" is as "dark" as it is "light," for its persistent task is to keep grounded plans in touch with the spaciness of space. Boyne describes the survival techniques for the production of the "truth" of being in ontology, provided by logocentrism, rhetoricity, and techniques of the self with the moral harshness of the desire that a critical philosophy offer dogmatic alternatives: "It is possible that an utterly pervasive self-deceit, together with all but unrecognized rhetorical deception and conceptual violence, is functionally necessary for social life." Here indeed is the "humiliation" expected by Rorty from the deconstructivist. It is hard for the dogmatic philosopher to grasp that a strategist is a trickster, since there is no free play. In his view therefore, a strategic essentialism becomes a "pessimistic essentialism."[78] When he reads Derrida as "invent[ing] a philosophical strategy which opposes reason from the inside," Boyne cannot see that the importance of this invention is in its confounding of the hope of success with the fear of failure. I am certainly in sympathy with Boyne when he writes: "the full confluence of the ideas of Foucault and Derrida may never be achieved," although what is a "full confluence"? But, in reading Foucault's interest in the care for the self as a finished project rather than a first step in the investigation of other *pouvoir/savoir* of a preontological ontology in the constitution of the subject of ethics, Boyne is both too upbeat and not upbeat enough:

> the vision, which is barely taking shape, of an aesthetics of existence oriented to the careful (in the fullest sense of the word) destabilization of hierarchical determinations of otherness, at least provides the possibility of an exit from the anti-social snares of liberal individualism.

This position is unfortunately open to Rorty's shots in "Moral Ideals." And the possibilities of the transformation of a care [*Sorge*]-ful acceptance of being-there [*Dasein*] into an aesthetics of existence are not necessarily socially fruitful. The critical exit is *in* liberal individualism, if that is our dominant historical moment, even as *we* are in it, by reading and writing this book. The critical (deconstructive/genealogicoethical) being can activate this exit within, without *full* hope (which may include having *some* hope) in teleological change, and therefore without letting up. That may be the name of ethical living, with some hope in working for political change. Indeed, this position too can be trivialized and made comfortable "loyal opposition" talk. It is hard to acknowledge that liberal individualism is a violating enablement. It is in postcoloniality and the hope for development that this acknowledgment is daily extracted; although postcoloniality—a wrenching coupling of epistemes—should not be taken as its only example.

It is customary to stage epistemes as national inclinations: France and the Anglo-U.S. Epistemes are of course not nationally determined. Or, to put it another way, they are as historically determined (or determining of history) as is "national character." Paul Bové is "American," and Jean

Baudrillard—expecting an ontological commitment to power from the same page of *The Will to Knowledge* that we have been reading—is "French." And in fact, since we have been speaking of the *pouvoir-savoir* circuits as layered, on a certain layer, the word "episteme" can stand in for "assent to the dominant."

Our notions of political activism are deeply rooted in the bourgeois revolution from whose inheritance Derrida and Foucault, descendants of 1789, have taken a distance. A call for individual rights, national or psychosexual liberation, constitutional agency, inscribed in a *pouvoir/savoir* deeply marked by the strategy-techniques of management (small m), cannot bring forth positive responses from them. As Foucault says, "knowing all the above, leave it to the people."[79] As Alessandro Pizzorno points out, "the 'victim' of power" is not, for Foucault, as s/he is "for Marx as for Weber, . . . the individual as such whom that structural power prevents from developing as he [sic] could have done in other conditions."[80] I suppose there is less harm in rewriting Derrida as a libertarian for the marginal, or Foucault as the successful practitioner of genealogy (Godot arrived on the bus, as it were) than in dismissing archaeology as nihilism, or saying, as I heard Anthony D'Amato, a lawyer stunningly ignorant of anything having to do with deconstruction, say at a conference in October 1989: "The fact that a black man is rotting away in prison for a crime is simply the real world byproduct of Judge Easterbrook's textbook exercise in deconstruction." I continue to think that the real usefulness of these two *is* in the lesson of their refusal to be taken in by victories measured out in rational abstractions, in the dying fall of their urge persistently to critique those dogmas for the few (in the name of the many) that *we* cannot not want to inhabit. By reading Foucault in Derrida, I have tried to repeat the practical lesson of history, the perennial critique: *qui gagne perd;* who wins (also) loses. "A cautious skepticism with regard to utopian politics and a neostoic almost Camusian[?] 'pessimistic activism' in the face of ultimate meaninglessness," writes Thomas Flynn, of the same lesson.[81] By reading Foucault in Derrida in the wake of a reconsideration of Heidegger, I have tried to distinguish this trajectory from the existentialist position.

This is not as mysterious or ethereal as one might think. Urging the reader to remember all that I have said about the narrow and general senses, let me give an example. In September 1989, I heard Ngugi Wa Thiong'o, the Kenyan writer and political exile, speak on Exile and Displacement at a panel on Third World Film in Birmingham. He spoke movingly of his sense of double exile, *in* his own country because of its betrayal of the democratic ideal, and in Britain, where he has sought *refuge,* because the worst elements in his country are collaborating with Britain. A South African from the audience asked him what he thought of recent developments toward a rapprochement in South Africa. Ngugi spoke with immense respect and support, very carefully made allowances for not being involved there, not being a savvy participant. But then said this: my greatest fear is that South Africa should fall into neocolonialism.

That is the voice of caution, raised at the moment of negotiated independence, a critique of what one cannot not want. It is not without interest that, in explaining his final move, Foucault uses the example of decolonization:

> When a colonized [*colonisé*] people tries to free itself of its colonizer, that is truly a practice [*pratique*] of liberation, in the strict sense of the word. But as we also know, this practice of liberation does not define [*définir*] the practices of liberty which will then be necessary for this people, this society and these individuals to define themselves [*se définir*] receivable and acceptable forms of their existence or of a political society.[82]

To elaborate Foucault's understanding of this double gesture into the productive unease of a persistent critique, I will move to Mahasweta Devi.

Critical-Dogmatic in the Postcolonial Subject

Mahasweta Devi is as unusual within the Bengali literary tradition as Foucault or Derrida within the philosophical or political mainstream in France. She is not representative of Third World feminism. Therefore my risk here is to feed too easily *our* academic *pouvoir/savoir,* that would like to familiarize her singularity into an example. Virago Press wanted to docket her as an *Indian* woman writer and put her in with Anita Desai or Bharati Mukherjee. On the other side, I have read a proposal where an effort is being made to put her within the pantheon of great Bengali woman writers in the bourgeois tradition, merely as a "complementary voice." Once again, that conflation of episteme with nation! At this moment, to slash her with an "ism," even *feminism,* puts her singularity at risk.

Mahasweta is almost exactly the same age Foucault would have been, slightly older than Derrida. She too is a sometime academic. She too lived through the Second World War, which for her was the prelude to the negotiated Independence of India. She has seen the need for the critical watchfulness of which Ngugi spoke. Mahasweta's involvement with the

Communist Party dates back nearly fifty years. Here too, seeing a beleaguered illegal party in British India move into electoral politics has made
it necessary for her to take a distance, though she is, of course, resolutely
"on the left."

It goes without saying that the real difference between Mahasweta and
the two French philosophers is by way of the place of woman in her texts.
In terms of the narrow sense/general sense or theory/practice argument,
however, a related difference is also significant. Unlike Foucault and
Derrida, Mahasweta was only incidentally an academic. She is, of course,
a writer of fiction. But, ever since the great artificial famine of 1942,
planned to feed British soldiers in the Asian theater, she has been continu-
ously a political activist. As she has taken a distance from party politics
on the left, her work has moved more and more into the area of the
politics of Indian tribals and outcastes. Paradoxically, her involvement is
away from the theater of armed struggle, in the arena of tribal self-
development and Constitutional rights. She is so involved in the immense
labor of making known and helping implement the sanctions for the
tribals and outcastes written into the Indian Constitution of 1947–49 that
the fine-tuning of her writing is beginning to suffer.

At the negotiated independence of the Indian subcontinent, the first
Indian constitution was written under the aegis of Lord Mountbatten and
came out of what Bhikhu Parekh has recently called "the claustrophobic
post-Enlightenment enclave."[83] It is Mahasweta's subject-position as the
"citizen" of a recently decolonized "nation" that puts her in a different
relationship to the inheritance of 1789 from Foucault and Derrida.[84] Her
position bears comparison, though is not identical, with reproductive
rights feminists in the West, who must also want a share of that inheritance, and must write the woman's body in a normative and privative
rational juridicolegal discourse. Mahasweta must therefore persistently
critique her involvement. She too is "aware" at some level that constitutional rights cannot take its end as an unquestioned good. I believe this
critique and anxiety are staged again and again in the theater of her fiction.
The fiction traffics in the untotalizable where the intending consciousness
cannot be privileged. Her political activism, which is not "described" in
the fiction, keeps its nose to a critiqued totality. The line between the two
is never very clear-cut.

With this brief introduction, let me flesh out my schema just a little
further. I will be anticipating some of the principal arguments animating
later chapters.

The subject-position of the citizen of a recently decolonized "nation"
is epistemically fractured. The so-called private individual and the public

citizen in a decolonized nation can inhabit widely different epistemes, violently at odds with each other yet yoked together by way of the many everyday ruses of *pouvoir-savoir*. "Literature," straddling this epistemic divide, cannot simply remain in the "private" sphere; and not only because it is at a "less developed stage" by some "Euro"-teleology. The embarrassing myopia of a statement like the following simply cannot see the script of the uneven epistemic violation in the decolonized theater:

> One would never guess, to read Foucault's analysis of the transformations operated in the last three centuries within European social institutions that that period has seen a considerable diminution in suffering and an equally considerable augmentation of the chances offered to the individual to choose his life-style himself.[85]

O brave new world.

The political claims that are most urgent in decolonized space are tacitly recognized as coded within the legacy of imperialism: nationhood, constitutionality, citizenship, democracy, socialism, even culturalism. In the historical frame of exploration, colonization, decolonization—what is being *effectively* reclaimed is a series of regulative political concepts, the supposedly authoritative narrative of the production of which was written elsewhere, in the social formations of Western Europe. They are thus being reclaimed, indeed claimed, as concept-metaphors for which no *historically* adequate referent may be advanced from postcolonial space. That does not make the claims less urgent. For the people who are making the claims, the history of the Enlightenment episteme is "cited" even on an individual level, as the script is cited for an actor's interpretation.

"Feminism," the named movement, is also part of this heritage of the European Enlightenment. *Within* the enclosure of the heritage, it is of course inscribed as an "irreducible vis-à-vis" the masculine dominant.

The space that Mahasweta's fiction inhabits is rather special, even within this specifying argument. It is the space of the "subaltern," displaced even from the catachrestic relationship between decolonization and the Enlightenment, with feminism inscribed within it.

Especially in cultural critique, the event of political independence can be automatically assumed to stand in-between colony and decolonization as an unexamined good that operates a reversal. As I am insisting, the new nation is run by a regulative logic derived from a reversal of the old colony from within the cited episteme of the postcolonial subject: secularism, democracy, socialism, national identity, capitalist development. There is however a space that did not share in the energy of this reversal, a space that had no firmly established agency of traffic with the *culture* of imperialism. Paradoxically, this space is also outside of organized labor, below the attempted reversals of capital logic. Conventionally, this space is described as the habitat of the *sub*proletariat or the *sub*altern. Mahasweta's fiction suggests that *this* is the space of the displacement of the colonization-decolonization reversal. This is the space that can become, for her, a dystopic representation of decolonization *as such*. In this context, "decolonization" becomes only a convenient and misleading word, used because no other can be found.

If neocolonialism is only seen from the undoubtedly complex and important but restrictive perspective of metropolitan internal colonization or the postcolonial migrant or immigrant, this particular scenario of displacement becomes invisible, drops out of sight. The *pouvoir-savoir* or know-it-as-this/can-do-it-as-this of the discourse of feminism is obviously counterintuitive to the inhabitants of this space, the space of Mahasweta's fiction. As she works actively to move the subaltern into hegemony, in her struggle in the field, she pushes them toward that other episteme, where the "intuitions" of feminism become accessible. I am not arguing a fiction/reality opposition here. The narrow and the general sense infiltrate each other, bring each other to crisis, although they are not inscribed into a continuum.

Thus, if we think back about the *pouvoir-savoir* example of mother-daughter relationships in new immigration, we can see another conjuncture of similar strands here: writer/activist, subaltern/citizen, in the same nation. Especially in the postcolonial womanspace, this is a much more "complex set of relationships" than Rorty's public-private.

Mahasweta's fictions are thus not stories of the improbable awakening of feminist consciousness in the gendered subaltern. They are also not spoken *for* them, whatever that might mean. She does not speak *as* them, or *to* them. These are singular, paralogical figures of women (sometimes wild men, mad men) who spell out no model for imitation. I will mention a few that I have tried to capture in commentary and translation and then talk about a couple that belong to my translation work in progress.

Draupadi and Jashoda are explosions of the Hindu traditional imagination of the female. In Mahasweta's stories, Draupadi stands finally fixed and naked, a figure of refusal, in front of the Police Officer, her breasts mangled and her vagina torn and bleeding. She is at a distance from the political activism of the male. Jashoda lies dead, her breast putrefied with cancer, a figure that blasts mothering right out of its affective coding. She is at a distance from the gradual emancipation of the bourgeois female.[86]

Mary Oraon in "The Hunt" is the child of the violation of a tribal

Christian servant-woman by the white planter who leaves the plantation at Independence. Child of violation, Mary Oraon is the very figure of postcoloniality, displaced to the subaltern level. At the end of "The Hunt," she has just murdered the exploitative rural contractor. Drunk on alcohol and violence, she is in flight, running along the railroad line. A half-caste, she is at a distance from the authentic ethnic.[87]

When we are not immediately involved in systemic politics, we are not necessarily exempt from the anxiety of being pushed into an alien, "scientific," or "constitutional" episteme. The philosopher-intellectual can offer nonspecific alternatives, a last-ditch hope that *might* inspire ecological activists in the postmodern economies (not the decolonized subaltern, for whom ancient utopias have become sites of terror under exploitation). But will those activists read literary journals, and can the aggregative apparatuses be made to listen? Michel Serre, for example, not immediately involved in what he calls the "Exact Sciences," can stage the anxiety and propose a utopian solution in the following way. First, the anxiety, here more Manichean, "terror":

> The terror comes, if I dare to say it, not from the fact of power, but from rightness. The thing is that science is right—it is demonstrably right, factually right. It is thus right in asserting itself. It is thus right in asserting that which is not right. Nothing is produced, no one is cured, the economy is not improved by the means of sayings, clichés or tragedies.[88]

And then the admirable solution (altogether restricted in its availability) which can, as he says, "chuck the death wish":

> I am seeking a knowledge that is finally adult. . . . The adult man is educated in a third way. Agronomist and man of the woods, savage and tiller of the fields, he has both culture and science. Criticism is fairly futile—only invention counts. This so-called adult knowledge is convinced and certain that the picture described above is full of sense.

But the anxiety still shows through, as does the binary ranking.

> Seeker, *if you need to find something* . . . take courses in the history of the sciences. . . . *My* hope [however] does not follow the straight road, the monotonous and dreary methodology from which novelty has fled; my hope invents the cut-off trail, broken, chosen at random from the wasp, the bee, the fly.

If you are actually involved in changing state policy on the one hand, and earning the right to be heard and trusted by the subaltern on the other, on behalf of a change that is both medicine and poison, you cannot choose to choose the cut-off trail, declaring it as a hope when for some it has been turned into despair. And, if, like Derrida and Foucault, you are a scrupulous academic who *is* largely an academic, you stage the crisis relationship between theory and practice in the practice of your theoretical production in various ways instead of legitimizing the polarization between the academy and the real world by disavowing it, and then producing elegant solutions that will never be seriously tested either in large-scale decision-making or among the disenfranchised.

Thus the figures of Mahasweta's fiction are at odds with the project of access to national constitutional agency for the tribal and the outcaste upon which Mahasweta is herself actively bent. This is not a contradiction, but rather the critical *rapport sans rapport* of which I spoke earlier. The most spectacular example is from "Douloti the Bountiful."[89] Here the affective nostalgic tribal world of the young central character, a bonded prostitute, is represented with great delicacy of a lyric sentiment that is at odds with the harsh, critical collectivity of prostitutes, and the armed struggle of the men in that gender-divided world. The aporia is staged *in* the fiction. These women of Mahasweta's fiction are almost like unconnected letters in a script neither archaic nor modern, caught neither in a past present, nor on the way to a future present. They are monuments to the anxiety of their inevitable disappearance as "justice is done," and the episteme is on the way to regularization. If you consider Mahasweta's fictive and social text together, "feminism" becomes a necessary but misfitting name. We keep pushing her: tell us, you *must* be doing this? She will say good-naturedly—yes, yes. Or, being irascible, and not as eager to placate as a senior academic—no.

I think now of the improbable hero of her novella "Pterodactyl, Pirtha, and Puran Sahay": a pterodactyl, discovered in a tribal area in the modern state of Bihar. It could not be kept alive, although the journalist and the child wanted to feed it. The look in its eyes could not be understood. The child drew its picture on the cave-wall. This latest entry into that collection of figures, mute guest from an improbable and inaccessible past, before the origin of paleonymy or archaeology, guardian of the margin, calling for but not calling forth the ethical antiphone, measures for me the risk of obliterating the rift between the narrow and the general in the name of a merely liberal politics.

3

Marginality in the Teaching Machine

This essay is not about the difference between Africa and Asia, between the United States and Britain. It is about the difference and the relationship between academic and "revolutionary" practices in the interest of social change. The radical academic, *when she is in the academy*, might reckon that names like "Asian" or "African" (or indeed "American" or "British") have histories that are not anchored in identities but rather secure them. We cannot exchange as "truth," in the currency of the university, what might be immediate needs for identitarian collectivities. This seems particularly necessary in literary criticism today, with its vigorous investments in cultural critique. If academic and "revolutionary" practices do not bring each other to productive crisis, the power of the script has clearly passed elsewhere. There can be no universalist claims in the human sciences. This is most strikingly obvious in the case of establishing "marginality" as a subject-position in literary and cultural critique. The reader must accustom herself to starting from a particular situation and then to the ground shifting under her feet.

In terms laid out in the previous chapter, we are dealing here with the aggregative apparatus of Euro-American university education, where weapons for the play of power/knowledge as *puissance/connaissance* are daily put together, bit by bit, according to a history rather different from our own. One of the structurally functional ruses of this manufacture or putting-together is to give it out as the cottage-industry of mere *pouvoir/ savoir* or the ontic, the everyday, the ground of identity. If we are taken in by this ruse, indeed propagate it through our teaching, we are part of the problem rather than the solution. Indeed, it may be that the problem and the solution are always entangled, that it cannot be otherwise. That may be the reason why persistent critique rather than academic competition disguised as the politics of difference is a more productive course.[1]

At the conference on Cultural Value at Birkbeck College, the University of London, on July 16, 1988, where this paper was first presented, the speaker was obliged to think of her cultural identity. From what space was she speaking, in what space was the representative member of the audience placing her? What does the audience expect to hear today, here?

Presumed cultural identity often depends on a name. In Britain in July of 1988 a section of underclass "Asians" was vigorously demanding to be recognized as different from underclass "Blacks," basically because they felt, by the deplorable logic of underclass racism, fed by poverty and encouraged by the ruling class, that on account of their cultural attributes of mildness, thrift, domesticity, and industriousness, they were, unlike the lazy and violent peoples of African origin, responsible and potentially upwardly mobile material.

Distinguishing between Africa and Asia in terms of kinship to Europe is an old story. As a politically correct Asian, of course, I find this story deplorable. Yet it can be said that first, a well-placed Asian academic can afford to find it deplorable; and, secondly, that academic insistence on a politics of difference may be equally as competitive in intent. To a London audience, academics and cultural workers, eager to hear a speech on cultural value, it is important that the speaker's identity that afternoon was "Asian," with underclass differentiations out of sight. Unless we continue to nurse the platitudinous conviction that the masses are necessarily identical with "the revolutionary vanguard," or conversely that, stepping into the university, "The truth has made us free," we must attend to the possibility of such dissension, and their imbrication with the history and burden of names. Identitarianism can be as dangerous as it is powerful, and the radical teacher in the university can hope to work, however indirectly, toward controlling the dangers by making them visible.[2]

In the United States, where the speaker lives and teaches, her cultural identity is not "Asian," although it would be recognized as a geographically correct description by most people. In the United States, "Asians" are of Chinese, Japanese, Korean, and, of late, Vietnamese extraction. The complex and class-differentiated scenario of the absence or presence of their solidarity with African-Americans is yet another story. In the United States, she is "Indian." Subterfuges of nomenclature that are by now standard have almost (though not completely) obliterated the fact that that name lost some specificity in the first American genocide.

The feeling of cultural identity almost always presupposes a language. In that sense, I suppose I feel a Bengali. Yet in the London of July 1988, that name was negotiable as well. The places of "Bengali" concentration are populated by disenfranchised immigrant Bangladeshis. This seems to me to have a real political logic, not unrelated to national languages, which probably escapes most metropolitan British users of the name. Yet, considering the two-hundred-year-old history of the British representation (in both senses) of Bengal and vice versa, my loss of that name in that place is not without a certain appropriate irony.[3]

To whom did they want to listen, then, this representative audience in London? Since, if they had been attending to the coding of proper names, the references were up for grabs.

The name "Third World" is useful because, for any metropolitan audience, it can cover over much unease. For these listeners, the speaker's identity might well have been "Third World." (In the United States this would undoubtedly have been the case. It nicely marks the difference between Britain as the central colonial, and the United States as a central neocolonial power.)[4] Sociologists have been warning us against using this expression, contaminated at birth by the new economic programs of neocolonialism.[5] And, indeed, in the discipline of sociology, in the decade spanning *The New International Division of Labour* and *The End of the Third World,* the genealogy of a culturalist use of that term seems rather shabby.[6] What need does it satisfy? It gives a proper name to a generalized margin.

A word to name the margin. Perhaps that is what the audience wanted to hear: a voice from the margin. If there is a buzzword in cultural critique now, it is "marginality." Every academic knows that one cannot do without labels. To this particular label, however, Foucault's caution must be applied and we must attend to its *Herkunft* or descent. When a cultural identity is thrust upon one because the center wants an identifiable margin, claims for marginality assure validation from the center. It should then be pointed out that what is being negotiated here is not even a "race or a social type" (as in the passage below) but an economic principle of identification through separation.

> The analysis of *Herkunft* often involves a consideration of race or social type. But the traits it attempts to identify are not the exclusive generic characteristics of an individual, a sentiment, or an idea, which permit us to qualify them as "Greek" or "English" [or "Third World"]; rather, it seeks the subtle, singular, and subindividual marks that might possibly intersect in them to form a network that is difficult to unravel.[7]

The Academy

In order to bypass that comparison, the speaker could provisionally choose a name that would not keep her in (the representation of) a margin so thick with context. With all the perils attendant upon a declared choice she "chose" the institutional appellation "teacher." The institution is, most often for such speakers and audiences, writers and readers, a university, and I am a university teacher. That context is in its own way no thinner, but at least speaker and audience share it most obviously.

When we begin to teach "marginality," we start with the source books of the contemporary study of the cultural politics of colonialism and its aftermath: the great texts of the "Arab World," most often Frantz Fanon, a Christian psychiatrist from Martinique.[8] (I mention these details in anticipation of the fifth section below).

It is also from this general context that we find the source book in our discipline: Edward Said's *Orientalism*.[9] (A word on *our* discipline: since the conference was held under the auspices of a Department of English with a small interdisciplinary component in Culture Studies, I took it to be the collective professional identity of the majority, with all genealogy suspended.)

Said's book was not a study of marginality, not even of marginalization. It was the study of the construction of an object, for investigation and control. The study of colonial discourse, directly released by work such as Said's, has, however, blossomed into a garden where the marginal can speak and be spoken, even spoken for. It is an important (and beleaguered) part of the discipline now.[10]

As this material begins to be absorbed into the discipline, the long-established but supple, heterogeneous, and hierarchical power-lines of the institutional "dissemination of knowledge" continue to determine and overdetermine its conditions of representability. It is at the moment of infiltration or insertion, sufficiently under threat by the custodians of a fantasmatic high Western culture, that the greatest caution must be exercised.[11] The price of success must not compromise the enterprise irreparably. In that spirit of caution, it might not be inappropriate to notice that, as teachers, we are now involved in the construction of a new object of investigation—"the third world," "the marginal"—for institutional validation and certification. One has only to analyze carefully the proliferating but exclusivist "Third World-ist" job descriptions to see the packaging at work. It is as if, in a certain way, we are becoming complicitous in the perpetration of a "new orientalism."

> No "local centers," "no pattern of transformation" could function if, through a series of successive linkages [*enchâinements successifs*], it were not eventually written into [*s'inscrivait*] an over-all strategy . . . The [disciplinary] apparatus [*dispositif*], precisely to the extent that it [is] insular and heteromorphous with respect to the other great "manoeuvres" . . .[12]

writes Foucault.

Let us attempt to read the possibility of our unwilling or unwitting perpetration of a "new orientalism" as the inscription of an "overall strategy":

It is not only that lines separate ethnic, gender, and class prejudice in the metropolitan countries from *indigenous* cooperation with neo-colonialism outside, in the Third World proper. It is also that arguments from culturalism, multiculturalism, and ethnicity, however insular and heteromorphous they might seem from the great narratives of the techniques of global financial control, can work to obscure such separations in the interests of the production of a neocolonial discourse. Today the old ways, of imperial adjudication and open systemic intervention, cannot sustain unquestioned legitimacy. Neocolonialism is fabricating its allies by proposing a share of the center in a seemingly new way (not a rupture but a displacement): disciplinary support for the conviction of authentic marginality by the (aspiring) elite.[13]

If we keep the possibility of such inscriptions in mind, we might read differently the specific examples of the working of "local forces," close to home. Here are three. The first two are more directly inscribed into the economic text as it rewards the construction of objects of investigation: funded proposals. What sells today? "A pattern of transformation." The third works through what one might call the text of metropolitan representation and self-representation. Here are examples:

(1) Quotation from a grant proposal written by a brilliant young Marxist academic: Taking the "magical realism" of García Márquez as a paradigmatic case of Third World literary production, I will argue that science fiction . . . may be considered, so to speak, the Third World fiction of the industrial nations . . .

How is the claim to marginality being negotiated here? The radicals of the industrial nations want to *be* the Third World. Why is "magical realism" paradigmatic of Third World literary production? I have touched upon this question in Chapter One. In a bit, and in the hands of the less gifted teacher, only that literary style will begin to count as ethnically authentic. There is, after all, a reason why Latin America qualifies as the norm of "the Third World" for the United States, even as India used to be the authentic margin for the British. It is interesting that "magical realism," a style of Latin American provenance, has been used to great effect by some expatriate or diasporic subcontinentals writing in English.[14] Yet as the Ariel–Caliban debates dramatize, Latin America has *not* participated in decolonization. Certainly this formal conduct of magical realism can be said to allegorize, in the strictest possible sense, a socius and a political configuration where "decolonization" cannot be narrativized. What are the implications of pedagogic gestures that monumentalize *this* style as the right Third World style? In the greater part of the Third World, the problem is that the declared rupture of "decolonization" boringly repeats the rhythms of colonization with the consolidation of recognizable styles.

(2) A feminist who has done inspiring and meticulous work on the European discursive text of mothering, a friend and ally. (Again, the interest of this essay lies in a general autocritique of our moment in criticism, not in the exposure of an imagined enemy. That indeed is why the speaker put aside the name "Asian/Indian/Bengali/Third World" and took the microphone as "literary/culturalist/academic.")

My friend was looking for speakers to comment on postmodern styles in the context of the third world. She did not want her funded institute on the avant-garde to be "Eurocentric." I told her that I could only comment on a handful of writers in my native language. Her question: but do these writers show their awareness of being in a minority, being marginals? No, I said, and asked a counterquestion: Isn't it "Eurocentric" to choose only such writers who write in the consciousness of marginality and christen them "Third World"? Answer: One must begin somewhere.

"One must begin somewhere" is a different sentiment when expressed by the unorganized oppressed and when expressed by the beneficiary of the consolidated disciplinary structure of a central neocolonialist power. If we were studying this move in the perspective of nineteenth-century colonial discursive production, what would we say about the margin being constituted to suit the institutional convenience of the colonizer? If the "somewhere" that one begins from is the most privileged site of a neocolonial educational system, in an institute for the training of teachers, funded by the state, does that gesture of convenience not become the normative point of departure? Does not participation in such a privileged and authoritative apparatus require the greatest vigilance?

"If a genealogical analysis of a scholar were made . . . his *Herkunft* would quickly divulge the official papers of the scribe and the pleading of the lawyer—their father—in their apparently disinterested attention. . . ." (*LCP*, 147). Should we imagine ourselves free of this analysis? Should we not attempt also to "write the history of the present"? Why, as we clear ourselves of the alibi of occupying the center or seeking validation by/as the center, should we think that we do not resemble "the confused and anonymous European" of the nineteenth century, "who no longer knows

himself or what name he should adopt," to whom "the historian offers
. . . the possibility of alternate identities, more individualized and substantial than his own" (*LCP*, 160)? Our disavowal can only feed the fast-consolidating forces of reaction in the Institution.

As a result of a decade of colonial discourse studies percolating into disciplinary pedagogy and its powerful adjuncts, and of the imbrication of techniques of knowledge with strategies of power, who claims marginality in the larger postcolonial field? What might this have to do with the old scenario of empowering a privileged group or a group susceptible to upward mobility as the authentic inhabitants of the margin? Should we not cast a genealogical eye over what we have spawned in literary criticism and the study of culture, since a study of the strategies of the margin must not be stopped?

> One must not suppose that there exists a certain sphere of "marginality" that would be the legitimate concern of a free and disinterested scientific inquiry were it not the object of mechanisms of exclusion brought to bear by the economic or ideological requirements of power. If "marginality" is being constituted as an area of investigation, this is only because relations of power have established it as a possible object; and conversely, if power is able to take it as a target, this is because techniques of knowledge [disciplinary regulations] were capable of switching it on [*investir*].[15] Between techniques of knowledge and strategies of power, there is no exteriority, even if they have specific roles *and are linked together on the basis of their difference* . . . Not to look for who has the power in the order of marginality . . . and who *is* deprived of it . . . But to look rather for the pattern of the modifications which the relationships of force imply by the very nature of their process. (*HS*, 98–99 emphasis and contextual modification added)

(3) My third example comes from Benita Parry. Ms. Parry is, once again, an ally, and she was kind enough to draw my attention to the fact that in a recent issue of the *Oxford Literary Review* on colonialism, she had charged Homi Bhabha, Abdul JanMohammed, and Gayatri Spivak basically with not being able to listen to the voice of the native.[16]

Postcoloniality

It is in my response to her that the name "postcolonial" comes fully into play, which, incidentally, makes the Latin American as paradigmatic (stylistic) example, tremble.

In a piece on J.M. Coetzee's novel *Foe,* I have approached Parry's question by contrasting Defoe's Robinson Crusoe, the mercantile capitalist who trains Friday, represented as the willing protocolonial subject, with Coetzee's Susan Barton, the anachronistic eighteenth-century Englishwoman who longs to give the muted racial other a voice.[17] Rather than repeat my argument, I will take the liberty of quoting myself, with contextual modifications:

> When Benita Parry takes us to task for not being able to listen to the natives, or to let the natives speak, she forgets that the three of us, post-colonials, are "natives" too. We talk like Defoe's Friday, only much better. Three hundred years have passed, and territorial imperialism has changed to neo-colonialism. The resistant post-colonial has become a scandal.
>
> Why is the name "post-colonial" specifically useful in our moment?
>
> Those of us present in that room in Birkbeck College, or indeed the writers and readers of this collection, who are from formerly colonized countries, are able to communicate to each other, to exchange, to establish sociality, because we have had access to the culture of imperialism. Shall we then assign to that culture, to borrow Bernard Williams's phrase, a measure of "moral luck?"[18] I think there can be no doubt that the answer is "no." This impossible "no" to a structure, which one critiques, yet inhabits intimately, is the deconstructive philosophical position, and the everyday here and now named "post-coloniality" is a case of it.[19]

Here a point made in the previous chapter will bear repetition. Whatever the identitarian ethnicist claims of native or fundamental origin (implicit for example, in Parry's exhortation to hear the voice of the native), the political claims that are most urgent in decolonized space are tacitly recognized as coded within the legacy of imperialism: nationhood, constitutionality, citizenship, democracy, even culturalism. Within the historical frame of exploration, colonization, decolonization—what is being effectively reclaimed is a series of regulative political concepts, the *supposedly* authoritative narrative of the production of which was written elsewhere, in the social formations of Western Europe. They are being reclaimed, indeed claimed, as concept-metaphors for which no historically adequate referent may be advanced from postcolonial space, yet that does not make the claims less important. A concept-metaphor without an adequate referent is a catachresis. These claims for founding catachreses also make postcoloniality a deconstructive case.

The center, on the other hand, still longs for the object of conscientious traditional ethnography: "where women inscribed themselves as healers, ascetics, singers of sacred songs, artisans and artists," writes Benita Parry.

I have no objection to conscientious ethnography, although I am a bit frightened by its relationship to the history of the discipline of anthropology. My especial word to Parry, however, is that her efforts as well as mine are judged by the exclusions practiced through the intricate workings of the techniques of knowledge and the strategies of power, which have a history rather longer and broader than our individual benevolence and avowals.[20]

Value

The persistent critique of what one must inhabit, the persistent consolidation of claims to founding catachreses, involve an incessant recoding of diversified fields of value. Let us attempt to imagine "identity," so cherished a foothold, as flash-points in this recoding of the circuitry.

Let us, then, for the moment at least, arrest the understandable need to fix and diagnose the identity of the most deserving marginal. Let us also suspend the mood of self-congratulation as saviors of marginality. Let us peer, however blindly, into the constantly shifting and tangling network of the techniques of knowledge and the strategies of power through the question of value. This is not an invitation to step into the sunlit arena where values are so broad that philosophers can wrangle about it with reference to imaginary societies: ethical universals and cultural particularity.[21]

"Value-form" is the name of that "contentless and simple [*einfach*]" thing by way of which Marx rewrote not mediation, but the possibility of the mediation that makes possible in its turn all exchange, all communication, sociality itself.[22] Marx's especial concern is the appropriation of the human capacity to produce, not objects, nor anything tangible, but that simple contentless thing which is *not* pure form, yet perceptible only formally; the possibility of mediation (through coding) so that exchange and sociality can exist: work—*any* work—standing over against the person working, becoming socially mediated into what Marx's desperately overreaching language would call value-measured work, ability to work, *pouvoir-faire*, which the protocols of English has forever monumentalized into "labor-power."[23] Marx's point of entry is the economic coding of the value-form, but the notion itself has a much more supple range. As Marx wrote, to Engels "the issue of the matter of value is too decisive for the whole book" (what subsequently became the three volumes of *Capital* and the *Theories of Surplus Value*).[24]

In the early 1970s, *Anti-Oedipus* attempted to extend the range of the Marxian argument from value by applying it to the production and appropriation of the value-form in affective and social rather than merely economic coding. This was their appeal against Althusser, to read again the first chapter of *Capital,* where the talk is of value—the contentless necessary paraindividual presupposition—*before* it gets fully coded into an economic system of equivalences and entailed social relations. Relating it to the poststructuralists' attention to the subindividual, they called it "desire," a word fully as misleading as "value." Their suggestion was that, since capital decoded and deterritorialized the socius by releasing the abstract as such, capitalism must manage this crisis via many reterritorializations, among which the generalized, *psychoanalytic* mode of production of affective value operates by way of a generalized systemic institution of equivalence spectacular in its complexity and discontinuity.

The coding of value in the politicocognitive sphere, through the discursive system of marginality, whether by way of psychoanalysis, culturalism, or economism, is still part of this crisis-management. In the discipline, to take the most familiar everyday examples: "What is worth [the German word for 'value'] studying, teaching, and talking about" appears as "What can best be parceled out into a fourteen- or ten-week format"; "What are the best available textbooks" (where "best" and the "production of the best" are altogether coded); "What are the most manageable paper topics" (produced by the techniques of knowledge in the United States' primary and secondary education system); "How best can it be proved that this can be integrated into the English curriculum without disturbing the distribution requirements"; "What projects funded"; "What books marketed." Paradoxically, as these necessary practicalities—"one must begin somewhere"—become tacitly accepted working rules for the planners, the recipients (students, audiences) often think in terms of pedagogy as only consciousness-transformation, conference speech as only agenda. I am not suggesting that there is a positive space of "marginality" to be recovered on the other side of the incessant coding. "Marginality," as it is becoming part of the disciplinary-cultural parlance, is in fact the name of a certain constantly changing set of representations that is the condition and effect of it. It is coded in the currency of the equivalencies of knowledge. That currency measures the magnitude of value in the sphere of knowledge.

We cannot grasp value as such; its form is a possibility for grasping, without content. But if we position ourselves as *identities* in terms of links in the chain of a value-coding as if they were persons and things, and go on to ground our practice on that positioning, we become part of the problem in the ways I am describing.[25]

Work in gendering in principle sees the socius as an affective coded site of exchange and surplus. The simple contentless presupposition of value as it allows gender-coded exchange has historically led to the appropriation of the sexual differential, subtracted from, but represented as, the theoretical fiction of sexual identity. (Economically codable value is the differential subtracted from the theoretical fiction of use-value in the identity of production and consumption.)[26] As I have suggested in Chapter One, Gayle Rubin's "The Traffic in Women: Notes on the 'Political Economy' of Sex" was a pathbreaking essay in the analysis of gender-coding. Kalpana Bardhan's writings on the status of Indian women is the only scholarly work in the frame of postcoloniality in the subaltern context that I have seen which shares the presupposition that gender determinacy is the coding of the value-differential allowing for the possibility of the exchange of affective value, negotiating "sexuality" rather than sexual identity. In the psychoanalytic sphere, Melanie Klein's work, appropriated into a curious practice, can be read as approaching the constitution of the value-form as a constantly shuttling self.[27]

The operation of the value-form makes every commitment negotiable, however urgent it might seem or be. For the long haul emancipatory social intervention is not primarily a question of redressing victimage by the assertion of (class- or gender- or ethnocultural) identity. It is a question of developing a vigilance for systemic appropriations of the unacknowledged social production of a *differential* that is one basis of exchange into the networks of the cultural politics of class- or gender-*identification*.

In the field of ethnocultural politics, the postcolonial teacher can help to develop this vigilance rather than continue pathetically to dramatize victimage or assert a spurious identity. She says "no" to the "moral luck" of the culture of imperialism while recognizing that she must inhabit it, indeed invest it, to criticize it.

(Indeed, the specificity of "postcoloniality" understood in this way can help us to grasp that no historically [or philosophically] adequate claims can be produced in any space for the guiding words of political, military, economic, ideological emancipation and oppression. You take positions in terms not of the discovery of historical or philosophical grounds, but in terms of reversing, displacing, and seizing the apparatus of value-coding. This is what it means to say "the agenda of ontocultural commitments is negotiable." In that sense "postcoloniality," far from being marginal, can show the irreducible margin in the center: We are always *after* the empire of reason, our claims to it always short of adequate. In the hands of identitarians, alas, this can lead to further claims of marginality. "We are all postcolonials . . .")

Claiming catachreses from a space that one cannot not want to inhabit and yet must criticize is, then, the deconstructive predicament of the postcolonial. It is my hope that this sense will put a particular constraint upon the metropolitan marginal or indigenous elite, in whose ranks I can belong, not to produce a merely "antiquarian history" which seeks the continuities of soil, language, and urban life in which our present is rooted and, "by cultivating in a delicate manner that which existed for all time, . . . tr[ies] to conserve for posterity the conditions under which we were born" (*LCP*, 162).

It is in this spirit that I will view *Genesis,* a film by Mrinal Sen.

Let me spell it out here. Postcoloniality in general is not subsumable under the model of the revolutionary or resistant marginal in metropolitan space. If "black Britain" or the "rainbow coalition" in the United States are taken as paradigmatic of, say, India or the new African nations, the emphasis falls on Britain or the States as nation-states. It is in this sense that the aggressive use made by an earlier nationalism of the difference between culture and political power has now been reversed only in political *intent.* The main agenda there is still to explode the fantasmatic "whiteness" of the metropolitan nation. In a powerful recent essay, Tim Mitchell has suggested that the typical Orientalist attitude was "the world as exhibition."[28] The "new orientalism" views "the world as immigrant." It is meretricious to suggest that this reminder undervalues the struggle of the marginal in metropolitan space. It merely points out that to remember that that struggle cannot be made the unexamined referent for all postcoloniality without serious problems. No "two-way dialogue" in "the great currents of international cultural exchange" forgets this.[29]

Thus an art film out of India (*Genesis*), or out of Mali (Cisse Souleymane's *Yeelen*) cannot resemble *Thé au harem d'Archimède* (Mehdi Charif, French/Algerian). The last sequence of Alain Tanner's new film *Une flamme dans le coeur,* placing Mercedes (the Arab woman in Paris) in Cairo, attempts to point at this problematic.

Genesis: A Film by Mrinal Sen (1986)

As I have been arguing, current postcolonial claims to the names that are the legacy of the European enlightenment (sovereignty, constitutionality, self-determination, nationhood, citizenship, even culturalism) are catachrestical claims, their strategy a displacing and seizing of a previous coding of value.[30] It can show us the negotiable agenda of a cultural commitment to marginality, whereas ethnicist academic agendas make a fetish of identity. The project, as always, is the recoding of value as the differential possibility of exchange and the channeling of surplus. Postcoloniality as agency can make visible that the basis of *all* serious ontological commitment is catachrestical, because negotiable through the information that identity is, *in the larger sense,* a text.[31] It can show that the alternative to Europe's long story—generally translated as "great narratives"—is not only short tales (*petits récits*) but tampering with the authority of storylines.[32] In *all* beginning, repetition, signature:

> In order for the tethering to the source to occur, what must be retained is the absolute singularity of a signature-event and a signature-form . . . But . . . a signature must have a repeatable, iterable, imitable form; it must be able to be detached from the present and singular intention of its production.[33]

The first sequence of the film, repeating the formula, "as always, yet once again," ends in a shot of recognizably North Indian men and women, peasantry or the urban poor dressed in their best, lining up to be perfunctorily interrogated and put their thumbprints on a long scroll. As the voice-over intones: "As always, yet once again, they lost everything they had and became slaves again." In the manner of didactic allegories, some signals are clear to some groups tied together by the various value-codings (systems of representation) the elements of which are being manipulated by Sen with a certain panache. Indigenous radicals sense the pervasiveness and ubiquity of bonded labor as a mode of production (see chapter four). India enthusiasts perceive the famous Indian cyclical time. Slightly more knowledgeable Indians perhaps catch an ironic reference to Kṛiṣṇa's famous promise in the *Gita:* "I take on existence from eon to eon, for the rescue of the good and the destruction of the evil, in order to reestablish the Law."[34]

Some would notice an *in medias res* reference to the sequential narrative of the modes of production, a reminder of the young Marx's impatience with the question of origins, an impatience that was never given up: "If you ask about the creation of nature and of man, then you are abstracting from nature and man. . . . Do not think and do not ask me questions, for as soon as you think and ask questions, your *abstraction* from the existence of nature and man has no meaning."[35]

In this articulation of history in terms of the mode of production of (economic) value, the "worker" is represented as collectively caught in the primitive signature (at its most proximate the thumbprint, the body's mark), the originary contract—the first codification/identification. Both of these things take on importance in the film's subsequent emphasis on the name of the father and its use of the radical counterfactual.

Banality and the Desert

At any rate, it is only after this pre-originary scene of repetition that the title flashes on the screen: GENESIS. It looks a bit self-consciously solemn, in large letters by itself on the screen. The ethnographically savvy viewer would find it banal, the savvy diasporic would find it embarrassingly prepostmodern, the metropolitan third worldist would perhaps suppress the embarrassment because it's a third-world allegory of the birth of a nation—"genesis" does mean birth—which unfortunately misses the appropriate style of magical realism. The "nontheoretical" metropolitan third worldist would prefer something more de Sica style, like the recent *Salaam Bombay* (Mira Nair) or Adoor Gopalakrishnan's *Face to Face* with its heavy contemporary cultural content, spelling out the fate of a Western theory in the context of the encroachment of industrial capitalism in rural India, or even Sen's earlier films, where the superrealistic technique achieved its obsessive brilliance by laying bare, for the most part, the workings of the urban lower middle class of West Bengal. The appropriate, indeed felicitous, viewer of the film, the participant in the active high-cultural life of New Delhi, would recognize that it taps a rather banal tourist genre, the perennial spate of Indian films celebrating the local ethnic color of Rajasthan. This is a crude taxonomy, but it is still slightly more complex than first world/third world, Eurocentric/marginal.

If we look at the coding of these positions, it is possible to speculate that the viewer is baffled because Sen assumes *agency* of re-inscription rather than the marginality of the postcolonial position. As the opening credits unroll, we notice that it is Sen's first collaborative film, with French and Belgian support. *Gandhi* (Richard Attenborough) had to pretend that its British and U.S. casting and production were not "part of the film." Sen uses international collaboration to put together a film as a postcolonial, not as a Bengali for Bengalis or even "Indians".

The postcolonial text is often the site of the renegotiation of the banal for its telescoping of "an infinity of traces, without . . . inventory."[36] When a so-called third world text speaks a postcolonial (rather than nationalist) allegory, what lexicon is, after all, most readily to hand? It's the difference between, let us say, the hermeneutic reinterpretation of Freud and a look at the operation of "pop-psych" in society to see how it has become an operative and allegorical lexicon: between fixing your glance at the thickness of signifiers and at the impoverishment of the referential.[37] In such a text the allegory works in bits and pieces, with something like a relationship with the postmodern habit of citing without authority. With a pedagogy that sees this as the mark of the fragmented postcolonial mode, the allegory can offer a persistent parabasis to the development of any continuous ethnocultural narrative *or* of a continuous reinscription.[38]

Genesis is the "original," not the translated, title of the film. Why should a mainland Indian film not appropriate English as one of its moments, without the usual coyness of magical or teratological realism? Generally, in diasporic English fiction written by authors with little productive contact with the native languages, the only way in which these native languages are denoted is through the monstrous mockery of a transformed standard English which "assigns" the writer's subject-position lacking creative access to the languages of the country. Here the English word is, and is not, a *sub*title when it flashes on the screen. That at least is the postcolonial Indian's relationship to English—a (sub)titular relationship that does not derive from an authentic title to the language. At the origin is something like a subtitle, something like a footnote, something like a postscript, and postcoloniality can be its scrupulous paradigm.

Among other things, the film records the origin myth of the Bible. Why should the so-called center of Hinduism not appropriate Judeo-Christianity with the haphazard points of contact and noncoherent reinscription, appropriate to the postcolonial mode, *without* the heavy trappings of transcendentalism, unitarianism, and the nineteenth-century legitimizing projects, such as the Brahmo Samaj or the semitized Hinduism that masquerades as "the real thing"? Postcolonial pedagogy must teach the overdetermined play of cultural value in the inscription of the socius. Such unacknowledged appropriative overdeterminations are the substance of contemporary globality. Think for instance of the appropriative weaving of the great "European" narratives of socialism and "Christianity" (in this context "Christianity" is not quite European, in its origins, either) with the "Asian" narratives of "ethnicity" and "Islam" in the fact that the trans-Caucasian autonomous region of Nagorno-Karabakh, representing five per cent of the territory of the Republic of Azebaijan, was, in that very July, attempting to secede, under *glasnost,* from its Muslim-majority base to form the seventy-five per cent Christian-majority Artsakh Autonomous Republic of Armenia.[39]

A postcolonialist pedagogy, looking at the title *Genesis* on the screen, can help us acknowledge the overdeterminations, see *glasnost* and its attendant and subsequent outbursts of subnationalisms and nationalisms in the former Soviet Union within the curious logic of postcoloniality. The fact that socialism can never fully (adequately) succeed is what it has in common with everything. It is *after* that fact that one starts to make the choices, especially after the implosion of the Bolshevik experiment.[40] And, in its perpetually postponed yet persistent establishment, there "should be no room" for the persistent moment of totalitarianism. The apparent contemporary success of capitalism ("democracy") depends on a seemingly benevolent identitarian ignoring of the shifting mechanics of value-coding in the interest of the socially and nationally "representative concrete individual." A postcolonial pedagogy in the literary case can help undermine the prejudices attendant upon such benevolence (a benevolence which would also fix a systemic "marginal") by suggesting that the word "catachresis" is at least no harder than expressions like "freedom of choice."

Genesis is not a continuist rewriting of the Judeo-Christian story as one episode in an eternal return by way of the celebrated Hindu cycles of time. By the time we come to the end of the film, we do not conclude that capitalism is just another turn of the wheel. On the other hand, the Hindu story (available from high myth to "folklore") of the ten consecutive incarnations, appearing accompanied by various natural cataclysms, allows Sen to offer parallel descendants for the two men and the one woman who are the central characters of the story, the two men's from a drought, the woman's from a murderous flood. The woman is not produced by man or men. They share the same story with a difference: natural (their drought/her flood) and social (their occupation weaving and farming; hers has been wifing, mothering, sharing work). This is not a story of "primitive communism," for Marx arguably a "presupposition," a theoretical fiction.[41] The snake appears at least twice, as a sort of reminder of one revised patriarchal story-line.

I have pointed out earlier that the film uses a banal tourist genre, recognizable by the felicitous viewer. It is not my intention to suggest that teaching within the postcolonial field of value should ignore the culturally "felicitous" and the scholarly. We must rather learn to recognize it as no more and, of course, no less, than a moment in the differential negotiation of ontological commitment to the object of investigation. We must, as teachers, make every effort to know what the appropriate diagnosis is (historically and in the present) and then speak of it as one case, rather than as the self-identical authority. The "essence of knowledge" is not merely "knowledge about knowledge."[42] This permits one not to be trapped by authority, to look at other codings, other constellations. Let us try this out on the space named "Rajasthan."

In Hector Babenco's *Kiss of the Spider Woman,* the use of early Hollywood technicolor at the end is carefully framed in diverse filmic idioms, so that we can adjust our look. In *Genesis,* the unframed yet noticeably regressive use of lyric space and the wide screen, unproblematic light, primary colors, can be seen as denoting "Desert." Yes, this *is* the desert area of North-West India, but we are, rather aggressively, not in veridical space. The stones of the ruins move, to denote insubstantiality, and the sound of an anachronistic airplane is the response of a god created out of a skull before the dawn of serious technology. North-West India pushes toward the desert of West Asia as the felicitous theater of *Genesis.* No garden in the beginning, but a desert in the middle of history. (West Asia, the Middle East, itself reveals the catachrestical nature of absolute directional naming of parts of the globe. It can only exist as an absolute descriptive if Europe is presupposed as the center.) This is no particular place, negotiable as the desert area of North-West India, pushing toward West Asia, but not quite West Asia; perhaps the very looseness of this reference questions the heavy, scholarly, period films, the benevolent anti-racist films (sometimes the benevolent racist films, one can hardly tell the difference) that have been made about the Bible story in its appropriate geographical context.

There is something of this loose-knit denotation of space in the language of the film as well. The film is made by an Indian whose native language is not Hindi, the national language. Do you see it now? To be in a new "nation" (itself catachrestical to the appropriate development of nations), speak *for* it, in a national language that is not one's mother-tongue. But what is a mother-tongue?

A mother-tongue is a language with a history—in that sense it is "insti-tuted"—before our birth and after our death, where patterns that can be filled with anyone's motivation have laid themselves down. In this sense it is "unmotivated" but not capricious. We learn it in a "natural" way and fill it once and for all with our own "intentions" and thus make it "our own" for the span of our life and then leave it without intent—as unmotivated and uncapricious as we found it (without intent) when it found us—for its other users: "The 'unmotivatedness' of the sign requires a synthesis in which the completely other is announced as such—without any simplicity, any identity, any resemblance or continuity—within what is not it."[43]

Thus the seemingly absurd self-differential of a nonnative speaker of a national language can be used to show that this *is* the name of the game, that this is only an instantiated representation of how one is "at home" in a language. There is no effort in *Genesis* to produce the rich texture of "authentic" Hindi, nor its Beckettized skeleton. This is just the spare Hindi of a man slightly exiled from his national language. And as such, one notices its careful focusing.

The extreme edge of Hindi as the "national language" is a peculiar concoction with a heavily Sanskritized artificial idiom whose most notable confection is the speech of the flight attendants on Indian airplane flights. By contrast, Hindi, as it is spoken and written, is enriched by many Arabic and Persian loan-words ("loan-words" is itself—you guessed it—a catachrestical concept-metaphor. "Those French words which we are so proud of pronouncing accurately are themselves only blunders made by the Gallic lips which mispronounced Latin or Saxon, our language being merely a defective pronunciation of several others," said Proust's Marcel).[44] And, in Sen's predictable stock Hindi, those are some of the words emphasized in an eerie light, adding, as it were, to that nonspecific desert aura, the cradle of genesis, Arabia and Persia, somewhere off the Gulf, real enough today as the stage of imperialist inhumanity. These "loan-words" move history out of the methodological necessity of a presupposed origin. You will see what I mean if I list the three most important: *zarurat* (necessity), *huq* (right), and the most interesting to me, *khud muqtar.*

The subtitle translates this last expression as "self-reliant" or "independent." The trader keeps repeating this phrase with contempt to the weaver and the farmer, whom he exploits, as a kind of scornful reprimand: "You went to the market yourself, to check up on the price of what you're producing for me. You want to represent yourself. You want to be *khud muqtar.*" "Independent" gives the exchange too nationalist an aura. The actual phrase would be something more like pleading your own case, and would underscore an everyday fact: in spite of efforts at Sanskritization, much of the language of legal procedure in India comes, understandably, from court Persian.

The aura of a place which is the semi-Japhetic desert, a semi-Japhetic language arranged by a nonnative speaker: the perfect staging for *Genesis.* In the beginning is an impossible language marked with a star. Progress is made by way of the imagined identity of an original caught between two translations.[45] This is neither Africa nor East Asia, nor yet the Americas. It is an old score being actively reshuffled, not the rather youthful debate about a third world identity.

The postcolonial teacher can renegotiate some of the deceptive "banality" of the film to insert the "third world" into the text of value.

Woman and Engels

The film loosens the tight logic of progression of the mode of production narrative most movingly by taking a distance from the tough, outdated, comprehensive, ambitious reasonableness of the Engelsian account of the origin of the family.[46] Rumor has it that the intellectuals of the majority left party in Calcutta have said about this part of the film that Sen hadn't really understood his Engels. Again, the authority of the authoritative account, the appropriate reading, are invoked. We are caught in a much more overdetermined web than one would think—inappropriate use of Hindi, inappropriate use of Engels, India Tourist Board use of Rajasthan: and you think you're just watching an *Indian* film, even that you want just to listen to the voice of the native.

Woman in *Genesis* marks the place of the radical counterfactual: the road not taken of an alternative history which will not allow the verification of a possible world *by the actual one*.[47] The two moments that I would like to discuss are in that sense not "true to history" but full of the possibility of pedagogic exactitude.

A work of art (I use this expression because I feel wary about our present tendency to avoid such old-fashioned phrases for no reason but to show that we are theoretically correct, although our presuppositions are in many ways unaltered) is a part of history and society, but its function is not to behave like "history" and "sociology" as disciplinary formations. My general argument that, *in terms of this characteristic*, and with a "nominalist" vigilance that will not allow "catachresis" to become a totalizing masterword, art or the pedagogy of art can point at the ultimately catachrestical limits of being-human in the will to truth, life, or power. But with the resistance to the menace of catachresis (use or mention, mention as use) comes a tendency to dismiss such arguments as "nothing but" the aestheticization of the political (the assumption being, of course, that the veridical is *eo ipso* political).[48] I leave the suggestion aside, then, and look at the representation of the woman as the radical counterfactual in history.

Engels finds the origin of class exploitation in the sexual division of labor needed for the structure of support around the reproduction of society. Woman's labor-power, measured by way of name-carrying or potentially exchangeable children, was, according to Engels, fetishized into a relationship of dependence and subordination. It is quite possible that this Engelsian script has written the woman as she suddenly appears on the screen in the *Genesis*, for she is shown *after* the monogamian family. The flood has killed her former husband and children. But, in *this* historical moment, in *this* text, in *this* "self-mediated birth," she negotiates reproduction as agent of production, able to articulate a position *against* the perversion of her agency.

In this counterfactual account, it is the woman who points out the fetish-character of the commodity. It is in answer to her question ("does the weaver have the right [*huq*] to satisfy the need [*zarurat*] of the farmer for a new cloth?") that the distinction between productive consumption and individual consumption and the meaning of bondage as nonowner-ship of the means of production emerge in the false haven. The trader lets the weaver weave a new cloth for his friend the farmer. This is not producing a use-value, but merely including the cloth as part of their real subsistence wage. But Sen represents another change in this moment inaugurated by the questioning of the curious woman (remember "Gene-sis"?). The trader gives the weaver money. The desert is being inserted into generalized commodity exchange.

Is this how it happened? Probably not. And certainly not according to most great narratives, anthropological or politicoeconomic. Yet why not? Women's story is not the substance of great narratives. But women are curious, they have a knack of asking the outsider's uncanny questions, even though they are not encouraged to *take* credit for what follows. Thus, here too, the two men will tell her "you won't understand" when they go to a distant market with their money, although her curiosity produced the money.

The point is not to contradict Engels but rather to see the counterfactual presentation of the woman as the motor of "effective" history. It is no disrespect to Engels to suggest, *in this way,* that his text too is held by a certain value-coding where women's victimage rather than agency is foregrounded. And is this sequence in the film also a fragmentary transval-uation of Eve's much maligned responsibility for the inauguration of knowledge?

It is perhaps not surprising that it is within the most touristic footage in the film that Sen fabricates the emergence of the autonomous aesthetic moment. No knowledge of Indic aesthetics or ethnics is required to flesh out the bold strokes, which I list below. (It is as if the sanctioned ignorance of a global audience is here being mobilized for political understanding.)

1.   The possibility of autonomous representation as one of the gifts of generalized commodity exchange: in order to dream, all you need is money.

2.   The framing of the aesthetic as such so that its production can be

hidden. The two men willingly hide themselves until the woman, decorated with silver anklets, appears as an aesthetic object.

3.   True to the autonomy of the aesthetic in this allegorical context, the aesthetic object is endowed with a hermetically represented subjectship. The woman sings, without subtitles. GENESIS in the beginning, in English (?) in the "original," marks postcolonial accessibility. Here, framed in the film, is a parody of culturalist art, inaccessible except to the authentic native; the audience of postcoloniality has no access to the authentic text. The song is in a Rajasthani dialect, ironically the only verbal marker that this is "Rajasthan." It is, however, the most stunningly double-edged moment in the film. For it is also a negotiation of a banality belonging to the internationally accessible idiom of a general "Indian" mass culture of long standing—the Bombay film industry: the woman breaking into a folk song. Unlike the rest of the film which creates interesting collages of musical idioms, this lilting singing voice is autonomous and unaccompanied. There is also an interesting manipulation of gazes here.

4.   As the sequence cuts to a scene at the well, the wordless tune infects the noise of the pulley. Labor is aestheticized.

Aesthetic objectification and commodity exchange bring out the supplement of sexual possessiveness that was implicit in the text. The two men are individualized by jealousy. If we must quote Engels, the here and now of the film, preceded by all those cycles of disaster, is clearly postlapsarian:

> Monogamy does not by any means make its appearance in history as the reconciliation of man and woman, still less as the highest form of such reconciliation. On the contrary, it appears as the subjection of one sex by the other, as the proclamation of a conflict between the sexes entirely unknown hitherto in prehistoric times. . . . The first class-antagonism which appears in history coincides with the development of the antagonism between man and woman in monogamian marriage, and the first class-oppression with that of the female sex by the male.[49]

The film is not an origin story, but a story of once again, once again. What we are watching here is not the "first class-oppression," but the discontinuity between developed class oppression and gender oppression. The woman had shared class oppression with the weaver and the farmer. The men join the merchant, their master, in the role of gender oppressor. Neither truth to Engels, nor truth to Rajasthani kinship patterns, is needed here, although both help in creating the aura of fields of meaning. Again, postcoloniality is a mode of existence whose importance and fragility would be destroyed by techniques of specialist knowledge as they work with strategies of power. To get a grasp on how the agency of the postcolonial is being obliterated in order to inscribe him and her as marginals, culture studies must use specialisms, but also actively frame and resist the tyranny of the specialist. It must, at all costs, retain its skill as a strategy that works on cases with shifting identities. "The overthrow of mother right was the *world-historic defeat of the female sex.* . . . In order to guarantee the fidelity of the wife, that is, the paternity of the children, the woman is placed in the man's absolute power."[50]

The woman in the film is finally pregnant. The men are obsessed by the question of paternity. In the spare dialogue, a point is made that does not apply only to the "third world" or "marginals"; the point that the real issue in the overthrow of mother right is not merely ownership but control. The woman is the subject of knowledge; she *knows* the name of the father in the most literal way. This scandalous power is modified and shifted into "a strange reversal": power is consolidated *in* the name of the father and the woman is reduced to the figure who cannot know. Again counterfactually, the woman is given the right to answer the question of the name of the father and of mother right:

SHE:	*I am the one to tell you?*
HE (THE FARMER):	Then who else can?
HE (THE WEAVER):	It's my child, isn't it?
SHE:	Why are you asking me?
HE:	Who else shall I ask?
SHE:	Ask yourself. Ask your friend.

When the question of right (*huq*) is posed, she answers in terms of the men's need (*zarurat*). In the simple language of affective exchange she speaks mother right. This, too, is counterfactual, for it has little in common with the heavily coded exchange-system of matriarchal societies.

SHE:	What difference will it make who the father is?
HE:	Who has the right over it?
SHE:	I don't know who has the right over it. I accepted you both. In three we were one. Now you talk of rights, you want to be master. The enemy is not outside, but in. This child is mine.

This moment does not belong in the accounting of history, and the men do not get her point. "Our first sin was to call her a whore," they mutter. The admission has, strictly speaking, no counterfactual consequence. The eruption of jealousy, the enmity between comrades, the defeat of the female sex seem to mark a moment of rupture. The tempo speeds up. This disaster is neither drought nor flood, but a quick succession of colonial wars—on camels, with bombs; succeeded by neocolonialism, "development"—a bulldozer.

In a completely unexpected final freeze-frame, what comes up from below is a Caterpillar bulldozer. You see the word CATERPILLAR on its nose and, again, it needs no subtitle; like GENESIS, it is a word that the postcolonial understands. The innumerable links between capitalism and patriarchy are not spelled out. The film ends with the immediately recognizable banality of the phallus—the angle of the shot focuses attention on the erect pipe so that we do not even quite know that it is a bulldozer. The subtitle becomes part of the text again, and the catachresis is brutally shifted into the literality of the present struggle.

Let us imagine a contrast between this bulldozer and the bulldozer in *Sammy and Rosie Get Laid* (Chapter Twelve), so textualized that it can work as a rich symbol. In Sen the lexicon is resolutely and precariously "outside." Pedagogy here must try to retrench from that outside the presence of a banal globality, which must not be retranslated into the autonomy of the art object or its status as ethnic evidence, the particular voice of the marginal. Our agency must not be reinscribed through the benevolence of the discipline.

Postscript

Not all "postcolonial" texts have to look like *Genesis*. In fact, I do not know what the paradigmatic postcolonial stylistic production would be. At any rate, this essay is as much about a postcolonial style of pedagogy as about the look of a postcolonial text.[51]

We must, however, attend to taxonomic talk of paradigms and such, for "no 'local center,' no 'pattern of transformation' could function if, through a series of sequences, it did not eventually enter into an over-all strategy" (*HS*, 99). But this attention cannot be our goal and norm. We must arrest the emergence of disciplinary currency by keeping our eye on the double (multiple and irregular) movement of the local *and* the over-all.

In Chapter 1 of *Capital* Marx speaks of four forms of value: the simple; the total or expanded; the general; and money.

The "simple" form of value (20 yards of linen = one coat) is heuristic or accidental. The "general," where all value is economically expressed in terms of *one* commodity, is on its way to the money form. The second form—"the total or expanded"—is where "z commodity A = u commodity B or v commodity C or = w Commodity D or = x commodity E or = etc." (C1,156).

In the Western European mid-nineteenth century Marx felt that the most appropriate object of investigation for an emancipatory critique was capital. In the analysis of capital (traffic in economic value-coding), which releases the abstract as such, it is necessary for both capitalist and critical activist to use the most logical form of value (general and then money) as his tool. This is a lesson that we cannot ignore. But in the analysis of contemporary capital*ism* in the broadest sense, taking patriarchy (traffic in affective value-coding) and neocolonialism (traffic in epistemic-cognitive-political-institutional value-coding) into account, it is "the Total or Expanded Form of Value," where "the series of [the] representations [of value] never comes to an end," which "is a motley mosaic of disparate and unconnected expressions," where the endless series of expressions are all different from each other, and where "the totality has no single, unified form of appearance" (C1, 156, 157), that Foucault or Deleuze, or indeed, implicitly, Gayle Rubin choose as their analytical field. "We must conceive discourse as a series of discontinuous segments whose tactical function is neither uniform nor stable" (HS, 100).

Rubin, Deleuze, and Guattari seem to know their relationship to Marx. Kalpana Bardhan, like Sen, although necessarily in a different form, gives us the ingredients for an expanded analysis from within the generalist position (adhering to the importance of the general or money form). Rubin's work is in some ways most exciting, because, as I have mentioned before, she comes to the threshold of the total expanded form (which she calls, somewhat metaphorically, "political economy") from a staunchly humanist-structuralist position; as does Melanie Klein from within psychoanalytic practice.

As for Marx's and Foucault's apparently opposed claims for their methodological choices, the only *useful* way to read them is as being determined by their objects of investigation.[52] Thus, *in the economic sphere,* "the total or expanded form" is "defective" as a form of analysis (C1, 156). And *in the cognitive-political sphere* "it is a question of orienting ourselves to a conception of power which *replaces* the privilege of the law with the viewpoint of the stake [*enjeu*]" (HS, 102; emphasis added). I have tried to imagine their relationship by reading the production of "marginality" as a taxonomic diagnosis in our trade; and suggesting that, here and now, "postcoloniality" may serve as the name of a strategy that repeatedly undoes the seeming opposition between poststructuralism (Foucault) and the Left.

4

Woman in Difference

The vast group that spans, *in the metropolis,* the migrant subproletariat at one end and the postcolonial artist, intellectual, academic, political exile, successful professional, or capitalist at the other end is articulated in many different ways. It is not surprising that it claims, in one way or another, a paradigmatic importance in the contemporary socius. By contrast, Mahasweta Devi lingers in postcoloniality and even there in the space of difference *on decolonized terrain* in the space of difference. Her material is not written with an international audience in mind. It often contains problematic representations of decolonization after a negotiated *political* independence. Sometimes this offends the pieties of the national bourgeoisie. A great deal can be said on this issue. Marie-Aimée Hélie-Lucas's words will suffice to make a closure here:

> In Algeria, many of us, including myself, kept silent for ten years after Independence, not to give fuel to the enemies of the glorious Algerian revolution. . . . I will certainly admit that Western right-wing forces may and will use our protests, especially if they remain isolated. But it is as true to say that our own rightist forces exploit our silence.[1]

The sheer quantity of Mahasweta's production, her preoccupation with the gendered subaltern subject, and the range of her experimental prose—moving from the tribal to the Sanskritic register by way of easy obscenity and political analysis—will not permit her to be an isolated voice.

Let me explain, somewhat schematically, what I mean by "postcoloniality in the space of difference, *on decolonized terrain.*" To do this, I will repeat, yet once again, one of the principal arguments in this book:

Especially in a critique of metropolitan culture, the event of political independence can be automatically assumed to stand between colony and decolonization as an unexamined good that operates a reversal. But the political goals of the new nation are supposedly determined by a regulative logic derived from the old colony, with its interest reversed: secularism, democracy, socialism, national identity, and capitalist development. Whatever the fate of this supposition, it must be admitted that there is always a space in the new nation that cannot share in the energy of this reversal. This space had no established agency of traffic with the culture of imperialism. Paradoxically, this space is also outside of organized labor, below the attempted reversals of capital logic. Conventionally, this space is described as the habitat of the *subproletariat* or the *subaltern*. Mahasweta's fiction focuses on it as the space of the displacement of the colonization-decolonization reversal. This is the space that can become, for her, a representation of decolonization *as such*. "Decolonization" in this context is a convenient and misleading word, used because no other can be found.

This space is not indeterminate or uninscribed. In Virginia Woolf's *Mrs. Dalloway,* for example, the historically invested cartography of London, charged with the task of positioning and cathecting the proper names inhabiting that novel, entails an unproduced mass variously named "India" or "Empire." Curiously enough, the structuring in Mahasweta's "Douloti" can be compared to this.[2] In "Douloti" too the historically produced proper name "India" is the name of a relatively unproduced and undifferentiated mass. However in "Douloti," the alias of "India" is not "Empire," as in *Mrs. Dalloway,* but "Nation." Mahasweta invites us to realize that, in the context of this fiction, for the subaltern, and especially the subaltern woman, "Empire" and "Nation" are interchangeable names, however hard it might be for us to imagine it. If *Mrs. Dalloway's* London is supported by the name and the implicit concept-metaphor "Empire" *from below,* the socially invested cartography of bonded labor in "Douloti" is animated and supported by the space of decolonization and the implicit presupposition "Nation" *from above.*[3] In this fiction, the space of decolonization is displaced out of the received version of the relay race between Empire and Nation, between imperialism and independence. If contemporary neocolonialism is seen only from the undoubtedly complex and important, but restrictive, perspective or explanatory context of metropolitan internal colonization of the postcolonial migrant or neocolonial immigrant, this particular scenario of displacement is cut out, becomes invisible, drops out of sight. (The solution is not necessarily to privilege the self-defensive liberal elite in the "new" nation.)[4]

Keeping this methodological proviso in mind, I should like now to cut the context in a different way, and focus on three points:

(1) How does Mahasweta inscribe this space of displacement, if not

with the lineaments of the nation? (2) What does it mean to say "socially invested cartography of bonded labor?" and (3) How does Mahasweta suggest, even within this space, that the woman's body is the last instance, that it is elsewhere?

Inscription of Displaced Space

As is her custom, Mahasweta uses a brilliantly simple strategy to inscribe the space of active displacement of the Empire-Nation or colonialism-decolonization reversal. She names.

On the very first page we read, "In Palamu, the communities of Nagesias and Parhaias are small. The bigger communities are Bhuyians, Dusads, Dhobis, Ganjus, Oraons, Mundas." We have not yet received the full treatment of naming or renaming. But the reader can already sense that this is different from the admittedly urgent situation of the United States or Britain (and Australia and Canada) as unacknowledged multiracial cultures, which view "India" as one of the minorities that must be affirmatively acted upon or mobilized into collective resistance. Without minimizing the importance of that other metropolitan struggle, attending to this one allows the reader to grasp that the word "India" is sometimes a lid on an immense and equally unacknowledged subaltern heterogeneity. Mahasweta releases that heterogeneity, restoring some of its historical and geographical nomenclature. We will have to go a little further into the text to grasp that this naming is not an invitation to monumentalize precapitalist tribal formations. Here the reader can prepare at least to think that, if in the metropolitan migrant context the invocation of heterogeneity can sometimes work against the formation of a resistant collectivity among all the disenfranchised, in the decolonized national context, the strategic deployment of subaltern heterogeneity can make visible the phantasmic nature of a merely hegemonic nationalism. Even a further step can be taken: to apply the requirements of the first case to the second is to be part of the problem, however innocently. The two cases are perhaps, even, *différends*.[5]

The *découpage* of "internal colonization"—colonization inside a metropolitan nation-state—can claim a normative globality only by leaving out this delicately outlined, displaced shadow space.

If the name "India" is undone here, the undoing is not coded in the terms regularly encountered in the international press—many languages, many religions. That scene of strife, again not to be ignored—especially today as India is on the brink of Fascism in the name of Hindu nationalism—is still within the hegemonic struggle over so-called national identity—still, that is to say, in the space of the empire-nation reversal. No Indian, expatriate or otherwise, could bypass the issue of violence in the subcontinent in the name of religious *identity*. But we must also keep our eye on the differences, where tribal animism does not even qualify as a religion.

In our childhood and adolescence, Indian history textbooks began with the invocation of "unity in diversity." This somewhat tired slogan is, quite understandably, still on the agenda of the "builders of the nation," even as the consumer elite is being constituted as the definitive citizen. As she inscribes this other displaced space, Mahasweta appropriates and transforms this worthy generalization by positing a unity in exploitation and domination, by giving in her story the generic name "bond-slave" (not the "miraculating" name "citizen") in many of the modern Indian languages. This is the unity in diversity of the many named groups of tribals and outcastes. If we look at the official map of India, we can see how meticulously the territory is covered and reinscribed; I have italicized the official proper names of the spaces of the new nation:

> In *Andhra* the people of Matangi, Jaggali, Malajangam, Mahar and other such castes become Gothi. In *Bihar* Chamar, Nagesia, Parhaia, Dusad become kamiya or seokiya. In *Gujarat* the Chalwaris, Naliyas, Thoris and such others become halpati. In *Karnataka* the low of birth become jeetho, in *Madhya Pradesh* haroyaha. In *Orissa* Gothi and in *Rajasthan* sagri. The Chetty Rayats of *Tamilnadu* keep bhumidases. In *Uttar Pradesh* the bhumidasas of the *Laccadive Islands* are Nadapu.

This is not an exhaustive list, just an indication of multiplicity. Contrasted with this is the Brahman and the Rajput, the contractor and the government, hereditary divinity indistinguishable from more recent forms of mastery: Boss-Gormen(government)-lord-Sir-Sarkar(government)-god.

These lists are scattered throughout the text, and the effect of the reinscription is sustained. It is through the lists that we can approach the second proposed question.

Social Investment of the Cartography of Bonded Space

Among these passages of lists, there are a few in which Mahasweta rather unexpectedly uses the Bengali word customarily used for "society": *shomaj*. (Since the English words are not exact equivalents, *shomaj* is quite appropriate for describing caste- or tribe-*communities*. It undergoes a startling transcoding into a broad collectivity when used in the context of the far-flung *society* of bonded labor.) The following passages are spoken by Bono Nagesia, an "unconventional personalit[y], . . . [a] fissure . . . for restructuring," to quote Kalpana Bardhan on the "strategies of indirect power within the authority hierarchy":[6] "Before I had left Seora [his village] I didn't know how many kamiyas there were in Chiroa, Chatakpur, Ramkanda, Daho, Palda, Chandoa, Banari. . . . Oh I didn't know before how large *my* society [*shomaj*] was" (emphasis added). And again, "that's why I no longer feel alone. Oh the society [*shomaj*] of kamiyas is so large. Very large. If you call it a society, there is no accounting for the number of people in it."

This access to collectivity, and the repeated use of *shomaj* to mark the access, might remind the Bengali reader that *shomaj* is also the word that gives us "socialism" in *shomajbad* or *shomajtantro*. All Eurocentric predictive scenarios to the contrary, it is not unreasonable to see here the prefiguration from primitive communism to the ground of socialism in the most general sense.

The youthful Marx suggested that, if the Hegelian system were wrenched into the sphere of political economy, its predictive morphology would prove itself wrong. Many readers still hold the implicit evolutionary assumption, sometimes in contradiction with their overt politics, that the true formation of collectivity travels from the family, through society, into the possibility of the ethicorational abstraction embodied in the nation-state. (Melanie Klein's subject-morphology can be a strong deterrent to this.) If this evolutionary narrative is wrenched into the sphere of decolonization or displaced into the sphere of transnational capitalism, the precariously manipulative *function* called "the nation-state," coded and reterritorialized with the heavy paleonymic (historically stuffed) baggage of reason and affect, reveals how problematic this assumption might be, both from the global and the local perspectives. We hear a good deal these days about the *post*national status of global capitalism and postcoloniality. Such conclusions ignore the ferocious recoding power of the concept/metaphor "nation-state," and remain locked within the reversal of capital logic and colonialism. If this entire way of thinking is displaced, the formation of a collectivity in bondage can accommodate an ethical rationality. Sharing this conviction, yet taking a distance from it, Mahasweta moves us further, further even from Bono Nagesia's access to *shomaj*, indeed to a space where the family is broken. Here the reader must recall that by the logic of the evolutionary narrative that is being displaced, the family is the first step toward collectivity.[7] Mahasweta moves us to a space where the family, the machine for the socialization of the female body through affective coding, has itself been broken and deflected.

Woman's Body Is the Last Instance, It Is Elsewhere

There is no avoiding this, even if the story is read by way of the broadest possible grid: in modern "India," there *is* a "society" of bonded labor, where the only means of repaying a loan at extortionate rates of interest is hereditary bond-slavery.[8] Family life is still possible here, the affects taking the entire burden of survival. Below this is bonded prostitution, where the girls and women abducted from bonded labor or *kamiya* households are thrust together as bodies for absolute sexual and economic exploitation. These bodies are connected to bond slavery but are yet apart. Detail by detail, in a spare narrative style that often resembles the schizo's "and then . . . ," "and then . . . ," Mahasweta relentlessly emphasizes this separation.

> The social system that makes Crook Nagesia [the father of the central character] a kamiya is made by men. Therefore do Douloti [the central character, a woman], Somni, Reoti have to quench the hunger of male flesh. Otherwise Paramananda [the boss of the house of prostitution] does not get money. . . . In the bond-slavery trade . . . the recourse to loans is the general regulator.[9]

Woman's body is thus the last instance in a system whose general regulator is still the loan: usurer's capital, imbricated, level by level, in national industrial and transnational global capital. This, if you like, is the connection. But it is also the last instance on the chain of affective responsibility, and no third world–Gramscian rewriting of class as subaltern-in-culture has taken this into account in any but the most sentimental way:

> [Her father] stumbled on his face when he tried to pull the cart, with the ox yoke on his shoulders, at [his boss] Munabar's command. His broken body gave him the name Crook. And Douloti has taken the yoke of Crook's bond-slavery on her shoulders. Now Latia is her client, her body is tight. Then going down and down Douloti will be as skeletal as Somni. She will repay the bond-slavery loan as a beggar.

The reader knows that Douloti will end her life not as a beggar but "destitute in quite another way." And, to begin the last movement of the story, which leads to this particular end, Mahasweta marks the impersonal indifference of the space of the woman-in-difference elsewhere, in a simple sentence starting the shift to this last sequence: "Douloti didn't know this news."

The "news" that Douloti doesn't know is the outcastes' and tribals' plans to appropriate and transform state and national legal sanctions for legitimizing armed struggle. The regular revolutionary line here is to suggest that, if women are drawn into national liberation, feminism is advanced. I have already spoken of the precariousness of the adjective "national" in this context. Further, if one considers recent historical examples, one is obliged to suggest that even if, in the crisis of the armed or peaceful struggle, women seem to emerge as comrades, with the return of the everyday *and in the pores of the struggle,* the old codings of the gendered body, sometimes slightly altered, seem to fall back into place. Mahasweta's "Draupadi" is a reminder of that.[10] Here she attends to the separate place of the woman's body.

In the previous paragraph, then, Mahasweta has been describing the politicization of male untouchables. Bono Nagesia has just joined Prasad Mahato's Freedom Party. Prasad, an untouchable who was associated with the now weakened legacy of Gandhian nationalism—*Harijan* (god's people was Gandhi's new name for the Hindu outcastes)—has just broken away and founded this militant party. Mahasweta treats these men with the sympathy they deserve. Yet, she assures us:

> The object of this account is not Prasad's quick transformation. Just as its object is not Bono Nagesia joining Prasad's party. Bono didn't value Prasad so much before. But the day Prasad, the son of a harijan, left the Gandhi Mission and the Harijan Association and joined the Liberation Party, Bono sought him out and mingled with him. . . . Douloti didn't know this news.

The final movement of the story will be considered later in this essay. Here let us note its place apart and continue the discussion of woman's relatedness to bond-slavery and the separateness or difference in the woman's body, by way of a few more examples.

There is, no doubt, an accession to sociality and collectivity through the male militants' survey of the cartography of bond-slavery. Yet the first invocation of collectivity in the story is in the women's voice, through the first of the few strange "poems" in the text that resemble somewhat the ritual choruses sung at folk festivals and ceremonies, but cannot be explained away as such. They are certainly not conventional to modern

Bengali fictional narrative. They have more in common with oral-historical modes of social critique. They are beside the site of this narrative as well, where groups or an individual customarily speak or speaks with typicality.

Thus, early in the story, it is the old *kamiya* women by the fire who provide the answer to the question: by what force does the boss turn human beings into slaves?

> By force of loans, by force of loans.
> Two rupees ten rupees hundred rupees
> Ten seers of wheat five of rice.

At the end of seventy-four lines they conclude:

> He has become the government [or lord, *sarkar*]
> And we have become kamiyas
> We will never be free.

The women and men are collectively connected by this regulative logic of loans. Yet in this fiction, woman's body is apart, elsewhere. This is made visible by another couple of "poems."

The first "poem" gives us the sociologist, producing knowledge about *kamiyas* within his context of explanation. (*Shomajbigyani*—"social scientist"—is also built on *shomaj*.) The poem speaks the well-known fact that the so-called "green revolution" has operated the transformation of a rural economy into agricapitalism and created a Kulak class.[11]

This poem comes from the position of the author analyzing the analysts, who wish to make a science out of structures that may be random. It is especially interesting to me that, whereas the old *kamiya* women speak the regulative cause of their condition with conviction, the author, parodying social scientific assignment of cause, first invokes "nothing" and then simply breaks off.[12] First the sentence about the experts: "The sociologists travel around Palamu and write in their files, every sonofabitch is becoming a kamiya because of weddings-funerals-religious ceremonies." Then the corrective poem:

> These savants want government support.
> The government wants the Kulak's support
> Land-lender, this new agri-capitalist caste
> This caste is created by the independent government of India
> The government wants the support of the Kulak and the agri-
>   capitalist

Because of nothing, nothing, nothing
Bhilai-Bokaro-Jamshedpur—[again, places on the map]
And Kulak, agri-capitalist, the king-emperors
Want free labor, free land—
So they recruit kamiya-seokia-haroaha
One mustn't know this, or write this, because—

When another authorial "poem," a bit later in the text and using a similar peculiar narrative, speaks woman's body, the narrative is not of the modes of production, land is *not-yet-and no-longer*-capital, and the question is *not-yet-and-no-longer* "what is productive labor?" but "what is called work?":

These are all Paramananda's kamiyas
Douloti and Reoti and Somni
Farm work, digging soil, cutting wells is work
This one doesn't do it, that one doesn't do it—
The boss has turned them into land
The boss ploughs and ploughs their land and raises the crop
They are all Paramananda's kamiya.

There is a break in the poem here. The next line is "They are all I don't quite know whose *maat*." *Maat* is one of the names for the bonded worker on Bono Nagesia's researched reinscription of the map of the nation-state. In the case of the woman's body defined and transformed into the field of labor, the author's diagnostic voice, inscribing "them" into a collective sociality they already inhabit, apart, is vague:

They are all I don't quite know whose *maat*.
Near the foot of the Himalayas in Jaunnar-Bauar
They don't say kamiya, they are called *maat*—
Tulsa and Bisla and Kamla
Kolta women are I don't quite know whose *maat*
Only farm work and shoveling soil is work
This one doesn't do it, that one doesn't do it, the other one doesn't
   do it
The boss has made them land
He ploughs and ploughs their bodies' land and raises a crop
They are all I don't quite know whose *maat*.

Mahasweta's fiction is impeccably researched. There is no "poetic license" here. But its rhetorical conduct shows me that it will not compete with "science." I have spent so long in discussing woman's logical connectedness and the separateness of woman's body in that connectedness because these problems are still sometimes "scientifically" dismissed as feudal, not feminist. Some feminists have described the broad spectrum of women's issues—from anorexia as resistance in the United States to the dowry system in India—as subsumable under the feudal mode of production.[13] Such gestures are, I think, incomplete. The woman is fully implicated in the mode of production narrative and, at the same time, also distanced from it. To quote Kalpana Bardhan again:

> In a stratified society, discrimination of wages and jobs/occupation by caste and sex is not a feudal remnant but perfectly consistent with the play of market forces. . . . If the wage-and-access differentials follow the lines of traditional privilege, then attention gets conveniently deflected from the adaptive dexterity of capitalist exploitation processes to the stubbornness of feudal values, when it is actually a symbiotic relationship between the two.[14]

I have suggested that Mahasweta displaces the woman's body even from the reversal logic of labor and capital. Kishanchand, a man who runs a house of prostitution on principles of Taylorism, says to one of the kamiya-whores: "Paramananda is boss, and this whorehouse is the factory. Rampiyari is Paramananda's overseer [in English] and you are all labor"; Jhalo, the most outspoken of the women's group, dismisses him by saying, "Again that nonsense!"

This part of the chapter, then, has been an extended discussion of three points: (1) inscription of displaced space, (2) social investment of bonded labor, and (3) the woman's body as last instance, and elsewhere. I would like to go back now to the phrase I began with: "postcoloniality in the space of difference in decolonized terrain."

Parliamentary Democracy and Nationalism

One of the gifts of the logic of decolonization is parliamentary democracy. Mahasweta treats with affectionate mockery the *kamiyas'* peculiar understanding of the voting booths and the census. Of the voting booth, she writes:

> What sort of thing is this that each person is put into an empty pigeon-hole? However much the election officer explains, shall I put the mark on the paper or on my hand? . . . The officer scolds him loudly. So Mohan Dusad says, now run away. No doubt there will be fighting. Everyone runs for their life. The representatives of the candidates run

to catch the voters. The police run to help them. When the police run, then Mohan Dusad says, the government doesn't mean well. In such glory do the General Elections come to an end.

And of the census:

> You'll write my age? Write, write, maybe ten, maybe twenty, eh? What, I have grandchildren, I can't have so few years? How old are people when they have grandchildren? Fifty, sixty? No, no, how can I be sixty? I have heard that our brave master is fifty? I am Ghasi by caste, and poor. How can I have more age than he? The master has more land, more money, everything more than me. How can he have less age? No sir, write ten or twenty. The 1961 Census took place in this way.

Where everything works by the ruthless and visible calculus of super-exploitation by caste-class domination, the logic of democracy is thoroughly counterintuitive, its rituals absurd. Yet here too, the line between those who run and those who give chase is kept intact.

Here, for example, is Latiya, on the occasion of the Sino-Indian war. Latiya is, among other things, a government contractor. He is also the first and sole owner and user of Douloti's body for as long as his taste for her lasts—serial monogamy pared down to its bare bones. He is noted for his physical prowess, of which an unbounded sexual appetite is an important part.

Latiya contributes a truck and gives a speech himself:

> Calls out, give whatever you have into this shawl.
> Why sir?
> Isn't there a war on?
> Where, I don't know.
> You will never know, bastard motherfucker. China has come to spoil India's honor.
> Yes, yes? But where is China? Where again is India?
> [Then the] Mye-lay or MLA [Member of the Legislative Assembly] says, this country is India.
> No, no, Madhpura.
> What! Contradicting the Mye-lay Sir?
> Latiya jumps into the sea of people with his club in hand and the people run away in every direction.
> Then Latiya comes again to Douloti's room.
> Here, too, the women keep their distance.
> Somni returned most troubled from the meeting.
> No, no this is not a good circus. What's the fight?

Who knows? They're fighting some China.
Whose fight?
Someone called India, his. I didn't understand anything.
Rampiyari [the manageress of the whorehouse] said, did you see
    Latiya?
He is shouting the most.
Then it's the contractors' fight. Come, make some tea.

Similar to this, somewhat later in the story, is the tribal and outcaste political activists' debate: "What is to be done?" With them is the white missionary Father Bomfuller. These seriously committed men speak of the advisability of nonviolent intervention, of armed struggle, and of agitating for legislation. The conversation takes place in the whorehouse, after the group has taken statements from the women and after we have heard that Douloti, simply one example among the women, taken for three hundred rupees ostensibly to repay her father's original loan, has brought in 40,000 rupees for the boss in eight years and is still taking five to twenty clients a day. In this context, the advocate of nonviolent intervention is found to be caste-specific. The women in his caste never enter bonded prostitution. Bomfuller's careful survey, entitled "The Incidence of Bonded Labor," is filed away in New Delhi and consigned to oblivion. It is agreed that since government officers in these areas themselves keep bond-laborers and since the police will not offend the bosses and moneylenders to enforce the law, mere legislation is no use. Only the untouchable Prasad Mahato understands that the law can be effectively claimed as justification for armed struggle. And only Bono Nagesia, with a strong affective tie to Douloti, understands the difference between the long haul and immediate action. "We will leave after hearing all this?," he asks twice, and then questions:

Who will light the fire Prasadji? There is no one to light the fire. If there was, would the kamiya society be so large in Palamu? There are people for passing laws, there are people to ride jeeps, but no one to light the fire. Can't you see the kamiya society is growing?

And, as we have heard, "Douloti didn't know this."
The alternative to this is not simply electoral education. And the most appropriate critique of that position does indeed come from migrant resistance in the metropolis.[15]
Let us move to the women's house, away from activist national debates, where Mahasweta meticulously charts a diversity of positions. First there

is Rampiyari, who manages the house and is herself a former bonded prostitute. Bardhan's statement can be used to analyze this character's situation:

> Female conservatism . . . is often explained in terms of "false consciousness" (or cognitive dissonance, an euphemism for underdeveloped psyche). . . . However, female conservatism develops logically out of women's strategies of influence and survival within patrilocal, patriarchal structures. They are . . . the product of resourceful behavior under extremely disadvantageous circumstances.[16]

For example, when her power is taken away from her by the man, she leaves, "promising to open another business."

The other women are differentiated not only in terms of themselves but also in terms of their attitudes to their children. As Mahasweta writes, "Even under such circumstances, children are born." Jhalo saves money. She says, "My husband is a kamiya, I am a kamiya, but I don't want my children to be kamiyas." Somni wants to put them in Father Bomfuller's mission, since she is not allowed to keep them with her.

The affective coding of mothering extends from sociobiology all the way to reproductive rights. Before the mobilization of the reproductive rights debate began in the West, demanding the full coding of the woman's body in constitutional abstractions, Simone de Beauvoir had suggested that, in the continuum of gestation, birthing, and child-rearing, the woman passes through and crosses over her inscription as an example of her species-body to the task of producing an intending subject.[17] Of gestation, Beauvoir remarks that, however much the woman might want *a* child, however much she may bestow an intentionality upon it, she cannot desire *this* child. Beauvoir suggests that the rearing of the child, once it is born, is a chosen commitment, not the essential fulfillment of a woman's being.

I defer here the necessary critique of Beauvoir's existentialist notion of commitment, in order to use her figuration of mothering as a site of passage.[18]

Among the women of this fiction, pregnancy as the result of copulation with clients allows the working out of the inscription of the female body in gestation to be economically rather than affectively coded. The obligation to abortion is deflected into that code, of maximum social need, and not written into the rational abstraction of individual rights. Children are not written into mother right. Somni scrupulously distinguishes between my man's or husband's children and Latiya's children.

Yet these women are absolutely committed, in the best sense of *engage-ment,* to the future of their children although they "can never do more than create a situation that only the child . . . can exceed."[19]

As is usual in Mahasweta's fictive texts, we are allowed an (impossible) step, before the coding of value. (In "Breast-Giver," for example, we see cancer rather than the clitoral orgasm as the excess of the woman's body. There, too, the minute particulars of mothering are under scrutiny by way of foster-mothering as labor.[20])

How do such gestures show up the fault lines in critiques that must assume a civil society to posit struggle, and in the efforts to recode? Let us consider Teresa de Lauretis's recent powerful essay "Sexual Indiffer-ence and Lesbian Representation."[21] As I will argue in Chapter Seven, one of the logical consequences of de Beauvoir's figuration of the mother is the possibility of reading gay parenthood as philosophically normative. De Lauretis, implicitly presupposing a multicultural Euro-American agent for the political struggles of this century, proposes:

> The discourses, demands, and counter-demands that inform lesbian identity and representation in the 1980s are more diverse and socially heterogeneous than those of the first half of the century. They include, most notably, the political concepts of oppression and agency developed in the struggles of social movements such as the women's movement, the gay liberation movement, and third world feminism, as well as an awareness of the importance of developing a theory of sexuality that takes into account the working of unconscious processes in the con-struction of female subjectivity. But, as I have tried to argue, the dis-courses, demands, and counter-demands that inform lesbian representation are still unwittingly caught in the paradox of socio-sexual (in)difference, often unable to think homosexuality and hommo-sexuality at once separately *and* together.[22]

"Douloti the Bountiful" shows us that it is possible to consider socio-sexual (in)difference philosophically prior to the reversal of the established codes, before or beside the bestowal of *affective* value on homo- or hommo- or yet heterosexuality. To think therefore that the story is an evolutionary lament stating that *their* problems are not yet accessible to *our* solutions and that they must simply come through into nationalism in order then to debate sexual preference is a mistake. On the other hand, this prior space, prior to the origin of coded sexual difference/preference, is *not* the neutrality of the Heideggerian *Geschlecht.*[23] This space is "unmotivated" according to the presuppositions of naturalized sexuality. (It reveals the lingering presence of such presuppositions even in our resolutely non-foundationalist discourses.) Although unmotivated, this space bears the instituted trace of the entire history and spacing of imperialism.[24]

It is not inappropriate to consider here the question not of lingering presuppositions of naturalized sexuality but of naturalized subject-agency. I am referring, of course, to the use of psychoanalysis in the study of colonialism and postcoloniality.

Frantz Fanon and O. Mannoni set the model for the diagnostic use of psychological types produced by colonialism. Mannoni was a practicing psychoanalyst; Fanon a clinical psychiatrist. We must put their written work in the perspective of the limits set by Freud's classic essay "Analysis Terminable and Interminable."[25] By the logic of that essay, psychoanalytic practice is founded in an originary limiting "mistake" about the presuppositions of psychoanalysis as a "science." When we use psychoanalysis in the production of taxonomic descriptives in literary and cultural critique, the arena of practice which persistently normalizes the presuppositions of psychoanalysis becomes transparent. Put another way, the shifting dynamics of the ethical moment in psychoanalysis, which is lodged in the shuttling of transference and countertransference, is emptied out.[26] What, apart from intelligibility, is the ethicopolitical agenda of psychoanalysis as a collective taxonomic descriptive in cultural critique? Lacan's simple and playful admonition to Anika Lemaire comes to mind: "Each of my écrits is apparently no more than a memorial to the refusal of my discourse by the audience it included: an audience restricted to psychoanalysis."[27] The current work being done in France on the implications of negative transference should also be kept in mind. And, finally, the powerful suggestions made by Deleuze and Guattari should generate an autocritique. Their suggestion, summarized here as in the last chapter, is that since capital decodes and deterritorializes the socius by releasing the abstract as such, capital*ism* manages the crisis by way of the generalized psychoanalytic mode of production of affective value, which operates via a generalized system of affective equivalence, however spectacular in its complexity and discontinuity.

By active contrast, the relationship between Marxist cultural critique and postimperialist practice can be a thoroughly foregrounded theater of contestation, not only in Western Marxism, but also in China, South and Southeast Asia, Central and South America, the African continent, and central and eastern Europe. I have attempted to indicate how Mahasweta's representation of woman in difference is apart even from this negotiation. I will now quote an example of how she makes visible a certain critique of a Marxian axiom against romanticizing "the rural commune." This will take me back to the idea of mothering as commitment among the bonded-labor prostitutes.

Douloti is the only member of the group of bonded-labor prostitutes who does not share in this commitment. She has only been a child, not a mother. Her relationship to her mother, who is still in the village, is filled with affect. In terms of the critical implications of our argument, it has to be admitted that this affective production, fully sympathetic, is yet represented *within* rather than prior to an accepted code. Here are mother and daughter when Douloti is about to leave with her powerful abductor by way of a fake proposal of marriage:

> Douloti and her mother were two stones clasping each other. The mother was running her hand gently and constantly over her daughter's body. A split broken hand. Running her fingers she was weeping and humming, what is this, my mother, I never heard such a thing? The Boss-moneylender always takes away our daughters-in-law from field and barn. When does a Brahman marry a daughter of ours?

Douloti, like the unresisting majority of the male outcastes, comes to terms with her existence by accepting bond-slavery as a law of nature. I have spoken of this in note 8. Mahasweta does not represent Douloti as an intending subject of resistance. Her ego splits at her first rape and stays split until nearly the end. We will see at the end that Douloti is not represented as the intending subject of victimization either. The coding of intention into resistance and the resisting acceptance of victimization animates the male militants and the fierce bonded prostitutes, for whom there is no opportunity for collective resistance.

Let us follow the buildup of Douloti as "character" through to the end. Like the affection between mother and daughter, Douloti's affect for her village, again gently and beautifully written, is *within* a recognizable coding of sentiment. And indeed, as we see in the following passage, this unresisting nostalgia, dismissing planned resistance as futile, seems to rely on a conservative precapitalist coding of the sexual division of labor.

Bono has come with the white missionary and other militants to take depositions from the bonded-labor prostitutes. Here is Douloti's silent communion with him:

> Douloti sat by Bono and started rubbing his feet with great sympathy. . . . Douloti's fingers said, why grieve Uncle Bono? . . . Why don't you rather speak to me silently just as I am speaking to you in silence? Let the gentlemen twitter this way. Those words of yours will be much

more precious. Remember that banyan tree. . . . Speak of it. When winter came . . . mother would put the little balls of flour into the fire. How sweet the smell of warm flour seemed to me. . . . Then I didn't know Bono Uncle that the world . . . held Baijnath, that it had so many clients. I lost those days long ago. I get all of it back when I see you.

Faithful to this characterological style, Douloti is here a catalyst to the passion of male militancy. It is at the end of *this* movement that Bono is made to burst out: "There are people for passing laws, there are people to ride jeeps, but no one to light the fire. Can't you see the kamiya society is growing?"

Douloti's affect for her home is thus staged carefully by Mahasweta as the "residual" bonding that works against social change and, ultimately, against the achievement of national social justice, a project in which the author is deeply involved as an activist. Mahasweta dismisses neither side, but presents Douloti's affect and, ultimately, Douloti herself, as the site of a real aporia. You cannot give assent to both on the same register. I am also arguing that, in terms of the general rhetorical conduct of the story, you also cannot give assent, in the same register, to the evocation of a space prior to value-coding, on the one hand, and the sympathetic representation of Douloti as a character, recognizable within an earlier discursive formation, on the other.

(An aporia is *not* a statement of preference, certainly not a dismissal. One genuinely cannot decide between the two determinants of an aporia. It is the undecidable in the face of which decisions must be risked.)

Mahasweta sublates both the coded nostalgia and the separate space of Douloti at the end of her story. The movement of sublation or *Aufhebung,* destroying the nostalgia and the space of displacement as well as preserving it, transformed, starts working through a lyrical celebration of the nostalgic affect. With a body broken by absolute exploitation, Douloti is stumbling home at night. "The smell of catkins by the wayside, around the necks of cattle the homecoming bells are chiming. Gradually the fireflies flew in the dark, the stars came out in the sky! People had lit a fire, the smoke was rising."

Marx wrote that the Hegelian *Aufhebung* was a graph of the denegation of political economy.[28] Derrida has suggested the undoing of the *Aufhebung* by setting wild the seedbed of the *seminarium* through acknowledging the Saturnalia—progressive parricide—of Absolute Knowledge.[29] In "Douloti the Bountiful" the *Aufhebung* of colony into nation is undone by the figuration of the woman's body before the affective coding of sexuality. This can be seen as follows: the rural schoolmaster, again sympathetically portrayed, tries to teach his students nationalism by in-scribing a large map of India in the clay courtyard of the school, in preparation for Independence Day. Douloti finds the clean clay comfort-ing in the dark and lies down to die there. In the morning the schoolmaster and his students discover Douloti on the map.

As she reinscribes this official map of the nation by the zoograph of the unaccommodated female body restored to the economy of nature, Mahasweta's prose, in a signature gesture, rises to the sweeping elegance of high Sanskritic Bengali. This is in sharpest possible contrast to the dynamic hybrid medium of the rest of the narrative, country Hindi mixed in with paratactic reportorial prose. Echoes of the Indian national anthem can also be heard in this high prose. Contemporary Bengali, although descended from Sanskrit, has in its historical elaborations by and large lost the quantitative measure of the classical parent language. In this sentence, however, the manipulation of the length of the vowels is to be felt. Mahasweta's sentence is scandalous in the planned clash between content and form. Not the least of the scandal lies in the fact that most of these words are, of course, so-called Indo-European cognates: "Filling the entire Indian peninsula from the oceans to the Himalayas, here lies bonded labor spreadeagled, kamiya-whore Douloti Nagesia's tormented corpse, putrified with venereal disease, having vomited up all the blood in her desiccated lungs."

The space *displaced* from the Empire-Nation negotiation now comes to inhabit and appropriate the national map, and makes the agenda of nationalism impossible: "Today, on the fifteenth of August [Indian Independence Day], Douloti [not as intending subject but as figured body] has left no room at all in the India of people like Mohan [the schoolmaster] for planting the standard of the Independence Flag."

The story ends with two short sentences: a rhetorical question, and a statement that is not an answer: "What will Mohan do now? Douloti is all over India."

In his book *Through Our Own Eyes: Popular Art and Modern History*, Guy Brett has described a kind of art

> that cross[es] over between . . . [the] silence . . . [for which] Paulo Freire invented the term "the culture of silence" to describe the condition in which the impoverished majority of the world's people are living—powerless, and with little access to the means of communication. . . . there is also [Brett continues] the silence and ignorance in which the affluent minority of the world is kept.[30]

In these last appropriative moments, I believe we are witnessing such a crossover. "Paradoxically," Brett says further, "the more intensely these images express a local reality and a local experience, the more global they seem to become." And indeed the last sentence of the story can push us from the local through the national to the neocolonial globe.

In Bengali, the word *doulot* means wealth. Thus *douloti* can be made to mean "traffic in wealth." Under the last sentence—"Douloti is all over India" [*Bharat jora hoye Douloti*]—one can hear that other sentence: *Jagat* [the globe] *jora hoye Douloti*. What will Mohan do now?—the traffic in wealth [douloti] is all over the globe.

I end, somewhat abruptly, with a text for discussion: Such a globalization of douloti, dissolving even the proper name, is not an overcoming of the gendered body. The persistent agendas of nationalisms and sexuality are encrypted there in the indifference of superexploitation, of the financialization of the globe.

5

Limits and Openings of Marx in Derrida

I have fallen into a habit of deconstruction over the last twenty-five years. Like most habits, it does not much resemble professional expertise. This habit has yielded three readings of some texts of Marx, to two of which I refer below. Derrida himself has taken various kinds of positions on Marx and, to my knowledge, written once on a specific Marxian passage; to these too I refer in what follows. I do, however, feel that claims to the built-in radicalism of deconstruction are as ill-advised as to its necessary elitism. I have written a good deal about the latter. Since Derrida's use of "Marxist" language is sometimes adduced as "evidence" for the radicalism of Derrida's thought, this is one of the rare pieces where I attempt to address the former. I have retained the allusions to the Conference on Derrida, where a shorter version of this essay was first presented.[1]

I have made no attempt to change the general format of the essay. Here I summarize the basic argument:

1. Derrida seems not to know Marx's main argument. He confuses industrial with commercial capital, even usury; and surplus-value with interest produced by speculation.

2. a) Marx defined the "social" by combining the "natural" with the "rational" and subtracting the evidence from "experience." This is "class-consciousness." "Class-consciousness" is a means to bring about the end of a better "society." Yet when Marx spoke of "society" as an "end," he used the term in an unexamined, humanist, colloquial sense.

b) Marx left the slippery concept of "use-value" untheorized.

3. The two "social"s (rational/natural and human) create a disavowed aporia. Systemic socialism fails by virtue of this disavowal, falling through a gap which it makes greater and greater efforts to deny by coercion. Here a Derridian critique of humanism (the "Ends of Man") can join with a feminist and antiracist critique, and can continue to supplement the principle of reason: the *es kommt darauf an* of the Eleventh Thesis (usually

translated "the point is") rethought as the future anterior. His so-called Marxian metaphorics are of little help here.

4. In the current situation of the financialization of the globe all critiques of hegemonic humanism must digest the rational kernel of Marx's writings in its own style of work, rather than attempt to settle scores with Marxism.

The essay as it stands attempts, after a preliminary topical critique of the conference, to demonstrate 1 and 2 with specific textual reference; and 3, with reference only to Derrida's work, appears mostly in parenthetical gestures, which I hope will be useful to the reader. Given that the original essay was written thirteen years ago, 4 does not appear there. I still thought it would be useful to cue the reader.[2]

Conference

The exile of philosophy has been under considerable discussion these last few days. Yet "The Ends of Man" are deduced from the history of philosophy in *France*—even if that country is defined as the "nonempirical site of a movement"—after the War.

It is in terms of this little detail that I have directed the opening questions of deconstruction at our own discourse.[3] At this meeting, we have distinguished carefully between LE *politique* and LA *politique*.[4] It seems to me that such a distinction too easily excludes LA *politique* as the other as such. On the side of LE *politique*, we mobilize the most generous and most philosophical principles, and on the side of LA *politique* we stockpile national and situational examples. And the ends of man remain unnoticeably deduced from a national instance dressed in the appropriate philosophical apology.

These gestures put me in mind of something Derrida maintained in *Of Grammatology:* that in elevating speech over writing, Western metaphysics opposed the *general* principle of speech, on the one hand, to writing in the narrowest sense on the other. We seem thus to have opposed a philosophical principle—LE *politique*, the political subject—to LA *politique*, divided among nations, or seen as a powerful and unary [*unaire*] "Marxism." Our desire to deconstruct LA *politique*, that other as such, might thus involve us in an unexamined binary opposition.

I should not be understood here to be speaking on behalf of the possibility for a "real" (rather than philosophical) subject of politics. I have rather attempted to argue in terms of the economy of the difference between Derrida's early and later work that he himself indicated to Jean-Luc Nancy: the economy, in the early work, of protecting and preserving [*garder*] the question and, in the later, of its transformation into the call to the wholly-other [*tout-autre*].[5] Let us say, echoing the early work, that I have not "ventured up to the perilous necessity" of thinking the undetermined wholly-other of the great, pure, unlivable, inappropriable outside. It is because of this that I "take shelter" in a certain vulgarity of tone (*OG*, 74).

For we must reflect upon the opposition between vulgar and pure, since it marks a gesture of disciplinary exclusion similar to the one I sketched above. If there is one word that can be isolated as the insignia of the nonreflexive discourse of this conference—it is "pure." Without any preparation or revision, "pure" emerged to distinguish philosophy from all other discourses, which it defined by implication as "regional."[6]

I draw my support from the curious fact that the discourse of deconstruction cannot be "purely" adequate to its own examples. I have questioned our own discourse in terms of that irreducible asymmetry which exists in the very definition of the operation of deconstruction.[7]

I should first like to indicate the most important "political" lesson that I have learned, the habit that I have acquired, from my own (mis)interpretation of Derrida: the awareness that theory is a practice. Saying such a thing, I think immediately, thanks again to Derrida, that even the provisional establishment of such a binary opposition is the condition and/or effect of certain norms by way of strategic exclusions. This special care not to exclude the other term of a polarity or the margins of a center has carried us also to a questioning of the normative character of institutions and of the disciplines in and by which we live. Derrida has repeatedly warned us, even in the title essay of this conference, that we cannot allow our practice, even of deconstructive critique, to become a continuation of business as usual after the appropriate apologies.

It is thus with a strong feeling of the political potential of Derrida's work that I shall make certain suggestions today. Let me remind myself here of my own stand in this regard with respect to the famous Franco-American break in the practice of deconstruction—another example of the imposition of nationality upon philosophies and philosophers:

> No discourse is possible . . . without the unity of *something* being taken for granted. It is not possible to attend to the trace *fully*. One's own self-contained critical position as attendant of the trace also refers back and forward. It is possible to read such references as one's "history" and "politics." Since the trace cannot be fully attended to, one possible alternative is to pay attention to the texts of history and politics as the trace-structuring of positions, knowing that those two texts are themselves interminable. . . . In other words, one must stop short of the

impossibly arrogant position that the deconstructor is politics free, oscillating freely in "the difficult double bind" of an aporia, like the Cumaean sybil in a perpetual motion machine.[8]

In the context of this understanding of deconstructive politics, this acquisition of the attention given to the desire for deconstruction, I will ask my first question: in spite of the renewed protestations of the deconstructor that, "operating necessarily from within, borrowing all the strategic and economic resources from the old structure, borrowing them structurally, without being able to isolate their elements and atoms, the enterprise of deconstruction always in a certain way falls prey to its own work," does not a certain deconstructive movement conceal a gesture of exclusion? I think of another sentence from the same book: "phonologism does not brook any objections"—let it play then on its own ground—"as long as one conserves the colloquial concepts of speech and writing which form the solid fabric of its argumentation" (OG, 24, 56).

Normally we consider it a resource of the greatest subtlety and political force that the deconstructive critique can acknowledge complicity with the world of vulgar positivism and with current concepts without being their dupe, "according to an operation [selon une opération] . . . which is [n'est] neither empirical nor meta-empirical."[9] I think of the exquisite choreography of the first two pages of the third chapter of the first part of Of Grammatology, ("Of Grammatology As a Positive Science") a dance-step of which I have myself availed in opening this piece (see pp. 1–2; OG, 74–75). I think of the brilliant operations in "Restitutions of the Truth in Pointing [pointure]": "Let us posit as an axiom that the desire for attribution is a desire for appropriation. . . . As a convenient simplification, let us retain the version [version] of Zeug as 'product'. . . . Retain [retenez] these facts and dates. Meanwhile, I shall isolate [isole] a few of them drily."[10]

But the so-called areas where positivist axiomatics are taken seriously are not simply Anglo-Saxon Speech Act theory, phonologism, or French anthropologism, nor yet New York art criticism; they are also taken seriously in "the world of politics and economics."

Unlike the well-elaborated filiations, however discontinuous, with Western thinkers from Plato to Husserl, the awareness of "political economy" is shown in Derrida's texts through many analogies and references which may be marked by the proper name of Marx only by a clandestine metonymy. No specific elaborations are forthcoming.[11] Here the unkept promise distances itself constantly, through a series of postponements and reservations: "But I will try to return to these difficult 'limits' elsewhere . . ."[12] I cannot ignore that it is Derrida himself who points at similar moves in the postponement of the necessary parasite in J.L. Austin, and thus invites us to take a close look at such marginalizations.

In new postscripts added to this earlier piece, I have considered the question I here ask, in terms of Derrida's later work: is it perhaps possible that what we as deconstructors relegate to the status of precritical methods duped by their own axiomatics, or to the status of studies still to be elaborated, might dupe *us* in their turn? Can there not be something like a relationship between our lack of interest and, for example, the typically reactive denegation of the academic intellectual who takes his own victimage as his mark of excellence?

> If deconstruction had neglected the principle of the *internal* destructuration of [political economy], it would . . . reproduce the classical logic of the frame. . . . This philosophical discourse is itself (in fact) determined by an enormous organization (social, economic, fantasmatic, on the level of psychic drives [*pulsionnelle*]), etc.[13]

I am suggesting that it is not only by naturalizing the frame that one neutralizes it. According to a certain "ideological" frame of reference of disciplinary philosophy, one may neutralize by "philosophizing" as well. Here is a quotation, obviously modified: " 'Philosophizing,' affecting to consider as 'purely philosophic' that which is not and never has been such, one neutralizes" (*CE*, 60). Could (and therefore will) there have been a socialism, a socialist ethic, if the critical had not been dogmatized on the one hand, and *only* philosophized on the other? The deconstructive cusp—*es kommt darauf an*—"the moment approaches," rather than an either/or of the eleventh thesis on Feuerbach changed into a mere opposition between revolution and philosophy? As Derrida says, "although it never occupies center stage, a politics acts in that discourse" (*E*, 3), the discourse of *choosing* within what limits philosophy can remain "pure."

Abdications and postponements may not only mime *différance* but spell exclusion. Commitments dissimulate the hidden agenda of an unacknowledged nation-emphasis, as strong here in France as it is at conferences in Britain or the United States. Here is an example: As defined by "the centralist and military structure of French national education" (*CE*, 72), the State is the most serious antagonist; Derrida has spoken and written this way about Nietzsche's relationship to the State and about Hegel's intervention in the nationalization of German education. Within the apparently decentralized academy of the United States, the problem is rather that the academy is inscribed in an economic text with less "direct" State interference.

In the ten years since the symposium at Cérisy, the need to attend to these differences, *and* not to remain confined within them, has become much more acute. It is the new transnational ordering of labor, the obliteration of the East-West relation, and the aggravation of the North-South, that makes U.S. education reiterate its differences from and similarities with the European Economic Community. Any consideration of "la politique" today should entertain the contamination of "the economic." In other words, the question of the ends of man is no longer merely a question of national differences, between, say, the U.S. and France.

Whatever, for example, might be the form of our institutions and disciplines, when we read in *Business Week,* a U.S.-international weekly with a few million readers, that "the new approach will tend to make money more costly for lenders—and, in turn, for borrowers," deconstruction would become a neutralizing methodology if it merely permitted us to point out how, in this case, the binary opposition between lenders and borrowers is without foundation.[14] To add, in a different tone, that such absolute control over reserves smells of "the language police," and finally to remark that, as long as the Federal Reserve Board conserves the colloquial concepts of borrowing and lending, their analysis "suffers no objection," allows them to *act* in their own domain; allows us to forget, *passively,* that we are what they act on.

Is there not also a risk that the active paleonymy of deconstructive methodology might be recuperated by a simple etymologism? The economy of economy (*oiko-nomia*) and politics (*politica*) can no longer play between the thematics of domestic society (the household) and civil society (the city). The cases of the economics and the politics which constitute the most general condition and effect of all our operations have been described thus by Silviu Brucan: "an international system that functions politically on the basis of nation-states and economically on the basis of capitalist principles is essentially a war system."[15] The excess that is produced by this heterogeneous opposition is a war hardly ever adjourned, not exactly the "pure" abyssal effect of a reading or a writing. The disbanding of the Soviet Union, coded within a nation-state rivalry with the United States, has caused a spillover in the region of excess which cannot be contained by the invocation of aporias innocent of the discourse of political economy.

Such a description would suggest that politiconationalist explanations are rationalizations—in an older idiom which is not yet distinctly distanced or other—of a contemporary transnational economic reality—

where capital—already far from "true" gold or cash—is identified in terms of the differences among industrial averages or in the superstructural languages of Eurocurrency—an unreal "reality" which renders the word "international" archaic.[16] A deconstructive mode of reading can of course help us situate the implicit metaphysics of presence in the passage from Brucan. But if that mode of reading reiterates the gesture of situating a vulgar political discourse and then going beyond, it participates in the marginalization-exclusion condemned by the Derridean critique since *Speech and Phenomena*. As he has himself indicated during this symposium, to avoid the intolerable, in the form of an opposition which irreducibly produces the possibility of war, rather than to deconstruct Marx's texts, should be the task of a philosophy confronting a politics.

Derrida

I might have kept these discomforts to myself if there had not been some important uses of the metaphors of money and political economy in Derrida's texts. (To attend to privileged metaphors in a philosophical text is of course a lesson learned from Derrida.) In *Limited Inc.*, one finds analogies between normative language taxonomies and capitalism and its crisis-management. In "The *Retrait* of Metaphor," Heidegger's metaphoric practice itself is described in economic terms. In "Restitutions of Truth in Pointing," criticism is presented in terms of use-, exchange-, and surplus-value. In "Economimesis," the naturalization of political economy by Kant is presented in terms of the God-poet relationship.

In *Limited Inc.*:

> Once this parasitism or fictionality can always add *another* parasitic or fictional structure—what elsewhere I call "supplement of the code" [*supplément de code*]—everything is possible against the language-police; for example "literatures" or "revolutions" that as yet have no model. . . . "Limited Inc.," which aside from its use-value in the legal-commercial code which marks the common bond between England and the United States [Derrida has an untranslatable pun between *trait d'union*—mark of union or hyphen—and trade union—which is interesting if one wished to compute his political position] (between Oxford and Berkeley) . . . *condenses* allusions to the internal regulation of the capitalist system which must limit concentration and decision-making power to protect itself against its own "crisis" (*LI*, 99–100, 84).

I have elsewhere cited the passage in *Capital* I that would be the other term of this analogy (CI, 178–179). Derrida's point is that, in order that the so-called exchange of intentions (the property of the subject in voice-consciousness) take place in communication, certain conventions must be decided upon by the guardians of the language. (It is interesting that the overdetermination of "Limited Inc.," implied by Derrida's use of the word "condensation"—in Freud[17] condensation is for the dreamer what overdetermination is for the analyst—is precisely the "everyday politics" of the French intellectual who, given the highly syndicalized French workplace, sees nothing but complicity between the capitalist system and the trade unions, a complicity that successfully deconstructs the binary opposition between management and labor.)

Derrida uses this analogy again in "Restitutions":

> The trap is that each one jumps in to fill it in, with his name or with the name of a Limited Liability Company (*SARL, société à responsabilité limitée*), of which he is more or less a stockholder or a bond bearer (Heidegger for an agricultural, earthy, rural sedentary company; Schapiro for an industrial, city-based, nomad emigrant company, without noticing that the check is crossed [*barré*]) (*RTP,* 279–280).

These are powerful analogies, especially noteworthy in Derrida because it is he who has instructed us that one cannot distinguish so easily between a simple analogy and a literal description. Precisely because of this insistent analogy, a certain set of questions refuses to disappear. Is the other—here the discourse of political economy—not authorized to penetrate what we prudently and provisionally call the "interior" of the deconstructive enterprise, except by the terms proper to the latter, the asymmetrical and irreducible differential material of the former having been reduced? Should we, in other words, not take into account that the management of global crisis is precisely the sort of devalorization or devaluation of the medium of exchange in the old and new colonies, so that, by way of a rapidly augmenting artificial internal inflation, a transnational equilibrium of exchange and capitalization can be "found"; within which any exchange between Britain and France has no more than a local interest *within* the theater of exploitation? The relationship between crisis-management and the establishment of language-taxonomies is a supportive and secondary one. To confine oneself to the study of this instrument of rational and affective (mis)representation can become a satisfactory source of alibis, shared by all studies confined to hegemonic representation. And at any rate, this decentralized and overdetermined management of language is, in my opinion, not what Derrida is objecting to. He is pointing, rather, at that establishment of systemic equilibrium that provides him with the analogy for Speech Act Theory; I argue below that his grasp of the system is confined to one restrictive manifestation of it. " . . . Denuding of the shoes that have become bare things again, without utility [*utilité*], stripped of their use-value?. . . . The naked thing (*blosse Ding*) is a sort of product (*Zeug*) but a product undressed (*entkleidetes*) of its being-as-product" (*RTP*, 300). The absence of the term "use-value" in Heidegger's commentary on Van Gogh and the fact that the two voices apparently dialoguing in "Restitution" seem here to be one another's iteration make it probable that this use of "use-value" is endorsed by Derrida.

Marx

To strip a thing of use-value is, according to Derrida's Heidegger, to expose the thing's proper nudity. By contrast, Marx's version of use-value institutes a qualitative exchange [*Stoffwechsel*, translated "metabolism," which is much more internalized] in the heart of species-life, the-human-being-in-nature:

> Labor, then, as the creator of use-values, as useful labor, is therefore a condition of existence [*existenzbedingung*] of human beings, which is independent of all social forms [*Gesellschaftsformen*], an eternal natural necessity for the mediation [*um zu vermitteln*] of the metabolism between human beings and nature, and thus human life itself. (*C*, 133)

There is no such thing as subtracting use-value from a thing in this sphere, for the prior mark of the material transformation with Nature is mutely testified to even by the "thing in its nudity." One can "subtract" use-value (a methodological abbreviation) only in the other direction (and that not by laying bare but setting in relation), to make quantitative exchange-value, "Value" in quotation marks, a necessary "parasite," appear:

> When, at the beginning of this chapter, we said in the customary manner that a commodity is both a use-value and an exchange-value, this was, strictly speaking, wrong. A commodity is a use-value or object of utility, and a "value." It appears as this doubled thing [*dies Doppelte*] that it is, as soon as its value possesses its own form of appearance [*Erscheinungsform*], which is distinct from its natural form, and is that of exchange-value, and the commodity never possesses this considered in isolation, but only when it is in a value- or exchange-relation with a second commodity of a different kind. Once we know this, our manner

of speaking does no harm; it serves, rather, as an abbreviation. (C1, 152)

How many of Marx's readers remember that use-value appears only *after* the appearance of the exchange-relation?

Indeed, use-value in Marx is a slippery idea, not necessarily connected to persons and things. By simple reckoning, it should be outside of the circuit of political economy, as the not necessarily historically prior product of an originary difference existing in a different temporality from the duration [*Zeitdauer*] that is the measure of value-magnitude. Yet this exorbitant thing has the sorts of intimate supplementary relationship with that very circuit which Marx's dialectical habit of thinking would produce. Use makes "value" vanish, yet without the moment of consumption of the commodity as use-value the value would not be "real"-ized. And, as I have indicated in a note to Chapter Two, capital "constantly . . . drive[s] beyond its own limits" by consuming the use-value of human labor-power, fluid abstract average labor. Capital cuts this flow by consuming its use-value. In full dress: labor-power as commodity is sublated into (exchange[able]) value by being negated as use-value.

As Derrida has written: "Reading should be aware of [philosophical specificity], even if, in the last analysis, it intends to expose the project's failure" (*OG*, 160). And use-value, like all the important words in Marx, takes its mercurial specificity from its place in a dynamic dialectical structure called a *Verhältnis* (relation or relationship).[18] Therefore, in the context under discussion, ignoring the specificity of the discourse of the critique of political economy, the use of the compound word use-value seems to give a confusing suggestion of the relationship between Heidegger and Marx in their thoughts on the relationship between work and art. They really do have nothing in common here except the German language (which is of course not nothing). Neither can enter the other's garden without a great deal of preliminary spade-work which might yield rather little in the end. Is it the thing in its nakedness that is inscribed in these speculations of Marx's?

> The commodity as such—its particularity—is therefore an indifferent, merely accidental, and in general imagined content [*en général vorgestellter Inhalt*], which falls outside the economic relation of form [*ökonomische Formbeziehung*]; or, the latter is a merely superficial form, a formal determination, outside the realm of which lies the real substance, a determination which stands in no relation at all to the substance as such; if this formal determination becomes fixed in money, the latter

transforms itself on the sly into an indifferent natural product, a metal, in which every trace of a connection, whether with the individual or with intercourse between individuals, is effaced.[19]

In these terms, should we be thinking of the formal determination of a substance becoming fixed in art? Such thoughts would lead us to rather different sorts of questions.

Surplus-value (more-worth) in Marx marks the necessary superadequation of the human to itself, a rather special definition of "creative potential." We have seen that "value" appears when use-value is subtracted. Labor-power "distinguishes itself [*unterscheidet sich*] from the ordinary crowd of commodities in that its use creates value, and a greater value than it costs itself" (C1, 342). The necessary labor adequate to the self-conservation ("reproduction" in the old sexist vocabulary) of the body can always be exceeded by the potential of the body which, because of the constitutive action of time, is susceptible to idealization as qualitative abstraction, that is to say, into transformation into value, which is the essential term of capital.

For there is no *philosophical* injustice in the *Verhältnis* of capital. Capital is only the supplement of the *natural* and *rational* teleology of the body, of its irreducible capacity for superadequation, which it uses as use-value. Capita*lism* manages the contradictions inherent in capital in its own interest. In order for his dream of the social to be calculated into Socia*lism* managing the contradictions of Capital in the interest of the socially human, Marx must therefore not only not emphasize the opposition between work and commodity (an emphasis necessary for all "human"ist theories of reification), but use their common double nature as commodity for the leverage necessary for an active calculus. (For a critique of this calculation, more specifically for discussions of the relationship between justice and the political calculus, the work of the more recent Derrida can indeed be useful.)[20] This double nature is revealed by subtracting the use-value of labor from labor-power on the natural (physiological) and the (supranatural) rational level.

First, the common double nature of commodity and work:

Initially the commodity appeared to us as pulling in two different directions [*Zweischlachtiges*], use-value and exchange-value [a convenient but erroneous description]. Later on it was seen that labor, too, in so far as it is expressed in value, no longer possesses the same characteristics as when it is the creator of use-values. This dual-conflicting [*zweischlachtig*] nature of the labor contained in the commodity was first critically demonstrated by me. Since this is the pivot [*Springpunkt*] around which the understanding of political economy revolves, it requires further eludication [a pivot fixed on a convenient error!] (*C1*, 131–132)

Second, the physiological level of possibility of the commodification of labor (whereas the level of possibility of use-values is individually vectored): "On the one hand, all labor is an expenditure of human labor-power in the physiological sense, and in this property [*Eigenschaft*] of being the same [*gleich*] human or abstract human labor that it forms the value of commodities" (*C1*, 137).

Third, the rational level of possibility of the commodification of labor— the "social": "Equality in the full sense between different kinds of labor can only consist in an abstraction from their real inequality, in their reduction to the common character that they possess as the expenditure of human labor-power, abstract labor" (*C1*, 166).

If the worker has arrived at this threefold understanding, the lesson can be further activated in the pages of the second volume of *Capital*, when Marx explains to the member of the German Social Democratic Workers' Party (*C 2*: 98), the destined reader of his text, that the commodity circuit is the best model of analysis for understanding the circuit of capital. (For a critique of the subsequent interception of a letter addressed to a collective *destinateur*, Derrida's speculations on *destinerrance* and the other rhythm of public opinion can indeed be useful.)[21] For in the essential inaugurative relationship of Capital analyzed as the commodity circuit, this double nature of labor-power, the special commodity among commodities, has to be unavoidably grasped. Without this grasping—this *begreifen*—of the concept—the *Begriff*—of this relationship—the special *character of labor-power* as a commodity cannot use itself as a lever for the sublation of Capital into the Social (using philosophical interpretation to change the world)—for as of now the worker understands it only in the middle ground of "human experience," somewhere between the natural and the rational: "*L* [labor-power] is always just a commodity for the worker and becomes capital only in the hands of the buyer, as a component part of *P* [productive capital]" (*C 2*: 169).

Marx's project is to create the force that will make appear the massive confrontation between capital and its complicit other (its *Gegen-Satz*, its counterproposition, literally contradiction)—Socialized Labor. "Between equal rights [*Rechten*], force decides" (*C1*, 344). To repeat, the "Social" here is the acknowledgment of the natural in the rational—with "human experience" subtracted. The Enlightenment project of "the public use of reason" must perforce be antihumanist in this displacement: and not only to correct the category mistake of humanist philosophy: the philosophical subject with the human face of the bourgeoisie and the ruling class.

And yet, the short-circuit teleological status of use-value, *materially* adequate to its proper consumption but inaccessible to evaluation (and not because of transcendentality) is, strictly speaking, a denegation of the natural and rational inscription of the possibility of surplus-value, the mark that a mere "humanism" cannot disappear, that it must be negotiated with. This is, in effect, the paradoxical excess or "surplus"-value of the entire system, conveniently yoked to exchange by deliberate error.

In the middle and final chapters of the third volume of *Capital*, when Marx begins to outline the task of the being in possession of a rational understanding of the "Social," the same word, used in justifying the task, carries the mark of the humanist domain of use-value, a "spare" time, precisely not a measure of value, the thing that was only ever subtracted in order to get on with the rational preparation for class-consciousness. I have emphasized the unprepared-for humanist "social" in the two following passages. Indeed, it was also that lack of preparation that allowed subsequent systemic Marxism to be only bureaucratico/economic, and for Western Marxism to be generally burdened by a positivist-humanist moral charge.

Here, now, are the two passages, among many. In the first passage "the forces of social production" carry the rational charge. "Pattern of life for the *society* of the producers" is informed by an unacknowledged humanism. The difference between the two goes unnoticed but contains the possible reasons for the failure of the Marxist calculus. In the second passage, the transformation of capitalism into socialism is given in terms of an end where the two uses of the word "social" carry that disavowed slippage:

> . . . the means of production [in capitalism] are not [as they should be in socialism] simply means for a steadily expanding pattern of the processes of life [*Lebensprozesses*] for the *society* [humanist] of the producers. . . . The means—the unrestricted development of the social [rational] forces of production [*gesellschaftliche Produktivskrafte*]— comes into persistent conflict with the restricted end, the valorization of the existing capital. (C 3: 358–359).

> . . . the relation [*Verhältnis*] of production to social [humanist] needs, the needs of socially [rational] developed human beings. (C 3: 367)

In these and similar passages, the humanist use of the word "social," slipping out of Marx's carefully constructed definition, offers an end by way of its general vague meaning in the history of the language. Here Derrida's reading of the "supplement" in Rousseau (*OG*, 141–268), written many years ago, as well as his reading of "spirit" in Heidegger, instructs us in the relationship between catachreses and their determination in practice.[22]

Surplus-value: "That half a working day [*ein halber Arbeitstag*] is necessary to keep the worker alive for 24 hours does not in any way prevent him from working a whole day. Thus the value of labour power, and its valorization [*Verwertung*] in the labour-process, are two different magnitudes. It is this value-difference [*Wertdifferenz*] that the capitalist had his eye on when he was purchasing labour-power" (*C1, 300*).

The term "surplus-value" may certainly be used to denote any and all textual effects beyond the adequate representation of the object or of so-called material utility when "it overflows (itself), in inadequation, excess, the supplement" (*RTP, 298*); such use has little to do with its place and use in Marx's critique of political economy. Should it matter? It is perhaps a disciplinary risk to attempt to go beyond such auratic borrowings. Yet the compound word "surplus-value" ("*plus-value*," *Mehrwert*) carries Marx's stamp on it; his most important discovery. And it is Derrida himself who has reminded us that, with every interpretive gesture "something irreducibly [specific to the author or discourse]" attaches itself, as "remains [*restance*]," and "at the same time [as] a yet quite unformed mass of roots, soil, and sediments of all sorts" (*OG*, 161). I would rather use or ab-use Derrida to remind myself of those limits of Marx that may, perhaps, still be reopened.

In any case, the project of "a radical shakeup [*ébranlement*] [which] can only come from the *outside* [and which] is played out in the violent relationship of the *whole* of the West to its other, whether it is the question of a 'linguistic' relationship . . . or ethnological, economic, political, military, relationships, etc" (*EM*, 134–135), is vitiated if the discourse of political economy continues to be reduced or metaphorized in this way. The tendency in Derrida has not altogether disappeared, as I will show in my discussion of the use of "Capital" and "absolute surplus value" in *The Other Heading*.

All the relations between East and West, today rewritten as South and North, still operate in terms of the possibility of the production of more "absolute" and less "relative" surplus-value, and that not in the "pure" sense of the excessive effect of a text. The body at work—the physiological part or moment of the flow of what may now only for archaic convenience be called "labor-power"—is not one text among many.

When consumed in use, surplus-value vanishes. When exchanged in the money-form, it is realized, and simple reproduction of the capital-relation may result. When further capitalized in exchange (productive consumption), there is accumulation. One can perhaps work out some elaborate analogy between the agent's relationship to the management of surplus-value and the subject's relationship to the agency of meaning. But need one? And have we not come rather far from Heidegger and the nudity of the object in art? At any rate, Derrida's analogies are with usury and the apparently infinite speculative possibilities of commercial capital.[23]

If we were to meditate upon the management of surplus-value we would focus our attention upon the Welfare State. And even there, Derrida's admonition must be kept in mind. For in *Limited Inc.*, even in a passage betraying the predictable impatience with "welfare economics" as with organized labor, with their promises of better things to come, Derrida writes: "but economics—even 'welfare economics'—is not one domain among others or a domain already recognized in its laws [*déjà reconnu dans ses lois*]" (*LI*, 76). My questions amount to no more than an appeal to these remarks by Derrida.

Derrida/Marx

Indeed, nearly fifteen years later, after many subtle changes in his thinking, Derrida seems not to have advanced his grasp of surplus-value. In *The Other Heading* (1991; translated 1992), where he admits to the identity of a supercolonized French-Algerian European, he relates deconstructively to Paul Valéry's reassertion, after the First World War, of the superiority of French intellectual capital. He explicates the relationship between this argument and assertion and the implicit acceptance of Paris as the intellectual capital. Derrida engages in serious play between the word *cap* (cape or heading) and "capital," and relates this to the assumption that Europe is and has been perceived by the "European" as well as a large number of admirers and detractors as the moving vanguard wedge (*cap*) of the (political economy of the) world's culture. In the present context, with the large number of migrants and the disappearance of Bolshevism, Europe (or the self-concept of the European intellectual-managerial class) must jump to "the other heading," and beyond that, "recall ourselves . . . to *the other of the heading*" (*OH*, 15). This doubling (another, something other than) is a common double gesture of deconstruction, pointing toward indefinite possibilities and impossibilities in an enigmatic formula. And, by way of another signature characteristic of the deconstructive relationship, it is hard to tell where Valéry ends and Derrida begins.

Strictly speaking, absolute surplus-value is obviously yet another theoretically necessary fiction in Marx. It is produced in the situation of the
"pure free" wage labor performed by an average labor-power calculated
upon nothing but bodies' labor unassisted by even the most primitive
machinery. It is a heliocentric fiction, for the measure of value here can
be nothing but time spent by average labor and the restriction on its
production is the time fixed between sunrise and sunrise, the limits of the
absolute working day. Clearly, Marx's analysis begins when this fiction
is necessarily disrupted (as it is, always and already) by the competition
in labor-saving devices, the rates of the relative surplus-value.

By contrast, Derrida/Valéry (the slash here means both, either, either/or,
and/or both/as well)'s use of "absolute surplus value" is totally confined to
an embarrassing lack of awareness of Marx's use of the term. They use
the phrase in a general way, as the infinite source of more and more value:
"Through this responsible memory, what was constituted as 'solid value'
(Valéry underlines these two words) produced at the same time an absolute surplus value, namely, the increase of a universal capital" (OH, 70).

Derrida's critique of Valéry in the second part of this provocative essay
is, in substance, not unlike my own critique of Derrida in this chapter:

> Valéry puts to work the regulated polysemy of the word "capital." This
> word compounds interests, it would seem; it enriches with surplus-value
> the significations of memory, cultural accumulation, and economic or
> fiduciary value. Valéry assumes the rhetoric of these tropes, the different
> figures of capital referring to each other to the point where one cannot
> nail them down into the propriety of a literal meaning (OH, 65).

Derrida begins the section with an exhortation to reread Marx's *Capital*, especially when

> the counter-dogmatism that is setting in today, (on the) right and (on
> the) left, exploiting a new situation, interrogating it to the point of
> banning the word "capital," indeed even the critique of certain effects
> of capital or of the "market" as the evil remnants of the old dogmatism
> (OH, 56).

Derrida yet once again identifies himself as a person who kept a Marxian
bent while separating himself from the totalitarian excesses of official
Marxisms; and this reader is always glad for those avowals. The point,
however, is that, if the project of reading *Capital* had been undertaken,
it would not have been difficult to launch a more rigorous critique of

Valéry's Eurocentric "idealism"—to have noticed that because the search for ever *more* absolute and less relative surplus-value continues unchecked in the post-Fordist New Europe—the feminization of superexploitation rages in the sweatshops of that very Turin where Derrida's words were pronounced. Derrida speaks of "sexual difference" when he comments on Valéry's cynical (because unconnected with the concept-metaphor of the proletariat as only laboring body) observation that the European body (*corps* in the French sense that is available in English as well) is its best source of capital. If *Capital* had indeed been reread, he would have known that this global feminization of superexploited labor is determined precisely by the gendering of sexual difference all over the world and Europe gains from it.

In the event, Derrida makes a good point, the best that intellectuals with strong leftist sympathies but not sufficient knowledge of the Marxian project can make these days: that Europe's "memory" as itself has colonialism inscribed in it; keeping contemporary Europe "pure" cannot escape that memory. (In the case of the United States cultural identity, a mere reminder of European imperialism is obviously not sufficient.) When Valéry, writing in 1939, suggests that in order to be the appropriate subject of European capital, one needs men "who have a thirst for knowledge and the power of inner transformation, for the creations of their sensibility" (*OH*, 68), and therefore men who are the inheritors of a European "memory," Derrida writes in response, in 1990, invoking, I think, the colonial past as well as a philosophical necessity:

> Hence the *duty* to respond to the call of European memory, to recall what has been promised under the name of Europe, to re-identify Europe, this *duty* is without common measure with all that is generally understood by that name [*sous ce nom*], though it could be shown that a wholly other duty supposes it [*tout autre devoir le suppose*] in silence. (*OH*, 76)

And therefore, in terms of this divided field of European identity, Derrida gives an excellent list of "double duties," as I have mentioned above. It is of course understood that this list is a tabulated representation of experience(s) of the impossible. *Es kommt darauf an,* to implement (and necessarily to betray) them in the mode of legal (and cultural) calculation.

Because this understanding does not come of course, let us pause for a moment on the rhetorical conduct of the tabulation. I am attempting to read Derrida's *a-venir*—the future anterior always around the corner in view of which one tabulates duties as events—as an affirmative différance of Marx's *darauf ankommen*.[24] It is because this was not, of course, understood, that systematized Marxism met its nemesis in the abstract dynamics of capitalism, its other différance.

For Derrida in the last decade, the responsibility of ethicopolitical practice comes from and is judged by an other who cannot be fully grasped. This is indeed a thinking of the "other of the *cap* or heading." And therefore this list of duties is supposed (not presupposed) in silence (not tabulated) by (a) wholly other duty. And the list that follows repeats like a drum beat that it is the *same* (not the wholly other) duty. You read this list with the assurance that (a) wholly other duty is supposing it in silence. You work it out, if you can. There will be a wholly other of that one too.

> "It could be shown" that this is so. Where? How? "Thought" requires *both* the principle of reason [tabulable duties for the new Europe with its memory of bringing the beyond into reason] *and* the beyond [*l'au-delà de*] of reason, the *arkhe* and an-archy [the untabulable other duty that supposes this in silence]. Between the two, the difference of a breath or an accent, only the putting-to-work [*mise-en-oeuvre*] of this "thought" can decide. The decision is always risky, it always risks the worst.[25]

This putting to work, of this thought, is being played out in the struggle between "sustainable development" by international agencies—the principle of reason—and the animist liberation theology of responsibility to the ecobiome—the non-Eurocentric ecology of rural survival.

> The same [here the tabulable duties], precisely, is *différance* (with an *a*) as the displaced and equivocal passage of one different thing to another, from one term of an opposition to the other. . . . the other . . . different and deferred in the economy of the same.[26]

Given my context, I can see the trace of this relationship between postcoloniality (strictly speaking) and migrancy (or the other way around). Derrida, given his, between "Europe" and migrancy (or the other way around). "The 'trace' . . . in and of itself, outside its text, is not sufficient to operate the necessary transgression" of thinking "the same"—"Europe" or national origin—as undifferentiated and prior, giving rise to difference and differences.

Whatever the tremendous problems lying implicit within this good list, one of Derrida's sentences shines out for the aspiring or assimilated migrant:

> If, to conclude, I declared in that I feel European *among other things*, would this be, in this very declaration, to be more or less European? Both, no doubt. Let the consequences be drawn from this. It is up to others, in any case, and up to me *among them*, to decide (*OH*, 83; emphasis author's).

She must digest and incorporate "Europe," rather than simply disavow our desire to be a new European (or new American) in the profound and justified reaction against European (or American) racism.

For a few years now, some of us have been suggesting that Marx's ethicoeconomic counsel, in its detail, should be digested, incorporated, and thus inscribed in the body of the feminist and antiimperialist struggles. When that is the case, we would be Marxists, among other struggles. The world's invisible and silent subaltern, superexploited women in the history of the present, might then become visible in the stream of the general struggles.[27] It is indeed the moment to reread *Capital*.

Reading "Economimesis," Derrida's 1981 essay on "the most pointed specificity of . . . [the] implication [of politics and political economy in Kant's] discourse on art and on the beautiful" (*E*, 3), one feels most strongly the absence of Marx. The essay itself is beautifully argued and self-contained. A certain trajectory of the economy of mimesis is traced through the third *Critique*. By means of this tracing it is demonstrated that

> what is absolutely foreclosed is not vomit, but the possibility of a vicariousness of vomit, of its replacement by anything else—by some other unrepresentable, unnameable, unintelligible, insensible, unassimilable, obscene other which forces enjoyment and whose irrepressible violence would undo the hierarchizing authority of logocentric analogy—its power of *identification* (*E*, 25).

I have considered the implications of this conclusion elsewhere.[28] Here I am more interested in the tracing of the trajectory of the economy of mimesis in Kant. Derrida is not obliged to refer to Marx in this tracing. But if he had been able to we would have received a critique of Kant which would have been richer in dimension and we might also have received the possibility of looking at the unexamined humanist moment in Marx's teleology of which we spoke a few pages above.

Derrida's consideration of the trajectory is grounded in the usual privileging of the money-form and the references to capital are contained within or constructed upon this grounding. There is nothing to indicate that Derrida is critical of this privileging; his critique seems to be directed at the "commerce between the divine artist and the human" (*E*, 9) through the natural inscription of genius in a general economy where "capitalization" (in the restricted Kant/Derrida sense of interest—sometimes called "profit"—accumulation) can take place without loss.

"Liberal art ought thus to be able to use mercenary art (without touching it, that is without implicating itself); an economy must be able to utilize (render useful) the economy of work" (*E*, 6). This seems understandable, especially if we have attended to the careful explanation of the relationship, in Kant, between the "higher faculties" (mercenary arts) and the "lower faculties" (liberal arts), offered by Derrida's reading of *The Conflict of the Faculties* in *Mochlos*."

Let us now consider Derrida's staging of Kant as a naturalizer of political economy: the analysis of "the figure of genius [who] capitalizes freedom but in the same gesture naturalizes all economimesis" (*E*, 10).

In the key-moment of the argument, Derrida's lack of awareness of the detail of the Marxian text vis-à-vis the capital relation makes itself felt most strongly. The text must ignore the subtle transformation of the heterogeneous and exploitative trans-action between capital and labor, by interpreting the role of the poet as both capitalist and worker in a confused tabulation. Utilizing the metaphorics of political economy: "God furnishes him his capital, produces and reproduces his labor power [*force de travail*], gives him surplus value and the means of giving surplus value" (*E*, 12). Marx: "The circulation of money, regarded as such, necessarily becomes extinguished in money as a static thing [*im Geld als einen unbewegten Ding*]. The circulation of capital ignites itself anew by itself and divides itself into its different moments: it is a *perpetuum mobile*" (*GR*, 516). Derrida, distinguishing Hegel from Kant: "As soon as the infinite gives itself (to be thought), the *opposition* tends to be effaced between restricted and general economy, between circulation and expendiary productivity" (*E*, 11).

Kant writes on the cusp of mercantile/commercial and nascent industrial capitalism. It is understandable that, as Derrida shows, the implicit political economy in his text should see the money-form as the matrix of the economy and salaried labor simply as "getting paid for working." Derrida hints at its antecedents in "a powerful traditional chain going back to Plato and to Aristotle" (*E*, 3). How would the essay have looked if the poet's genius had been put over against the rational physiology of the industrial worker? What other critique of idealism might we have received? We might recall here Marx's tribute to Aristotle,

> the first to analyze the value-form. . . . "There can be no exchange," he says, "without equality, and no equality without commensurability." . . . Here, however, he falters, and abandons the further analysis of the form of value. . . . What is the same [*das Gleiche*], i.e., the common substance [?] . . . human labor. However, Aristotle himself was unable to decipher [*herauslesen*] this . . . from the form of value, because Greek society was founded on the labor of slaves, hence had as its natural basis the inequality of men and of their labor-powers (*C1*, 151–152).

Since, in the Marxian reading, money (the "universal equivalent") does not create value, Derrida's comment that poetry in Kant "is the universal analogical equivalent, and the value of values" does not allow for a comparable reading of Kant.

Reading the essay, I muse on what might have been: on the benefit of Derrida's microscopic reader's eye on a comparison of Kant's "free" poet and Marx's "free" worker, on Capital's systematization of the worker's freedom, on the more interesting analogy between the tautology of total Social capital (*C* 3: 327) and "God who makes a present of himself to himself" (*E*, 13), on the relationship between the hieroglyph on the forehead of the commodity and Kant's "nature . . . who loves to encrypt herself and record her signature on things" (*E*, 15). Instead, precisely because the singularity of Kant's notion of "moral surplus value" is seen as a "moral revenue . . . without interest," we cannot hope to see this reading of Kant's phonocentrism, grounded on the privileging of a hearing-oneself-speak which "tears the problematic away from its anthropological space in order to make it pass, *with all the consequences that can entail,* into a psychological space . . . because its 'form' is time" (*E*, 20), produce a practical critique of the space, in Marx, between the rationalized socially necessary time that is the measure of value and the untheorized human time that is the teleology of the rational use of rational time.

Given these musings, I offer the following summary:

From a Marxian point of view, Kant's claim is precisely part of the general problem with what may loosely be called a "humanist idealism." Whereas in political economy, when money is spent for individual consumption, it drops out of circulation, in Kant's world, the poet, in his special status as God's capitalist, can spend the universal equivalent and yet produce more for circulation. So does Marx's worker, of course, except that the argument is not in terms of money, a relatively unimportant explanatory instrument that is ignorantly grabbed for purposes of explanation, but in terms of the infinite value-productive potential of capital. Viewed "socially," the individual consumption of the worker is part of the reproduction of the "living labor" component of variable capital. The term "expendiary productivity," used by Derrida to explain the Kantian poet's special gift, would be uninteresting in Marx, since it is not the circulation of money as such, but rather the circulation of capital that is the more robust dynamic for him. And in that dynamic, there is of course the act of "productive consumption," where, money, among other things, is consumed so that more constant capital may be produced. It is only the individual consumption of the capitalist that genuinely interrupts the circuit of capital. If we give the benefit of the doubt to Derrida (and Kant) and transcode the analogy from money to capital, we might say that, in that particular respect, Kant's poet trumps the capitalist; a conclusion interesting only for teachers of literature and perhaps of philosophy.

It becomes difficult to extend this benefit, however, when we notice that the circulation of money restricted by the spending of money is designated as a "restricted" and the "expendiary productivity" as a general economy. For Marx the circulation and the expenditure of money belong to a highly restricted sphere. It is the circulation of capital and its constitutive interruptions that make visible to him the generality of a deconstructible economy: "The *true barrier* to capitalist production is *capital itself*" (C 3: 358). I have already argued, and hope to argue at greater length elsewhere, that the subtracted domain of use-value remains the unquestioned possibility of this deconstruction. But I cannot be sure that Derrida's use of a politicoeconomic vocabulary, confined to money and interest-bearing capital, allows for the emergence into this argument.

A similar restriction to the money-form and usurer's capital is noticeable in "*Retrait* of the Metaphor," in the description of the catachrestic or invaginated use and place of the metaphor in Heidegger.[29] First Derrida clears himself of Paul Ricoeur's misunderstanding of his position:

> I am precisely putting into question, far from assuming that . . . the process of metaphoricity in general would be understood under the concept or the scheme of *usure* (wear and tear) . . . and not as *usure* (usury) in another sense, as the production of surplus-value (*plus-valu*) according to laws other than those of a continuous and linearly accumulative capitalization (*RM*, 13).

It is again noticeable that, since one is confined to usurer's capital, the irreducible moment of rational-social "living" labor-power in capital accumulation does not produce an inconvenient interruption here. The same characteristic appears when Derrida tells the reader that he must

> speak ... economically of economy ... in order to articulate what I am going to say about the other possible tropical system (*tropique*) of *usure* (usury), the one of interest, of surplus value, of fiduciary calculus or usury rate which Ricoeur indicated but left in the dark ... (*RM*, 17).

It is upon this basis that Derrida teases out the peculiar (non)relationship between tenor (vehicle) and vehicle (tenor) in Heidegger's practice. It is beyond the scope of this essay to rehearse that brilliant reading. Yet my question remains: how would these readings have been enhanced if Derrida had betrayed an awareness of the capital relation?

In "Economimesis" Derrida comments that in Kant "the poet merely proposes an entertaining play of the imagination and proceeds as if he were handling the business of the understanding ... giv[es] more than it [the imagination] promises" (*E*, 17). There is a gap, in other words, between what the poet thinks he does and what he in fact does. Would it have mattered if Derrida had known that in the so-called capital exchange, Marx's genius was to have shown that the worker thinks s/he sells labor as commodity (for use), whereas the capitalist in fact receives an advance of labor-power already capitalized as commodity; and that Marx exhorts the worker, his implied reader, to grasp this gap between "experience" and "the social," of this giving more than one thinks, and finally, that the history of "Marxism"s is the *destinerrance* of this exhortation? I quote again that crucial sentence, not rhetorically fleshed out in the unrevised pages of *Capital,* volume two: "*L* is always just a commodity for the worker and becomes capital only in the hands of the buyer, as a component part of *P.*"Habituated to the morphology of Hegel's logic, Marx's immense effort to confront the false-other of that philosophy was to push in *by force and by force of reason* a performative or revolutionary contingency into the philosophical justice of the formal scheme of values: to try to operate the heterogeneity of being and knowing on the one hand and of being and doing on the other. Deconstruction's share in the undoing of the dialectic has been, as Derrida has often pointed out, by way of a detranscendentalized transcendental phenomenology: to risk the trace-structure *at every step*: to rememorate (con)textuality whenever the desire to universalize appears. The map of this risk, wishing to pose the question of LE *politique,* cannot be uncovered by following the deployment of the metaphorics of political economy in Derrida's work; but otherwise.

6

Feminism and Deconstruction, Again: Negotiations

The previous chapter looked at Derrida's use of Marxian metaphors. This chapter shows how feminism might use deconstruction. Again, it is the habit of deconstruction that I deal with, not so much the relationship between feminism and postmodernism, for which one must turn to scholars such as Alice Jardine and Linda Nicholson.[1] I give below a summary of my general argument: It is not just that deconstruction cannot found a politics, while other ways of thinking can. It is that deconstruction can make founded political programs more useful by making their in-built problems more visible. To act is therefore not to ignore deconstruction, but actively to transgress it without giving it up. (A slightly tougher formulation which clarity-fetishists can ignore: deconstruction does not aim at *praxis* or theoretical practice but lives in the persistent crisis or unease of the moment of *techñe* or crafting.) Feminism has a special situation here because, among the many names that Derrida gives to the problem/solution of founded programs, one is "woman." I explain in this chapter why feminism should keep to the critical intimacy of deconstruction but give up its attachment to that specific name for the problem/solution of founded programs (also named "writing"). I put it so awkwardly because so-called "political" academics will still insist that writing is only script and make the blindingly brilliant critique that Derrida ignores mothers speaking to infants, or ignores orature.[2]

This is a more charitable position on the usefulness of deconstruction for feminism than I have supported in the past. It is a negotiation and an acknowledgment of complicity. This is a result of a growing sense that, at home and abroad, postcolonials and migrants are still coming to terms with unacknowledged complicity with the culture of imperialism, in a whole range of experiences including the failure of secularism and the Eurocentrism of economic migration. There may be something like a relationship with how feminists and indeed women in general deal with patriarchy and feminist theory.[3]

The chapter is written in the musing style of speaking to my "school-mates," the occasion being Teresa Brennan's invitation to speak to feminists generally sympathetic to poststructuralism and psychoanalysis in a seminar series at Cambridge in 1987.

I first conceived of the line of thought pursued in the following pages immediately after six months of teaching in Delhi and Calcutta. Teaching for the first time in the country of my citizenship, and occasionally in my own language, was an unsettling and ambivalent experience. The measure of my unease will be sensed when I point out that I found a resonance in Thomas Nagel's reflections on the Vietnam years:

> the United States was engaged in a criminal war, criminally conducted. This produced a heightened sense of the absurdity of my theoretical pursuits. Citizenship is a surprisingly strong bond, even for those of us whose patriotic feelings are weak. We read the newspaper every day with rage and horror, and it was different from reading about the crimes of another country. Those feelings led to the growth in the late 1960s of serious professional work by philosophers on public issues.[4]

Rajiv Gandhi and his centralized power-structure were attempting to redefine India as the habitation of the tiny percentage of the taxpaying upper crust. That is my class alliance, which I felt much more strongly than my class-position as an academic in a trivial discipline in the United States. Those were also the months of the crisis of the Bofors arms scandal, not much publicized in the international press but certainly disturbing to a critic who regularly theorized the "epistemic violence" of imperialism. It did not help that that particular crisis was later managed by the Indian intervention in the Sri Lankan Civil War. (Again, the intervening years have left their mark on this narrative. Does one ever catch up with the history of the present? I have come to sense that my unease had something to do not only with the culture of "old" imperialisms, but with the relationship between the new economic migrant to the United States and the country of her origin, thus the "new" imperialism; citizenship as a pious mark of perceived difference rather than sameness, on both sides. This sense bleeds into forthcoming work. In that balance, two fresh entries, adding to the bond of [a] citizenship there, [b] migrancy here: [a] Religious fundamentalism and the relationship between secularism and the culture of "old" imperialism [more about this in Chapter Twelve]; [b] the Gulf War and the New World Order, the breakup of the remnants of India's old protected economy and the much greater role played by the

IMF and the World Bank in the new "liberalized" polity, perceived by the *New York Times* as the end of "the political era in which India emerged from colonialism.")[5]

The position of academic feminism in the elite universities in the two Indian cities where I worked was not strikingly different from the United States, where I habitually teach. And I am not given to unquestioning benevolence towards that dubious category—"Third World Woman." Yet, there was produced in me, not infrequently during my time in India, "a heightened sense of the absurdity of my theoretical pursuits." When I spoke in Cambridge in response to Teresa Brennan's invitation, immediately after leaving India, I found myself considering the relationship between feminism and deconstruction in terms of that sense of absurdity.

Before I could embark on such a chastening project, it seemed necessary to situate a sympathetic misrepresentation of the connection between the two movements. In that spirit I offered a reading of a few pages from a book then recently out, Jacqueline Rose's *Sexuality in the Field of Vision.*[6]

At the end of Rose's introduction to her book, there is a dismissal of Derrida as a certain kind of subjectivist essentialist. Unlike Elaine Showalter's or, more recently, Margaret Homan's dismissals of deconstruction, Rose's text is based on a *reading* of Derrida.[7] When I deal with this dismissal, you see me defending a sort-of-Derrida against Rose defending a sort-of-Lacan. This is yet another instance of "the [necessary] absurdity of [our] theoretical pursuits." Those few months in India, spent as a diasporic Indian and a working academic, gave me a sense of how peculiarly uneasy people were about the cultural legacy of imperialism. This was certainly true in my own class but was also pervasive, however inarticulately, across the classes. The unease straddled the genders, and in its context, varieties of elite nativism or isolationist nationalism seemed peculiarly out of touch with national and international "realities." The practical effects of this legacy will escape theoretical negotiations into the veining of traces even as those negotiations become more possible, more authoritative.[8] As a reminder of this unease, and in response to Brennan's specific invitation, I felt I must reckon with the legacy of patriarchy which, like the culture of imperialism, is a dubious gift that we can only transform if we acknowledge it. In the strictest sense, feminism is "subsumed" in patriarchy (C3, 1015). My entire discussion of Rose must be read as framed by this necessary absurdity.

I agree with Rose that "to understand subjectivity, sexual difference and fantasy, in a way that neither entrenches the terms nor denies them" remains a crucial task for today.[9] On these terms, in fact, there is not much difference between how she understands Lacan and how I understand deconstruction. For Rose, "only the concept of a subjectivity at odds with itself gives back to women the right to an impasse at the point of sexual identity, with no nostalgia whatsoever for its possible or future integration into a norm."[10] This desire for an impasse is not unlike the desire for the abyss or infinite regression for which deconstruction must perpetually account. I do, of course, declare myself bound by that desire. The difference between Rose and myself here is that what she feels is a right to be claimed, I am obliged to recognize as a bind to be watched.[11] I think the difference between us in this context comes from Rose's understanding of deconstruction as *only* a narrative of the fully dispersed and decentered subject. I am not myself suggesting a strict opposition between structure and narrative, or morphology and narrative. But I do want to insist that when it is understood only as a narrative, deconstruction is only the picture of an impossibility that cannot help *any* political position. Or perhaps it can, only too easily. (I am thinking here of other arguments, relying on a trivialized description of deconstruction as a narrative, arguments which suggest, for example, that since women are naturally decentered, deconstruction is good for feminism and vice versa.)

In her introduction to *Sexuality in the Field of Vision,* Rose is by no means a trivializer, but seems still to understand deconstruction only as a narrative. One way of showing this is to bring a different understanding of deconstruction to bear on Jacqueline Rose's general presentation of psychoanalysis as a project.

It seems to me that, for Rose, the psychoanalytic project is a kind of epistemological project, through which women and men understand their ontology in terms of (or at least not excluding) sexual difference:

> Feminism must depend on psychoanalysis because the issue of how individuals recognize themselves as male or female, the demand that they do so, seems to stand in such fundamental relation to the forms of inequality and subordination which it is feminism's objective to change.[12]

This sentence is, I think, about male and female subjects construing themselves as knowable objects, especially if I am right in thinking that the word "recognize" is doing duty here for the more critical "cognize." Now the antisexist project of feminism bases itself upon the conviction that distinctions arising in social practice out of the declaration of a fundamental ontic difference are, more often than not, incorrect, because, like most declarations of difference, these involve a dissimulated ranking. The range of such social practices runs from sociobiology to corporate (civil) and familial (domestic) practice. Rose's new epistemological itinerary will allow us to correct this. It will use the epistemology of sexual difference as an answer to the ontological question: what am I (woman)? and then to an accounting of that epistemology: how do I recognize myself (woman)?

It is, however, the next step, contained in the last part of the sentence from Rose quoted above, which gives me trouble. That step covers the quick shift from epistemology/ontology to the ethicopolitical project. The subject recognizing herself (woman) seems in Rose's reading to do so in order to act in the interests of psycho-social justice: in a "fundamental relation to the forms of inequality and subordination which it is feminism's objective to change." Rose's position is of course sufficiently subtle. She is aware that "femininity [the formula for this ontic secret that we discover through the epistemological itinerary of the divided subject— woman] in psychoanalysis, is neither simply achieved nor is it ever complete." It none the less involves that unacknowledged shift I have described between epistemology/ontology on the one hand and ethicopolitics on the other. If, as Rose suggests, it is crucial to admit the division in the subject, it seems to me no less crucial to admit the irreducible difference between the subject (woman) of that epistemology, and the subject (feminist) of this ethicopolitics.[13] In the previous chapter, I have touched upon the fact that Marxism foundered on this difference. In my new and forthcoming work, I am concentrating upon this difference straddling the division between the women's movement and feminist theory.

If one looks at the deconstructive *morphology* (rather than simply reading it as the narrative of the decentered subject), then one is obliged to notice that deconstruction has always been about the limits of epistemology. It sees the ontological impetus as a program implicated in the writing of the name of Man.[14]

Let me emphasize this by reopening *Spurs*, where Derrida comments on Heidegger and his reading of Nietzsche.[15] Simplifying Derrida's argument a little, we could read it as follows: there is a question which is precomprehended even by the careful subtlety of the Heideggerian articulation of the ontico-ontological difference. Simplifying that Heideggerian subtlety, we might summarize it as follows: Heidegger suggests that *Dasein* is ontically programmed to ask the ontological question, *and* not to be able to answer it. This is undoubtedly a corrective for any account which assumes that when we look for an epistemological itinerary to cleanse the ontological account of ourselves, this might contribute or, indeed, lead to correct psychosexual ethicopolitical action. (One may argue that "correct" epistemologies can be the basis of "correct" public policy—but that seems not to be Rose's argument. Indeed, the relationship between research and public policy is another link on the chain of knowing/doing [*pouvoir/savoir*] that is under discussion.)

Even this Heideggerian corrective is critiqued by Derrida because it does not attend to the naming of woman.

> For not having posed the sexual question, or at least for having subsumed it in the general question of truth, Heidegger's reading of Nietzsche has been idling offshore ever since it missed the woman in the *affabulation* of truth.[16]

Spurs gives an account of how one can read Nietzsche's master concept-metaphors. The most interesting one for Derrida is "woman." Like all concept-metaphors, "woman" is here used in such a way that one cannot locate an adequate literal referent for the word. There *is* something special about it, however, for the question of sexual difference in Nietzsche is not "a regional question in a larger order which would subordinate it first to the domain of a general ontology, subsequently to that of a fundamental ontology, and finally to the question of the truth of being itself."[17]

Derrida rescues this reading of the concept-metaphor "woman" in Nietzsche, and also suggests that Nietzsche's own *analysis* of sexual difference is caught within a historical or narrative understanding/misunderstanding of "propriation," making a being proper to itself.

(This notion, of the originary and therefore structurally inaccessible autoposition of the subject, is a fairly common one in generally non-foundationalist "Marxist" philosophers such as Louis Althusser or Theodor Adorno. Althusser's ill-fated remark about the "apparently paradoxical proposition which I shall express in the following terms: *ideology has no history*" belongs to this family of notions; as does Adorno's carefully articulated statement, "the subject is appearance in its self-positing and at the same time something historically altogether real."[18] Derrida places the question of sexual difference, at least, as he sees it in Nietzsche, in this space. (For Althusser, by contrast, sexual difference is one of the ideologies [rather than Ideology], which are within history: "it is in this implacable and more or less pathological . . . structure of the familial ideological configuration that the former subject-to-be will have to . . . (become) the sexual subject [boy or girl] which it already is in advance."[19] For Adorno the question of sexual difference cannot be entertained on this level.)

In Derrida's reading, Nietzsche is able to sketch sexual difference as preontological propriation perhaps *because* he is bound by and gives his assent to significations and values that define sexual difference in terms of the eternal war between the sexes, and the mortal hatred of the sexes in love, eroticism, etc. Thus propriation in Nietzsche may at first glance seem to have nothing but a series of restricted meanings: appropriation, expropriation, taking possession, gift and barter, mastering, servitude.[20] You have, then, on the one side, Heidegger with his extraordinarily subtle account of the ontological difference, *not* posing the sexual question, at least in this context. You have, on the other, Nietzsche, using or having to use the concept-metaphor "woman" to point at preontological difference, using it, none the less, inside male-dominated historical narratives of propriation.

Jacqueline Rose, when she writes about propriation in a couple of sentences in her introduction, is obliged to keep within the Nietzschean historical assumptions about propriation, without the emancipating moment of emergence of woman as "catachresis," as a metaphor without a literal referent standing in for a concept that is the condition of conceptuality: Nietzsche privileges the metaphor as condition of possibility of "truth." "Woman" is a necessary and irreducible misnomer for this prior or primal figurative. Any program which assumes continuity between the subject of epistemology/ontology and that of ethicopolitics, must actively forget that the call to/of the wholly-other, that which is the undiffarantiated (radically precontinuous) ethical, is the condition of possibility of the political, and that the propriation of a subject for ontology/epistemology has already also become possible by way of this condition. I will discuss Luce Irigaray's "ethics of sexual difference" in this context in the next chapter.

The distinction between the narrow sense and the general sense of catachresis is never clear-cut in deconstruction, although the difference is always acknowledged. According to Derrida, if one looks at propriation in the general sense in Nietzsche, one sees a question that is "more powerful than the question, 'what is?'," more powerful than "the veil of truth or the meaning of being,"[21] because before one can even say that *there is being,* there must be a decision that being can be proper to itself to the extent of being part of that proposition. (In German, before the gift of being in *Es gibt Sein,* one has to think the propriety to itself of the *Es.*) Outside of all philosophical game playing, the irreducible predicament pointed at here is that the ontological question cannot be asked in terms of a cleansed epistemology, for propriation organizes the totality of "language's process and symbolic exchange in general," caught in the catachresis, snarled in the false analogy, not in "pure" metaphor.[22]

I believe that in "Displacement and the Discourse of Woman," I missed the fact that in Derrida's reading of Nietzsche in *Spurs*, there is an insistence that "woman" in that text was a concept-metaphor that was also a *name* marking the preontological as propriation in sexual difference.[23]

When one of us defends Derrida against the other of us defending Lacan we are moving away from the suggestion in deconstruction (indeed European post-Hegelian theory in general) that a thinker does not make a point on the full steam of his sovereign subjectivity. Nietzsche, even as he depends upon propriation in the patriarchal, restricted, or narrow sense, reaches the general sense of propriation by putting the *name* of woman on it through the conduct of his text. And Derrida, grasping his reach as reader, does it not to trump Nietzsche but to make his text more useful for us. I hope the rest of this chapter will make clear how crucial it is not to ignore the powerful currents of European antihumanist thought that influence us, yet not to excuse them of their masculism while using them. This is what I am calling "negotiation."

Thus we can read Nietzsche's text in a way that suggests that the name of woman makes the question of propriation indeterminate. Let us look at the sentence: "there is no truth of woman, but because of that abyssal self-apartness of truth, this non-truth is 'truth.' "[24] If one takes the crucial term "woman" out of the sentence, it would be possible to suggest that this is what Nietzsche thinks is new about his philosophy of truth, that the nature of truth is such that it is always abyssally (in a structure of repeated indefinite mirroring) apart from what one appropriates as the truth in terms of which one can act. This non-truth is "truth." The quotation marks indicate a catachrestical setting apart, comparable to the quotation marks around "value" that Marx places in the passage quoted in the previous chapter. "Truth" here is not only not the literal, it is rather that for which there is no *adequate* literal referent.

Because, in Nietzsche's understanding of propriation in the narrow sense, woman is seen as the custodian of irreducibly inadequate literal referents; she is also seen as a model. In other words, when Nietzsche suggests there is no truth of woman in his historical understanding, a certain *kind* of woman is a model for the "no truth." Woman is thus "one name for that non-truth of truth:"[25] *one name* for that nontruth of truth.

My previous position on this essay of Derrida's was polemical. I suggested that it was not right to see the figure of woman as a sign for indeterminacy. Reading my analysis of appropriation in this polemic, Jacqueline Rose gives me the benefit of the doubt by claiming solidarity on this particular position.[26] And, within its own context, I accept this gesture. But today, negotiating, I want to give the assent for the moment to Derrida's argument. Affirmative deconstruction says "yes" to a text twice, sees complicity when it could rather easily be oppositional. As we have seen in the previous chapter, Derrida has described his first phase as "guarding the question," "keeping the question alive." The question is no particular question, of course, but its slippage into the form of *a* particular question is a "necessary transgression." In that spirit, and in this case, let us protect the question that we urge Rose to ask: is there not a difference between knowing-being—the epistemo/ontological—and right doing—the ethicopolitical? [27] He described the second phase as calling to the wholly other. (If sexual difference is indeed pre-comprehended by the ontological question then, miming Derrida's Nietzsche, *we* might think "philosophers," by way of the same historical narrative that gave Nietzsche "woman," as one misname for the forgetfulness of the nontruth of "truth." The quick defensiveness to save philosophy from this charge, discussed in the previous chapter, will then match our anger at these "philosophers" ' use of the name of "woman," and show that the difference between the philosopher and woman conceals a violence (truth/non-truth::theory/practice) that will not be undone by repeating the theory-practice quarrel in the women's quarter. Luce Irigaray's "ethics of sexual difference," which I have already once invoked, gives us a way out in the thinking of ethics. I have tried to think a politics that will not repeat that violence, more carefully than I have been able to in this book, in "Gender in Contemporary Colonization," as yet unpublished.

At this stage, still discussing feminism and deconstruction, let us consider how this shift from the first phase to the second translates into a strategy of reading, a strategy of giving assent. Let us look at Derrida's relatively recent study of Nietzsche, *The Ear of the Other,* a piece on the politics of reading.[28] He suggests there that the reader should not excuse the texts of Nietzsche for their use by the Nazis. There is no reason to say that that was a mere misreading. On the contrary, the reader should note that there is something in Nietzsche's text which leads exactly to that kind of appropriation. This is one paradoxical way of saying "yes" to the text, but it entails understanding from within, as it were, so that the moments that lend themselves to the so-called misappropriation are understood in the text's own terms. It is then that one can begin to develop a politics of reading, which will open up a text towards an as yet unknown horizon so that it can be of use without excuse. Let us now call this: negotiating with structures of violence. It is in that spirit of negotiation that I propose to give assent to Derrida's text about woman as a name for the nontruth of truth, upon the broader terrain of negotiation with other established structures, daily practiced but often disavowed, like the

Law, institutional education, and, ultimately, capitalism. Negotiation, not collaboration; producing a new politics through critical intimacy. Affirmative deconstruction of this kind was already signaled in *Grammatology*. Let us repeat that passage:

> The movements of deconstruction do not destroy structures from the outside. They are not possible and effective, nor can they take active aim, except by inhabiting those structures. Inhabiting them *in a certain way*, because one always inhabits, *and all the more when one does not suspect it.* Operating necessarily from the inside, borrowing all the strategic and economic resources of subversion from the old structure, borrowing them structurally, that is to say without being able to isolate their elements and atoms, the enterprise of deconstruction always *in a certain way* falls prey to its own work (*OG,* 24; emphasis mine).

It is this particular attitude that presages the crucial difference between the first and the second phases. The second attitude towards that which is critiqued, the giving of assent without excuse, so much that one inhabits its discourse—a short word for this might be "love."[29]

Deconstruction is not an exposure of error, nor a tabulation of error; logocentrism is not a pathology, nor is the metaphysical closure a prison to overthrow by violent means. Looking for irreducibles, realizing the theoretical absurdity of my position, it is with that "love" that I am reading texts already read, and questioning the usefulness of reading deconstruction merely as the narrative of the decentered subject, of the fully dispersed subject. This is where I began, with the suggestion that Rose's case against deconstruction was based on such a reading.

Let us look in more detail at why it is unsatisfactory to reduce deconstruction to a narrative.

One focus of deconstruction as a morphology is the graphematic structure. In this brief compass, I will present the morphology also as a narrative (perhaps this is inescapable)—the narrative of a narrative if you like—and contrast it to the narrative of a decentered subject which deconstruction offers not only to Jacqueline Rose, but to readers such as Jürgen Habermas and Fredric Jameson.

One focus, then, of deconstruction is the graphematic structure. The adjective "graphematic" comes from Derrida's analysis that writing is historically the structure that is supposed necessarily to operate in the presumed absence of its origin, the sender.

Any act must assume unified terms to get started. The implicit mechanics by which these assumptions are established or taken for granted spell out, if examined, a structure of repetition, which yet overtly posits self-evidence. These mechanics are generally found to be suppressed or finessed, so that beginnings do not seem problematic. Nearly all of Derrida's writing has been a discussion of such gestures—sometimes even self-conscious gestures of dismissal as difficulties or counterexamples—performed in different ways in different discourses. Let us decide to call this gesture the suppression of a graphematic structure. The graphematic structure that seems to orchestrate the inauguration of all acts (including acts of thought) is a structure *like* writing (although it is passed off as the self-identity of definitions present to themselves), something that looks more like the mark of an absent presence, writing commonly conceived. As in the case of writing commonly conceived, we cannot be necessarily sure of the identity of the originator, so in the case of the graphematic structure, we cannot endorse the "fact" that it *is* an absent presence of which the trace-structure at the origin is the mark. (I remind the reader of the origin of Marx's socialist teleology in a "convenient error," discussed in the previous chapter.) This unendorsable naming of the discovery of the repetition at the origin as "graphematic," by way of "writing" as a catachresis, is the double bind that founds all deconstruction. In other words, hidden agendas might pass themselves off as the goes-without-saying-ness of truth, to fools and knaves alike; but to show them up as writing *and mean it* is to buy into that very agenda, unless we put scare-quotes around the word, and say: can't do better for the time being, must keep moving. To call by the name of man all human reality is move number one: humanism; to substitute the name of woman in that mode is move number two; to put scare-quotes around "woman" is move number three, not a synthesis but a provisional half-solution that always creates problems because it is or is not mistaken for the second move; therefore always looking forward, while making do, toward a fourth move, that never happens but always might.

By these alleyways, human beings think themselves unified also by finessing the assumption of a repressed graphematic structure. There is no way to get hold of a subject before this two-step. This is the narrative of the famous decentered subject. In early work such as "Structure, Sign, and Play" and the first chapter of *Of Grammatology*, Derrida does invoke "our epoch," meaning, specifically, an "epoch" that privileges language and thinks (impossibly) to have got rid of centrisms.[30] To turn this critique—of a claim to have decentered method, by pointing out that the subject can only ever be posited by the finessing of a graphematic structure at the origin—into merely the story of the individual becoming decentered with late capitalism (Jameson), the passing of the pre-Socratics (Heidegger), the inception of modernity (Habermas via Weber), or with Derrida's new tricky bolstering of Eurocentric patriarchy (Rose), is a plausible but unexamined move.

The useful part of deconstruction is in the suggestion that the subject is always centered. Deconstruction persistently notices that this centering is an effect-structure with indeterminable boundaries that can only be deciphered as determining. No politics can occupy itself with only this enabling epistemological double bind. But when a political analysis or program forgets this it runs the risk of declaring ruptures where there is also a repetition—a risk that can result in varieties of fundamentalism, of which the onto/epistemo/ethicopolitical confusion is a characteristic symptom. International communism has died of the risk.

Différance is one of the names for the necessity to obliterate the graphematic structure, *and* the necessity to misname it "graphematic," since there is no other way one can call it. This double bind—the double session of "defering"—is at the origin of practice.[31]

Rose suggests, and she is not alone, that there is in Derrida a desire to suppress sexual difference in the interest of *différance,* and a privileging of *différance* as *the* name. (It seems to go unnoticed that, in his later work, the word is hardly ever used.)

Différance is, and it cannot be repeated often enough, only *one* name for the irreducible double bind that allows the very possibility of difference(s). Sexual *identity* is sexual *différance,* not sexual difference; it produces sexual difference. We are obliged to assume a pre-originary wholly other space without differences in the interest of suppressing that "graphematic" structure at the inauguration of our texts; and *différance* is only *one* name for that necessity. There is no harm in admitting that it's not just the production of *sexual* difference that's being framed here but the possibility of thinking difference itself.

I invite you to consider again that, in the discourse of this critic of phallogocentrism, "woman" is another name for this irreducible double bind. This is a difficult consideration when we want to claim deconstruction for or against feminism, but I now see no way around it. Here *différance* as the ungraspable ground of propriation *is* (but the copula is a supplement) sexual difference.[32] The *name* (of) woman occupies this site in Derrida. *Différance* and "woman" are two names on a chain of nominal displacements where, unmotivated names, neither can claim priority. "Man" is the duped name of the undivided origin. We are rather far away from the "subject" of feminist ethicopolitics. In fact, we are still looking at the (im)possibility of broaching the epistemo/ontological.[33]

If *différance* (or "woman," as well as the other names) opens up the question of symbolic possibility in general, it is not, as Rose writes, by suppression of thoughts of cultural form. The thought of cultural forms, which implies the differentiation of one culture from another, or of sexual difference, and indeed all other kinds of difference; the difference between being and nonbeing, if you like the ontico-ontological difference in this particular understanding, our desire to have an impasse which can only be between two things, our desire even for the undecidable; all of these are limited by the possibility that at the beginning is a suppression which we cannot get a handle on. *Différance* is in a (con)text, never pure. That's all it is, it's no big deal, but it's *not* a story-line which dismisses these differences as culturally unacceptable. We are still circling around the possibility of story-lines, even the story-lines that put one "culture" over against another. (I have learned this all the better in terms of the politics of the postcolonial clamor for cultural difference and the current demands of liberal multiculturalism.) If all this seems too ethereal remember we wouldn't have to do this if "deconstruction" had not been diagnosed in the first place as a story-line suppressing sexual and cultural difference in the interest of *différance*. As you will, I hope, see in the end, I prefer a more pragmatic line of reasoning (by way of a persistent active and only immediately forgetful transgression of theory) myself when I am thinking/ doing as a feminist.[34]

"Woman," then, is a name that is the nontruth of "truth" in Derrida reading Nietzsche. We have considered the status of a *name* in thinkers of this type in our discussion of Foucault's "nominalism" in Chapter Two. This particular species of nominalism, an obsession with names that are necessarily misnames, names that are necessarily catachreses, "writing," "*différance*," "power" ("woman" in this case), names that have no adequate literal referent, characterizes poststructuralism in general, in spite of local differences (and via "Value," and the "Social," makes one suspect a kinship between the Marxian project and the implicit politics of poststructuralism—thinking of Marx's critical intimacy with Hegel's *Verhältnis*-obsessed dialectical structuralism—so inaccessible to the polemical eye, yet perhaps among the most important reasons for its failure in the hands of positivist sentimentalists). It is important to remember that each of these names is determined by their historical burden in the most empirical way. (Derrida calls this "paleonymy.") I hope it is by now clear that Nietzsche uses a name such as "woman" because he has inherited it, and thus he uses all the contemporary allegorical, sociological, historical, and dismissive stereotypes about woman. On the other hand, since Nietzsche also wants to welcome this name as a name for his own practice—"my truths"—what one sees in his text is the site of a conflict or a negotiation. Nietzsche, or Derrida, or for that matter Lacan, is here fully complicit with masculism (quite as Nietzsche is with the possibility of the grafting of Nazism onto his left), yet it is also possible to see, and Derrida is asking us to see this in Nietzsche because if we do this we can make the text useful, that within this itinerary there is that peculiar affirmation. This is the model Nietzsche wants—woman in that sense is *twice* model (modeling the nontruth of "truth," and being as unlike the dogmatic philosopher of truth as possible by way of some of the dubious historical stereotypes). It might be useful for us to *accuse* the text responsibly, and then lift this lever and *ab-use* the text, rather than not use it at all and follow the mistake of the truth of (wo)man. Derrida himself is also bound (as is Lacan, and as are we in our taste for a pragmatic feminism that claims to be theoretical even as it forgets the difference between the subjects of onto/epistemology and ethico-politics) by a certain set of historical presuppositions. After all, one never hears a claim not to use anything from the other side except as it is made possible through institutional affiliation, the International Book Trade, fiscal support of a nation-state, consumerist support of transnational ("postmodern") capitalism, and so on. It is never heard from women involved in primary health care, literacy, or alternative (not "sustainable"—that new cant word) development. (The crisis of so-called national liberation is a different case and must have its share of gesture politics.) In the persistent struggle against gendering ("internalized constraint seen as choice"),[35] it is better to ab-use the enemy's enemies than to be a purist while sitting in the enemy's lap—a lap so colossal and shape-changing that you can forget you are sitting in it.

Derrida gives proof of being bound by the paleonymy of "woman" when, at the end of *The Ear of the Other,* speaking still about his politics of reading, he sounds a theme that has been sounded by him before: the patronymic (the father's name), because through it the man can continue to survive after death, is a kiss of death. By contrast, the nameless feminine is the name of living. And it is this peculiar *livingness* of the feminine that is in some ways contaminated or betrayed by what Derrida perhaps understands as "feminism." "No woman or trace of woman. And I do not make this remark in order to benefit from that supplement of seduction which today enters into all courtships or courtrooms. This vulgar procedure is what I propose to call 'gynegogy.' "[36]

It must be acknowledged that this perspective, constituted by the historico-legal tradition of the patronymic in patriarchy, exists in Derrida's text just as much as a perspective constituted by *his* historical legacy exists in Nietzsche's catachrestical use of "woman" as name. Thus, because of the necessity of the historical determination of the name "woman" for the double bind at the origin of the production of "truth(s)," there is no sense in talking about the relationship between deconstruction and feminism as if women were naturally decentered.[37] It takes its place, in its productivity, with the claim that women are naturally anything.

Yet the name of woman as the nontruth of "truth" *can* have a significant message for us if we, refusing fully to honor the historically bound catachresis, give the name of woman to that *disenfranchised* woman who is *historically* different from ourselves, the subjects of feminist theory, and yet acknowledge that she has the right to the construction of a subject-effect of sovereignty in the narrow sense. Then we, as those by now relatively enfranchised agents, will share and understand the philosophers' anxiety about the nasty historical determinations which allow this name to exist. Since these philosophers are not essentialists, they have a real anxiety about the loss of the name "woman" because it survives on these precariously sketched, basically essentialist historical generalizations. This is what is reflected in the kind of masculinist noises we noticed above at the conclusion of *The Ear of the Other*.[38]

There is a passage in Lacan's "Love Letter," an essay translated by Jacqueline Rose in *Feminine Sexuality*, where he talks about the understanding of the place of woman beyond the question of sex, in soul-making and in naming God, which I think can be put together with Nietzsche's longing for affirming the name of woman as the nontruth of "truth," and Derrida's anxiety about compromising the living feminine in the interest of a gynegogy which would sell itself to the death-story of the patronymic.[39] This, to my mind, marks a moment of the need for taking the name of woman in the interest of a philosophical practice. It is, in fact, no more and indeed no less than the need for a name. It is easier to grasp this if we look at the way in which Derrida writes about *différance*. In "Différance," the essay by that name, he repeats tediously that *différance* is neither a concept nor a metaphor, nor indeed a word, and yet, in the end, the entire essay is argued in terms of the conceptuality and metaphoricity of the term. This particular tactic, of marking the anxiety by keeping the name intact against all disavowals unreadable without the name of that graphematic structure which can only be misnamed, makes work open to traditional masculism, in the case of the name of "woman," as it makes it open to traditional modes of language use in the case of *différance*.

What can we do about this? I have already mentioned that I welcome the idea of the embattled love of the text that is given to us by deconstruction. Yet I cannot err too long on that path. Deconstruction is not androgyny, phallocentrism is not a pathology. After we have repeated these lessons, we must still insist on the project of antisexism, because sexism *is* also a pathology.[40] In that perspective, women can no longer only be names for "writing" or the nontruth of *différance*. We cannot claim both the desire to identify with the oppression of woman in terms of an ontological deception, and the desire for the right to an impasse, to a deconstructive feminism which would take woman as a name for the graphematic structure and the nontruth of truth. We have to give up the one or the other. I would propose that we should not share this anxiety for the name, we should not identify the guarding of the question with *this* particular name. This would allow us to use the ontological and epistemological critiques found in deconstruction (and indeed psychoanalysis) and appreciate poststructuralist "nominalism." We must remember that this *particular name*, the name of "woman," misfires for feminism. Yet, a feminism that takes the traditionalist line *against* deconstruction falls into a historical determinism where "history" becomes a gender-fetish.

What I have described in the paragraph above is an ethical aporia, backed up by intellectual preparation and its relationship to a political decision. "Pessimism of the intellect and optimism of the will," if you like formulas, or, "ethics as the experience of the impossible." Derrida has written about this with the philosopher's anxiety in "The Force of Law." By contrast, guarding this particular name for the graphematic structure is perhaps the most essentialist move of all—this turning of deconstruction into a narrative whether in praise or dispraise. If *we* lose the "name" of specifically woman for writing there is no cause for lament.

It is *in the interest of* diagnosing the ontological ruse, on the basis of which there is oppression of woman, that we have to bring our understanding of the relationship between the name "woman" and deconstruction into crisis. If we do not take the time to understand this in our zeal to be "political," then I fear we act out the kind of play that Nietzsche figured out in *The Genealogy of Mortals:* in the interest of giving an alibi to his desire to punish, which is written into his way of being, in other words in the interest of a survival game, man produces an alibi which is called justice. And in the interest of that alibi, man has to define and articulate, over and over again, the name of man. It seems to me that if *we* forget that *we* cannot have a deconstructive feminism which decides to transform the usefulness of the name "woman," itself based on a certain kind of historical anxiety for the graphematic structure, into a narrative, and thus take up arms against what we sometimes call essentialism, *then* we might be acting out this particular scenario, adequately contradicting and thus legitimizing it—by devising newer names of woman—in the interest of giving the desire to punish the alibi of justice. And if you ask me whether the disenfranchised can think this critique, I would say yes. It is the disenfranchised who teaches us most often by saying: I do not recognize myself in the object of your benevolence. I do not recognize my share in your naming. Although the vocabulary is not that of high theory, she tells us if we *care* to hear (without identifying our onto/epistemological subjectivity with *her* anxiety for the subjectship of ethics and the agency of the political) that she is not the literal referent for our frenzied naming of woman in the scramble for legitimacy in the house of theory. She reminds us that the name of "woman," however political, is, like any other name, a catachresis.

(I am not being ethereal here. I know the kind of woman I am thinking about. And I also know that this person is not imaginable by most friends reading these words. I cannot enter into the immense and complicated logic of why this is so. Let this remain a lost parenthesis, being fleshed out through a laborious program of a learning not yet accessible to the production of knowledge—a promissory note that you are under no obligation to endorse in the competition for "the most oppressed feminist.")

The claim to deconstructive feminism (and deconstructive antisexism—the political claim of deconstructive feminists) cannot be sustained in the name of "woman" within the Derridian problematic. Like class consciousness, which justifies its own production so that this historical class-formation can be undone, "woman" as the name of writing must be erased in so far as it is a necessarily historical catachresis.

The name of woman cannot be the "reality" of writing or of the necessary graphematic structure unless you turn the theory into nonsense. Let us say, speaking from within, that we have to deconstruct our desire for the impasse, neutralize the name of "woman" *for deconstruction* and be deconstructive feminists in that sense. If we want to make political claims that are more useful all around than the general bourgeois academic feminist toothsome euphoria, this seems now to be the only way.

This point is not quite identical with the other note I have been sounding on and off: the object that is known to us through the epistemic project, the cleansed object that knows the itinerary of its recognition of itself as male or female, cannot be identical with the constituency of antisexism, the subject of ethicopolitics. I will bring the two together by way of a consideration of Foucault's double-play with "power" and power, and compare it to ours with "woman" and woman: the name and, as it were, the thing, the phenomenal essence. It should be a lesson to us that *if* we do not watch out for the historical determinations for the name of woman as catachresis in deconstruction, and merely seek to delegitimize the name of man, we legitimize what is diagnosed by Nietzsche and acted out by Foucault.

"Objective" precedes the famous chapter on "Method" in *History of Sexuality I*. By the end of this section, everything happens as if the lessons learned from Nietzsche, precisely the alibi for the ontological compulsion to articulate as epistemology (name of man as subject of justice as alibi for the ontological need to punish), could be undone by an act of will. Thus Foucault is able to say, "We must at the same time conceive of sex without the law, and power without the king" (*HS*, 91). This sentence leads into the section entitled "Method." Arrived here, the *name* "power" is systematically sold short for the "thing" power, and we are able to get a method because we know the objective, not reduced to an act of willed thought. (The best way to deconstruct this is through Foucault's own notion of the "referential" in the *Archaeology of Knowledge*, which I attempt in Chapter Two.)

This bit of short-circuiting is comparable to the way that we would naturalize the *name* "woman" if we transformed it into the central character in that narrative of woman's recognition within gendering, however deferred. Foucault's naturalizing of the *name* "power" allows the coding of the phenomenality of power as something like an arithmetical system of equivalences: "And it is doubtless the strategic codification of these points of resistance that makes a revolution possible somewhat similar to the way in which the state relies on the institutional integration of power relationships."[42] We see here a case of Foucault's desire to get beyond the ontological/epistemological bind, comparable to our equation of the subject of ontoepistemology and ethicopolitics.

I have warned against an abuse of theory, because we cannot stop when the analytic philosopher can stop, with "the heritage of Socrates" behind him.[43] I quote the following words, continuing my very first quotation in this essay not in mockery, but recognizing how self-critical they are. "Moral judgment" Nagel writes, "and moral theory certainly apply to public questions, but they are notably ineffective." What I have been arguing so far about the relationship between feminism and deconstructive feminism, feminism and the confusion between the object of the epistemic project and the constituency of antisexism might translate to what is being said here.

> Moral judgment and moral theory certainly apply to public questions, but they are notably ineffective. When powerful interests are involved

it is very difficult to change anything by arguments, however cogent, which appeal to decency, humanity, compassion, and fairness. These considerations also have to compete with the more primitive moral sentiments of honor and retribution and respect for strength. The conditions under which moral argument can have an influence are rather special, and not very well understood by me. They need to be investigated through the history and psychology of morals, important but underdeveloped subjects much neglected by philosophers since Nietzsche. It certainly is not enough that the injustice of a practice of the wrongness of policy should be made glaringly evident. People have to be ready to listen, and that is not determined by argument.[44]

In the end Nagel says, in a kind of melancholy self-distancing from Marx's Eleventh Thesis on Feuerbach: "I do not know whether it is important to change the world or to understand it, but philosophy is best judged by its contribution to understanding, not to the course of events." In the previous chapter, it has been argued that Marx tried to redo the role of philosophy in the divided but related activities of interpreting and changing the world. Yet Marxism foundered in the relationship between class-*consciousness* and agency of "revolution," not to mention the running of a bounded "post-revolutionary state." If, in fact, we do not acknowledge that the object of the epistemic search and the constituency of antisexist work are not identical, that gendering is within "the history and psychology of morals," and we simply finesse the fact that the feminist challenge must combine method *and* act, we might be able to echo the nobility of Thomas Nagel's sentiments. I myself think we cannot stop here, because in the cultures now dominating the world, women have not had an acknowledged code of "honor and retribution and respect for strength" except as victims/supporters. I will, then, repeat my modest solution.

Incanting to ourselves all the perils of transforming a "name" to a referent—making a catechism, in other words, of catachresis—let us none the less name (as) "woman" that disenfranchised woman whom we strictly, historically, geopolitically *cannot imagine,* as literal referent. "Subaltern" is the name of the social space that is different from the classed social circuit, the track of hegemony. By proposing the irreducible other in that space as holding the name "woman," I am attempting to deflect attention from the "poor little rich girl speaking *personal* pain as victim of the *greatest* oppression"-act that multiculturalist capitalism—with its emphasis on individuation and competition—would thrust upon us. Let us divide the name of woman so that we see ourselves as naming, not merely named. Let us acknowledge that we must change a morphology to a story-line, acknowledge that we participated in obliterating the traces of her production, stage the scene of the effacing of the graphematic—her biography—in the crudest possible way. The anxiety of this naming will be that, if we must think a relationship between the subject of onto/epistemology (ourselves, roughly, in this room at Cambridge, or Elaine Showalter at Princeton) and the object of onto/axiology (that disenfranchised woman, not even graduated into that subject, whose historicity or subjectship we cannot imagine beyond the regulation "women's union" or "personal pain" human interest anecdote), the hope behind the political desire will be that the possibility for the name will be finally erased. Today, here, what I call the "gendered subaltern," especially in decolonized space, has become the name "woman" for me. "Douloti" (see Chapter Four)—traffic-in-wealth—financialization—may be one such name. In search of irreducibles, after the chastening experience of coming close to the person who provides that imagined name, I want to be able not to lament when the material possibility for the name will have disappeared.

In the five years between first publication and second, the name "woman," in this sense, has shifted for me into the subaltern of contemporary colonization. Once again I point at the beginning of the intellectual consolidation of that shift, "Gender in Contemporary Colonization," a speech in Galway as this was a speech in Cambridge. The promissory note is being redeemed in installments, somewhere else.

In a staged "improvisation" with Hélène Cixous, in October 1991, on "Readings of Sexual Difference," Derrida shuttles to the other side: all readings are of/from (the double-jointed French *de*) sexual difference from inside sexual difference. One is never completely on one side of it, it is the story of a constant untimely interruption [*histoire d'un contretemps*]—of getting to the in-different *human* perspective?

To relate it to the subtitle of my chapter: the two sides (can there be two) of sexual difference are thus, in the reading that is living, in constant ground-level negotiation, with no leisure [*nec-otium*] at all, before sides can be taken.

To relate it to the end of the next chapter: sexual difference is the critical intimacy—in bits as well as all of a piece (Derrida finds the model for such a form in the Latin word for insect)—that can presumably think sexual difference as radical alterity, always from within sexual difference, of course.[45]

7

French Feminism Revisited

Algeria has a highly diversified structure of women's movements. Inter-acting with part of that diversified network, starting from the now rela-tively venerable FLN-based national women's organization through more recent grass-roots movements, one would receive the impression that workers like Marie-Aimée Hélie-Lucas, of whom I speak in the body of my text, with their attention fixed on the Family Code, are felt by some in the interior to be more remote from other emancipatory women's issues on the domestic front, by which the former are not as deeply touched. Thus my original argument, that the face of "global" feminism is turned outward and must be welcomed and respected as such, rather than fetish-ized as the figure of the Other, gains confirmation from my first research visit to Algeria. Subsequent visits have strengthened the conviction that the Family Code occupies a space within a diversified womanspace. The possibility of the exercise of the Law as right is class-stratified. Further research will, I hope, flesh out the domestic space in such a way that this postcolonial feminist will no longer need to revisit French feminism as a way in, although it might remain an exigency in academic Cultural Stud-ies. And indeed, current work on Assia Djebar and Gender in Contempo-rary Colonization is creating bypasses from recognizably "French" feminisms.

The way in through French feminism defines the third world as Other. Not to need that way in is, paradoxically, to recognize that indigenous global feminism must still reckon with the bitter legacy of imperialism transformed in decolonization:

> Current research on the family in Algeria and in the Maghreb cannot be evaluated without a retrospective view, however brief, of the move-ment of ideas that have emerged in Europe, and in Anglo-Saxon and transatlantic countries. . . . The paradigms of academic intelligibility of feminism in Algeria and in the Maghreb have been, for the large part,

modulated in the intellectual configurations of Western thought: They have offered the frame and the genesis. . . .[1]

This intelligent passage defines my charge: to see that the view is retrospective, and that the requirements are of academic intelligibility, in the service of which we write for publication. I must first show how the frame and the point of genesis are themselves contested, and then remind myself that within the frame, and after the genesis, is a patchwork of which I have not yet learned to speak (for ethnography/sociology must be unlearned here) without the legitimation-by-reversal of mere admiration.

Second Thoughts

Texts open when you talk to groups of others, which often turn out to be classes, public audiences. Yet these openings are not beginnings, for the staging of each such talking is secured by politics: classes at least by the individualism and competition of the academy "at its best," public lectures by the politics of funding and the thematics of travel and lodging; the gender, race, and class politics of custodial staff in both arenas. No attempt such as ours can begin without a grounding mistake, cutting off the space where theory is persistently normed by politics.

Texts open when you talk to groups of others, which often turn out to be classes, public lectures. The most intimate alterity or otherness defines and offers up our so-called selves to ourselves. Most intimate, yet least accessible. So close that we cannot catch it through the self or selves that it frames for us. As for those clusters of alterity—groups of others—that we call classes or audiences, conversation says that the best way to reach them is to assume them as collections of selves and adjust your pitch. (And, if you move globally—from the U.S. via Algeria to France, for example—the imagining of pitch and collectivity inscribes the political centering of the speaker's theoretical burden).

Every craftsperson knows that unless she is sure of the effectiveness of every detail of her craft, what she is making will not hold. Assuming that classes and audiences are collections of selves ignores the details of their intimate and inaccessible alterity. In the previous chapter we invoked the alterity of the woman whose selfhood or, better, mental theater, to borrow a phrase from Wittgenstein, was unimaginable. Here we attend to the alterity of women whose selves are, or so we think, only too easily imagined. These details mark the limits of teaching and talking, so that the certainty that texts are opening remains framed by a radical uncertainty. I was teaching "My Chances/*Mes Chances:* A Rendezvous with Some

Epicurean Stereophonics" for the first time when I wrote the first draft of this paper, and the conventionally ignored details of class and audience insistently became clear to me as they never had before.[2] And now, reading Patricia Williams's uncanny attention to the blank part of the text, I feel my affection for deconstruction grow, that it can claim such friends:

> I would like to write in a way that reveals the intersubjectivity of legal *constructions,* that forces the reader both to participate in the *construction* of meaning and to be conscious of that process. Thus, in attempting to fill the gaps in the discourse of commercial exchange, I hope that the gaps in my own writing will be self-consciously modeled, filled by the reader, as an act of forced mirroring of meaning-invention. To this end, I exploit all sorts of literary devices. . . .[3]

It is from the far end of the track which talks of intersubjectivity as forced mirroring and the exploitation of rhetoric, even as it undoes construction, that we can ask: What is it to write for you? What is it to teach? What is it to learn? What is it to assume that one already knows the meaning of the words "something is taught by me and something is learned by others"?

In one sense, this uncertainty is the ground of the academic institution, if we consider that institution to be, not only an ideological apparatus, but also an apparatus with the help of which we believe we produce a critique of ideology.[4] Yet it is in the face of this felt uncertainty that we must risk the generalizations that we feel are opened up by the convenient assumption that a class learns, an audience hears, readers read as we teach, talk, write. The greatest fear, and the greatest hope, is that once the generalizations emerge, the convention of taking others as collections of selves should take over only too easily and something be grasped from whatever is offered. In that grasping, the working of the academy as ideological apparatus has an operative role.

This is the first essay in the book where I touch *women* "of another kind." How can I hope that the generalizations I offer here will miraculously escape this violating yet enabling convention? Yet how can anyone not care? Especially since they have been opened up for me by talk with others, even, in one case where talk was not permitted and the necessary misfiring of teaching and learning was turned into deliberate arson.

Bio-Graphy

Eleven years ago I wrote "Displacement and the Discourse of Woman," believing that men on women could only be set right by women.[5]

Ten years ago I wrote "French Feminism in an International Frame," believing that no Europeanist should ignore the once and future global production of "Europe."[6]

Three years ago I wrote "Feminism and Deconstruction, Again," as a sort of second take on "Displacement." I had come to think that in the production of feminist theoretical practice, negotiation based on acknowl-edgment of complicity with the male-dominated history of theory was also in order. Chapter Six is a revised version of this essay.

And here is "French Feminism Revisited," which feels to me like a second take on "International Frame." I have come to think that in the face of patriarchal reappropriation of decolonization, isolationist nationalisms, and internalized gendering, there can be exchange between metropolitan and decolonized feminisms.

When I wrote "French Feminism in an International Frame," my subject position, even if only partly assigned by the workings of the ideological apparatus, was that of an ethnic minority who had broken into the university in the United States. I was not fully aware of this, of course, just as I was not fully aware of the convictions of single-issue feminism guiding my reading in "Displacement."

"International Frame," like "Displacement," was the beginning of a certain kind of revisionary work for me. A decade later, what little I have learned—may I not forget to question: what is it to assume that one already knows the meaning of the words; something is taught by others and something is learned by me—seems to point at three different general-izations for this resistant reader's subject position: ethnic in the U.S., racial in Britain, negotiating for decolonized space. These are generaliza-tions that now seem good for teaching and learning in classes, lecture halls. They will not travel directly, of course, to all situations of struggle in the three arenas, as some of us, impatient with the grounding uncer-tainty of teaching, talking, writing, seem too quickly to presume.

After the rupture of negotiated political independence or national liber-ation, racialization or ethnicization of resistance is no longer the most urgent emancipatory generalization in decolonized space, is indeed increasingly used for mobilizing on the right. As I have repeatedly empha-sized in this book, the most urgent political claims in decolonized space are tacitly recognized as coded within the legacy of imperialism: nationhood, constitutionality, citizenship, democracy, socialism, even culturalism. "Feminism," the named movement, is also part of this so-called heritage of the European Enlightenment, although within the enclosure of the heritage it is often inscribed in a contestatory role. It is obvious that these positions, logically defined, swirl in the inaccessible intimacy of the everyday, giving hue to being. To fix it in paint is to efface as much as to disclose. Yet the agenda of agency remains: to wrench these regulative political signifiers out of their represented field of reference. And the instrument of such a wrenching, such a reconstellating or dehegemonizing, cannot be ethnophilosophical or race-ideological false and simulated pride. Given the international division of labor and the consequent pattern of leisure and dominance in the imperialist centuries, it is to be expected that the "best" critique of the European ethical-political-social universals, those regulative concepts, should come from the North Atlantic.[7] But what is ironically appropriate in postcoloniality is that this critique finds its best *staging* outside of the North Atlantic in the undoing of imperialism.

When I wrote "French Feminism in an International Frame" my assigned subject-position was actually determined by my moment in the United States and dominated my apparent choice of a postcolonial position. For my own class in the decolonized nation vaguely conceived, I had little else but contempt. Now it seems to me that the radical element of the postcolonial bourgeoisie must most specifically learn to negotiate with the structure of enabling violence that produced her; and the normative narrative of metropolitan feminism is asymmetrically wedged in that structure. Simply to resist it as "white feminism" is to yield privilege to the migrants' and the diasporics' struggle, crucial *on* their terrain, and to forget that they too want to inhabit the national subject by displacing it: Black Britain, Arab France; it is to neglect the postcolonial's particular generalization in the vaster common space of woman.

I remain, of course, a Europeanist by training. My belief remains the same: no Europeanist should ignore the once and future global production of "Europe." My question has sharpened: How does the postcolonial feminist negotiate with the metropolitan feminist? I have placed three classic texts of French feminism before an activist text of Algerian feminism that speaks of negotiation.[8] I imagine a sympathy with Marie-Aimée Hélie-Lucas's subject-position because hers too is perhaps fractured and I help to crack it further, for use. She too is revising an earlier position. As she does so, she speaks *of* solidarity with Islamic women around the world. She speaks *to* a British interviewer. And I, a non-Islamic Indian postcolonial, use her to revise my reading of French feminism.

The texts in this essay were opened up for me in teaching; subsequently in speeches. This, then, might be the moment to remember that, even when—in class, in a lecture room—the other seems a collection of selves and nothing seems displaced or cracked, what "really happens" remains radically uncertain, the risky detail of our craft. To remember both that "within the range of our calculations we can count on certain probabilities"; and, that "to believe in chance can just as well indicate that one believes in the existence of chance as that one does *not*, above all, believe in chance, since one looks for and finds a hidden meaning at all costs."[9] Can it be imagined how this mischief conducts traffic between women's solidarity across two sides of imperialism?

Simone de Beauvoir

In a few paragraphs hidden in the curious chapter on "The Mother" in *The Second Sex,* Simone de Beauvoir rewrote the figure of the Mother as possible existentialist subject.[10]

We have judged Beauvoir harshly. Juliet Mitchell's remark remains representative and definitive: "*The Second Sex,* strictly speaking, is not a part of the second feminist movement."[11] The implications of Antoinette Fouque's harsh words after Beauvoir's death, which Toril Moi sums up in the following way, were quickly shared by many in France: "Now that Beauvoir is dead, feminism is finally free to move into the twenty-first century."

I want to reopen the chapter on "The Mother" in the face of the judgment of these daughters. First, and most curious, the chapter seems to focus teleologically on the child and thus frees daughters from mothers. In *our* time-space of feminism, we have kept uncertainties at bay by binding mother to daughter in our theories and strategies. But we cannot make the whole world fit forever into that devoutly wished embrace. A section of the generation of emancipated bourgeois colonial women whose daughters can be and are the agents of negotiation in decolonized feminist space, represented by Hélie-Lucas in this essay, were inspired by Beauvoir's book or sentiments similar to the ones to which she gave coherent articulation. Secondly, her reduced or pared-down structural picture of the Mother, so intimate that it is intuitively inaccessible (and thus protected against dominant universalizing), is theoretically inclusive of "situations" (an existentialist word) often considered beside the point of the norm: gay parenting, mothering by the gendered subaltern.

"Situation" is an existentialist word. Beauvoir's chapter on "The Mother" is one among other descriptions of "situations" for the second sex. I would like to make this my point of entry into the chapter. On the threshold I place a generalization about deconstructive reading to ward off uncertainty: it is unexcusing, unaccusing, attentive, and situationally productive through dismantling.

I attempt to follow the protocols of Beauvoir's text into existentialism.

As a daughter, I sense her hesitation between the role of object/Other that is offered to her. I sense her assertion of a difficult liberty—both as daughter and as the mother philosophized. And I think I am able to sketch the lineaments of a counternarrative that would bring her forward to Hélène Cixous's figuring of the Mother, which must finally be supplemented by Melanie Klein.

Reading against the grain of the text, then, I will suggest that, in the figure of the mother, and in the making of an anthropos, Beauvoir has set down or made visible, perhaps without intent (given her commitment to patriarchal humanism, but then, what is it to teach?), a critique of the very philosophical anthropology of which Derrida accused Sartre twenty years after the publication of *Being and Nothingness* and *The Second Sex*.[12]

In the chapter on "Existential Psychoanalysis," Sartre describes how the mother *does* create the possibility for the child to "exist." This is a much-discussed passage, but I want to quote it as if nothing has been written on it:

> On the contrary it is only through another—through the words which the mother uses to designate the child's body—that he [the pronoun makes a difference in the applicability of this conceptual scheme, surely? Although it is not distinguishable in French] learns that his anus is a *hole*. It is therefore the objective nature of the hole perceived in the world which is going to illuminate for him the objective structure and the sense [*sens*] to the erogenous sensations which were hitherto limited to merely "existing." In itself then the *hole* is the symbol of a mode of being which existential psychoanalysis must elucidate. . . . Thus to plug up a hole means originally to make a sacrifice of my body in order that the plenitude of being may exist; that is, to subject the passion of the for-itself so as to shape, to perfect, and to perceive the totality of the in-itself (*BN*, 781).

In order to frame Beauvoir's critique, I will quote a passage from the conclusion to *Being and Nothingness*. This passage is in effect introduced by the last sentence of "Existential Psychoanalysis": "Man is a useless passion."

" 'There is' being," Sartre writes, "because the for-itself is such that there should be being. The character of the *phenomenon* comes to being by [way of] the for-itself" (*BN*, 788). Let us recall that it is by way of a reading of the Heideggerian sentence *Es gibt Sein* (there is being), that Derrida introduces the question of the being's prior access to the proper through sexual difference. *Es gibt Sein* is guarded by the properties or definitive characteristics of different languages. If you translate that German sentence into literal English, yet retaining the trace of German clandestinely, it gives Being, the gift of Being becomes in German a *Gift* or poison. By such ruses Derrida tries to protect the status of a sentence that can only mark a limit by betraying it, since there are languages. Sartre has no such problem. He treats the "to have" of the literal French translation *il y a* (it there has) as a verb and declines it, and ignores the other implications of the linguistic specificity of this apparently generalizable sentence. The *différance* at the origin, disclosed (as it is concealed) by language differences, is forgotten. What is it to learn?

Sartre can thus rewrite the ontico-ontological difference (what is most intimate is also inaccessible) in the following way: "the phenomenon of the in-itself is an abstraction without consciousness but its *being* is not an abstraction" (*BN*, 791). Let us proceed to examine how, in the figure of the mother and child, Beauvoir writes this difference philosophically into the name of woman. This reduced or pared-down structural picture of the mother, shorn of heterosexual affect, can take on board gay parenting, or mothering by the gendered subaltern.

It is possible to read Beauvoir's description of the female body in gestation as exactly not biologism. The pregnant body here is species-life rather than species-being, to follow Marx's famous distinction in the *Economic and Philosophical Manuscripts*.[13] It is the site of the wholly other, rather than the man-consolidating other that woman is supposed to be. This is where "the whole of nature . . . is woman's *body without organs*."[14] There are no proper names here. To read this as bio-*logy* is abreactive, for that assumes that someone reads where being is nature. A bio-*logized* reading makes this mode—if mode it can be called—merely intuitively inaccessible. It then becomes a space before access to the properness of the species-being of each female subject, where she is proper to herself; thus prepropriation. "For the great difficulty is to enclose within the given frames an existence as mysterious as that of animals, turbulent and disordered like natural forces, yet human" (*SS*, 575).

Cixous and Irigaray, in their different ways, will be concerned with an *ethics* of sexual difference. And it is in the domain of the "ethical," pointed at in the last section of *Being and Nothingness*, that Beauvoir's consideration of child *rearing* must be placed.

Here is Sartre: "Ontology allows us to catch a glimpse of what will be an ethics which will assume its responsibilities in the face of a *human reality in situation*" (*BN*, 781; my emphasis). And then come his final questions, proved to be merely rhetorical by subsequent work:

Is it a question of bad faith or of another fundamental attitude? And can one *live* this new aspect of being? In particular, will freedom by taking itself for an end escape all *situation*? Or on the contrary, will it remain situated? Or will it situate itself so much the more precisely and the more individually as it projects itself further in anguish as freedom on condition and accepts more fully its responsibility as an existent by whom the world comes into being? All these questions . . . can find their reply only on moral terrain. We shall devote to them a future work (*BN*, 798).

I have emphasized the words "human reality in situation." Derrida's strongest critique of Sartre's philosophical anthropology is contained in his rejection of Sartre's translation of *Dasein*—in Heidegger a catachresis to name being where it is so intimate that it is inaccessible—as "human reality." It is possible to read Beauvoir's Mother as figuring forth the fundamental difference—between proximity and accessibility to knowing—that marks *Dasein*. "Human reality in situation" stages this difference in the it-gives-being of birth.

Here the binary opposition between the "philosophical" and the "empirical" is on its way to being undone. One can read here the ontico-ontological difference being redone into the difference between species-life and species-being, as well as the scenario of mothers forever deferred in their children rather than fathers preserved in them.[15]

Here is also the assumption of care in a situation where situating oneself is not allowed. This is the "other fundamental attitude" that Sartre cannot quite imagine. It is not just another way of living, as species-being, as it were. Let us not forget that Beauvoir sees the Mother as a situation. The following passage writes the Mother as the situation that cannot situate itself but must take responsibility—the risk of a relationship in view of the impossibility of relating—*un rapport en vue de rapport sans rapport*:

The child brings joy only to the woman capable of disinterestedly desiring without reflexion [*retour sur soi*] the happiness of another, who seeks to exceed [*dépasser*] her own existence.[16] To be sure, the child is an enterprise which one can validly take up [*se destiner*]; but it does not represent a ready-made justification more than any other project; and it must be willed for itself [*voulue pour elle-même*] (*SS*, 583).

Again,

the child does not snatch her from [*l'arrache*] her immanence. . . .
[S]he can only ever create an actual situation [*situation de fait*] whose
exceeding belongs to the liberty of the child alone [*appartient à la seule
liberté de l'enfant de dépasser*] (*SS*, 585).

I have substituted "exceeding" for Parshley's misleading translation of
dépassement as "transcendence." I find in this and comparable passages
of Beauvoir the description of what Sartre calls the acceptance of "responsibility as an existent by whom the world comes into being" in a men-
only universe. I must insist that, in Beauvoir's plotting, the line between
philosophical and empirical begins to waver. And again, this acceptance
of responsibility is radically differed-and-deferred between mother and
child, rather than confined internally to men defined as self-contained
beings-for-itself. (I can suggest that it is this possibility of the alternative
feminization of human ontology that Irigaray will see refracted by men
into the thinking of women as "the envelope.")

Again, Beauvoir captures the critical potential of existentialism in the
discontinuous figuration of gestation-birthing-rearing. "It is [the] perpetual failure," writes Sartre, "of the integration of the *en-soi* and *pour-soi*
which explains at once the relative indissolubility of the in-itself and of
the for-itself and their relative independence" (*BN*, 792). In Beauvoir, the
in-itself "is" woman in nature's laws—gestation—species-life, and the
for-itself "is" the rearing mother and the child as adult.

Sartre appropriates this relative independence into the thematics of
anguish and freedom: the worldly staging of the difference entailed by
moral responsibility without moral authority. Beauvoir acknowledges it
as the real failure that is the name of history. Convention, as I indicated
at the beginning of this essay, *must* allow us to assume alterity to be
another self, even the convention of mothering for the expectant mother:
"justified by the presence in her womb of an other, she rejoices finally
and fully in being herself." Beauvoir does not animate this with *en-soi/
pour-soi* talk. But mark the final words in the French, especially the use
of *jouir:* "Justifiée par la présence dans son sein d'un autre, elle jouit enfin
pleinement d'être soi-même" (*SS*,314).

Quite apart from the restraining of the *jouissance* of the woman into
the inauguration of reproduction, the inscription of the body into the
species in gestation is a rupture with any model of intersubjectivity, as
much a guardian at its margin as the pterodactyl I mention at the end of
Chapter Two. In spite of anything the antichoice lobby might say, the
pregnant mother cannot decide to desire *this* child (the "propriated"
child, the child as for-itself). Beauvoir, concentrating on the existentialist

project, accepts birthing as a severing from gestation into the nurturing of an intending subject, a violent origin of the possibility of intentionality. (Margaret Atwood thus questions the phrases *"giving birth," "delivering a baby,"* and suggests that the *mother*—I presume as mother *of* daughter or son—is delivered at birth.)[17]

If, however, we turn to what is pre-originary in this scheme, the time of gestation *for* the mother, it is a peculiarly contaminated exile from herself as subject. It cannot be claimed as a pure rupture, for the physical "events" marking the progress of gestation must also be read as the body's textuality that is the daily weave of human beings pregnant with nothing but their own death, always alive and dying until the completed "life" is delivered at death, for others. (I think Elaine Marks judges Beauvoir too harshly here by reading death with the full force of humanist passion.)[18] Gestation is thus inscribed into this larger economy of death. Indeed, it undoes the binary opposition of life and death. I must consign to chance your understanding that I am saying nothing against or indeed about the feelings of joy, fulfillment, or continuity attending pregnancy and gestation. And, indeed, sonar pictures can even create a strongly anthropomorphic sense of the fetus which has become a bargaining point for the opposition in the debate about reproductive rights. In the certainty, or uncertainty, then, of not being misunderstood in that particular way I will say further, that, within this limited indeterminacy, there is also an intimation (necessarily effaced as it is disclosed) of radical exile, the only other reminder of which is the mysterious anonymity of the earth as temporary dwelling place, the anonymity of the self when newborn, the only certainty its anonymization in death.

To sum up what I have said in the last few pages: Derrida criticized Sartre for anthropologizing the Heideggerian *Dasein* (and Heidegger for ignoring the question of woman as "before propriation," although the latter critique was later partially recovered in a discussion of *Geschlecht*). If read with sympathy, though against the grain, Beauvoir's figure of the Mother provides an asymmetrical site of passage with the possibility of a strong framing of propriation that has been protected from a philosophical anthropology yet not preserved in transcendental talk.

Rights Talk

It is not possible to leave this topic without some consideration of its implication for the reproductive rights debate. Before I turn to Cixous, Hélie-Lucas, and Irigaray, then, I will engage in such a consideration briefly. I am of course aware that this issue has been part of feminist ethical philosophy for some time now. My remarks cannot possibly take into account the complexity of the legal and ethical problems here.

The reproductive rights debate can only begin after the body has been written into the normative and privative discourse of a law predicated on agency. The prepropriative description of gestation and the figure of the Mother as a site of passage *for* the Mother *from* species-life to the project of the child as species-being (rigorously to be distinguished from the patriarchal view of the person of the mother as a passageway for the child) is irreducible to that discourse. The question of agency—which in this view is distinct from the question of the subject—cannot be decided with reference to prepropriation. Indeed, the prepropriative cannot be a referent. It is rather the undecidable in view of which all decisions *must* be risked. If the prepropriative is figured into the discourse of decision, it is possible to use it to support a woman's right over her body, for it could be argued that the fetus is part of the species-life of the body. But, and this is why it remains undecidable, it would also be possible to use it against that position—for, *in the specific case of childbearing,* the question of the possibility of the origin of intention in the fetus is philosophically inaccessible to the mother, as indeed to anyone else, and therefore, for the opposition, might well have an affirmative answer. Therefore the decisions involving agency must be taken on rational grounds.[19] The prepropriative figuration of the mother in species-life serves as a reminder that those grounds cannot be finally grounded and thus stand guard against what is perhaps the necessary possibility of failure written into all the rational abstractions of democracy: the possibility of their use as alibis, to deflect critique.

It is his lack of concern for this last position that allows Richard Rorty to dismiss deconstructive vigilance as a monotonous litany, best ignored in the field of action, a field into which he has chosen to step without much preparation because of his disappointment with philosophy.[20] I am inclined to take Zillah Eisenstein's strategic violations of what she *calls* deconstruction more seriously.[21]

There is an impasse here between rights talk and undecidability. Of course one *prefers* rights talk because of the general inscription of the globe within the culture of the European Enlightenment. Rosalind Petchesky offers a brilliant possibility of recoding here. She orchestrates the rupture between totalizing social programs and the untotalizable by suggesting, in her book *Abortion and Woman's Choice,* that abortion should be shifted from human rights talk to social needs talk.[22] Coding within the rational abstraction of the rights of the sovereign subject commits feminism to a totalizing telos. Coding as a social need makes visible who does and who does not merit access to social totality. And here is how, *from within a positivist notion of self*, Petchesky reaches out to articulate the warning against a totalizable future present as a result of a constitutional guarantee for abortion:

> To deny that there will always be a residual conflict between this principle—which is the *idea* of concrete individuality, or subjective reality—and that of a social and socially imposed morality of reproduction seems not only naive but dismissive of an important value. For any society, there will remain a *level of individual desire that can never be totally reconciled with social need* without destroying the individual personalities whose "self-realization" is the ultimate object of a social life.[23]

In the very last sentence of her book, she invokes "tension" rather than balance, and writes, "this very tension can be, for feminism—and through feminism, socialism—a source of political validity." It seems important to point out that her invocation of "socialism" is based on a recognition of the discrepancy between the two "social"s in Marx (see Chapter Five). In solidarity, I would rewrite "validity" as "persistent critical effort."

Since we are within the discourse of "French" philosophy, and for no other reason, I should mention that in "The Force of Law," Derrida has articulated the difference between undecidability and rights talk as the *différance* between justice and the Law. It is in this sense that rights talk can only be grounded in presuppositions that ignore the prepropriative, actively as well as passively. The possibility of such an ignoring/ignorance (task or event) is not derived from any accessible model of faithfulness.[24]

I should, however, also mention that any discussion of abortion outside of the entire network of the necessarily normative and privative discourse of rights talk operates on more situational principles, that will engage (disclose/efface) the prepropriative as figure in different ways. Simone de Beauvoir's own words on the *affective* coding of abortion in the French society of the time must be read with this in mind. In quite another context, the sharp break between the arena of abortion and sterilization issues and the well-organized movement against reproductive engineering in some Third World countries with well-developed women's activist organizations should also be considered with thorough familiarization with situational imperatives.

Hélène Cixous, Giving the Mother

Back now to the mysterious thickets of French feminist philosophy. I want to touch briefly upon Hélène Cixous's use of the figure of the mother and her staging of plurality. If Simone de Beauvoir belongs basically to the language of the very Enlightenment that she questions, Cixous belongs to that stream of French writing announced as having happened by Stéphane Mallarmé in the 1880s: *on a touché au vers*—. She calls, therefore, for a somewhat different style of reading.

She calls for a different style of reading also because she writes as a writer, not as a philosopher, although she is deeply marked by her own version of the philosophies of writing and of the Other. We must attend more closely to the detail of her style as we attempt to explain her positions.

I want to look at the moment of the mother and of plurality in the famous essay, written many years ago, "The Laugh of the Medusa."[25] This essay falls into two modes of address—one where, addressing one woman intimately as *"tu,"* Cixous gives advice about writing and publishing on the then current French scene. By using the second-person *style indirect libre,* Cixous characterizes this person fairly elaborately. The bit about mothering is still in the *"tu-toi"* form, but it seems to dissolve the lineaments of the character of the addressee. By the time the talk moves on to the historical plurality of woman, the mode of "address," if one can even use such a term for this part of the essay, is the implicit and impersonal one of expository prose. Let us consider the two moments without ignoring their mode of presentation.

Whatever Cixous's intent in *arranging* the modes of address in her essay in quite this way, here is a *reading* of it. Strictly speaking, an ethical relationship with the other entails universalizing the singular. And there is no room for an ethicotheological I-thou in the space where the mother is in species-life rather than species-being, as the prepropriative figure. In the first part of the I-thou situation of "The Laugh of the Medusa," by contrast, it is the extreme specificity of the situation—the Parisian publishing scene in the mid-1970s—that will not allow a transposition into a too-easy ethical exchange.

But what of the moment when the Parisian literary scene unobtrusively fades out and, although the *"tu"* is retained, the usefulness of the addressee's characterization is also dissolved by an entry into a strange injunction? "It is necessary and sufficient," Cixous writes first, "that the best be given to woman by another woman for her to be able to love herself and return in love the body that was 'born' to her" (*LM,* 252). And "Mother" is the name of this "giving." Then she moves to the injunction: "You [*toi*], if you wish, touch, caress me, give me you the living no-name, even me as myself." I would like to suggest that by thus framing the moment, Cixous releases the peculiar threshold of an ethical "I-thou" which has nothing to do with the theological. Such devices of foregrounding are not uncommon in practice that is recognizably "literary" and is routinely noticed in minimally efficient literary criticism. By releasing this threshold, Cixous might be bringing into the feminine familiar that space described by Heidegger as a space of prior interrogation, "a vague average understanding of Being . . . [which] up close, we cannot grasp at all."[26]

We know that Derrida has reread such Heideggerian passages as the effaced/disclosed trace (not a past present), and the differed/deferred end (not a future present), inscribing what we must stage as our present, here and now, here only insofar as it is also away, elsewhere. Cixous's genius is to take these ways of thinking and straining to turn them into something doable. I think she is helped in this by her somewhat unexamined belief in the power of poetry and art in general which she has never lost. To be sure, in the hands of essentialist enthusiasm, this doability can turn into precious posturing. But, then, in the hands of rationalist convictions, attempts to bring the aesthetic into the *Lebenswelt* can lead to interminable systems talk bent on the simple task of proving that the aesthetic is coherent. And, in the grip of *anti*essentialist enthusiasm, the Derridean maneuvers can *also* turn into precious posturing. I think it is in this spirit that Cixous has recently written: "I believe the text should establish an ethical relation to reality as well as textual practice."[27] The task here is not to suspend reading until such time as a text is out of quarantine.

All precautions taken, then, we can say that Cixous is staging the thought that, even as we are determined in all kinds of other ways—academic, philosopher, feminist, black, homeowner, menstruating woman, for example—we *are* also *always* in the peculiar being-determination that sustains these. She is staging that dimension in the name of the place of mother-and-child. This is not really a space accessible to political determinations, or to specific determinations of mothering in specific cultural formations. Following a chronological notion of human psycho-biography, this is where, at the same *time* as we mature into adulthood and responsibility, we continue to exist in a peculiar being-determination to which the name "child" can be lent:

> The relation to the "mother," in terms of intense pleasure and violence,
> is curtailed no more than the relation to childhood (the child that she
> was, that she is, that she makes, remakes, undoes, there at the point
> where, the same she mothers herself).[28]

I have argued at length in the previous essay and in an earlier chapter, that this sort of poststructuralist nominalism brings with it the burden of

"paleonymy," imposed by the fact that the name belongs to the imbrication of a so-called empirical-historical account which is the condition and
effect of the role of the word in the history of the language. Cixous makes
a selective use of the paleonymy of the name "mother," comparable to
Derrida's selective use of the paleonymy of words such as "writing" or
"justice." *Not* the narrow sense: "Listen to me, it is not the overbearing
clutchy 'mother' but, rather, it is, touching you, the equivoice that affects
you" (*LM*, 252).

It is almost as if Beauvoir's female child is beginning to take responsibility toward the situation of the mother.

Notice that determinative essentialisms become irrelevant here. No
matter if I have no children and therefore no "experience" of "giving the
mother to the other woman." It is a general sense of mothering—its
minimal definitive and presupposed cultural predication as self*less* love,
reinscribed in Beauvoir as the species-other passing into loved subject—
that is supposedly also a defining characteristic of woman in the narrow
sense—that Cixous is turning into a relationship with the other woman—
who is precisely not a child of my body. If read seriously, this must be
rigorously distinguished from being motherly or maternal, matronizing,
et cetera. The other woman's age is not specified, only that she is other.

In the previous chapter, I wrote as follows: "Incanting to ourselves all
the perils of transforming a 'name' to a referent—making a catechism, in
other words, of catachresis—let us none the less name (as) 'woman'
that disenfranchised woman whom we strictly, historically, geopolitically,
cannot imagine as literal referent." Indeed, responsibility to the trace of
the other seems to have literalized itself as a reminder of the limit-case as
other rather than self throughout my work.

Try to think of what Cixous is actually asking you to do and you
will begin to see what an amazing formulation of responsibility this is,
especially since the dimension is inaccessible and therefore the responsibility is effortful. If you want to reduce to conceptual logic some of the more
obviously metaphoric passages, there are handles, such as "woman does
not defend herself against these unknown women whom she's surprised
at becoming, pleasuring [*jouissant*] in this gift of alterability" (*LM*, 258).
We must be able to read this "present tense" in that nondimensional
verbal mode of which I spoke earlier: not a future present but a persistent
effortfulness that makes a "present." This practice "does and will take
place in areas other than those subordinated to philosophico-theoretical
domination." Up close, we cannot grasp it at all. The undecidable in view
of which decisions *must* be risked.

Marie-Aimée Hélie-Lucas. Flash

Is this of any use to Hélie-Lucas? Yes, because she lives in a classed space of power as well.

Should Hélie-Lucas listen to Hélène Cixous? Not necessarily. But the cultural politics of asking Hélie-Lucas to listen only to purely "traditional" Algerian things comes quite often from the most Frenchified. Since Hélie-Lucas is not a member of an Algerian minority in the United States, in decolonization, she has to negotiate actively with the trace of the French until it becomes unrecognizable as such and useful; with Hélène Cixous, or with much worse, especially when unacknowledged. And Cixous's text has put a limit to its *own* power in the field of negotiation. The ethical field of the I-thou requires that the I earn the right to *tutoyer* the interlocutor. Indeed, that felicitous *tu-toi*-ing is itself a case of what she is speaking of: "Everything will be changed once woman gives woman to the other woman" (*LM*, 260). In "Laugh of the Medusa," Cixous earns the right by narrowing the entry—a published feminist writer speaking to a novice woman writer upon the Parisian scene of writing.

In the heritage of imperialism, one of the peculiar by-products is the "emancipated" woman *in* the decolonized nation, not her sister in metropolitan space, whom we know much better. However unwilling she may be to acknowledge this, part of the historical burden of that "emancipated" postcolonial is to be in a situation of *tu-toi*-ing with the radical feminist in the metropolis. If she wants to turn away from this, to learn to "give woman to *the other woman*" in her own nation-state is certainly a way, for it is by no means certain that, by virtue of organizational and social work alone—doing good from above, itself infinitely better than doing nothing—she is in touch with the Algerian gendered subaltern in that inaccessible I-thou.[29]

At any rate, my agenda is not to recommend Hélène Cixous to Marie-Aimée Hélie-Lucas or to prescribe Hélène Cixous for Marie-Aimée Hélie-Lucas, but in a sense to judge Hélène Cixous's text to see if it can live in Hélie-Lucas's world, which is not the grass-roots world of Algeria. This is a particularly interesting challenge because, like Derrida, Cixous is, in the strictest sense, a Creole, a Frenchwoman born and raised in early childhood in Oran in the days before the Revolution.[30] It is in that spirit that I have lingered on this moment in "The Laugh of the Medusa." I want now to pass on to the thought of plurality, which is lodged in one of the islands of comparatively expository prose coming immediately after the passage I have read.

Back to Cixous, Subject for History

As subject for history [*sujet à l'histoire*], woman always occurs simultaneously in several places. Woman un-thinks or squanders the unifying,
ordering history that homogenizes and channels forces, herding contradictions into the practice of a single battlefield. In woman, the history
of all women blends together with her personal history, national and
international history. *As a fighter,* woman enlists [*fait corps*] in all
liberations. She must be far-sighted. Not blow for blow. She foresees
that her liberation will do more than modify relations of force or toss
the ball over to the other camp; she will bring about a mutation in
human relations, in thought, in all practices: it is not only the question
of a class struggle, which she sweeps along in fact into a much vaster
movement. Not that in order to be a woman-in-struggle(s) one must
leave the class struggle or deny it; but one must open it up, split it, push
it, fill it with the fundamental struggle so as to prevent the class struggle,
or any other struggle for the liberation of a class or people, from
operating as an agent of repression, pretext for postponing the inevitable, the staggering alteration in relations of force and in the production
of individualities (*LM,* 252–252).

In her exchange with Catherine Clément, later published as *La Jeune-
née,* Cixous shows herself to be somewhat ethereal in her take on "hard"
politics.[31] But perhaps Catherine Clément is not her best interlocutor.
Here, in "The Medusa," under the surface of an often-read passage, some
surprising points are being made. Certain seeming generalizations are
being advanced about woman's role as subject *for* history. Remember the
ordinary-language double charge of the word "histoire" in French. It is
almost as if Cixous is speaking of a narrativization or figuration of woman
that would be appropriate *for* this new story. This is not, in other words,
an account of woman as world-historical subject or, in a humbler vein,
subject *of* history.

The "is," "will," "must" of the passage are articulated within *this*
framework. Thus these straightforward lines do not necessarily mark a
forgetfulness of the deconstructive lesson of timing that Cixous seems to
know elsewhere. The general point is that the appropriate subject *for* such
a new story is the one that makes visible all the plural arenas that are
suppressed when history is written with the representative man as its
subject. This temporality operates within the task of producing a subject
for a story—at the other end from ethical intimacy. Within this peculiar
time, then, woman as subject *for* history will not merely modify but
mutate and alter relations of force. This is not a liberatory promise but a

feminist alliance with relevant bits in Foucault/Derrida and, later, Lyotard's position, a development out of Nietzsche via Heidegger which
freezes and takes a distance from Marxism. The effort to renarrativize
and the relationship to Beauvoir can be grasped by way of Melanie Klein.[32]
If the manifold, irreducibly plural, and incessantly shifting strategic exclusions required by a coherent systematic account of history are incessantly
attended to, power/knowledge (*pouvoir/savoir*) relations are thoroughly
displaced and productively disrupted, framing in undecidability the sure
ground of decision. This feminism is a persistent critique of history.

Cixous finesses the question of agency delicately. Not for her the Derridean unfleshed figuration/nomination, but rather the task of conceiving
an agent of pluralization, alteration. This is unusual in metropolitan
feminism, yet may be a requirement in decolonized feminism. Thus Cixous
opposes single-issue feminism. *If* and *when* woman as subject *for* storying
or history is conceived as militant, she must be faithful to the subversive
logic or graphic of plurality and thus become part of the body of all
struggles (*faire corps* in French is more charged, especially in military
metaphors, than the English "integrate").[33] Like most French radicals,
Cixous sees the class struggle as the only *struggle* that operates out of
a coherent narrative.[34] Therefore it presupposes exclusions and invites
supplementation by repression. Yet the fundamental struggle as such is
not woman's struggle alone. It is to split, open, and fill all generalized,
unified struggles with plurality. (In the headnote to Chapter Five, I suggest
eating and digesting the rational kernel of Marx's lesson.) Within the
framing of the putting together of a subject for a new story, the status of
the last phrase "production of individualities" is rhetorically charged. An
"individuality" here is not merely an exclusionist repressive construction,
but a necessary underived fiction, the agent's springboard for a decision
in the face of radical undecidability, affirmative deconstruction performed
in the way of a writer rather than a philosopher.

Is Cixous able to become part of the body of the struggle for national
liberation, or against imperialism? That struggle too is pluralized—traveling up and down, and in a discontinuous way—from the familiar to the
aggregative and out, from the epistemic to the legal and away. The way
in which Cixous attaches to this moving base is, inevitably, interpretable.
When she writes her Indian and Indonesian plays, her take on the complexity and hybridity of so-called postcolonial nations is shaky. Her work
with the *Theater of the Sun* can unfortunately be seen as perpetuating a
kind of inspired, too-admiring ethnography and a romanticizing historiography.[35] And one does not hear her name in activist circles in Algeria.
If one understands the serviceability of underived fictions, one is obliged

to know more intimately the contaminated fictions of the empirical, and for this we must turn to Marie-Aimée Hélie-Lucas.

Marie-Aimée Hélie-Lucas

As I have often insisted, deconstructive subversion when affirmed in the political sphere can perhaps find its best theater outside of the Atlantic tradition. With all the reservation that I have already stated, it is still to be noted that the argument from plurality becomes something different in the hands of Marie-Aimée Hélie-Lucas.

Her statement engages two arenas of generalization: the first a national liberation movement that is also a revolution in the strictest sense of the word—the establishment of a "more progressive" mode of production through armed struggle—and the second the coding of gender difference. The second arena is also the field of play of two sets of normative and privative discourses—the extended French Law on personal status under French rule, the Islamic Code under Algerian.

In the conclusion to the next chapter, I discuss the historical discursive spaces of the possible socialization of the two great monotheisms: the Judeo-Christian and the Islamic. Hélie-Lucas does not concern herself with that problem of choice here. She comments rather on the repressive logic of a race and class struggle not open to plurality. She treats the women monumentalized in the earlier struggle for decolonization with sympathy but also instrumentally, as do many other Algerian postrevolutionary feminist women: "Usually any kind of demonstration is just crushed, but this time we had in the front line six women who had been condemned to death under the French, so the police didn't beat them" (*BG*, 4).

Cixous's register can be roughly described as the European literary romantic, deployed to release the intimate-ethical as well as the fictive-historical in a woman-defined field. This register has been as often used to question as to supplement the more recognizable, reasonable discourse of philosophy. The relationship between Cixous's mother and plurality and Beauvoir's mother and passage can be plotted on this circuit as well. By contrast, Hélie-Lucas's register is postcolonial where the nation cannot be taken for granted. Here is her tabulation of a repressive homogenization.

(It is never, has never been the right moment to protest . . . [in the name of women's interests and rights]: not during the liberation struggle against colonialism, because all forces should be mobilized against the principal enemy: French colonialism; not after independence, because all forces should be mobilized to build up the devastated country; not now that racist imperialistic Western governments are attacking Islam and the Third World, etc.). Defending women's rights "now" (this "now" being ANY historical moment) is always a betrayal—of the people, of the nation, of the revolution, of Islam, of national identity, of cultural-roots, of the Third World . . . according to the terminologies in use *hic et nunc*. . . . (*BG,* 13)

What Hélie-Lucas is speaking of is, clearly, the *postponement* of the production of individualities. "There is a constant ideological confusion," she reminds us, "between religion, culture and nationality" (*HL,* 15). But if Cixous's individuality is short of the "real individual" because it is posited *in* the possibility of fiction, Hélie-Lucas's is beyond the "real individual" because posited *as* the possibility of collectivity. Each should presuppose the other, as each leaves the space of the "real individual" negotiable. When Cixous imagines collectivity, Hélie-Lucas must thicken it. When Hélie-Lucas naturalizes individuality, Cixous can stand as a warning. The enabling violation of imperialism laid the line for a woman's alliance in decolonization. Hélie-Lucas can only ever animate that line with the implicit metaphor of sisterhood. Cixous's impossible dimension of giving woman to the other woman can split up and fill that thought of sisterhood so that it does not become the repressive hegemony of the old colonial subject. To imagine that Hélie-Lucas's distance from the subaltern Algerian woman is any less than Cixous's from the scared novice writer or Beauvoir's from the French peasant or working-class unmarried mother in need of abortion is to decide to forget the plurality of the Third World. From within decolonized space, Hélie-Lucas productively uses her specific subject-production and calls out to women around the world: "We should link our struggles from one country to the other for reasons of *ethics*. . . . We have everything to gain in being truly internationalist" (*HL,* 14).

The word "true" in truly internationalist can be read as an affirmative "misuse," a wrenching away from its proper meaning. This is among the important dictionary meanings of "catachresis." One of the offshoots of the deconstructive view of language is the acknowledgment that the *political* use of words, like the use of words, is irreducibly catachrestic. Again, the possibility of catachresis is not derived. The task of a feminist political philosophy is neither to establish the proper meaning of "true," nor to get caught up in a regressive pattern to show how the proper meaning always eludes our grasp, nor yet to "ignore" it, as would Rorty, but to accept the risk of catachresis.

A "true internationalism." The antagonist here is clearly the strained Marxist ideal of internationalism-after-national-liberation. It is only when we see that that we can begin further to see that the word being really put into question here is "nation." Everyone who gets embroiled in the real politics and history of nationalism begins to get the uneasy sense that the nation-state, spring and source of nationalisms, is not altogether a good thing. This is not really an unease for the North Atlantic radical when it comes to the history and development of nationalism in that part of the world. When it comes to the development of national identity in the Third World, it is harder to acknowledge the mysterious anonymity of space, to acknowledge that all nationalism is, in the last instance, a mere inscription on the earth's body.[36] Yet this is where, to use two of the formulas I use most, the persistently critical voice must be raised at the same time as a strategic use of essentialism—in other words this is the crucial scene of the usefulness of catachresis. (It may be said that the tone of recantation of the introductory essay of this book is a result of the failure of catachrestic strategy in the face of essentialism in the highly personalist middle-class culture of the United States.) Hélie-Lucas is using the historical empirical definitive predication of women in exogamous societies: a woman's home is radical exile, fixed by her male owner. A woman's *norm* of *pouvoir/savoir* is a persistent passive *critique* of the idea of the *miraculating* agency or identity produced by a home. Thus the simple conviction of exchangeability, bred in the little girl in sorrow and joy, is the internalized critique that *can* be mobilized against all essentialist notions of the home as base of identity.[37] This is a particularly important practical resource because the rational aggregative consolidation of this notion *is* the apparatus of the nation, presupposed by the great aggregative teleological system of internationalism. And this is the telos that Hélie-Lucas shakes up through the *pouvoir/savoir* of the feminine. This is a perspective that is almost always lacking in North Atlantic calls for female solidarity, whether metropolitan or migrant. This is an internationalism that takes a distance from the project of national identity when it interferes with the production of female individualities. And the *critique* of individualities, not merely individualism, will bring us back to Cixous.

This model of true inter-nationalism is also in an oblique relationship with the diversified Algerian womanspace (the northern, predominantly urban, class-hatched socius; the South predominantly rural, subalternity shared by Arab and Berber women, shading off into "Africa") with all its discontinuous and sometimes contradictory relationships to the culture of Islam and the culture of imperialism, because the model belongs to the organization called Women Living Under Muslim Law.[38] Although the impetus in the organization is clearly against Islamic patriarchy, what it signals by sheer opposition is the (gendered) internationality of Islam, rather different from the (masculinist) demonized image that is projected in the West. This internationality is, on one plane, written in the civil machinery of many different forms and stages of nation-state consolidation, in many different economic and political alignments, stretching from Morocco through Bangladesh, to Indonesia: on another plane, this internationalism is not among nations, not *inter* but *antre* whatever is hyper-realized as "nation" in the "real world."[39] And woman/individuality is crucial here. These women persistently and affirmatively deconstruct political theory on the ground, although they are not identical with women on ground level.

Irigaray: Ethics

Earlier I suggested a supplementary and contrastive relationship between the literary-romantic and the recognizably reasonable discourses of Cixous and Beauvoir respectively. By some accounts, the general critique of humanism in France has summoned up a style of philosophizing which would use both. I believe that Luce Irigaray writes more and more in that style. The usual critique of Irigaray, that she is an "essentialist," generally springs from an ignoring of the aggressive role of rhetoricity in her prose. Derrida has framed his remark about writing and woman in the possibility that he is himself acting out the male fetish, *if* Freud were right.[40] Those precautions taken, *if* Derrida were right, the writing of the woman called Luce Irigaray is written like writing and should be read that way, although the other way of reading, involving the history of the language, should also be taken into account.

Any consideration of Irigaray as a feminist philosopher should consider her extended reading of Plato in "Plato's *Hystera*."[41] Here I will point at its rhetorical conduct in passing.

Like Derrida, Irigaray as philosopher defines herself as critic within the enclosure of Western metaphysics. Any argument about how deconstructively she in-habits this enclosure might also look at the rhetorical detailing of the timing of "Plato's *Hystera*." Here let me simply quote the passage that might be read as a staging of how the name of the mother can be used to homogenize multiplicity into intelligibility. Please remember that this comes toward the end of a spectacular reading of, among other texts, *Republic* V that is almost impossible to summarize:

> The dilemmas of Plato's *hystera* will . . . have concealed the fact that there is no common measure with the unrepresentable *hystera protera,*

[think of the virtuoso play of use and mention in this catachrestic, because pluralized, invocation of, of all things, the *rhetorical* figure of *hysteron proteron,* putting last things first, here] the path that might lead back to it and the diaphragm that controls the cavity opening . . . the mother.[42]

Then a section break. Then: "The confused and changing multiplicity of the other thus begins to resolve itself into a system of intelligible relationships." And so on.

In the lectures collected under the general title "Ethics of Sexual Difference," the question of the maternal-feminine (mistranslated mother-woman) is reopened. Let us read two passages to outline cryptically how, from within the problematic that Beauvoir and Cixous can be made to inhabit, Irigaray wants to move to a final dialogue with the passive-masculist philosopher Emmanuel Levinas in "The Fecundity of the Caress," the last piece in the book.[43]

The maternal-feminine is a limit, an envelope, the other place consolidated into *her* norm. The maternal-feminine must incessantly envelop herself twice, as mother and as woman. Yet the *ethical* question for woman is played out in the realms of nudity and a perverse self-decoration through envelopes:

> If, traditionally, in the role of mother, woman represents *place* for man [Sartre's silence about the French version of *Es gibt Sein*—*il y a* (it *there has*)—comes to mind], the limit signifies that she becomes a *thing,* undergoing resultant mutations from one historical period to another. She finds herself caged as a thing. Moreover, the maternal-feminine is also used as *envelope* in terms of which man limits things. *The relationship between the envelope and things* constitutes . . . the aporia of Aristotelianism and the philosophical systems which are derived from it. . . . The mother woman remains the *place separated from "its" place,* deprived of "its" place she ceaselessly is or becomes the place for the other who cannot separate himself from it. . . . She would have to re-envelop herself by herself, and do so at least twice as a woman and as a mother. This would entail a modification in the entire economy of space-time. In the mean time, this ethical question is played out in the realms of *nudity* and *perversity.* Woman is to be nude, since she cannot be situated in her place. She attempts to envelop herself in clothes, make-up, and jewelry. She cannot use the envelope that she is, and so must create artificial ones.[44]

Taking a distance from the entire problematic of claiming a proper place within this tradition, Irigaray thinks sexual difference as the separation from the *absolutely* other. Commenting on Descartes's passage on wonder, she writes:

> Who or what the other is, I never know. But this unknowable other is that which differs sexually from me. This feeling of wonder, surprise, and astonishment in the face of the unknowable ought to be returned to its proper place: the realm of sexual difference (*SD*, 124).

This is no separatist politics, but a full-blown plan for an ethics where sexual difference, far from being located in a decisive biological fact, is posited as the undecidable in the face of which the now displaced "normal" must risk ethicopolitical decisions. An ethical position must entail universalization of the singular. One can wish not to be excluded from the universal. But if there is one universal, it cannot be inclusive of difference. We must therefore take the risk of positing two universals, one radically other to the other in one crucial respect and keep the "real universal" on the other side of *différance*. If Derrida had dared to think of minimal idealization, Irigaray dares minimal alterity. Each is a same-sexed ethical universal, operating in a social cooperation that must conventionally assume others to be collectivities of othered selves. This is to provide the (im)possible ethical base for rewriting gendering in the social sphere.

For Irigaray, sexual *difference* is the limit to ethics. As in Derrida's essay on Levinas ("Violence and Metaphysics"), so also for her, there can be no ethics of ethics. But for her that impossibility is determined (an "impossible determination," for alterity cannot determine) by the alterity of sexual difference. Thus, if coded within reproductive ethics, the fecund caress can become indistinguishable from violence. This is the supplement to Cixous's imagination of the alteration of fields of force in the family.

For Levinas the erotic accedes neither to the ethical nor to signification. In Beauvoir, it is in gestation that the mother/child in species-life is prepropriative, but intended, in so far as the Mother is a "situation," toward the rupture of the proper in species-being: mother *and* child. Since, as we shall see, "fecundity" for Levinas is the "transubstantiation" of paternity, it is in the male-dominant heterosexual embrace that he locates the issueless prepropriative which,

> prior to the manifestation of attributes . . . qualifies alterity itself. . . .
> [In it] *the essentially hidden throws itself toward the light, without becoming signification*. . . . The relationship established between lovers in voluptuosity, fundamentally refractory to universalization, is the

very contrary of the social relation. . . . Only the being that has the
frankness of the face can be "discovered" in the non-signifyingness of
the wanton.[45]

However subtle Levinas's thought of the impossible "subject"ship of
ethics in general, upon the heterosexist erotic scene, the subjectship of
ethics is certainly male. I have been speaking of the "empirical" narrative
with which these catachrestic morphologies secure themselves. The empirical scene of sexual congress behind Levinas's "Phenomenology of Eros"
is almost comically patriarchal, so generally so that the bourgeois male
colonial subject from various parts of the world can be fitted into the slot
of "the lover." The "forever inviolate virginity of the feminine," "frail
and animal-like," is completely excluded from the public sphere: "It
excludes the third party . . . [and is] the supremely non-public" (*TI*, 258,
263, 265). Being prior to attribution, this scene is supposedly before the
emergence of value. Yet value drips from words such as "profanation,"
"indecency," "obscenity," "interdiction," "indiscretion," "exhibition-
ism," ubiquitously part of the descriptive vocabulary of the phenomenology of eros. As for "fecundity," it defines the "distinction within
identification" (*TI*, 267). Here "the *encounter* with the Other [not *Autre*
but *Autrui*—"all around?"] as feminine is required" so that the father's
"*relation* with the future [may be transformed] into a *power* of the
subject" (*TI*, 267, emphasis mine).

In this patriarchal discourse, "equivocation" is not the activation of
Cixous's delicate "equivoice" of the mother but simply the old-fashioned
nasty word describing woman's civil duplicity, her only access to power
(over men), her only access to the public sphere, indeed to phenomenality
itself, her epiphany:

> Equivocation constitutes the epiphany of the feminine—at the same
> time interlocutor, collaborator and master superiorly intelligent, so
> often dominating men in the masculine civilization it [the feminine as
> master] has entered, and woman having to be treated as a woman, in
> accordance with rules imprescriptible by an orderly [*policé*] society. The
> face, all straightforwardness and frankness, in its feminine epiphany
> dissimulates allusions, innuendos. It laughs under the cloak of its own
> expression, without leading to any specific meaning, alluding to it in
> empty space [*en faisant allusion dans le vide*], signaling the less than
> nothing (*TI*, 264).

Just as I find it difficult to believe that Hegel's virulent racism is written
off (not by Derrida) when we worship at the shrine of the dialectic; so do

I find it difficult to take this prurient heterosexist, male-identified ethics seriously.[46] Irigaray is more generous. She undoes Levinas's sexism by de-gendering the active-passive division. The lover is *amant and amante,* the beloved *aimé and aimée.* She does indeed also notice the features of Levinas's treatment of the erotic that I mention above: "Infantile and animal, for him? Irresponsible in order to give him back freedom" (*FC,* 240). Irigaray's rhetoric makes the question apply not only to the invari-ably male-gendered lover in Levinas's scheme, but to Levinas the philoso-pher; he makes the invariably female-gendered beloved infantile and animal in order to win back his freedom. Let us read the next few paragraphs with this robust philosophical equivocation in mind: "the lover leads her back to the *not yet* of the infant, the *never like that* of the animal—outside human becoming. This gesture perpetrated [*ce geste perpétré*], [he] separates himself to return to his ethical responsibilities" (*FC,* 241). Let us notice also Irigaray's comment on the surreptitious equivocation of the philosopher:

> the seduction of the loved one makes a bridge [*fait pont*] between the Father and the son. . . . In the [female] loved one's fragility and weakness the [male] lover loves himself as a [male] loved one without power [*en lesquelles l'amant s'aime comme aimé sans pouvoir*] (*FC,* 244).

Voluptuousness, in this reading, is irreducibly male, that which "does not know the other. That which seduces itself of her [*d'elle*] in order to return to the abyss and take up ethical seriousness again" (*FC,* 246).

The most noticeable thing about Irigaray's "Fecundity of the Caress" is the practical crispness of its tone. It is obviously a text that assumes that both partners do things, and are not inevitably heterosexual. Again, it is not surprising that, in the world of this text, although the scene of sexuality is prior and exterior to the son or daughter, there is such a thing as pregnancy, the womb, and its ontological inaccessibility to some mother's son and some mother's daughter, as they meet in the fecundity of the caressing hands. Their faces are not the only ethical surfaces. Their hands take part in shaping otherness. And each one reminds the other of that prepropriative site, the impossible origin of the ethical that can only be figured, falsely, as the subject as child-in-mother:

> The fecundity of a love whose gesture or the most elementary gesture remains caress [*dont le geste ou le geste le plus élémentaire demeure caresse*]. . . . The other's hand, these palms with which he approaches me without crossing me [*m' approche sans me traverser*], give me back

the borders of my body and call me to the remembrance of the most profound intimacy [of the child-in-the-mother]. Caressing me, he bids me neither to disappear nor to forget, but to rememorate [*remémorer*] the place where, for me, the most secret life holds itself in reserve. . . . Plunging me back into the maternal entrails [*entrailles*] and, before that conception [*en deça de cette conception*], awakening me to another— amorous—birth (*FC*, 232).

This is not a past present, this act of rememoration that we are all mothers' children. This is "birth that has never taken place, unless one remains a substitute for the father and the mother. Which signifies a gesture radically non-ethical" (*FC*, 233). If Beauvoir had spoken only of the child as project and Cixous had only exhorted women to give the mother to the other woman and Hélie-Lucas had spoken of the female individual in a political rather than a familial collectivity, then Irigaray exhorts lover *and* beloved to give the woman to the other, indeed to rememorate being-in-the-mother as the impossible threshold of ethics, rather than inaugurate it as the Law of the Father. Not all of us are mothers, but we have all been children. We recall how the vocabulary of Melanie Klein's mature essays is accessible to agency.

What is it that is born in the sexual embrace? The possibility of two spaces, un-universalizable with each other:

A (time) to come [*àvenir*] which is not measured by the surmounting of death but by the call to birth for self and other [*naissance pour soi et l'autre*]. Of which each arranges and rearranges the environment, the body, and the cradle without closing up anything at all of a room, a house, an identity (*FC*, 232).

For Irigaray the fecund caress gives birth to the (im)possible threshold of the ethical.

[T]he most intimate perception of the flesh escapes every sacrificial substitution. . . . This memory of the flesh as the place of approach is ethical fidelity to incarnation. To destroy it risks suppressing alterity, both God's and the Other's (*FC*, 256).

Otherwise, "the aporia of a tactility which cannot caress itself and needs the other to touch itself" gives itself the usual alibi: ethics as such. The scene of the caress is in fact porous to the (im)possibility of ethics.

This is not just philosophical or literary talk, but Christian talk, of incarnation. This talk will have to be fleshed out in the future with a consideration of Derrida's current work (still in seminar form): *aimer/ manger l'autre*—to love/eat the other. Irigaray would restore the (im)possible garden—therefore the threshold of the garden—where woman's sin does not make man's difficult access to knowledge possible: "Not perceptible as profanation. The threshold of the garden, a welcoming cosmic home, remaining open. No guard other than love itself. Innocent of the knowledge of the display and the fall" (*FC*, 244).

Is this a new regulative narrative? Perhaps so. It is hard for me to enter this garden. But can Hélie-Lucas?

In principle, yes. Muslims, Christians, and Jews are all "people of the book," as the recent effort of the *Intersignes* group would show.[47] This attempt to see two different ethical worlds, opened up by the gender-divided caress is, I believe, operative in Farhad Mazhar's "To Mistress Khadija," a poem I have translated and quoted in Chapter Eleven.

Yet in *Intersignes* I, which deploys the impulse to transfer discourses from one Book to another by correcting the errors of Freud's *Moses and Monotheism* in the text of the life of Muhammad, the one discordant note is struck by Martine Medejel, a Frenchwoman married to a Moroccan, whose piece allows us to see, in overdetermined ways, the *global* power difference between French and Arabic. And therefore simply redoing the stories will, again, not suffice. If the new Irigaray, revising Levinas, tries to restore a sexual encounter that is the threshold of ethics, it is still true that, in acceding to the agency of the caress, the woman must *violate* the historical narrative—time as sequence, told in numbers—in which she is written:

> But there is time [*il y a le temps*]. Too linked [*trop lié*] to numbers, and to what has already been. And how repair, in a second, an evil that has lasted for such a long time? . . . And if others continually meddle with this expectation of alliance [*alliance*], how to maintain a candor that neither cries out for remission nor burdens the lover with the weight [*poids*] of the healing of wounds? (*FC*, 243)

This is a serious question: how indeed? The ethics of sexual difference are persistent and to come. In *all* patriarchal cultures, *all* classes, it is an immense move for the wife to become the fecund *agent* of the caress, someone who inaugurates, beyond the right to say "yes" or "no," preventing conjugal sex as rape. Nawal el-Saadawi recently made the point that one could not raise a collective voice against the war if one could not raise an individual voice against a husband.[49] How much more immense to inscribe the agency of the fecund caress in "woman" collectively, rather than in site- and situation-specific exceptions. In fact, it is not excessive to say that this ethical charge illuminates every immediate practical undertaking for women's liberation. There is even something like an analogy between Saadawi/Irigaray and Hélie-Lucas/Cixous. Saadawi exhorts women to be the sovereign agent of resistance: Irigaray, having learned from (by learning resisting) Freud and the Marx of Ideology and Commodity-Hieroglyph, reminds us that this future (à venir) is not totally under our control, for we spell out the truth there as if our being were a rebus. If Levinas had relegated eros to a short-circuiting of signification, Irigaray shows the couple as being written, être-écrit. Here face and hand come together in the structural possibility of writing rather than articulation in a language. Once again that intimate (ontic) space:

> The [female] loved one's face radiates the secret that the lover touches. . . . It says [dit] the hidden [le caché] without exhausting it in a meaning [un vouloir dire]. . . . A giving of form to matter [mise en forme de la matière] that precedes any articulation in a language (FC, 251).

What have I said so far but that Irigaray has rewritten the fecundity of the caress as the figuring of the prepropriative into an (im)possible appropriation? What is it, indeed, to learn the agency of the caress? Perhaps to keep on unlearning agency in the literal sense and allowing space for the blankness of the être-écrit(e), even in the pores of struggles recognizably "political." To acknowledge that, however urgent the need of time measured in numbers, "the limit to the abyss [or the abyssal; la limite à l'abîme] is the unavoidable alterity of the other" (FC, 246).

The discourse of the clitoris in the mucous of the lips still remains important in Irigaray's work. Trying to think the international from within a metropolized ethnic minority, I had given this discourse a general structural value a decade ago. Much talk, flying, and falling, from known and unknown women, has shown me that that evaluation runs no more than the usual risks of intelligibility. It is just that the generalization of a bicameral universal, or even two universals, to provide the impossible differed/deferred grounding of the ethics of sexual difference in the fecund caress seems to respond to the call of the larger critique of humanism with which postcoloniality must negotiate, even as it negotiates daily with the political and cultural legacy of the European Enlightenment.

What of the Irigaray who rereads Plato and Levinas? Can Hélie-Lucas have no use for her?

On the contrary. Here again we revert to the task of decolonizing the mind through negotiating with structures of violence. One cannot be sure that, in a specific cluster of others (such as the readership of this book), with all its attendant insecurities, there will be someone who is in that peculiar subject position—a feminist citizen of a recently decolonized nation concerned with its domestic/international political claims, not merely its ethnocultural agenda. To such a person I would say—whenever the teleological talk turns into unacknowledged, often travestied, articulations of the Plato of *The Republic* or *Laws;* or, indeed to the rights of the self-consolidating other, Irigaray's readings must be recalled in detail. If such a person—I must assume her without alterity—holds a reproduction of this page, she will know, alas, that such occasions will not be infrequent. But how can I be certain? And what is it to know, or be sure that a knowing has been learned? To theorize the political, to politicize the theoretical, are such vast aggregative asymmetrical undertakings; the hardest lesson is the impossible intimacy of the ethical.

8

Not Virgin Enough to Say That [S]he Occupies the Place of the Other*

Chapter Five interrupted the deconstructive establishment in the name of the language of Marx. This piece does it in the name of religions outside the Book (see the end of the previous chapter). It was uttered at a conference on Deconstruction and the Call to the Ethical where I was given five minutes to speak.[1] I have not revised its cryptic and distracted tempo.

It used to seem necessary to remind metropolitan, literary-philosophical panels of the international division of labor. Now it seems necessary to remind them also of the polytheist everyday.[2] (A case in point: before contextualization, the transcript picked up this phrase as "policies everyday.") For those who find this predictable and repetitive, this word: notice how often, in panels like this one, people invoke God, the Death of God, the Bible, the Talmud, the Law of the Father—an ensemble. Even "the secular" carries upon its exergue the history of a "world" facing a specific "ecclesia," that inscription now effaced into the universal name of an enlightened world that has sublated religion. Assimilated polytheist ex-colonials were brought up to presuppose that the European "secular" imagining of ethics, which has not lost touch with its God even in His Death, is the only space, of critique *or* dogma.

I had thought to let the immense problem of the word "polytheism" rest buried in my discreet first footnote. In the meantime a letter arrived from Jean-Luc Nancy, in which he quite appropriately reminded me that "polytheism is a completely Western, Greek, word and there would be a lot to say about that."[3] To honor my friend's good critique, here is a first quotation from the work with which, at first, I had hoped merely to end:

> Whatever the philosophers say, I think it is important that mono- as
> well as poly- would be mistranslations of *advaita* or *dvaita* that would

---

*Jacques Derrida, *Glas*

take away the agility of the popular ethical mind set that makes nothing of this undecidability. Mono is "un-two-ed," a strange way of saying One! Omni- (science or potence) does not fit into this too well. And the "two-ed," without a precise authority of a One to stand guard over it, can stand in for an indefinite swarm. Translation of *advaita* and *dvaita* into monism (non-dualism) and dualism has a lot to answer for.

These institutions cannot be reasonably *verified*, but they are a coherent way of repeatedly taking a distance from the inflexible principle of reason (*dharma* as code, *karma* as determinism) in the everyday performance of the sense that the type case of the ethical predicament is the dilemma. What reason plots as an asymptote is founded by an epistemic shuffle where god and man are indeterminately in each other's corner. It is also no less plausible as a description of something as tenuous as a "mind set" than the structural orientalism of a *homo hierarchicus*.[4]

As you have repeatedly pointed out, the "West" is not without its discomforts about the inconsistencies in the omniscient-omnipotent God. I have worked my way away from the question of omnipotence to Indic performative ethics by starting where you end. My subtext has of course been that the question of God is too monotheist. Over against it is not polytheism but the *dvaita-advaita* habit of mind. Hence my questions earlier: is there an invariable word for God? Is it at least vestigially susceptible to a noncompetitive one-person model?[5]

Within this predictable and repeated staging, an unbelieving, middle-class, contemporary *dvaitin* might beg leave to invoke that other staging of an "origin." She might crave for that invocation a singular space on the agenda because the March of History that some of you have recalled is not quite (please mark the "quite") the March of her History. The Second World War, much on the mind of our conference, brought in for her kind, in a circuitous way, not all at once, not as a cause leading to a consequence, a certain kind of freedom, which then demanded an imagination of a world other than the old *European* monotheist world, which in turn led to a near total loss of ethical authority, partly because the old *European* monotheist time had miraculated into the new secular time of ethics. It is indeed the resurgence of "polytheist" violence against the forcibly justified violence of the State that places on her this responsibility: to ask, in an assembly such as this, if it is possible to think of an unromanticized, contemporary, hegemonic, corrupt "polytheism" in the house of ethics.

And if the response comes back, from those friends who have some claim outside of a cartographic Europe, we too could choose to speak as non-Europeans; here is a gentler word: it is upon the intractability of that itinerary that the assimilated ex-colonial intellectual must meditate. No cheap thrills here, no "freedom of choice." And therefore, finally, the gentlest word of all: why not "choose" that indefinite miasma? Why avoid the avoidable in an attitude? Perhaps this question receives an answer in Geoffrey Bennington's and Jacques Derrida's *Jacques Derrida*, a book that I have not yet read. At first glance, it seems soaked in Algeria and Saint Augustin's Italo-Maghreb, though no doubt the letter press will be differential to that too-obvious immersion.[6]

The assimilated ex-colonial is trained in the European secular imaginary. She "knows" nothing on the other side. (I am making a philosophical point here; this absence of "knowledge" is also true of radical Indianists. It has to do with the nature of contemporary "knowledge," not with disciplinary expertise.) From within that long-inhabited residential hotel then, she will first share with you what she understands our title to be. I may not have got it quite right. She enters her hotel room with that epistemic sleight of hand and this is what she understands:

The Call to the Ethical is, almost, the call *of* the ethical. If the Call to the Ethical is the definitive being-called-ness of Being, then it might just as well be called the call to the *non*-ethical, it would not make a difference. Only with the call *of* do we begin to get even the most general *sense* of the first part of our title: the Call to the Ethical, an originary relatedness that might just as well be called the ethical relationship. There is something like a relationship between this being-called-ness and the fact that being human might be to be in excess, to be *in*adequate even as the being is *super*-adequate. But these general senses are constantly bled into by all kinds of narrow senses. It is not possible to get a grip on the call to the ethical as the ethical relationship in the general sense. The necessary violence, it may be called a "mistake," of thinking the ethical subject cannot be avoided. And the transportation of the cannot to the should not must be the ruse of ethical education.

It is of the first interest to me, from within this hotel room, looking out of the window, as it were, to consider how Marx, in positing the being in excess, as secreting a simple, contentless, unavoidably and immediately codable thing misnamed the value-form, attempted to contaminate the economic by the ethical, and failed, taking the most fragile European constitution of the ethical subject for granted and basing a spurious internationalism on an example that could only be located in Victorian England.

Still within the hotel room but getting restless now, it is of great interest to me to consider how the unavoidable, violent slippage between the general and the narrow has been creatively anthropomorphized by feminist thinking: (a) the definitive being-called-ness as gestation, a formal analogy with the human being pregnant with (its own) death, and the rupturing of birth as a severing into the ethical relationship with the possible subject; (b) plotting justice as the impossible balance between sexual difference, ethics to be thought with a gendered subject (Chapter Seven). The assimilated colonial Hindu—what is that name in the context of contemporary religious violence in India?—can move this far, even in two minutes, practicing the performative-constative ruse learned before memory—the human being has a (European) history: Europe's monotheism or Europe's monotheism effaced is the only space of dogma or critique. Enabled by this ruse, I can desist forever, and even with no time at all, put in a word for Foucault, insist that he was not only concerned with the microphysics of power.[7]

The assimilated ex-colonial's next step, then, in half a minute, is a willed move, and, this too is a wrestling with deconstruction. And, precisely because the law of the forum now allows only half a minute, she must spend that time to disclose what she cannot do, and not because of lack of time. Ten or fifteen years ago, at the inauguration of marginality studies in metropolitan humanities, it used to be enough simply to bring in a so-called non-European example to monumentalize a politically correct ritual moment. Now that the empowerment of ethnic and sexual others in the metropolis has got its own Trinity Formula of race-class-gender, it has become increasingly important for members of ethnic minorities who can sit at a table like this one—a historical displacement of the assimilated ex-colonial—to emphasize that on the other side is the indefinite.[8]

For the Call to the Ethical in general, as it is differed/deferred in its differantial contaminations, forces us to think the subject of ethics. If the assimilated-colonial-ethnic-minority (ACEM) should make herself believe that she unperforms that sleight of the episteme, she still cannot get a grip on what makes up the subject of an ethics on the other side. All the prior questions have been asked and unasked in colonized space. Yet the subjectship of ethics cannot be thought as logically *after* equality-before-the-law of even "phenomenological symmetry" (Drucilla Cornell's phrase).[9] So ACEM, in her willfully undone mode of questioning, must still assume the differantially contaminated other as the subject of an ethics that remains unthinkable.

The only way to "do research" in that predicament is the most literal-minded "hanging out," resisting anthropology, resisting history, resisting revolutionary tourism. Hanging out on that terrain is a naive planned miming of *Da-sein* as *Weg-sein*, being there as being away. And here she can find nothing in her "own tradition"—that curious thing miscalled

Hinduism—a hegemonic, middle-class "polytheism" mired in bad politics and "semitized" in its nationalist face. In search of the differantially contaminated face of the absolutely other she has to wander into subaltern Islam on the subcontinent, and into the by-her-unnameable aboriginal preindic animism: Bangladesh and Purulia.

Keeping her presuppositions examined, her theoretical nose clean, the only way she can question the woman it seems eerie to call the "subaltern," when one is face to face, when the moment seems right in her hanging-out times, is by way of questions cooked on the hot plate in the hotel room: What is it to vote? What is it to hope to save? What is the good life? Anthropological questions, or oral historians' questions will not do when you want, not to produce knowledge about others, but to open yourself to an other's *ethic*. What is it to "open," what does one open? ACEM cannot talk feminism because that comes packaged with the Enlightenment material that allowed her assimilation.

These questions—political (what is it to vote?), economic (what is it to hope to save?), social (what is the good life?)—and their answers cannot teach her enough to make up an account of the ethical subject distinguishable from the celebration of a transcoded, anthropological subject/object. How can the questioner not acknowledge that the arrival of the moment between her and the other woman is not just good chemistry between the two, but also vast aggregative violating systemic work which is precisely from that hotel lobby that she is trying to leave?

The preconference plan had been to proceed now, time permitting, to an example from a hegemonic Indic text, a feminist rereading of a famous moment in the *Mahābhārata* as a call to an ethical *à-venir*. But time did not permit, and it now seems more in keeping with the spirit of the piece simply to indicate some of the conclusions from that reading and end inconclusively. If there is an interested reader, she will follow it through in a text where the question—"what is it to 'read' the text of a different ethics?"—is played out at leisure.

In conclusion, then, the conclusions, literal self-citations from a postscript to a friend's work:[10]

> Draupadi's question is modest, not mad. Or, it is mad only in its boldness, only in its nonrecuperability by narrative logic. She is not a great criminal showing up the violence of the law. Or the greatness of the crime is in its daring to invoke legal justice.
> The momentary imagination of the menstruating, lorded-yet-lordless, questioning-though-property, woman in suspension does not need to be covered over, for it as yet threatens nothing.

This postscript ends in unverifiable hearsay: that at the end of the whole devastating battle, she laughed aloud from inside the encampment. As a "Hindu" woman, I have the responsibility to put a gloss for our times on this unauthorized epic detail. She laughed to think of a time—always to come, à-venir— when unlorded women would choose to ask the question of the law's relationship to ethics across sexual difference, again, and perhaps intelligibly.

9

The Politics of Translation

The idea for this title comes from the British sociologist Michèle Barrett's feeling that the politics of translation takes on a massive life of its own if you see language as the process of meaning-construction.[1]

In my view, language may be one of many elements that allow us to make sense of things, of ourselves. I am thinking, of course, of gestures, pauses, but also of chance, of the subindividual force-fields of being which click into place in different situations, swerve from the straight or true line of language-in-thought. Making sense of ourselves is what produces identity. If one feels that the production of identity as self-meaning, not just meaning, is as pluralized as a drop of water under a microscope, one is not always satisfied, outside of the ethicopolitical arena as such, with "generating" thoughts on one's own. (Assuming identity as origin may be unsatisfactory in the ethicopolitical arena as well, but consideration of that now would take us too far afield.) I have argued in Chapter Six that one of the ways of resisting capitalist multiculturalism's invitation to self-identity and compete is to give the name of "woman" to the unimaginable other. The same sort of impulse is at work here in a rather more tractable form. For one of the ways to get around the confines of one's "identity" as one produces expository prose is to work at someone else's title, as one works with a language that belongs to many others. This, after all, is one of the seductions of translating. It is a simple miming of the responsibility to the trace of the other in the self.

Responding, therefore, to Barrett with that freeing sense of responsibility, I can agree that it is not bodies of meaning that are transferred in translation. And from the ground of that agreement I want to consider the role played by language for the *agent*, the person who acts, even though intention is not fully present to itself. The task of the feminist translator is to consider language as a clue to the workings of gendered agency. The writer is written by her language, of course. But the writing of the writer writes agency in a way that might be different from that of

179

the British woman/citizen within the history of British feminism, focused on the task of freeing herself from Britain's imperial past, its often racist present, as well as its "made in Britain" history of male domination.

Translation as Reading

How does the translator attend to the specificity of the language she translates? There is a way in which the rhetorical nature of every language disrupts its logical systematicity. If we emphasize the logical at the expense of these rhetorical interferences, we remain safe. "Safety" is the appropriate term here, because we are talking of risks, of violence to the translating medium.

I felt that I was taking those risks when I recently translated some eighteenth-century Bengali poetry. I quote a bit from my "Translator's Preface":

> I must overcome what I was taught in school: the highest mark for the most accurate collection of synonyms, strung together in the most proximate syntax. I must resist both the solemnity of chaste Victorian poetic prose and the forced simplicity of "plain English," that have imposed themselves as the norm . . . Translation is the most intimate act of reading. I surrender to the text when I translate. These songs, sung day after day in family chorus before clear memory began, have a peculiar intimacy for me. Reading and surrendering take on new meanings in such a case. The translator earns permission to transgress from the trace of the other—before memory—in the closest places of the self.[2]

Yet language is not everything. It is only a vital clue to where the self loses its boundaries. The ways in which rhetoric or figuration disrupt logic themselves point at the possibility of random contingency, beside language, around language. Such a *dis*semination cannot be under our control. Yet in translation, where meaning hops into the spacy emptiness between two named historical languages, we get perilously close to it. By juggling the disruptive rhetoricity that breaks the surface in not necessarily connected ways, we feel the selvedges of the language-textile give way, fray into *frayages* or facilitations.[3] Although every act of reading or communication is a bit of this risky fraying which scrambles together somehow, our stake in agency keeps the fraying down to a minimum except in the communication and reading of and in love. (What is the place of "love" in the ethical? As we saw, Irigaray has struggled with this question.) The task of the translator is to facilitate this love between the original and its shadow, a love that permits fraying, holds the agency of the translator and the demands of her imagined or actual audience at bay. The politics of translation from a non-European woman's text too often suppresses this possibility because the translator cannot engage with, or cares insufficiently for, the rhetoricity of the original.

The simple possibility that something might not be meaningful is contained by the rhetorical system as the always possible menace of a space outside language. This is most eerily staged (and challenged) in the effort to communicate with other possible intelligent beings in space. (Absolute alterity or otherness is thus differed-deferred into an other self who resembles us, however minimally, and with whom we can communicate.) But a more homely staging of it occurs across two earthly languages. The experience of contained alterity in an unknown language spoken in a different cultural milieu is uncanny.

Let us now think that, in that other language, rhetoric may be disrupting logic in the matter of the production of an agent, and indicating the founding violence of the silence at work within rhetoric. Logic allows us to jump from word to word by means of clearly indicated connections. Rhetoric must work in the silence between and around words in order to see what works and how much. The jagged relationship between rhetoric and logic, condition and effect of knowing, is a relationship by which a world is made for the agent, so that the agent can act in an ethical way, a political way, a day-to-day way; so that the agent can be alive, in a human way, in the world. Unless one can at least construct a model of this for the other language, there is no real translation.

Unfortunately it is only too easy to produce translations if this task is completely ignored. I myself see no choice between the quick and easy and slapdash way, and translating well and with difficulty. There is no reason why a responsible translation should take more time in the doing. The translator's preparation might take more time, and her love for the text might be a matter of a reading skill that takes patience. But the sheer material production of the text need not be slow.

Without a sense of the rhetoricity of language, a species of neocolonialist construction of the non-Western scene is afoot. No argument for convenience can be persuasive here. That is always the argument, it seems. This is where I travel from Barrett's enabling notion of the question of language in poststructuralism. Poststructuralism has shown some of us a staging of the agent within a three-tiered notion of language (as rhetoric, logic, silence). We must attempt to enter or direct that staging, as one directs a play, as an actor interprets a script. That takes a different kind of effort from taking translation to be a matter of synonym, syntax, and local color.

To be only critical, to defer action until the production of the utopian translator, is impractical. Yet, when I hear Derrida, quite justifiably, point out the difficulties between French and English, even when he agrees to speak in English—"I must speak in a language that is not my own because that will be more just"—I want to claim the right to the same dignified complaint for a woman's text in Arabic or Vietnamese.[4]

It is more just to give access to the largest number of feminists. Therefore these texts must be made to speak English. It is more just to speak the language of the majority when through hospitality a large number of feminists give the foreign feminist the right to speak, in English. In the case of the third world foreigner, is the law of the majority that of decorum, the equitable law of democracy, or the "law" of the strongest? We might focus on this confusion. There is nothing necessarily meretricious about the Western feminist gaze. (The "naturalizing" of Jacques Lacan's sketching out of the psychic structure of the gaze in terms of group political behavior has always seemed to me a bit shaky.) On the other hand, there is nothing essentially noble about the law of the majority either. It is merely the easiest way of being "democratic" with minorities. In the act of wholesale translation into English there can be a betrayal of the democratic ideal into the law of the strongest. This happens when all the literature of the Third World gets translated into a sort of with-it translatese, so that the literature by a woman in Palestine begins to resemble, in the feel of its prose, something by a man in Taiwan. The rhetoricity of Chinese and Arabic! The cultural politics of high-growth, capitalist Asia-Pacific, and devastated West Asia! Gender difference inscribed and inscribing in these differences!

For the student, this tedious translatese cannot compete with the spectacular stylistic experiments of a Monique Wittig or an Alice Walker.

Let us consider an example where attending to the author's stylistic experiments can produce a different text. Mahasweta Devi's "Stanadāyini" is available in two versions.[5] Devi has expressed approval for the attention to her signature style in the version entitled "Breast-Giver." The alternative translation gives the title as "The Wet-Nurse," and thus neutralizes the author's irony in constructing an uncanny word; enough like "wet-nurse" to make that sense, and enough unlike to shock. It is as if the translator should decide to translate Dylan Thomas's famous title and opening line as "Do not go gently into that good night." The theme of treating the breast as organ of labor-power-as-commodity and the breast as metonymic part-object standing in for other-as-object—the way in which the story plays with Marx and Freud on the occasion of the woman's body—is lost even before you enter the story. In the text Mahasweta uses proverbs that are startling even in the Bengali. The translator of "The Wet-Nurse" leaves them out. She decides not to try to translate these hard bits of earthy wisdom, contrasting with class-specific access to modernity, also represented in the story. In fact, if the two translations are read side by side, the loss of the rhetorical silences of the original can be felt from one to the other.

First, then, the translator must surrender to the text. She must solicit the text to show the limits of its language, because that rhetorical aspect will point at the silence of the absolute fraying of language that the text wards off, in its special manner. Some think this is just an ethereal way of talking about literature or philosophy. But no amount of tough talk can get around the fact that translation is the most intimate act of reading. Unless the translator has earned the right to become the intimate reader, she cannot surrender to the text, cannot respond to the special call of the text.

The presupposition that women have a natural or narrative-historical solidarity, that there is something in a woman or an undifferentiated women's story that speaks to another woman without benefit of language-learning, might stand against the translator's task of surrender. Paradoxically, it is not possible for us as ethical agents to imagine otherness or alterity maximally. We have to turn the other into something like the self in order to be ethical. To surrender in translation is more erotic than ethical. In that situation the good-willing attitude "she is just like me" is not very helpful. In so far as Michèle Barrett is not like Gayatri Spivak, their friendship is more effective as a translation. In order to earn that right of friendship or surrender of identity, of knowing that the rhetoric of the text indicates the limits of language for you as long as you are with the text, you have to be in a different relationship with the language, not even only with the specific text.

Learning about translation on the job, I came to think that it would be a practical help if one's relationship with the language being translated was such that sometimes one preferred to speak in it about intimate things. This is no more than a practical suggestion, not a theoretical requirement, useful especially because a woman writer who is wittingly or unwittingly a "feminist"—and of course all woman writers are not "feminist" even in this broad sense—will relate to the three-part staging of (agency in) language in ways defined out as "private," since they might question the more public linguistic maneuvers.

Let us consider an example of lack of intimacy with the medium. In

Sudhir Kakar's *The Inner World,* a song about Kālī written by the late nineteenth-century monk Vivekananda is cited as part of the proof of the "archaic narcissism" of the Indian [sic] male.[6] (Devi makes the same point with a light touch, with reference to Kṛṣṇa and Siva, tying it to sexism rather than narcissism and without psychoanalytic patter.)

From Kakar's description, it would not be possible to glimpse that "the disciple" who gives the account of the singular circumstances of Vivekananda's composition of the song was an Irishwoman who became a Ramakrishna nun, a white woman among male Indian monks and devotees.[7] In the account Kakar reads, the song is translated by this woman, whose training in intimacy with the original language is as pains-taking as one can hope for. There is a strong identification between Indian and Irish nationalists at this period; and Nivedita, as she was called, also embraced what she understood to be the Indian philosophical way of life as explained by Vivekananda, itself a peculiar, resistant consequence of the culture of imperialism, as has been pointed out by many. For a psychoanalyst like Kakar, this historical, philosophical, and indeed sexual text of translation should be the textile to weave with. Instead, the English version, "given" by the anonymous "disciple," serves as no more than the opaque exhibit providing evidence of the alien fact of narcissism. It is not the site of the exchange of language.

At the beginning of the passage quoted by Kakar, there is a reference to Ram Prasad (or Ram Proshad; 1718–85). Kakar provides a footnote: "Eighteenth century singer and poet whose songs of longing for the Mother are very popular in Bengal." I believe this footnote is also an indication of what I am calling the absence of intimacy.

Vivekananda is, among other things, an example of the peculiar reactive construction of a glorious "India" under the provocation of imperialism. The rejection of "patriotism" in favor of "Kālī" reported in Kakar's passage is played out in this historical theater, as a choice of the cultural female sphere rather than the colonial male sphere.[8] It is undoubtedly "true" that for such a figure, Ram Proshad Sen provides a kind of ideal self. Sen had retired with a pension from a clerk's job with a rural landowner, when the English were already in Bengal but had not claimed territory officially. He was himself given some land by one of the great rural landowners the year after the battle that inaugurated the territorial enterprise of the East India Company. He died eight years before the Permanent Settlement would introduce a violent epistemic rupture.[9] In other words, Vivekananda and Ram Proshad are two related moments of colonial discursivity translating the figure of Kālī. The dynamic intricacy of that discursive textile is mocked by the useless footnote.

It would be idle here to enter the debate about the "identity" of Kālī or indeed other goddesses in Hindu "polytheism." But simply to contextualize, let me add that it is Ram Proshad about whose poetry I wrote the "Translator's Preface" quoted earlier. He is by no means simply an archaic stage-prop in the disciple's account of Vivekananda's "crisis." Some more lines from my "Preface": "Ram Proshad played with his mother tongue, transvaluing the words that are heaviest with Sanskrit meaning. I have been unable to catch the utterly new but utterly gendered tone of affectionate banter"—not only, not even largely, "longing"—"between the poet and Kāli." Unless Nivedita mistranslated, it is the difference in tone between Ram Proshad's innovating playfulness and Vivekananda's high nationalist solemnity that, in spite of the turn from nationalism to the Mother, is historically significant. The politics of translation has shifted into the register of reactive nativism. And that change is expressed in the gendering of the poet's voice.

How do women in contemporary polytheism relate to this peculiar mother, certainly not the psychoanalytic bad mother whom Kakar derives from Max Weber's misreading, not even an organized punishing mother, but a child-mother who punishes with astringent violence and is also a moral and affective monitor?[10] Ordinary women, not saintly women. Why take it for granted that the invocation of goddesses in a historically masculinist polytheist sphere is more feminist than Nietzsche or Derrida claiming woman as model? I think it is a Western and male-gendered suggestion that powerful women in the Sākta (Sakti or Kāli-worshipping) tradition *necessarily* take Kāli as a role model.

Mahasweta's Jashoda tells me more about the relationship between goddesses and strong ordinary women than the psychoanalyst. And here too the example of an intimate translation that goes respectfully "wrong" can be offered. The French wife of a Bengali artist translated some of Ram Proshad Sen's songs in the twenties to accompany her husband's paintings based on the songs. Her translations are marred by the pervasive orientalism ready at hand. Compare two passages, both translating the "same" Bengali. I have at least tried, if failed, to catch the unrelenting mockery of self and Kāli in the original:

Mind, why footloose from Mother?
Mind mine, think power, for freedom's dower, bind bower with
    love-rope
In time, mind, you minded not your blasted lot.
And Mother, daughter-like, bound up house-fence to dupe her
    dense and devoted fellow.
Oh you'll see at death how much Mum loves you
A couple minutes' tears, and lashings of water, cowdung-pure.

Here is the French, translated by me into an English comparable in tone and vocabulary:

Pourquoi as-tu, mon âme, délaissé les pieds de Ma ?
O esprit, médite Shokti, tu obtiendras la délivrance.
Attache-les ces pieds saints avec la corde de la dévotion.
Au bon moment tu n'as rien vu, c'est bien là ton malheur.
Pour se jouer de son fidèle, Elle m'est apparue
Sous la forme de ma fille et m'a aidé à réparer ma clôture.
C'est à la mort que tu comprendras l'amour de Mâ.
Ici, on versera quelques larmes, puis on purifiera le lieu.

Why have you, my soul [*mon âme* is, admittedly, less heavy in
    French], left Ma's feet?
O mind, meditate upon Shokti, you will obtain deliverance.
Bind those holy feet with the rope of devotion.
In good time you saw nothing, that is indeed your sorrow.
To play with her faithful one, She appeared to me
In the form of my daughter and helped me to repair my enclosure.
It is at death that you will understand Ma's love.
Here, they will shed a few tears, then purify the place.

And here the Bengali:

মন কেন মার চরণ-ছাড়া ।
ও মন, ভজ শক্তি, পাবে মুক্তি, বাঁধ দিয়ে ভক্তি-ডোর ॥
সময় যাকালে, না দেখলে মন, এইমা তোমার কপালগোড়া ।
আপন ভক্তে ছলিতে, তনয়া রূপেতে রাঁধিন আসি ধারের বেড়া ॥
মায়ে মত জানাগামে, মরণ পাবে শক্তিশেষ,
সোনার দুঃ-ছুঁয়ে কান্নাকাটি, শেষে দিবে গোররছড়া ।

I hope these examples demonstrate that depth of commitment to correct cultural politics, felt in the details of personal life, is sometimes not enough. The history of the language, the history of the author's moment, the history of the language-in-and-as-translation, must figure in the weaving as well.

Mere reasonableness will allow rhetoricity to be appropriated, put in its place, situated, seen as only nice. Rhetoricity is put in its place that way because it disrupts. Women within male-dominated society, when they internalize sexism as normality, act out a scenario against feminism that is formally analogical to this. The relationship between logic and rhetoric, between grammar and rhetoric, is also a relationship between social logic, social reasonableness, and the disruptiveness of figuration in social practice. These are the first two parts of our three-part model. But then, rhetoric points at the possibility of randomness, of contingency as such, dissemination, the falling apart of language, the possibility that things might not always be semiotically organized. (My problem with Kristeva and the "presemiotic" is that she seems to want to expand the empire of the meaning-ful by grasping at what language can only point at.) Cultures that might not have this specific three-part model will still have a dominant sphere in its traffic with language and contingency. Writers like Ifi Amadiume show us that, without thinking of this sphere as biologically determined, one still has to think in terms of spheres determined by definitions of secondary and primary sexual characteristics in such a way that the inhabitants of the other sphere are para-subjective, not fully subject.[11] The dominant groups' way of handling the three-part ontology of language has to be learned as well—if the subordinate ways of rusing with rhetoric are to be disclosed.

To decide whether you are prepared enough to start translating, then, it might help if you have graduated into speaking, by choice or preference, of intimate matters in the language of the original. I have worked my way back to my earlier point: I cannot see why the publishers' convenience or classroom convenience or time convenience for people who do not have the time to learn should organize the construction of the rest of the world for Western feminism. Five years ago, berated as unsisterly, I would think, "Well, you know one ought to be a bit more giving etc.," but then I asked myself again, "What am I giving, or giving up? To whom am I giving by assuring that you don't have to work that hard, just come and get it? What am I trying to promote?" People would say, you who have succeeded should not pretend to be a marginal. But surely by demanding higher standards of translation, I am not marginalizing myself or the language of the original?

I have learned through translating Devi how this three-part structure works differently from English in my native language. And here another historical irony has become personally apparent to me. In the old days, it was most important for a colonial or postcolonial student of English to be as "indistinguishable" as possible from the native speaker of English. I think it is necessary for people in the third world translation trade now to accept that the wheel has come around, that the genuinely bilingual postcolonial now has a bit of an advantage. But she does not have a real advantage as a translator if she is not strictly bilingual, if she merely speaks her native language. Her own native space is, after all, also class-organized. And that organization still often carries the traces of access to imperialism, often relates inversely to access to the vernacular as a public language. So here the requirement for intimacy brings a recognition of the public sphere as well. If we were thinking of translating Marianne Moore or Emily Dickinson, the standard for the translator could not be "anyone who can conduct a conversation in the language of the original (in this case English)." When applied to a third world language, the position is inherently ethnocentric. And then to present these translations to our unprepared students so that they can learn about women writing!

In my view, the translator from a third world language should be sufficiently in touch with what is going on in literary production in that language to be capable of distinguishing between good and bad writing by women, resistant and conformist writing by women.

She must be able to confront the idea that what seems resistant in the space of English may be reactionary in the space of the original language. Farida Akhter has argued that, in Bangladesh, the real work of the women's movement and of feminism is being undermined by talk of "gendering," mostly deployed by the women's development wings of transnational nongovernment organizations, in conjunction with some local academic feminist theorists.[12] One of her intuitions was that "gendering" could not be translated into Bengali. "Gendering" is an awkward new word in English as well. Akhter is profoundly involved in international feminism. And her base is third world. I could not translate "gender" into the U.S. feminist context for her. This misfiring of translation, between a superlative reader of the social text such as Akhter, and a careful translator like myself, speaking as friends, has added to my sense of the task of the translator.

Good and bad is a flexible standard, like all standards. Here another lesson of poststructuralism helps: these decisions of standards are made anyway. It is the attempt to justify them adequately that polices. That is why disciplinary preparation in school requires that you write examinations to prove these standards. Publishing houses routinely engage in materialist confusion of those standards. The translator must be able to fight that metropolitan materialism with a special kind of specialist's knowledge, not mere philosophical convictions.

In other words, the person who is translating must have a tough sense of the specific terrain of the original, so that she can fight the racist assumption that all third world women's writing is good. I am often approached by women who would like to put Devi in with just Indian women writers. I am troubled by this, because "Indian women" is not a feminist category. (In Chapter Two I have argued that "epistemes"— ways of constructing objects of knowledge—should not have national names either.) Sometimes Indian women writing means American women writing or British women writing, except for national *origin*. There is an ethno-cultural agenda, an obliteration of third world specificity as well as a denial of cultural citizenship, in calling them merely "Indian."

My initial point was that the task of the translator is to surrender herself to the linguistic rhetoricity of the original text. Although this point has larger political implications, we can say that the not unimportant minimal consequence of ignoring this task is the loss of "the literarity and textuality and sensuality of the writing" (Barrett's words). I have worked my way to a second point, that the translator must be able to discriminate on the terrain of the original. Let us dwell on it a bit longer.

I choose Devi because she is unlike her scene. I have heard an English Shakespearean suggest that every bit of Shakespeare criticism coming from the subcontinent was by that virtue resistant. By such a judgment, we are also denied the right to be critical. It was of course bad to have put the place under subjugation, to have tried to make the place over with calculated restrictions. But that does not mean that everything that is coming out of that place after a negotiated independence nearly fifty years ago is necessarily right. The old anthropological supposition (and that is bad anthropology) that every person from a culture is nothing but a whole example of that culture is acted out in my colleague's suggestion. I remain interested in writers who are against the current, against the mainstream. I remain convinced that the interesting literary text might be precisely the text where you do not learn what the majority view of majority cultural representation or self-representation of a nation state might be. The translator has to make herself, in the case of third world women writing, almost better equipped than the translator who is dealing with the Western European languages, because of the fact that there is so much of the old colonial attitude, slightly displaced, at work in the translation racket. Poststructuralism *can* radicalize the field of preparation so that simply boning up on the language is not enough; there is also that special relationship to the staging of language as the production of agency that one must attend to. But the agenda of poststructuralism is mostly elsewhere, and the resistance to theory among metropolitan feminists would lead us into yet another narrative.

The understanding of the task of the translator and the practice of the craft are related but different. Let me summarize how I work. At first I translate at speed. If I stop to think about what is happening to the English, if I assume an audience, if I take the intending subject as more than a springboard, I cannot jump in, I cannot surrender. My relationship with Devi is easygoing. I am able to say to her: I surrender to you in your writing, not to you as intending subject. There, in friendship, is another kind of surrender. Surrendering to the text in this way means, most of the time, being literal. When I have produced a version this way, I revise. I revise not in terms of a possible audience, but by the protocols of the thing in front of me, in a sort of English. And I keep hoping that the student in the classroom will not be able to think that the text is just a purveyor of social realism if it is translated with an eye toward the dynamic staging of language mimed in the revision by the rules of the in-between discourse produced by a literalist surrender.

Vain hope, perhaps, for the accountability is different. When I translated Jacques Derrida's *De la grammatologie*, I was reviewed in a major journal for the first and last time. In the case of my translations of Devi, I have almost no fear of being accurately judged by my readership here. It makes the task more dangerous and more risky. And that for me is the real difference between translating Derrida and translating Mahasweta Devi, not merely the rather more artificial difference between deconstructive philosophy and political fiction.

The opposite argument is not neatly true. There is a large number of people in the third world who read the old imperial languages. People reading current feminist fiction in the European languages would probably read it in the appropriate imperial language. And the same goes for European philosophy. The act of translating into the third world language is often a political exercise of a different sort. I am looking forward, as of this writing, to lecturing in Bengali on deconstruction in front of a highly sophisticated audience, knowledgeable both in Bengali and in deconstruction (which they read in English and French and sometimes write about in Bengali), at Jadavpur University in Calcutta. It will be a kind of testing of the postcolonial translator, I think.[13]

Democracy changes into the law of force in the case of translation from the third world and women even more because of their peculiar relationship to whatever you call the public/private divide. A neatly reversible argument would be possible if the particular Third World country had cornered the Industrial Revolution first and embarked on monopoly imperialist territorial capitalism as one of its consequences, and thus been able to impose a language as international norm. Something like that idiotic joke: if the Second World War had gone differently, the United States would be speaking Japanese. Such egalitarian reversible judgments are appropriate to counterfactual fantasy. Translation remains dependent upon the language skill of the majority. A prominent Belgian translation theorist solves the problem by suggesting that, rather than talk about the third world, where a lot of passion is involved, one should speak about the European Renaissance, since a great deal of wholesale cross-cultural translation from Greco-Roman antiquity was undertaken then. What one overlooks is the sheer authority ascribed to the originals in that historical phenomenon. The status of a language in the world is what one must consider when teasing out the politics of translation. Translatese in Bengali can be derided and criticized by large groups of anglophone and anglograph Bengalis. It is only in the hegemonic languages that the benevolent do not take the limits of their own often uninstructed good will into account. That phenomenon becomes hardest to fight because the individuals involved in it are genuinely benevolent and you are identified as a trouble-maker. This becomes particularly difficult when the metropolitan feminist, who is sometimes the assimilated postcolonial, invokes, indeed translates, a too quickly shared feminist notion of accessibility.

If you want to make the translated text accessible, try doing it for the person who wrote it. The problem comes clear then, for she is not within the same history of style. What is it that you are making accessible? The accessible level is the level of abstraction where the individual is already formed, where one can speak individual rights. When you hang out and with a language away from your own (*Mitwegsein*) so that you want to use that language by preference, sometimes, when you discuss something complicated, then you are on the way to making a dimension of the text accessible to the reader, with a light and easy touch, to which she does not accede in her everyday. If you are making anything else accessible, through a language quickly learned with an idea that you transfer content, then you are betraying the text and showing rather dubious politics.

How will women's solidarity be measured here? How will their common experience be reckoned if one cannot imagine the traffic in accessibility going both ways? I think that idea should be given a decent burial as ground of knowledge, together with the idea of humanist universality. It is good to think that women have something in common, when one is approaching women with whom a relationship would not otherwise be possible. It is a great first step. But, if your interest is in learning if there *is* women's solidarity, how about stepping forth from this assumption, appropriate as a means to an end like local or global social work, and trying a second step? Rather than imagining that women automatically have something identifiable in common, why not say, humbly and practically, my first obligation in understanding solidarity is to learn her mother-tongue. You will see immediately what the differences are. You will also feel the solidarity every day as you make the attempt to learn the language in which the other woman learned to recognize reality at her mother's knee. This is preparation for the intimacy of cultural translation. If you are going to bludgeon someone else by insisting on your version of solidarity, you have the obligation to try out this experiment and see how far your solidarity goes.

In other words, if you are interested in talking about the other, and/or in making a claim to be the other, it is crucial to learn other languages. This should be distinguished from the learned tradition of language acquisition for academic work. I am talking about the importance of language acquisition for the woman from a hegemonic monolinguist culture who makes everybody's life miserable by insisting on women's solidarity at her price. I am uncomfortable with notions of feminist solidarity which are celebrated when everybody involved is similarly produced. There are countless languages in which women all over the world have grown up and been female or feminist, and yet the languages we keep on learning by rote are the powerful European ones, sometimes the powerful Asian ones, least often the chief African ones. We are quite at home, and helpful, when large migrant populations are doing badly in the dominant countries, our own. The "other" languages are learned only by anthropologists who *must* produce knowledge across an epistemic divide. They are generally (though not invariably) not interested in the three-part structure we are discussing.

If we are discussing solidarity as a theoretical position, we must also remember that not all the world's women are literate. There are traditions and situations that remain obscure because we cannot share their linguistic constitution. It is from this angle that I have felt that learning languages might sharpen our own presuppositions about what it means to use the sign "woman." If we say that things should be accessible to us, who is this "us"? What does that sign mean?

Although I have used the examples of women all along, the arguments apply across the board. It is just that women's rhetoricity may be doubly obscured. I do not see the advantage of being completely focused on a single issue, although one must establish practical priorities. In the book where this chapter was first anthologized, the editors were concerned with poststructuralism and its effect on feminist theory. Where some poststructuralist thinking can be applied to the constitution of the agent in terms of the literary operations of language, women's texts might be operating differently because of the social differentiation between the sexes. Of course the point applies generally to the colonial context as well. When Ngugi decided to write in Kikuyu, some thought he was bringing a private language into the public sphere. But what makes a language shared by many people in a community private? I was thinking about those so-called private languages when I was talking about language learning. But even within those private languages it is my conviction that there is a difference in the way in which the staging of language produces not only the sexed subject but the gendered agent, by a version of centering, persistently disrupted by rhetoricity, indicating contingency. Unless demonstrated otherwise, this for me remains the condition and effect of dominant and subordinate gendering. If that is so, then we have some reason to focus on women's texts. Let us use the word "woman" to name that space of parasubjects defined as such by the social inscription of primary and secondary sexual characteristics. Then we can cautiously begin to track a sort of commonality in being set apart, within the different rhetorical strategies of different languages. But even here, historical superiorities of class must be kept in mind. Bharati Mukherjee, Anita Desai, and Gayatri Spivak do not have the same rhetorical figuration of agency as an illiterate domestic servant.

Tracking commonality through responsible translation can lead us into areas of difference and different differentiations. This may also be important because, in the heritage of imperialism, the female legal subject bears the mark of a failure of Europeanization, by contrast with the female anthropological or literary subject from the area. For example, the division between the French and Islamic codes in modern Algeria is in terms of family, marriage, inheritance, legitimacy, and female social agency. These are differences that we must keep in mind. And we must honor the difference between ethnic minorities in the first world and majority populations of the third.

In conversation, Barrett had asked me if I now inclined more toward Foucault. This is indeed the case. In "Can the Subaltern Speak?," I took a rather strong critical line on Foucault's work, as part of a general critique of imperialism.[14] As I have indicated in Chapter Two, I do, however, find, his concept of *pouvoir-savoir* immensely useful. Foucault has contributed to French this ordinary-language doublet (the ability to know [as]) to take its place quietly beside *vouloir-dire* (the wish to say—meaning to mean).

On the most mundane level, *pouvoir-savoir* is the shared skill which allows us to make (common) sense of things. It is certainly not only power/knowledge in the sense of *puissance/connaissance*. Those are aggregative institutions. The common way in which one makes sense of things, on the other hand, loses itself in the sub-individual.

Looking at *pouvoir-savoir* in terms of women, one of my focuses has been new immigrants and the change of mother-tongue and *pouvoir-savoir* between mother and daughter. When the daughter talks reproductive rights and the mother talks protecting honor, is this the birth or death of translation?

Foucault is also interesting in his new notion of the ethics of the care for the self. In order to be able to get to the subject of ethics it may be necessary to look at the ways in which an individual in that culture is instructed to care for the self rather than the imperialism-specific secularist notion that the ethical subject is given as human. In a secularism which is structurally identical with Christianity laundered in the bleach of moral philosophy, the subject of ethics is faceless. Breaking out, Foucault was investigating other ways of making sense of how the subject becomes ethical. This is of interest because, given the connection between imperialism and secularism, there is almost no way of getting to alternative general voices except through religion. And if one does not look at religion as mechanisms of producing the ethical subject, one gets various kinds of "fundamentalism." Workers in cultural politics and its connections to a new ethical philosophy have to be interested in religion in the production of ethical subjects. There is much room for feminist work here because Western feminists have not so far been aware of religion as a cultural instrument rather than a mark of cultural difference. I am currently working on Hindu performative ethics with Professor B.K. Matilal. He is an enlightened male feminist. I am an active feminist. Helped by his learning and his openness I am learning to distinguish between ethical catalysts and ethical motors even as I learn to translate bits of the Sanskrit epic in a way different from all the accepted translations, because I rely not only on learning, not only on "good English," but on that three-part scheme of which I have so lengthily spoken. I hope the results will please readers. If we are going to look at an ethics that emerges from something other than the historically secularist ideal—at an ethics of sexual differences, at an ethics that can confront the emergence of fundamentalisms without apology or dismissal in the name of the Enlightenment—then *pouvoir-savoir* and the care for the self in Foucault can be illuminating. And these "other ways" bring us back to translation, in the general sense.

Translation in General

I want now to add two sections to what was generated from the initial conversation with Barrett. I will dwell on the politics of translation in a general sense, by way of three examples of "cultural translation" in English. I want to make the point that the lessons of translation in the narrow sense can reach much further.

First, J.M. Coetzee's *Foe*. This book represents the impropriety of the dominant's desire to give voice to the native. When Susan Barton, the eighteenth-century Englishwoman from *Roxana,* attempts to teach a muted Friday (from *Robinson Crusoe*) to read and write English, he draws an incomprehensible rebus on his slate and wipes it out, withholds it. You cannot translate from a position of monolinguist superiority. Coetzee as white creole translates *Robinson Crusoe* by representing Friday as the agent of a withholding.

Second, Toni Morrison's *Beloved.*[15] Let us look at the scene of the change of the mother-tongue from mother to daughter. Strictly speaking, it is not a change, but a loss, for the narrative is not of immigration but of slavery. Sethe, the central character of the novel, remembers: "What Nan"—her mother's fellow-slave and friend—"told her she had forgotten, along with the language she told it in. The same language her ma'am spoke, and which would never come back. But the message—that was—and had been there all along" (*B,* 62). The representation of this message, as it passes through the forgetfulness of death to Sethe's ghostly daughter Beloved, is of a withholding: "This is not a story to pass on" (*B,* 275).

Between mother and daughter, a certain historical withholding intervenes. If the situation between the new immigrant mother and daughter provokes the question as to whether it is the birth or death of translation (see above, 000), here the author represents with violence a certain birth-in-death, a death-in-birth of a story that is not to translate or pass on. Strictly speaking, therefore, an aporia. And yet it is passed on, with the mark of *un*translatability on it, in the bound book, *Beloved,* that we hold in our hands. Contrast this to the confidence in accessibility in the house of power, where history is waiting to be restored.

The scene of violence between mother and daughter (reported and passed on by the daughter Sethe to her daughter Denver, who carries the name of a white trash girl, in partial acknowledgment of women's solidarity in birthing) is, then, the condition of (im)possibility of *Beloved.*

> She picked me up and carried me behind the smokehouse. Back there she opened up her dress front and lifted her breast and pointed under it. Right on her rib was a circle and a cross burnt right in the skin. She said, "This is your ma'am. This," and she pointed . . . "Yes, Ma'am," I said. . . . "But how will you know me? . . . Mark me, too," I said . . . "Did she?" asked Denver. "She slapped my face." "What for?" I didn't understand it then. Not till I had a mark of my own" (*B,* 61).

This scene, of claiming the brand of the owner as "my own," to create, in this broken chain of marks owned by separate white male agents of property, an unbroken chain of rememory in (enslaved) daughters as agents of a history not to be passed on, is of necessity different from Friday's scene of withheld writing from the white woman wanting to create history by giving her "own" language. And the lesson is the (im)possibility of translation in the general sense. Rhetoric points at absolute contingency, not the sequentiality of time, not even the cycle of seasons, but only "weather." "By and by all trace is gone, and what is forgotten is not only the footprints but the water and what it is down there. The rest is weather. Not the breath of the disremembered and unaccounted for"—after the effacement of the trace, no project for restoring (women's?) history—"but wind in the eaves, or spring ice thawing too quickly. Just weather" (275).

With this invocation of contingency, where nature may be "the great body without organs of woman," we can align ourselves with Wilson Harris, the author of *The Guyana Quartet*, for whom trees are "the lungs of the globe."[16] Harris hails the (re)birth of the native imagination as not merely the trans-lation but the trans-substantiation of the species. What in more workaday language I have called the obligation of the translator to be able to juggle the rhetorical silences in the two languages, Harris puts this way, pointing at the need for translating the Carib's English:

> The Caribbean bone flute, made of human bone, is a seed in the soul of the Caribbean. It is a primitive technology that we can turn around [trans-version?]. Consuming our biases and prejudices in ourselves we can let the bone flute help us open ourselves rather than read it the other way—as a metonymic devouring of a bit of flesh.[17] The link of music with cannibalism is a sublime paradox. When the music of the bone flute opens the doors, absences flow in, and the native imagination puts together the ingredients for quantum immediacy out of unpredictable resources.

The bone flute has been neglected by Caribbean writers, says Wilson Harris, because progressive realism is a charismatic way of writing prize-winning fiction. Progressive realism measures the bone. Progressive realism is the too-easy accessibility of translation as transfer of substance.

The progressive realism of the West dismissed the native imagination as the place of the fetish. Hegel was perhaps the greatest systematizer of this dismissal. And psychoanalytic cultural criticism in its present charismatic incarnation sometimes measures the bone with uncanny precision. It is perhaps not fortuitous that the passage below gives us an account of Hegel that is the exact opposite of Harris's vision. The paradox of the sublime and the bone here lead to non-language seen as inertia, where the structure of passage is mere logic. The authority of the supreme language makes translation impossible:

> The Sublime is therefore the paradox of an object which, in the very field of representation, provides a view, in a negative way, of the dimension of what is unrepresentable . . . The bone, the skull, is thus an object which, by means of its *presence,* fills out the void, the impossibility of the signifying *representation* of the subject . . . The proposition "Wealth is the Self" repeats at this level the proposition "The Spirit is a bone" [both propositions are Hegel's]: in both cases we are dealing with a proposition which is at first sight absurd, nonsensical, with an equation the terms of which are incompatible; in both cases we encounter the same logical structure of passage: the subject, totally lost in the medium of language (language of gesture and grimaces; language of flattery), finds its objective counterpart in the inertia of a non-language object (skull, money).[18]

Wilson Harris's vision is abstract, translating Morrison's "weather" into an oceanic version of quantum physics. But all three cultural translators cited in this section ask us to attend to the rhetoric which points to the limits of translation, in the creole's, the slave-daughter's, the Carib's use of "English." Let us learn the lesson of translation from these brilliant inside/outsiders and translate it into the situation of other languages.

Reading as Translation

In conclusion, I want to show how the postcolonial as the outside/insider translates white theory as she reads, so that she can discriminate on the terrain of the original. She wants to use what is useful. Again, I hope this can pass on a lesson to the translator in the narrow sense.

"The link of music with cannibalism is a sublime paradox." I believe Wilson Harris is using "sublime" here with some degree of precision, indicating the undoing of the progressive Western subject as realist interpreter of history. Can a theoretical account of the aesthetic sublime in English discourse, ostensibly far from the bone flute, be of use? By way of answer, I will use my reading of Peter de Bolla's superb scholarly account of *The Discourse of the Sublime* as an example of sympathetic reading as translation, precisely not a surrender but a friendly learning by taking a distance.[19]

P. 4: "What was it to be a subject in the eighteenth century?" The reader-as-translator (RAT) is excited. The long eighteenth century in

Britain is the account of the constitution and transformation of nation into empire. Shall we read that story? The book will at least touch on that issue, if only to swerve. And women will not be seen as touched in their agency formation by that change. The book's strong feminist sympathies relate to the Englishwoman only as gender victim. But the erudition of the text allows us to think that this sort of rhetorical reading might be the method to open up the question "What is it to be a postcolonial reader of English in the twentieth century?" The representative reader of *The Discourse of the Sublime* will be postcolonial. Has that law of the majority been observed, or the law of the strong?

On p. 72 RAT comes to a discussion of Burke on the sublime:

> The internal resistance of Burke's text . . . restricts the full play of this trope [power . . . as a trope articulating the technologies of the sublime], thereby defeating a description of the sublime experience uniquely in terms of the enpowered [sic] subject. Put briefly, Burke, for a number of reasons, among which we must include political aims and ends, stops short of a discourse on the sublime, and in so doing he reinstates the ultimate power of an adjacent discourse, theology, which locates its own self-authenticating power grimly within the boundaries of godhead.

Was it also because Burke was deeply implicated in searching out the recesses of the mental theater of the English master in the colonies that he had some notion of different kinds of subject and therefore, like some Kurtz before Conrad, recoiled in horror before the sublimely empowered subject? Was it because, like some Kristeva before *Chinese Women*, Burke had tried to imagine the Begums of Oudh as legal subjects that he had put self-authentication elsewhere?[20] *The Discourse of the Sublime*, in noticing Burke's difference from the other discoursers on the sublime, opens doors for other RATs to engage in such scholarly speculations and thus exceed and expand the book.

Pp. 106, 111–112, 131: RAT comes to the English National Debt. British colonialism was a violent deconstruction of the hyphen between nation and state. In imperialism the nation was subl(im)ated into empire. Of this, no clue in *The Discourse*. The Bank of England is discussed. Its founding in 1696, and the transformation of letters of credit to the ancestor of the modern check, had something like a relationship with the fortunes of the East India Company and the founding of Calcutta in 1690. The *national* debt is in fact the site of a crisis-management, where the nation, sublime object as miraculating subject of ideology, changes the

sign "debtor" into a catachresis or false metaphor by way of "an acceptance of a permanent discrepancy between the total circulating specie and
the debt." The French War, certainly the immediate efficient cause, is
soon woven into the vaster textile of crisis. *The Discourse* cannot see the
nation covering for the colonial economy. As on the occasion of the race-
specificity of gendering, so on the discourse of multinational capital, the
argument is kept domestic, within England, European.[21] RAT snuffles off,
disgruntled. She finds a kind of comfort in Mahasweta's livid figuration
of the woman's body as body rather than attend to this history of the
English body "as a disfigurative device in order to return to [it] its lost
literality." Reading as translation has misfired here.

On p. 140 RAT comes to the elder Pitt. "Although his functionality is
initially seen as demanded . . . by the incorporation of nation," it is not
possible not at least to mention empire when speaking of Pitt's voice:

> the voice of Pitt . . . works its doubled intervention into the spirit and
> character of the times; at once the supreme example of the private
> individual in the service of the state, and the private individual eradi-
> cated by the needs of a public, nationalist, commercial empire. In
> this sense the voice of Pitt becomes the most extreme example of the
> textualization of the body for the rest of the century.[22]

We have seen a literal case of the textualization of the surface of the body
between slave mother and slave daughter in *Beloved*, where mother hits
daughter to stop her thinking that the signs of that text can be passed on,
a lesson learned *après-coup,* literally after the blow of the daughter's
own branding. Should RAT expect an account of the passing on of the
textualization of the interior of the body through the voice, a metonym
for consciousness, from master father to master son? The younger Pitt
took the first step to change the nationalist empire to the imperial nation
with the India Act of 1784. *Can The Discourse of the Sublime* plot
that sublime relay? Not yet. But here, too, an exceeding and expanding
translation is possible.

Predictably, RAT finds a foothold in the rhetoricity of *The Discourse*.
Chapter Ten begins: "The second part of this study has steadily examined
how 'theory' sets out to legislate and control a practice, how it produces
the excess which it cannot legislate, and removes from the center to
the boundary its limit, limiting case" (230). This passage reads to a
deconstructive RAT as an enabling self-description of the text, although
within the limits of the book, it describes, not itself, but the object of its

investigation. By the time the end of the book is reached, RAT feels that she has been written into the text:

> As a history of that refusal and resistance [this book] presents a record of its own coming into being as history, the history of the thought it wants to think differently, over there. It is, therefore, only appropriate that its conclusion should gesture towards the limit, risk the reinversion of the boundary by speaking from the other, refusing silence to what is unsaid.[23]

Beyond this "clamor for a kiss" of the other space, it is "just weather."

Under the figure of RAT (reader-as-translator), I have tried to limn the politics of a certain kind of clandestine postcolonial reading, using the master marks to put together a history. Thus we find out what books we can forage, and what we must set aside. I can use Peter de Bolla's *The Discourse on the Sublime* to open up dull histories of the colonial eighteenth century. Was Toni Morrison, a writer well-versed in contemporary literary theory, obliged to set aside Paul de Man's "The Purloined Ribbon"?[24]

> Eighteen seventy-four and white folks were still on the loose . . . Human blood cooked in a lynch fire was a whole other thing . . . But none of that had worn out his marrow . . . It was the ribbon . . . He thought it was a cardinal feather stuck to his boat. He tugged and what came loose in his hand was a red ribbon knotted around a curl of wet woolly hair, clinging still to its bit of scalp . . . He kept the ribbon; the skin smell nagged him (*B*, 180–181).

Morrison next invokes a language whose selvedge is so frayed that no *frayage* can facilitate full passage: "This time, although he couldn't cipher but one word, he believed he knew who spoke them. The people of the broken necks, of fire-cooked blood and black girls who had lost their ribbons" (*B*, 181). Did the explanation of promises and excuses in eighteenth-century Geneva not make it across into this "roar"? I will not check it out and measure the bone flute. I will simply dedicate these pages to the author of *Beloved,* in the name of translation.

10

Inscriptions: Of Truth to Size

In the previous chapter, I argued something like a relationship between translating from third world languages and postcolonial reading as translation. In the latter category, some of my examples included inside/outsiders, writers who had had English thrust upon them in one way or another: Morrison, Coetzee, Harris. It is not by chance that the themes in their writings should be of this species of translation as well, translation in the general sense, accession to the owner's mark, transplanting the mother tongue, as the heart is transplanted (or a hybrid strain produced). In this chapter I look at two exhibitions of visual art where this theme is respectively foregrounded and foreclosed. The first, Jamelie Hassan's *Inscription*. The second, the comparatively more opulent *Magicians of the Earth* at the Pompidou Center in Paris.

In the Dunlop Art Gallery in the Regina Public Library in Regina, Saskatchewan, where I look at Jamelie Hassan's *Inscription,* I stop at *Inscription,* the title piece, before I enter the gallery space. The entire exhibit is an act of solidarity with Pakistani-British writer Salman Rushdie, whose novel *The Satanic Verses* provided an excuse for the late Ayatollah Khomeini to issue a death sentence against the author in the name of Islam. In the title piece, Hassan inserts Rushdie into the company of other censored writers from the Arab world. Their names are block-printed on the door of the glass case. Covers of their books, imaginatively reproduced by Hassan, are on display. And on the base are bright brass bowls, made by Egyptian artisan Aly Aly Hassan. In the bottom of the bowls are pools of India ink, replenished every day. Under the ink, in some of the bowls, is the proper name of the censored author. In others, merely an Islamic motif. The ink dries in different patterns every day, covering (something that might be) the proper name of the author. I read this simply: it is a miming of the trace left by the laws of nature in the ink of writing by which the author covers over her proper name. For writing is that which makes sense in the absence of the writer. That is why writing is censored. It is too powerful.

I walk in to *Meeting Nasser*, a video installation.[1] I work this out like a puzzle that mimes the ways in which our "truth"s are woven together.

Jamelie Hassan, whose parents came to Canada in 1914 and 1932 from Lebanon, grew up in an Arabic-speaking household. Yet she is not merely nostalgic about the place of origin. She sees it as a place in the history of the present, not just in the history of her own displaced migration. This installation is a text-ing (a weaving as in text-ile) of that seeing. Hassan "sees" the place of Gamal Abdel Nasser (1918–1970), the "Liberator" of Egypt, through the writing of one of the censored writers named in *Inscription*: Naguib Mahfouz, censored precisely by Nasser:

> We live in the age of unknown forces, invisible spies and day ghosts. I keep releasing images from my imagination and memory. My information about contemporary brutality remained based on the imagination until many years later the locked hearts were opened to me, explaining the mysterious events I failed to understand while they were taking place (adapted from *Al-Karnak*).

This is a text about the restitutions of truth to history through rememoration. Because Hassan recognizes the place of origin as a place other than simply an endorsement for herself as cross-cultural Canadian "other," she can respect the immigrant as agent of historical rememoration. The photographs lining the walls in this installation were found in the family album.

Who is the little girl presenting the bouquet to Nasser in the blown-up photo in the wall, overshadowed by grinning men? Is it Jamelie Hassan, herself younger? We cannot know. Nor can she. All we have is another blown-up snapshot on the wall, of herself full face, without Nasser. With Nasser, the little girl's back is turned to the camera.

A simple sign—nothing as heavy as a metaphor or a symbol—of the recovery of identity in politics. You can't have a true fit, just the approximate size, a hand-me-down to others who must stage the same collective origin as yourself.

Experience is a staging of experience. One can only offer scrupulous and plausible accounts of the mechanics of staging. . . . One of the most tenacious names as well as strongest accounts of the agency or mechanics of staging is "origin." I perform my life this way because my origin stages me so: national origin, ethnic origin. And, more pernicious, you cannot help acting this way because your origin stages you so. The notion of origin is as broad and robust and full of affect as it is imprecise. History lurks in it somewhere. To feel one is from an origin is not a pathology. It belongs to the group of grounding "mistakes" that enables us to make sense of our lives. But the only way to argue for origins is to look for institutions, inscriptions; and then to surmise the mechanics by which such institutions and inscriptions can stage such a particular style of performance.

The video monitor mimes the scene (or stage) of the writing of history. This girl, dressed quite like the girl in the photo, faces us. She is Elizabeth Hassan, Jamelie's niece. The photo of meeting Nasser is behind her on the small screen, as well as blown up on the wall of the gallery. Again and again, this agent of rememorating history turns her back and "enters" the picture in the picture, though the superimposition is never adequate. Again and again, she moves forward and reads the lines. The (ethnic) Canadian—who is the nonethnic Canadian?—has her face turned back and front. She must understand the place of origin as politically present without her. She must also speak that politics to the metropolis in the words censored in that other space, but translated into the metropolitan language. The child reads an adaptation into English.

The child as agent of reading a history written elsewhere, *for* this space, prompted by the artist's audible whispers for the big words "imagination," "event," "mysterious." This is a much more complex and overdetermined scenario than claiming otherness. But the agent of history has her own lesson to teach. It is a lesson about learning, learning "the practice of freedom" after the "act of liberation."[2] Little Elizabeth Hassan tells her artist-foremother confidently why she still needs prompting. She can still only read big letters—in English, of course. She has stepped off the staged origin. She is a Canadian, the agent of new Canadian history.

If I should dwell on this apparently minor moment, about the size of letters, in this exhibit about the written word, entitled *Inscription,* my catalogue essay would become interminable. To catalogue is to inscribe an account or a legend—*legein*—that is a downward movement—*kata*— from the being-there-in-the-gallery of the exhibit. A downward movement—as in "scrolling down" on my computer screen as I inscribe my essay in my temporary dwelling place across from the temporary home of *Inscription,* the hotel across the park from the gallery in the library. The child as reader of writing speaks again and again of the *size* of letters on the electronic stage—a simulacrum of the opening up of history. (It is interesting that she might be making a "mistake," she might be meaning the "size" of words. Just such a mistake is Hassan's patronymic, her father's first name transposed by the immigration agents seventy-five years ago. The comradeship with the Egyptian artisan of the brass bowls— Aly Aly Hassan—is fake but real.)

This measure of the unit of learning, the size of letters, may be the place of the *technē* or (art) of art and history. The child's repetitiveness in the work of art "makes the expert speak, and he will not take long to say": the work represents the text-ing of history.[3] If we believe we can restore the (personal, political, historical, cross-cultural) "truth" of art, we are silenced by the child/apprentice-in-art who reminds us that one learns inscription letter by letter. Therefore one must think of restitution not of truth in art (or *peinture*) but of size (*pointure*). "[Restitutions: Of Truth to Size]. . . . 'Number of stitches [the size] in a shoe or glove' (—Littré). . . . 'But truth is so dear to me, *and so is the* seek*ing to make true,* that indeed I would still rather be a cobbler than a musician with colors' (—Van Gogh)."[4] Restitutions: Of Truth to Size of Letters. How different to learn the agency of reading the borrowed script of history from talking about learning.

> One is not only disappointed when . . . academic high seriousness, . . . [the] severity and rigor of tone give way to this "illustration." . . . One is not only disappointed by the consumerlike hurry toward the content of a representation, by the heaviness of the pathos, by the coded triviality of this description . . . and one never knows if it's busying itself around a [video], [a] "real" [child], or [children] that are imaginary but outside [the artwork]. . . . One is not only disappointed, one sniggers.

The limits of theory, the limits of representation, restitutions of truth to size. The rest of this misleading downward scroll, this *cata-legein,* this essay (or attempt) at a catalogue, must proceed under the sign of that snigger.

I saw a child sit in front of the video monitor, and rise. Was this the child who had written in the visitors' book, "For a child this is confusing"? If so, Jamelie has anticipated her. Part of Jamelie Hassan's diverse cultural activities is to place "art" in the living areas of the Embassy, a working-class hotel in London, Ontario. "When people sleep with art," she says, "some respond to it, some write or make their mark on it, some take it away, some turn away, some do nothing. Last week a fight between

N'Amerindians and taxi-drivers bloodied the carved tree we had placed in the bar."

How fragile these fragments. Like the shards, the ceramic kerchiefs with the "real" names of the "disappeared," Hassan's representation of the kerchiefs of the mothers who held vigil in the Plaza de Mayo in Buenos Aires. Yet with such fragments is the substance of history mantled and dismantled in a series of everydays. Political art that respects this history, forever the present ruin of a past pushing into an intact utopia, changes minds as drops of water groove stone. Hassan has anticipated this. No quick fixes here.

From *Meeting Nasser* I step back to "Is This Pornography?" This is the first installation of "Trilogy," focusing on Rushdie's three novels: *Shame* (1983), *Midnight's Children* (1981), and *The Satanic Verses* (1989).

"Is This Pornography?" begins with a dial phone and an answering machine, and a little clay figure in a nest of shredded paper. Four messages on the answering machine, in "real" time, play on, over and over, easily drowned when people speak. A bland Anglo voice promises to return Hassan's art work, thus serving, for the artist, the purpose of pointing incidentally and without fuss at the working of the institution that is the condition of possibility for an exhibition for a practicing artist. Then the artist *as* artist, away from home, leaves a reassuring message for her son. In between are two grotesque "real" obscene phone calls that Hassan has defused by citing them as "art." (Although this particular installation relates to *Shame,* in my viewing it undoes perhaps the weakest part in the *denouement* of *The Satanic Verses,* the destruction of Farishta and Alleluia through anonymous telephone messages.)

"Is This Pornography?" is blazoned in large golden letters on the gallery wall. The question was asked in 1987, by one customs agent in Brownsville, TX of another, about a pre-Columbian Mexican figurine that Hassan was bringing in from Mexico. Hassan was suspect because she was perhaps born in "Arabia," although she assured the good men that she was Canadian.

(Among the many rave comments in the visitors' book, three or four citizens of Regina decide to answer for the customs agent's colleague: "Yes, this is pornography." Drops of water on stone . . .)

In a flash of genius the artist places by the side of this recorded exchange a virulently misogynist passage from the celebrated twelfth-century Arabic romance of *Layla wa Majnun.* No "cross-cultural" us-and-them-ing here. In the middle is an enlarged photograph of the stylized, naked, haughty figurine. Standing against the wall are two huge bold-stroke water-color and gold-acrylic representations of these figurines, one young, one old, on slightly buckling cardboard. The tackiness of the material gives a special pleasure to this postcolonial viewer. Much of global cosmopolitan public culture is a mix of hi-tech, hi-tack, trad, and post-mod. The card-board fits right in with the tiny figurine on the telephone table, nestling in its tacky nest of shredded paper in a cardboard box. It makes sense that the packing paper should be printed mostly in an East Asian script. In transnational global economy the Asia-Pacific is plausible in Mexico. I must confess I am more excited by all this than the textual connection of the 3+1 ladies with the three sisters in *Shame*.

The next station—*Midnight's Children*—has powerfully wrenched the title of Rushdie's novel from its context. I applaud Hassan's feeling for "becoming involved and taking a stand on issues that may not necessarily affect you directly,"[5] especially in the face of the fierce turf-battles in radical cultural studies, where the only possible politics seems sometimes to be the politics of identity in the name of being the "other." But this is my own turf! This puts my own identity in parenthesis! I was awake as a child upon that midnight, between the 14th and 15th of August, 1947, when an India divided into India and Pakistan became independent. Hassan makes me learn the ropes. She has unmoored the date away from Rushdie's India and Pakistan and given it over to the children of Egypt, who seem, to most spectators in Canada, to be the children of Palestine. And I say, it's all right.

On the wall, flanked by the photographs of children, is a large brass plate by Aly Aly Hassan inscribed "Midnight's Children" in English and Arabic, with "Salman" in Arabic in the center. The final sentence of *Midnight's Children,* written in a spiral on the wall, now speaks the fate of the dispossessed children who lost a country in 1948, although neither photograph nor novel represents them.

Part of this installation is a sizable brass table with wooden legs, focused on the theme of fortune-telling, reading the thick coffee grounds in the bottom of an Arab coffee-cup. These inscriptions, like the random tracings in ink, haunt Jamelie Hassan. After *Meeting Nasser,* I find it easy to understand that the traces of the future at the bottom of these cups are the photographs of children, her own son among them, fired into the porcelain. In between are those little ceramic open-books that you find in hobby-shops, with photos of the flames consuming *The Satanic Verses*.

Move now to *The Satanic Verses,* the "final" installation inside the room. No reconstellation here, no tracking of the random trace, no sign-language. This installation refers to "what really happened," a robust use of "truthspeak."[6] These are newspaper crowd-shots of book-burning Bradford Muslims. The censors and pornographers and children and writers of the other installations enrich from a distance this scene that "is rich by reason of the poverty of its objective context."[7] The great ladies of *Shame* and the little girl in *Nasser* make the point that there are no women here. Not overdetermination but only superimposition is the form. Some of the newspaper photographs are blown up and stuck on pictures of the awful modernist fountain in the Bradford public square where the book was burned at the stake. What sign can you make when the sign is turned into a thing for the flames? I look at the bewildered faces of the male children, the fanatic faces of the igniters, the dull faces of the media men and ask: Do they read? In the name of that most philosophical religion whose opening injunction is "read"? The death of a human being is to bring the possibility of narrative to an end.

It seems right that the relationship between wall and floor here is stark, not subtle. Cut from banal public fountain to soft-stone much-mended junk-antique cake-tier found-fountain on sturdy well-made octagonal three-legged wood table made by the artist's son. All those books burned on the walls have floated to the foot of this fountain—a great pile of ragged *Satanic Verses,* some in plain brown wrappers, easy reference to booksellers' cowardice. A bullet-case wrapped in script . . .

If you look for it, there is a heavily coded bit of history-book history in one corner of these photographs that will lead you right out of the gallery into the last installation of the show. It is the late nineteenth-century campanile of one of Bradford's public buildings, clumsy imitation of the soaring masonry of the Italian Renaissance, pointing back, in Venice and Urbino, to the so-called Moorish centuries before the fall of Constantinople. How brilliant, then, to make us move to "the real thing" on video-tape, the tenth-century minaret of the Al-Ahzar mosque in Cairo, in "the present" of the Islamic world, to bring that call to prayer into the library in the Canadian prairies.

This is the last installation, "You're Gonna Blow It, Mom!" which is what Jamelie Hassan's seventeen-year-old son Tariq says when she decides to reveal to Aly Aly Hassan what he is really making his brass stuff for. Hassan keeps the text of the conversation printed in front of the video monitor, separate from the four-and-a-half-minute soundtrack of Muslims at prayer, played every half-hour. Unlike the frozen-faced migrant Muslims of Bradford, these men, photographed from above, move in a certain flow. The static affective subculture of the migrants, when it fetishizes the origin, is kept separate from the dynamic fluidity of the place of the origin "in the present." The Bradford Muslims have not graduated into the truth of size. Hassan mimes the "sovereignty" of Islam in Egypt, by translating the dialogue on paper.

In her halting Arabic, Jamelie puts Aly Aly on the spot, makes him admit that he personally would not kill Rushdie if he were standing in his shop. And she locates Aly in the praying crowd. Simple gestures: to intervene in the Arab artisan's "practice of freedom," to humanize the Muslim crowd for her own Canadian audience.

Of course it doesn't always work. The first evening at closing time, standing in front of the final piece, I overhear a young staff person say, "I love writing—committing to paper—it really takes my stress off." "Ah Inscription! You are at home in this public library," think I. But the last day, leaving in the afternoon, with the Sunday crowd coming and going, I heard the (same?) staff woman speak across to the checkout lady, "That thing is sure loud today!"

I thought then of Sartre's example of an *acte gratuit*—shouting in the library. Jamelie Hassan's "noise(s) in the Library" is not just an existentialist's free act. It is the clamor of her responsibility, to the trace of the historical other, in her self, an agent of history. She breaks the peace of the complacent identity of British Canada by noisily breaking apart the imaginary institution of "cross-cultural alterity."

What follows is a briefer response, to a much grander show. The first part of this chapter is a catalogue essay. The catalogue for *Magiciens de la terre* is a hefty affair. It was waiting for us, a panel of critics invited to participate in a private miniconference which would inaugurate the exhibition. I was allowed, in other words, much more attention before uttering on *Inscription* than on *Magiciens,* and that is reflected in the length and thickness of specific reference in the two halves of the essay. And, since I have long held that trying to disclose the frame is tangling with cultural politics—"telling tales out of school," to extend Mieke Bal's powerful metaphor in "Showing, Telling, Showing Off"—I have made no attempt to flesh out the commentary by referring later to the reproductions in the catalogue.

As in the case of Chapter Five, there was also here a sense of daring, to critique an *art* exhibition *in Paris,* questioning authority with no authoritative preparation—I am not an art critic—as well of breaking decorum as an invited guest—an awful sense of being "ill-" or "under-bred"—words that normally do not cross my consciousness—which gives rise both to self-contempt at feeling it as well as fierce loyalty to my principled parents, not to mention the shallowness of being merely "well-bred"—an imperialist notion if ever there was one—in the former colonies—a dizzying spiral only too susceptible to postcolonial pop-psych, but laid aside. Let me, however, note the result: a desire to hide behind Hegel. These are the only pages in this book where disclosure is also veiled. I hope the reader will be able to share my embarrassment, read the symptom of the very predicament I analyze, that a "raised consciousness" would hasten to delete after the fact.

I have said in the opening that *Inscription* foregrounds the migrant's transplanted heart and the makers of *Magiciens* foreclose it.

I am overwhelmed by the visual impact of this exhibition. It seems too soon to speak. I must also say at the outset that I do not know how to make plastic art "mean."

I am not unacquainted with our desire for *signifiance*, and these last two days, I have been compelled to acknowledge its presence in us. About these objects, we seem to have to repeat what they *are*, what they *mean*, or at least what they *indicate*. We seem to have to show them incorporated into various sign-systems, or incorporate them, even if into a political meta-semiotic. We seem to have to read them between what we imagine to be the curator's desire for the artist's desire and ours, or at least, to quote Rasheed Araeen's phrase, "in the crossroads of history."[8]

Yet, as I have walked through these silent or near-silent objects, I have felt more and more that there is no innocent gaze, that the space of a museum is a space which assigns *us*, makes *us* visible, for we are necessarily unable to work with the structural possibility that every signification ascribed here is parasitical, beside itself.

It is under the sign of that para-sitical near-silence that I speak, first, of Hegel.

We have heard a good deal about Hegel's prediction of the death of art. Most of us here know that that death, indeed *Aufhebung* or sublation, is not just the denouement of a story-line. It is also shorthand for a moment in a morphology. Let us remind ourselves of it: The *Lectures on the Aesthetic* offers us an epistemograph of the Mind, separated from its Knowledge, slowly closing the gap. Different varieties of art are the by-product of the Mind's separation from Knowledge. When the gap closes, art will no longer happen. In Absolute Knowledge there is no art.[9]

It is also well-known that there is a misfit between morphology and narrative in Hegel. Absolute Knowledge at the end, like Absolute Necessity at the beginning, cannot find narrative instantiation. What you find is manifestos announcing the death of art, works of art that can respond to the desire for *signifiance* by seeming to represent the imminence of death, death-as-absence, the unease of not-quite-not-death, programmed artificial intelligence in an empty room. Let us name as such Tatsuo Miyajima's *The Counter Room,* Louise Bourgeois's *Articulated Lair,* Marc Couturier's *Fin, ver, or,* Enzo Cucchi's black painting with a light bulb, and others, no doubt. Thus does the philosopher sometimes offer a system of self-representation that secures a cultural moment, Japan in the group of seven, hooking on its traditional cultural traffic with silence and indirect representation to this register.

But there is something else that "happens" with the extinction of Art in Absolute Knowledge. Theology sublates into philosophy, or by another philosopher's version, religion proves to be a *pre*figuration of the moral law or the ethical imperative. Michel de Certeau has written brilliantly on the social substitution of ethics for religion, especially in France, in the seventeenth and eighteenth centuries (See Chapter Eleven). This access to the secular ethical imperative was very largely used as the ideology of imperialism. This too is the subtext of the surreptitious narrativization of Absolute Knowledge: the relegation of "other" arts to religion. In Hegel that would be a "normative deviation" fixed for the folks who are mere stages on the Mind's journey. Those who think to supersede Hegel re-write this normative deviation as a *special* grace. Yet the two positions legitimize each other. For example, because we the Europeans are secular ethical subjects, it would be extremely dubious and perhaps illegal for us to say this exhibition is the Temple of the Living Christ. We can let it be the temple of other religions for a season, because we know that those spirits are tamed. Thus does the philosopher sometimes offer a system of the representation of the other that secures a cultural moment. We have not moved far from Hegel.

Perhaps it is true that the visual arts in the West have not been globalized in the same way as literature or music. Our exhibition, then, marks the desire for a rupture. This is reflected in the beautiful title: *Magiciens de la terre.* But every rupture is also a repetition. I think we must acknowledge this if we focus, not only on the word *magiciens,* but also on the word *terre.* Our desire for a rupture with previous practice lives in the separation between the two expressions *artistes du monde* and *magiciens de la terre.* Heidegger long ago in "The *Origin of the Work of Art*" claimed that a work of art worlded a world on uninscribed earth, wrote a *monde* on a virgin *terre.*[10] (Please note the play of gender here. I will come back to it.) Three things can be said about this:

First. The actual practical presupposition, all theoretical work to the contrary, that the new world is a *terre* rather than a *monde* belongs to the previous practice that we so desperately want to annul.

Second. That the single work of art worlds a world on an uninscribed earth may be valid as a morphological assumption. But, if we assume this to be an empirical narrative, we are in trouble, as Peter Bürger reminded Jürgen Habermas in quite another context, for art has already been separated from the *Lebenswelt*, and not only in the West. We cannot wish it otherwise by fiat. Not even by the choice of so-called traditional art as metonymic of the entire nation. We have to remember that the geo is already graphed. There *is* geography. Every desire for a wholly new re-inscription of the *terre* can only ever be a palimpsest.

Third. This is staged for us in Alfredo Jaar's *La géographie sert, d'abord, à faire la guerre.* This is the affirmative deconstruction of a postcolonial global cartography, not of a parahistoric uncharted earth or *terre.* The returned glance of the other is not of the Africa—a Roman proper name inscribed on a bit of earth long ago—not of the African of magic, but of the naked and benignly ironic African child, grave with the wisdom of the brutality of modern geography learned in its blood. I was assured that the photographs were not posed.

In our letter of invitation, we were asked to ponder our general topic from our own point of view. *Identité, alterité, métissage: centre et périphérie.* The subtitle comes from the very dependency theory that, once again, the curators want not so much to annul but to reverse. I sympathize with this wish, as it is reflected in the world projected in the upper right-hand corner of each page of the catalogue, with the center marked in the artist's country of origin. I cannot of course credit or honor the centrality of the creative spirit, individual or collective, as anything but a necessary survival technique, most spectacularly seen today perhaps in political mobilization or the kind of Atlantic appropriation that Mr. Robert Farris Thompson has described. If I had the time I would develop this notion a bit further by way of that old term—species-Being, *Gattungswesen.* But let us turn now to the main title: *Identité, alterité, méttissage.* I have to continue to be cryptic here.

I. Identity: Names like "Asian" or "Africa" or "Madhuban" or "Nago" or "Zavrugo" or "Warputali" are not anchored in identities. They are incessant fields of recoding that secure identities. The immediate *need* for identitarian collectivities must *not* take on truth-value by the monumentalizing solemnity of our exhibition, which takes the identity of a fantasmatic "West" for granted. Some of the best efforts in the metropolis today is to make the "West" see that its "identity"—the proper word against "alterity" is, of course, "ipseity"—to make the "West" see that its "ipseity" is phantasmatic. I am referring to such revised proper names as "black Britain" or the "rainbow coalition" in the United States. As Jean-Hubert Martin, the curator, has reminded us, all "identities" are fields of recoding, *in their different ways*.

II. The English language has recently received the word "alterity" from French, in the human sciences perhaps through discussions of the work of Emmanuel Levinas. This is not always recognized. So much so, that Johannes Fabian, an anthropoligist, wrote a book called *Time and the Other, Le Temps et l'Autre,* the same title as Levinas's, nearly forty years later, *without being aware of it.*[11] One of Fabian's arguments is that anthropology posits distance in space as distance in time, and this hides an agenda. This line of thought has already been pursued in our discussions. Let me step back and consider one of Levinas's warnings: the wholly other, *le tout-autre,* cannot be selved or samed. It is not susceptible to *ipseité* or *mêmeté.* The face of the wholly-other is without a name. The "other" that we narrativize or grasp consolidates the self, through a kind of *stade du miroir.* Thus, before a fundamental ontology, or a transcendental phenomenology, there must be an ethic of ethics. This too is an impossible requirement. It cannot be fulfilled, for example, by wondering what were, and I quote the press-release of January 1989, what were "the work[s] which completely escape[d] our aesthetic categories and criteria," or "works . . . which we cannot 'see.' " This requirement for an ethic of the ethics of the *tout-autre* can also *not* be fulfilled by thinking "of all those places—cultural, linguistic, political, etc.—where the organization of [an international exhibition] simply would have no meaning, where it would be no more meaningful to investigate it than to prohibit it" (*EM,* 112–113).

Let us turn from such impossible warnings to something more humdrum. Let us consider how the identity-alterity couple is being reversed in the so-called "new" nations in decolonized space as it happens. In India, Algeria, or yet Ireland today, from Ministry of Culture through fundamentalism, down to a certain underclass, varieties of talk of national or religious identity are always to hand. One pathetically neutral position, favored as condition and possibility of "reasons," is to see the former colonizer as no more than an "other" on terms of equality. The only representative of such a position among the speakers is Jyotindra Jain, who is from the country of my own citizenship. In his innocent and confident defense of the curators we saw a mark of that seeming reversal. In Algiers, in May 1992, I heard Benjamin Storra make the remark that French pain over Algeria was simply the obverse of Algerian suffering, and over a hundred Algerian intellectuals let that one go by. In Ireland, later that same month, I heard that one of the problems with mentioning "colonialism" in the Humanities was the embarrassment of the bourgeoisie. As far as I can see, this reversal is being operated on two fronts, one recoding the other. Remember, I am generalizing, mis-representation is inevitable.

On two fronts, then: political and cultural. For the political claims, I turn back to Chapter Four: Politically, whatever our identitarian ethnicist claims of nativist or fundamentalist origin, the political claims that are most urgent in decolonized space are tacitly recognized to belong to the old culture of imperialism: at least the European post-Enlightenment. Nationhood, citizenship, democracy, socialism, secularism, even culturalism. Within the historical frame of restoration—colonization/*de*colonization—what is effectively reclaimed is a series of regulative political concepts the authoritative narrative of whose production was written elsewhere, in the metropolis. They are being reclaimed as catachreses: concept-metaphors for which no historically adequate referential may be advanced, and yet their seriousness cannot be ignored.

This deep traffic with rational abstraction is incessantly recoded and reterritorialized by a highly sophisticated form of nativism, securing a national identity, quite different from the static ethnographer's community, where every "individual" emerging out of repetition is to be elaborately congratulated. In terms of available systems of cultural representation, Europe or the West is being "othered" within the same discursive formation. It is Europe that occupies the space of alterity here. (It would be different to speak of the United States in this context, and I will not do so. Afro-America is neither new nation nor *méteque*. As I have already remarked, the extraordinary cultural exchange between Africa and Afro-America, to be matched in energy if not in scope only by the exchange between Palestine and Arab-America, is a different phenomenon.) The phenomenon of reversal I am describing here is by no means unknown by political-cultural activists of those nations—in Asia, the Maghreb, and sub-Saharan Africa. It is especially hotly debated in Africa, North, Central, Southern.

I have always been interested in the space that is not covered by this vivacious dynamic of politics and "culture," political culture, cultural politics, culture for politics, and so on. This is the area of subalternity.

This space is not "uncontaminated" by the West, and certainly not "apart" by collective social choice. Although cultural or political institutions, by definition, do not give them any support for them to be constituted as social agency of judgment, for my own work, I have come to presuppose them as the arena of judgment, or testing; precisely of the reversal operated by politics or culturalism or reconstellation in museums. The giving of the name "woman" to the other woman (Chapters Six and Seven), as well as my discussions of Mahasweta and Foucault, share this presupposition. To this space the logic of parliamentary democracy or the logic of socialist planning or yet the logic of cultural identity is, as I think Mahasweta's fiction shows, counterintuitive. This is the space where the organization or prohibition of an exhibition is meaningless. Therefore I will say no more than that it is for us a space of anxiety. It is also a space of a genuine aporia of history. Both culturalism and the politics of the nation-state will transform this ambiguous place. And today there is a clandestine seepage from here into superexploitation where resistance to hybridity is the only affect to be found. Ganga Devi, the Madhubani painter celebrated by Jyotindra Jain, no longer lives in this space, but must continue to represent it. I thought of the colossal battered wooden figure of Bhima, once-bright paint faded and chipped, "authentic" but neglected-in-use, around the bend of a track in the village of Manasri in southern West Bengal, where the women complained that the "Government" required Rs.400 (under $15 with the most recent IMF devalorization) for a birth-certificate (someone was pocketing the money, there is no such law in the books), and without a certificate there was no hope for primary education for their children, and there were no teachers at the local primary school anyway, and the village-level social workers, themselves poorly educated, devoted some of their heavily burdened energies on agitating for teachers rather than doing ad hoc literacy and numeracy, and if there were teachers, more boys than girls go and/or continue.[12] ... What magician of the earth had fashioned that Bhima? A fruitless line of thought.

III. *Métissage.* Beginning from the migrant subproletariat here we can go all the way to the postcolonial artist intellectual academic. In different ways, this whole group is an embarrassment to both Eurocentric or nationcentric visions of identity and alterity. Yes *we* are the children of the enabling violation of imperialism. We should not be defined as having "been to school" in the West and thus disqualified everywhere. We should be *used,* and here I go back to an earlier point. We should be *used* to explain or make visible the ethicopolitical agenda in your tendency to conserve a center that you can then cede, only in a certain way. Certain artists in the exhibition speak this loud and clear. John Knight putting the uranium symbol in a Navajo sand-painting. Jean-Michel Alberola with his *porte bouteille.* Rasheed Araeen has expressed this forcefully as a denial of access to modernity. One look at Jeff Wall's Tran Duc Ran will suffice. This is a perspective that has been ably elaborated by Homi Bhabha. I want therefore to talk just a little bit about womanspace. I am using the word for that site which, in every group, dominant or subordinate, is presupposed as inhabited by secondary human beings as defined by primary and secondary biological sexual characteristics. These human beings give crucial support for the operation of the group's narrative without being primary agents in it. Representations of the female body can either figure or contest this siting, this territorialization.

The *terre* or the terrain of the exhibition, as Homi Bhabha has pointed out, is quite effectively graphed. And, if I may make a gentle critique, I do not think that this careful deployment of space attends to the aesthetics of sexual difference.

This is not a special pleading for a special interest. For some years now, that part of the Women's Movement that is not taken in by simple declarations of global sisterhood, has been mobilizing around the question of the problematics of the *ethics* of sexual difference. Problematic because an ethical position entails a universal presupposition, that must at the same time inhabit empirical singularity. Is there such a common ground inscribed by sexual difference? From any exhibition tacitly celebrating the move from *le monde* to *la terre,* an attempt at graphing an aesthetics of sexual difference, *as offered* by the constellation of objects, can, I think, be expected.

As it is, woman remains, as usual, in the pores of the exhibition. Both Professor Thomson and Homi Bhabha have pointed at some of these porous presences. I am thinking also of the extraordinary fecundity-figures of Seni Camara from Senegal. In the few words she's quoted as saying, there is a witting or unwitting reappropriation of the subjectship of ethics: "I reflect," she apparently said, "I have an inspiration, I work." On the other side, there is the violent misogyny of the male schizostate of Zevrugo, where the anti-Oedipus is, again, not constellated by spatial organization. You have the play of gendering and postcoloniality in Cheri Samba'a *Marche sur le S.I.D.A.* And even the unacknowledged and eerie phallo-uterine mechanicity of Rebecca Horn's *Kiss of the Rhinoceros.* The woman viewer is obliged to put in there, somewhere, Sherazi Houshiary's *Fire and Water.*

I want to end by invoking again the overwhelming pleasure of seeing so much. I have found an image of our efforts at drawing lines of reasonableness out of all this heaping in my exchange with the Cult '89 videocar. The first evening, jet-lagged, I was full up with art, or if you prefer, magic. I kept waiting for James Coburn to reappear, wondering what movie, what sequence. A humble paradigm of the need for informational coherence, call it reason or mysticism, your choice. Another image, another message: those postcards by Frédéric Brouly Bouabré. Two on racial difference. One shows a human being and a termite. Another a European and an African.[13]

If there is a universal principle it is in the incessant renegotiation of difference. Such a principle is an impossible starting point for anything. It is better to keep working away at the impossible, than to make things seem possible by way of polarizations.

I end, therefore, in spite of everything, with congratulations and thanks to the organizers. It is, for better or for worse, the moment for a step such as this exhibition, in this place. It is better to take it than not to. Many of us hope that you will remember that first steps must often be taken again. We have offered you our participatory and persistent critique, the best sign of interest, in the hope of a new next time.

11

Reading *The Satanic Verses*

In postcoloniality, every metropolitan definition is dislodged. The general mode for the postcolonial is citation, reinscription, rerouting the historical. *The Satanic Verses*[1] cannot be placed within the European avant-garde, but the successes and failures of the European avant-garde are available to it.

Peter Bürger pointed out to Jürgen Habermas some time ago that all deliberate attempts at integrating the aesthetic sphere with the *Lebenswelt* must take into account their profound and continued separation.[2] Metropolitan curators must contend with this when they imagine the periphery as seamlessly integrated. But, in postcoloniality, all metropolitan accounts are set askew. The case of the *The Satanic Verses* is a case of the global *Lebenswelt*—the praxis and politics of life—intercepting an aesthetic object so that a mere reading of it has become impossible.

The case of Mr. Fukuyama—fully "assimilated" Asian-American, who, put off as a graduate student by the nihilism of Derrida and Barthes, wrote an article on Hegel's End of History as USA Today, bored but in charge, indolently defending freedom of expression against terrorism—is not outside of this contemporary fact of life. The United States is not outside the postcolonial globe.[3]

Here is a metropolitan aphorism: "The birth of the reader must be at the cost of the death of the Author."[4] Faced with the case of Salman Rushdie, how are we to read this sentence? I have often said, and said again in Chapter Two, that the (tragic) theater of the (sometimes farcically self-indulgent) script of poststructuralism is "the other side." The aphorism above is a case in point. Let us read slowly, word for word.

Barthes is writing here not of the death of the writer (although he *is* writing, quite copiously, of writing) or of the subject, or yet of the agent, but of the *author*. The author, who is not only taken to be the authority for the meaning of a text, but also, when possessed of authority, possessed *by that fact* of "moral or legal supremacy, the power to influence the conduct or action of others;" and, when authorizing, "giving legal force to, making legally valid" (*OED*). Thus, even on the most "literal" level of the dictionary, "the birth of the reader must be at the cost of the death of the Author" takes on a different resonance.

Barthes is speaking of the birth not of the critic, who, apart from the academically certified authority of the meaning of a text is, also, in the strictest sense, a judge. It is not of such a being that Barthes announces the birth. He announces the birth of the reader who "is simply that *someone* who holds together in a single field all the traces by which the written text is constituted." It is the birth of this someone that is conditional upon the death of the author. The writer is, in this robust sense, a reader at the performance of writing. Or, as Barthes writes, "*writing* can no longer designate an operation of recording . . . , rather, it designates exactly what linguists, referring to Oxford philosophy, call a performative . . . in which the enunciation has no other content . . . than the act by which it is uttered."[5] When Barthes writes, further, that "the reader is without history, biography, psychology," I believe he means there is no specific set of history, biography, psychology, belonging to the writer-as-privileged-reader or the ideal reader implied in the text, that gives us the reader as such. When the writer and reader are born again and again together, the author(ity)-function is dead, the critic is not mentioned. There is the pleasure of the text.

In the next decade and a half, Roland Barthes will tone down the binaries that seem entailed by these pronouncements. But the words "the Death of the author" have become a slogan, both proving and disproving the authority of the author. And Foucault's question "What is an Author?" has been construed by most readers as a rhetorical question to be answered in the negative.[6] I reckon with these signs of the times by turning, as usual, toward Derrida.

Derrida usually comes at these things from the other end. He is not an overthrower of myths but rather is interested in seeing how a myth works both as medicine and poison. For him the author is present in excess. I have not yet read *The Critical Difference,* but I believe I will agree with Barbara Johnson's distinction between Barthes the anti-constructionist and Derrida's *de*-construction.[7]

Moving with Derrida, I can say, that when Barthes and Foucault are monumentalized as marks for the death and nothingness of the author, everything happens as if the sign "Author" has no history, no linguistic or cultural limits. I turn back to the dictionary, where I began, and I see that, in the Rushdie affair, it is the late Ayatollah who can be seen as filling the author-function, and Salman Rushdie, himself, caught in a different cultural logic, is no more than the writer-as-performer. I will say more about this in the body of my paper. Let me now turn to another aspect of the excessive presence of the author in Derrida's reading habits: what he calls "the politics of the proper name."[8]

In order to read the politics of the proper name, Derrida pays close attention to the staging of the author *as* author by the author. "We would," he writes, "be mistaken if we understood it as a simple presentation of identity. (Me, such and such, male or female, individual or collective subject.)"[9] I believe the author of *The Satanic Verses* is "staged" rather than "simply presented" in the vestigial rememoration of a face and a proper name in the poem published in *Granta* last autumn.[10] Because the author-function dies hard, that poem is *hors de reproduction,* but also, and strictly speaking, an artwork, an *hors d'oeuvre,* an exergue or a flysheet, whose topos, like (its) temporality, strangely dislocates what we, without tranquil assurance, would like to understand as the time of life and the time of life's *récit,* or the writing of life by the living.[11]

As I will go on to propose, *in* the novel, Rushdie's staging of the author is more recognizably "modernist" (not what Barthes, or indeed French critics as a rule would call "modern"), not decentered but fragmented by dramatic irony, the question of authorship repeatedly and visibly suspended by foregrounding. But the violence of the *fatwa* continuing the signature after its author's death, has jolted modernist playfulness into a Nietzschean *Ecce Homo* in Rushdie's irreproducible poem.

In the first part of my paper, I will attempt the impossible: a reading of *The Satanic Verses* as if nothing has happened since late 1988. The second part will try to distinguish the cultural politics of what has happened, by assembling a dossier of responses from various subject-positions in contemporary political geography. In the third part, I will try to make parts I and II come together in the element of an intellectual history. And perhaps this will allow me a conclusion.

I

First, then, the reading:

The Satanic Verses, in spite of all its plurality, has rather an aggressive central theme: the postcolonial divided between two identities: migrant and national.

As migrant, the postcolonial may attempt to become the metropolitan: this is Saladin Chamcha (ass-kisser) in his first British phase: "I am a man to whom certain things are of importance: rigour, self-discipline, reason, the pursuit of what is noble without recourse to that old crutch, God.

The ideal of beauty, the possibility of exaltation, the mind" (*SV*, 135–136). This self-definition of the migrant *as* metropolitan is obviously not the book's preferred definition.

The postcolonial way, also, to keep himself completely separated *from* the metropolis *in* the metropolis as the fanatic exile. This is represented in the least conclusive section of the book, the place of dark foreboding, the subcontinental Imam ("desh" is a north Indian word which signifies his country), who must destroy the woman touched by the West. This is also not preferred: "Exile is a soulless country" (*SV*, 208).

What we see in process in the greater part of *The Satanic Verses* is the many fragmented national representations coming together in serious and comic—serious *when* comic and vice versa—figures of resistance. In the hospital, a highly paid male model based in Bombay,

> now changed into a "manticore" . . . [with] an entirely human body, but [the] head of a ferocious tiger, with three rows of teeth . . . whisper[s] solemnly . . . [while] break[ing] wind continually . . . "They describe us. . . . They have the power of description, and we succumb to the pictures they construct" (*SV*, 167–168).

These monsters organize a "great escape," and "take . . . the low roads to London town . . . going their separate ways, without hope, but also without shame" (*SV*, 170–171).

On another register, and two-hundred odd pages later, "a minute woman in her middle seventies gives us a related but more upbeat message:

> We are here to change things. . . . African, Caribbean, Indian, Pakistani, Bangladeshi, Cypriot, Chinese, we are other than what we would have been if we had not crossed the oceans. . . . We have been made again: but I say we shall also be the ones to remake this society, to shape it from the bottom to the top (*SV*, 413–414).

There is framing and dramatic irony everywhere, but never all the way. For example, it is at this meeting that Saladin encounters

> a young woman [who gives] his [conservative British] attire an amused once-over. . . . She was wearing a lenticular badge. . . . At some angles it read, *Uhuru for the Simba*; at others, *Freedom for the Lion*, "It's on account of the meaning of his chosen name," she explained redundantly. In African, "Which language?" . . . she shrugged. . . . It was African: born, by the sound of her in Lewisham, or Deptford, or New

Cross, that was all she needed to know. . . . As if all causes were the same, all histories interchangeable (*SV*, 413, 415).

Most strongly in the hospital section of the book, aptly called "Ellowen Deeowen," the effect of fragmentation, citation, fast-shifting perspectives is sustained through echoes from British literature. This embedding in the history of the literature of England and Ireland—the echoes from *The Portrait of the Artist As a Young Man* are a text for interpretation in themselves—may prove the most seductive for metropolitan readers.

But the book will not let us forget that the metropolitan reader is among "the describers." The postcolonial is not only a migrant but also the citizen of a "new" nation for which the colonial experience is firmly in the past, a past somewhat theatrically symbolized in Gibreel Farishta's dream of Mirza Sayeed Akhtar's house *Peristan*, "built seven generations ago," perhaps "a mere contraction of *Perownestan*," after "an English architect much favoured by the colonial authorities, whose only style was that of the neo-classical English country house" (*SV*, 230).

Mirza Akhtar is a *zamindar*—member of a landowning class, collecting land-revenue for the British, transmogrified at the end of the eighteenth century. He and his wife thus mark modern Indian elite postcolonial public culture in rather an obvious way:

> In the city [they] were known as one of the most "modern" and "go-go" couples on the scene; they collected contemporary art and threw wild parties and invited friends round for fumbles in the dark on sofas while watching soft-porno VCRs (*SV*, 227).

Because the migrant as paradigm is a dominant theme in theorizations of postcoloniality, it is easy to overlook Rushdie's resolute effort to represent contemporary India. Whereas the topical caricature of the Bombay urban worlds of the popular film industry, of rhapsodic "left" politics, of Muslim high society, of the general atmosphere of communalism, carries an idiomatic conviction, it is at least this reader's sense that so-called "magical realism" becomes an alibi in the fabrication of Titlipur-Chatnapatna, the village and the country town. But then, these might be the constitutive asymmetries of the imagination—itself a fabricated word—that is given the name "migrant."

(And perhaps it is only in this sense that the drifting migrant imagination is paradigmatic, of the "imagination" as such, not only of the historical case of postcoloniality. Here migrancy is the name of the institution that in-habits the indifferent anonymity of space and dockets climate and soil-type and the inscription of the earth's body. In this general sense, "migrancy" is not derived.)

But since this general sense is never not imbricated with the narrow sense—our contemporary predicament—the trick or turn is not to assume either the metropolitan or the national as the standard and *judge* some bit of this plural landscape in terms of it. In learning to practice the turn, if only to sense it slip away, we can guess that the deliberate oppositional stance of the European avant-garde is itself part of an instituted metropolitan reversal, among the "describers"—again.

Thus every canvas will have a spot that is less "real" than others. Excusing it away as an entailment of migrancy in general is no less dubious a gesture than accusing it as a historical or sociological transgression. I do therefore note that, within the protocols of *The Satanic Verses*, it is contemporary rural India that clings to magical realism as an alibi and thus provides a clue to the politics of the writing subject, the scribe. This would lead us to a deconstructive gesture toward the claim of magical realism as a privileged taxonomic description, of decolonization, a gesture already made in Chapter Three, and a consideration of alternative styles and systems of the representation of rural India.[12]

Within the labyrinth of such gestures, we must acknowledge that, writing as a migrant, Rushdie still militates against privileging the migrant or the exilic voice narrowly conceived, even as he fails in that very effort. A *mise-en-abyme,* perhaps, the eternal site of the migrant's desire, but also a persistent critique of metropolitan migrancy, his own slot in the scheme of things. The message and the medium of his book are marked by this conflict.

In other words, I do not think the "cosmopolitan *challenge* to national culture" is perceived by Rushdie as only a challenge.[13] Perhaps it is even an aporia for him, an impossible decision between two opposed decidables with two mutually canceling sets of consequences, a decision which gets made, nonetheless, for one set, since life must operate as a passive or active *différance* of death, as we know from our most familiar experiences: "I wanted to write about a thing I find difficult to admit even to myself, which is the fact that I left home."[14]

The Indian world of the book is Muslim-based. India's Islamic culture, high and low, is too easily ignored by contemporary hegemonic constructions of national identity as well as international benevolence. (These words have become derisive in the context of the genocide of Indian Muslims undertaken by Hindu fundamentalists since 1992.) Islamic India is another theme of migrancy, unconnected with the recent colonial past. For Islam as such has its head turned away from the subcontinent, across the Arabian Sea, perpetually emigrant toward Mecca. Within this turned-away-ness, Rushdie plants the migrant's other desire, the search for roots as far down as they'll go. The name of this radical rootedness is, most often, religion. Thus in the section called Mahound, Rushdie re-opens the institution of Revelation, the origin of the Koran. It is paradoxical that the protection against desacralization, writing in the name of the false prophet, Mahound rather than Mohammed, has been read, quite legitimately, by the Law where Religion is the "real" (there can be no other Law), as blasphemy.

The question is not if the book is blasphemous. The question is not even the profound belief of heretics and blasphemers. The question is rather: how is blasphemy to be punished? Can it be punished? What is the distinction between punishment and nourishment? And further, in the name of what do we judge the punishers? We will look at these questions in the two following sections.

The story of Mahound in *The Satanic Verses* is a story of negotiation in the name of woman. As so often, woman becomes the touchstone of blasphemy.

One of the most interesting features about much of Rushdie's work is his anxiety to write woman into the narrative of history. Here again we have to record an honorable failure.[15] (But I am more interested in failed texts. What is the use of a "successful" text? What happens to the recorder of failed texts? As a postcolonial migrant, "a tall, thin Bengali woman with cropped hair" [*SV*, 536], like Swatilekha—the "real" name of the woman playing the lead character in Ray's film version of Tagore's *The Home and the World*—an "actress" acting out the script of female Anglicization—read emancipation—by male planning in the colonial dispensation, I am part of Rushdie's text, after all.) In *Shame*, the women seem powerful only as monsters, of one sort or another. *The Satanic Verses* must end with Salahuddin Chamchawalla's reconciliation with *father* and nationality, even if the last sentence records sexual difference in the idiom of casual urban fucking: " 'My place,' Zeeny offered. 'Let's get the hell out of here.' 'I'm coming,' he answered her, and turned away from the view" (*SV*, 547).

All through, the text is written on the register of male bonding and unbonding, the most important being, of course, the double subject of migrancy, Gibreel Farishta and Saladin Chamcha. The two are tortured by obsession with women, go through them, even destroy them, within a gender code that is never opened up, never questioned, in this book where so much is called into question, so much is reinscribed.

Gibreel is named after the archangel Gabriel by his mother. But his patronymic, Ismail Najmuddin, is "Ismail after the child involved in the sacrifice of Ibrahim, and Najmuddin, *star of the faith*; he'd given up quite a name when he took the angel's" (*SV*, 17). And that name, Ismail, comes in handy in an echo of *Moby Dick*, to orchestrate the greatest act of male bonding in the book as an inversion of the angel of death, when Gibreel saves Saladin's life in the glazing Shaandaar Cafe: "The adversary: there he blows! Silhouetted against the backdrop of the ignited Shaandaar Cafe, see, that's the very fellow! Azraeel leaps unbidden into Farishta's hand" (*SV*, 463). The allusion in the otherwise puzzling "there he blows" is the white whale, of course.

Yet it must be acknowledged that in Mahound, we hear the satanic verses inspired by possible *female* gods. Gibreel's dream of Mahound's wrestling with himself, acting out an old script, restores the proper version, without the female angels, man to man. By the rules of fiction in the narrow sense, you cannot assign burden of responsibility here; although by the law of Religion, in the strict sense, the harm was already done. Rushdie invoked those rules against these Laws, and it was an unequal contest. We will not enter the lists, but quietly mark the *text's* assignment of value. The "reality" of the wrestling, the feel of the voice speaking through one, is high on the register of validity, if not verifiability. By contrast, in "Return to Jahilia," prostitution is mere play. Ayesha, the female prophet, ("historically" one of his wives) lacks the existential depth of "the businessman" prophet. To her the archangel sings in popular Hindi film songs. Her traffic with him is reported speech.

If postcolonial plurality is one aggressive central theme of *The Satanic Verses*, the artist's identity is another. Rushdie's tactic is boldly old-fashioned here, and the tone reminds one of, says, George Meredith's "Authorial voice" in *The Egoist*. Everything is taken care of by this overt comic self-undermining miming manipulation of "dramatic irony" on so many levels. The multiple dreams, carried to absurdity, support as they take away the power of this planning genius. Here is the entire shift from Religions' God to Art's Imagination—a high European theme—played out in the staging of author. Ostentatiously appearing as God or Devil (*upparwala* or *nichaywala*—the one above or the one below), he clearly produces error in Gibreel, who has a delusion of angelic grandeur and nearly gets run over by a motorcar as a result. Almost a hundred pages later, the authorial voice reveals that it had been the authorial voice posing as the Almighty, capable of "mobiliz[ing] the traditional apparatus of divine rage . . . [making] wind and thunder [shake] the room" (*SV*, 319), and looking like photographs of Salman Rushdie "medium height, fairly heavily built, with salt-and-pepper beard cropped close to the line of the jaw . . . balding . . . suffer[ing] from dandruff and [wearing] glasses." Does this make the author less reliable or more? Does this make the voice less real or more? Does this make the dream more true than truth? Is this a serious use of Romantic Irony in a contemporary comic format or a caricature of Romantic Irony? In an era of industriously decentered subjects and radicalized citationality, these questions are disarmingly cozy. Are we obliged to repeat the argument that, as metropolitan writing is trying to get rid of a subject that has too long been the dominant, the postcolonial writer must still foreground his traffic with the subject-position?[16] Too easy, I think. Not because the migrant must still consider the question of identity, plurality, roots. But because fabricating de-centered subjects as the sign of the times is not necessarily these times de-centering the subject. There in the wake of the European avant-garde is also a confusion of the narrow and general senses of the relationship between subject and center. The trick or turn is not to assume the representation of decentering to *be* decentering, and/or judge styles by conjunctures.

All precautions taken, there is no risk in admitting that Rushdie's book reads more like a self-ironic yet self-based modernism ("a myopic scrivener" setting two gentlemen a-dreaming) than an object-coded or subject-decentered avant-garde. Although he does broaden out to other empires—notably Argentina through the Rosa Diamond sequence which also stages the Norman Conquest as immigration—once you have finished the phantasmagoric book, the global slowly settles into the peculiar locale of migrancy.

What are these dreams, these phantasmagoria, these shape-changes that convince not only the shape-changers themselves but the inhabitants of the world of the book as well? Like the taxonomy of migrancy, Rushdie provides what may be called an oneiric multiplicity, the dream as legitimizing matrix. The story begins in a miracle, a series of supernatural events tamely accommodated into the reasonableness of the everyday. Vintage "magical realism"—Asturias or Márquez—has taught us to expect a more intricate mosaic. Alleluia Cone's "visions" can be validated by her personality and experience. Gibreel's fantasies have a firm diagnostic label: paranoid schizophrenia. But what about the peculiar authority of the many times repeated "Gibreel dreamed" . . . and then a noun of event or space? What is the relationship between this and the claim of "and then . . ." "and then . . ." that Deleuze and Guattari assure us is the mode of narrativization of the schizo?[17]

And what about the metamorphosis of the migrants in the hospital where Saladin is brought after the embarrassment of the discovery that he is a British citizen? What about his physical transformation into the Devil, setting a trend in the fashion world of "Black Britain," only to be canceled when he learns to hate Farishta? Saladin is never "diagnosed"; he is the sidekick that negotiates the book from beginning to end. And isn't that story about eating kippers at public school supposed to be a bit from Rushdie's own life-story? Is this a clue? Is Rushdie graphing his bio here as President Schreber, British-citizen-escaping-the-angel-of-god-by-demonic-metamorphosis-and-returning-home-for-a-wished-for-entry-into-the-real?[18]

In *Capitalism and Schizophrenia,* Deleuze and Guattari have suggested that the schizo as a general psychic description entailed by capitalism stands as a critique of the Oedipal recuperation of the great branching-out of social—and desiring—production inscribing the unproduced. I should like to think that *The Satanic Verses* presents a portrait of the author as schizo under the desiring/social production of migrancy and postcoloniality, a displacement of the Oedipal project of imperialism as bringing into Law of the "favorite son."

Farishta finds *The Marriage of Heaven and Hell* in Alleluia Cone's house. But the genius of this book is more the paranoid Schreber than the visionary Blake. This is no Prophet Against Empire, to quote the title of a well-known book on Blake.[19] The confident breaching of the boundaries between dream and waking in the *text*—not merely in the characters—and, indeed, in a text that sets store by the paradox of the so-called "creative imagination"—can earn for *The Satanic Verses* a critic's subtitle: "Imperialism and Schizophrenia." Not because empire, like capital, is abstract, but because empire messes with identity.

Good and Evil, set up with such pomp and circumstance, have therefore no moral substance in the persons of the protagonists. They are no more than visual markers, inscribed on the body like special effects—a halo, a pair of horns. I am uncomfortable with this of course, but then ask myself if this is not the peculiar felicity of postcoloniality, good and evil as reactive simulation, overturning the assurance in the prediction that "a performative utterance will be *in a peculiar way* hollow or void if said by an actor on the stage, or if introduced in a poem."[20] Postcolonial women and men, in many different ways, utter metropolitan performatives on the stage of migrancy as they utter "cultural-origin" performatives in a simultaneous shadow play; thus perhaps revealing the constitutive theatricality of all performatives.

I can anticipate critics suggesting that I give resistance no speaking part here. But the point is that a book such as this might at least be inviting us to consider the following question: who am I, or my critics, or indeed

Salman Rushdie, to *give* resistance a speaking part? To "state the problem" is not bad politics. In fact, it might be poor judgment to consider academy or novel as straight blueprint for action on the street. Chamcha gives himself the assurance that if a " 'chimeran graft' . . . were possible," as shown on TV, "then so was he; he, too, could cohere, send down roots, survive. Amid all the televisual images of hybrid tragedies . . . he was given this one gift" (*SV*, 406). In that very section, Rushdie's "authorial voice" puts it in the first person singular in the classic tones of the psychotic as savant:

> But, it had to be conceded, and this was his [Chamcha's] original point, that the circumstances of the age required no diabolic explanation. I[authorial voice]'m saying nothing. Don't ask me to clear things up one way or the other; the time of revelations is long gone (*SV*, 408).

It is after this that we come to the only real act of intended, gratuitous, cunning cruelty and persecution represented in the book: the destruction of Farishta and Alleluia through the anonymous telephoned messages, in the pluralized ventriloquilism of the radio-waves, of sexual innuendo couched in childish doggerel. No conceivable high allegorical connection with the great narrative of postcoloniality can be found in this important nexus of the book's narrative energy: this is rather the absurd discontinuity of the hyper-real. *Etre-pour-la-mort* is *être-au-telephone*.

(A final word about the "tall, thin Bengali woman with cropped hair," whom I cannot really leave behind. Rukmini Bhaya Nair gives her some importance:

> Narration in Rushdie's novels is shaped as gossip, an undervalued form of everyday talk that is now creatively empowered to reclaim the metaphors of an elite history. In *S[atanic]V[erses]*, Rushdie, tongue very much in cheek, presents the following case through one of his minor characters, an intellectual Bengali woman. ["]Society was orchestrated by what she called *grand narratives;* history, economics, ethics. In India, the development of a corrupt and closed state apparatus had 'excluded the masses of people from the ethical project.' As a result, they sought ethical satisfactions in the oldest of the grand narratives, that is, religious faith.["][21]

Ms. Nair goes on to make a persuasive case for *The Satanic Verses* as "satirical gossip."[22]

The case that I have made for religious faith as a counternarrative with a generalized subject focused on the moment when, *within the colonial rather than postcolonial context,* religious discursivity changed to militancy, gossip changed to rumor as vehicle of subaltern insurgency.[23] In the present essay, my opening point is that, in *post*coloniality, the praxis and politics of life (the *Lebenswelt*) intercept aesthetic objects away from their destined ends. Thus, if the project of the *novel* is gossip, the postcolonial *Lebenswelt* wrenched it into rumor, criticism by hearsay, a text taken as evidence, talked about rather than read.[24] Upon the wings of that rumor, the metropolitan migrant heterogeneity (rather different from the colonial subaltern in the colony, though we tend to forget this) forged a collectivity which they could stage as a strike *for* the Imam *against* the West. The narrative of the State and the narrative of religion overdetermined the rumored book into a general mobilizing signifier for crisis.

II

I come now to the cultural politics of the specific (mis)reading of the book as disposable container of blasphemy, signifier of cultural difference, rather than the field of the migrant's desiring/social production. As Aziz Al-Azmeh comments:

> The enracinations, deracinations, alienations, comforts, discomforts and mutations which constitute the novel are kept entirely out of view by Rushdie's islamist critics, and his putative treatment of Muhammed and Abraham brought into view.[25]

Literature is transactional. The point is not necessarily and exclusively the correct description of a book, but the construction of readerships. "The birth of the reader must be at the cost of the death of the Author."

A great deal has been written and said about the Rushdie affair in the last half-year. I will concentrate on a spectrum of historically constructed readerships here and assemble a highly selective dossier.[26] My main argument attempts to lay out the full implications of the statement made by Gita Sahgal, a member of the Southall Black Sisters, based in Britain: "It is in this crisis where our own orthodoxies have collapsed that the doubters and transgressors must once more create a space for themselves."[27]

India banned the book first: on October 5, 1988. Of the twenty-one deaths associated with *The Satanic Verses* to date, nineteen took place on the subcontinent. Of these, twelve were Muslim anti-Rushdie demonstrators, shot in Rushdie's hometown, Bombay, on February 24, 1989. Ayatollah Khomeini called for Rushdie's death on February 14.

Why did India ban the book? In the name of the rights of a religious minority in a secular state, Syed Shahabuddin, an opposition Muslim MP, launched a campaign against the book. "Doubters and transgressors must create a space for themselves" by taking a distance from mere rational abstraction, and here is the first one: "rights of a religious minority in a secular democratic-socialist state." Rational abstractions can be staunch allies, but *they can always also be used as alibis.* Gita Sahgal's *"this* crisis" is *always* implicit in the principle of reason. Her "once more" is the activist's shorthand for what must be *persistent.*

I have insisted throughout this book upon the catachrestic relationship between Enlightenment rational abstractions and postcolonial practice: theatrical performatives. In India thus, it was not an islamist decision, but a decision related to the functioning of the rational abstractions claimed catachrestically by the postcolonial state that banned the book. Artists and intellectuals were immediately vociferous against the decision, but, from personal accounts that I have heard, the logic of the protests was extremely hard to manipulate, still in the realm of rational abstractions.

In addition, perhaps precisely because the rational abstractions of democracy are claimed catachrestically and therefore critically by the secularist in the postcolonial state, there was a voice raised in India against the West's right to claim freedom of expression. The best succinct statement of this may be found in a letter to the *Economic and Political Weekly* signed by, among others, Asghar Ali Engineer, one of the strongest analysts and critics of "communalism" (religious sectarianism) in India: "We do not for a moment belittle [the] Ayatollah's threat. . . . But we also see the danger of 'freedom of expression' being fetishized and the embattled context in which a writer finds her/himself oversimplified."[28]

Wole Soyinka, traveling in India in December wrote, as a native of Nigeria:

a nation which is, in the estimation of many, roughly equally divided amongst Muslims and Christians and animists, with the former two constituting a floating adherent population of the "animist" in addition to being what they publicly proclaim. . . . I caught some flak from sections of the artistic and intellectual community for commenting that I quite understood the action of the Indian government in banning Salman Rushdie's book. . . . I stated that, given India's harrowing situation of religious unrest, I probably would have done the same if I were the Prime Minister. I did not condone the ban; I merely tried to understand the horrible dilemma in which the government of India was placed.[29]

A dilemma, a crisis, an aporia, peculiar to democracy as checks and balances, rights and duties computed on the normative grid of rational abstractions inherited from the culture of imperialism. Bhikhu Parekh, a British-Indian political theorist has asked: "Is there a release from this highly claustrophobic post-Enlightenment world-view?"[30]

Rushdie's own reaction was straightforward:

> The right to freedom of expression is at the foundation of any demo-
> cratic society. . . . My view is that of a secular man for whom Islamic
> culture has been of central importance all his life. . . . You know, as I
> know that [the Muslim parliamentarians] and their allies don't really
> care about my novel. The real issue is the Muslim vote.[31]

Still within "the claustrophobic post-Enlightenment world-view," let us step back and ask, what exacerbated the situation of the Muslim vote so dramatically? It is of course idle to assign a single efficient cause to such trends but, for strategic reasons that I hope will be evident to at least a section of my readership, I choose the successful censoring of a woman, contained within national boundaries, a national *cause célèbre* for a time, but nothing about which it can be said "Islam today has displayed its enormous mobilizing power." I refer, of course, to the Shahbano case. I quote a few passages from "Shahbano" by Rajeswari Sunder Rajan and Zakia Pathak:

> In April 1985, the Supreme Court of India . . . passed a judgment in
> favor of Shahbano in the case of Mohammed Ahmed Khan, appellant,
> versus Shahbano and others, respondents. The judgment created a furor
> unequalled, according to one journal, since "the great upheaval of 1857
> [the so-called Indian Mutiny]" . . . awarding Shahbano, a divorced
> Muslim woman, maintenance of Rs. 179.20 (approximately $14) per
> month from her husband . . . and dismissed the husband's appeal
> against the award of maintenance under section 125 of the 1973 Code
> of Criminal Procedure. . . . When some by-elections fell due in Decem-
> ber 1985, the sizeable Muslim vote turned against the ruling party (the
> Congress-I) partly because it supported the judgment. . . . When Hindu
> fundamentalists offered to "protect" her from Muslim men, her reli-
> gious identity won. . . . In an open letter, she denounced the Supreme
> Court judgment "which is apparently in my favour; but since this
> judgment is contrary to the Quran and the *hadith* and is an open
> interference in Muslim personal law, I, Shahbano, being a Muslim,
> reject it and dissociate myself from every judgment which is contrary
> to the Islamic Shariat." . . . When the battle was carried to Parliament
> and the government of India passed the bill that threw her on the mercy

of the male relatives of her natal family, her gender status was again activated. She became a Muslim woman pursuing the case for the return of her *mehr* (dower) under the provisions of the new act.[32]

Sunder Rajan and Pathak are quite right in saying that what is at issue here is not "whether this spacing, temporalizing self is a deferral of the unified freely choosing *subject* or whether the latter is itself only a metaphysic."[33] What we are concerned with here is the question of *agency*, even *national* agency within the effect of the nation in the real—just as Rushdie's novel is concerned with the *migrant* agency represented in a magical but none the less serious layout. "Agent" and "subject" are different codings of something we call "being." Shahbano, as citizen of the same postcolonial nation invoked by Rushdie in his letter to Rajiv Gandhi, has her *agency* censored by the script of religion and gendering. In this context, to bring up the question of the staging of free will in the *subject* has a hidden ethicopolitical agenda that may give support to the very forces that recode her as gendered and therefore make her dependent upon the institution of heterosexual difference. This has something like a relationship with what militants in the Rushdie case have pointed out: that arguments from cultural relativism are profoundly complicit, when invoked at certain moments, with racist absolutism. It is quite correct to point out the immense mobilization of national resistance—the provisional fabrication of a collective agency on the occasion of Shahbano. But woman *as* woman (unavailable to class agency in the particular context) is still only an occasion here. The question of free will should not be inscribed within arguments from subject-production; it is rather to be seen in connection with the presupposition of individual agency in collectivities. It is here that Shahbano stands censored. Within this frame, there is no real polarization between self-censoring and other-censoring (conversion and coercion); that is the opposition we must learn to undo. The definition of "choice" as "internalized constraint" is invaluable here. In the sphere of the production of political value, the mute as articulate in the service of "orthodoxy" (to borrow Gita Sahgal's word)—a discontinuous naming of collective agency in the name of the "sacred" rather than the "profane" (in the other coding called "secular," "national")— is more spectacularly muted because so abundantly audible. And, in the context of the international collectivization brought about by way of Rushdie's book, of which she is among the first efficient causes, she has dropped out, become invisible. How can she *become* one of "the doubters and transgressors" before she can participate in their "clearing a space for themselves"? By counter-coercion through the orthodoxy of reason?

Paradoxically, it is the rationalist who can think reason as internalized constraint. *This* is the genuine dilemma, the aporia, the double-bind of the question of agency. The condition of (im)possibility of rational collectivites must be seen, not as instrument, but as last instance.

> By being categorized as a vagrant—the destitute woman—widow, divorcée, or abandoned wife . . . fulfills her (anti-)social role. The psychological damage of potential vagrant status is partially minimized by the depersonalizing effects of legal action. Section 125 offers women "negative" subjectivity: the new act responds by reinserting the divorcée within the family, this time as dependent on her natal family and sons.[34]

As impersonal instrument, rational abstractions can operate as *pharmakon,* a poison that can be a healing drug.[35] It is thus that one must turn to the extraordinary and (ex)orbitant category of "legal vagrant." In the subordinate, gendered, decolonized *national* space, the category of *female* "vagrant" as "access to public space" (section 125 of the Uniform Civil Code) must be recognized beside the category of "migrant" within ex-colonial metropolitan space, where, as the migrant feminist group "Women Against Fundamentalism" have pointed out, "women's voices have been largely silent"—and, I repeat, audible as muted ventriloquists— "in the debate where battle lines have been drawn between liberalism and fundamentalism."[36] Paradoxically, categorization as vagrant is "psychologically damaging" only if the religious coding of gendered heterosexuality is implicitly accepted by way of a foundational concept of subject-formation. The freeing pain of a violent rejection from a system of self-representation (a mode of value-coding) is not confined to the franchised or disenfranchised.

This would take me into the arena where the reversal empire-nation is displaced, about which I have written in Chapter Four. Here we are obliged to go forward to the most visible agent, the late Ayatollah Khomeini.

Who punishes? How was the Ayatollah produced?

Although we cannot afford to forget, as Albert Memmi writes in the context of the Rushdie case, that "monotheism, philosophically and pragmatically speaking, is totalitarian," we must of course also see that the stake in Khomeini's agency (in every sense) is not Islam, but islamism.[37] And, at first glance, islamism is the regulation of diaspora/migrancy. In the words of Farzaneh Asari, a pseudonymous and exiled Iranian writer, "it is the Muslims of America, Britain, India, Lebanon and so on whom the Islamic Republic wants to persuade of its continued hold on the

Iranian people."[38] It is important to underline that "virtually all the pronouncements from Teheran on *The Satanic Verses* begin and end with the denunciations of *imperialism* and *colonialism,* accusing Rushdie of complicity in a crusade aimed at Islam," writes Mehmet Ali Dikerdem.[39]

But who punishes? How was the Ayatollah produced? These are still merely the question of stakes. In answer to this question, Asari offers an account of Khomeini's bio-graphy, that concept-metaphor whose importance I have learned from Derrida:

> He . . . chose his "transcendent" self, the one that had been made into an almost Gandhian leader, over his "real" theocratic self—what by temperament and belief he was and has remained. Khomeini's [political appointments] . . . following the victory of the revolution to testify to the primacy of this "transcendent" self in the crucial pre-revolutionary period.

Asari relates "his gradual loss of popular support" as due to the overcoming by the "real" of the "transcendent."

> This loss has been more than made up for by the reconstruction and vast extension of the Shah's repressive apparatus . . . (though the social base of the present Iranian regime is still . . . much broader and deeper than that of the Shah . . .)

Here is a rather convincingly proposed doubling, then, of the man playing the monolith.[40] To sacrifice the heretic in a defense of the faith is a ruse to "recover lost territory," to cover over the political and military defeat in the war with Iraq. (This political text has new patterns now; the present piece records the initial phases of "the Rushdie case.")

This monolithic face, defending an unchanging word, this "construct"—with the piercing eyes under the iconic turban—"at the center of attention, [desperately attempting to] mak[e] . . . reading, writing, and meaning seem to be very close to the same thing" is a product of complicity between Khomeini's "direct interest in presenting Iran as a static monolith defined by the steadfast devotion of its people to a 'fundamentalist' brand of Islam" and a sanctioned ignorance, "the accepted wisdom which makes . . . ignorant lines eminently reasonable" (Asari).[41] "Reason" and "religion" are thus clandestine cooperators. Asari describes the conflation of "the estimated five million that celebrated Khomeini's return in the streets of Teheran in February, to the fewer than three thousand that greeted his call for Rushdie's murder . . . in the same city in February 1989." It is

234 / Outside in the Teaching Machine

not certain that the corporeal textuality of Khomeini's body, levitated by helicopter, will do anything to rip apart this conflation. For this conflation of collectivities in fact projects a "central image" of the "omnipresent if often physically absent Ayatollah . . . when a crowd is large enough to fill the small screen, how is the viewer to know the number of people involved or the significance of such a number?"

Once again I emphasize the implausible connection-by-reversal—the simulated Khomeini as Author and the dissimulated Shahbano marking the place of the effaced trace at the origin: an invocation of collective support projecting a singular agent filled with divine intention; an invocation of collective resistance displacing a censored patient as cross-hatched by discursivities. If we yield ground and grounding by deliberately "writing otherwise," analyzing a Shahbano by subject-formation rather than agency-deformation, the forces of the Author claiming as Author to write "the same" come forward to occupy the space cleared. The case of *The Satanic Verses,* a realist reading of magical realism, makes visible the violent consequences.

Deliberate cultural relativism is a seemingly benevolent rational abstraction that shows its insidious credential here. Al-Azmeh calls it "apartheid—expressed in culturalist and religious tones." Mehmet Ali Dikerdem calls it "infecting . . . into . . . ethnic pathology"; Gita Sahgal insists that

> fundamentalism has been the main beneficiary of the adoption of relativist multi-cultural norms by large sections of the political establishment. . . . Anti-racist rhetoric . . . sees only that a black religion feels powerless in a racist society. Any debate within the community—among Muslims, between believers and non-believers, men and women—is irrelevant from this viewpoint.

Asari again:

> Clearly the explanation for [BBC's documentary *Inside the Ayatollah's Iran* (14 February 1989)] *Panorama's* account lies in the basic assumption of the radical otherness of "the Ayatollah's Iran." But Iran does not consist entirely of Ayatollahs.

The radically other is a warning to the power of reason, not a featured face blocking out accessible heterogeneity. Those of us who have been troubled by the fetishization of Levinas into a prophet of marginality feel comforted by Asari's enviably sober tones.[42]

Cultural relativism and the recognition of the limitations of Eurocentrism have been important achievements in the radical consciousness and cultural anthropology that have developed in this century and whose wisdom must be preserved. But in the current climate these insights are being used or abused in unexpected ways.

I must, of course, insist that the "use *and* abuse" are both entailed by institutionalized relativism, even as use and abuse are entailed by "the principle of reason" that generates "the post-Enlightenment claustrophobia" that such a relativism would contest. The answer is not the "preservation" of the positive and perennial and the "elimination" of the negative and contextual. It is not even to attempt to sublate—preserve and destroy. My peculiar theme is always *persistent* critique—and, I must emphasize, an *asymmetrical* persistent critique, focusing on different elements in the incessant process of recoding that shifts the balance of the *pharmakon's* effect from medicine to poison; while insisting on the necessity of the broad grounding position. Admittedly this brings practice to a breaking point in its acknowledgment of the everyday, but what else is new? I cannot develop this here, for, in this brief compass, I think it is more urgent to dramatize a diversity within the dossier that I have been presenting, in order to close this section by reminding ourselves first of an often unacknowledged desire and, second, of the United States, for we migrants in the U.S. are parked in a spot claimed by some to be united by democratic reason.

Gita Sahgal speaks as a migrant fighting for racial equality in a metropolitan space and sexual justice within the migrant community. Soyinka speaks as a national in a space where speaking of a *minority* religion would involve recasting dominance in the inaccurate language of numbers. Asghar Ali Engineer speaks as a national of a *religious* minority in a *secular* state. And Farzaneh Asari, speaking necessarily in a false name, speaks as an exile from Iran, *one* nation united under God. Standing in the United States, and accepting the responsibility for that highly dangerous positioning we must ask the question that Homi Bhabha has recently brought to our attention: "what do these people want?" These people: migrant, national in an equally-divided-religion state, national in a majority-religion state, exile from a theocratic state.

Seen as collectivities (and that is not the only way to see them) they all want an access to generality *and* difference through the mediation of access to national agency. The migrant wants to redefine the nation, the postcolonial wants to identify the nation, the exile wants to explain and restore the nation and be an agent in terms of its normative and privative discourse. Rushdie's novel is not only a novel of migrancy, but also a novel of return. Thus Al Azmeh hears religion as the cry of the oppressed heart living in ghettos in a land of false dreams, "impervious to the logic of cultural relativism and multi-culturalism but not to the logic of capitalism." Soyinka wants to ban "everything which is Iran . . . as long as Ayatollah Khomeini remains accepted as a leader in Iran, everything except the voices of Iran's political and cultural dissidents and the protests of her repressed womanhood." But to the Muslims in Bradford, where it all began, who wanted to conserve and establish Islamic education in Britain, the Ayatollah showed the fantasmatic vision of a nation, not a religion but a theocratic state. And Sahgal puts it this way:

> When [we] went to Bradford to make a documentary on *The Satanic Verses* . . . it emerged that their main problem was to maintain faith in a secular society. What would future generations of Muslim children believe in, one asked rhetorically, if the book remained in circulation and was seen to be sanctified by society?

Yet the desire of these British Muslims is not to abdicate from the nation, but to insert Islamic education into the state. To participate in the nation in general, and yet to remain an enclave. And in the statement of the collective to which Sahgal belongs, it is the word "nationality" that carries this contradiction: "We will take up the right to determine our own destinies, not limited by religion, culture or nationality."[43]

It is only if we acknowledge the heterogeneous desire for that great rational abstraction, agency in a nation, that we postcolonials will be able to take a distance from it. It is here that the transgressor must persistently critique that transgressed space, which she cannot not want to inhabit, even if coded another way. We can sometimes be released from the claustrophobia of the post-Enlightenment bunker if we acknowledge that we also want to be snug in it. What is punishment is also nourishment. It is only then that we can sense that the spectacular promise of democracy— those rational abstractions coded as Human Rights—is desirable precisely because those abstractions can be used as alibis to deflect critique. In fact, it is only then that we can begin to suspect that the ethical, without which any hope for civil society or social justice must crumble, and which must therefore remain eminently desirable, bases itself upon what might be the lowest common denominator of being-human, objectivity, and the universal, and yet *must* code itself as the highest.[44] *Neither* radical alterity *nor* universal ipseity is an unquestionable value.

The United States is the dream of post-Enlightenment Europe. It is here that the bunker is a *trompe-l'oeil* of the wide-open spaces. It is here that the rational abstractions of formal democracy are most resolutely trotted out on behalf of cultural relativism, sanctioned ignorance, idiot goodwill, as well as racism and classism. As Rushdie himself said in a less harried time, American liberals just can't shake the habit of wanting to take care of the world. By the logic of this coding, Communism and Capitalism have of course already been recoded as State Censorship versus Free Choice.[45] And the Rushdie affair has been coded as Freedom of Speech versus Terrorism and even as "a triumph of the written word." It has been domesticated into a possible "Western" (why?) "martyrship" for literature, or rather for the book trade!—"to the cause that we [as an industry] supposedly espouse!"[46]

It is only if we recognize that we cannot not want freedom of expression as well as those other normative and privative rational abstractions that we on the other side can see how they work as alibis. It is only then that we can recode the conflict as Racism versus Fundamentalism, demonizing versus disavowal.[47]

In the name of what do we judge the punisher? In the name of right reason, of course, but from what does it detract our attention? It hides, and I quote Mehmet Ali Dikerdem again:

> one of the most elemental fears and phobias of European cultural consciousness which regarded this new faith as the incarnation of the "anti-Christ" . . . Islam and Christianity confronted one another for a millennium in possibly the longest and bitterest "superpower struggle" of all time. . . . Islam is thus the opposite of the accumulated values and institutions of the evolution from Renaissance and Reformation to the Industrial Revolution via the American and French Revolution.[48]

Dikerdem relates this adroitly to the political history of the Middle East since the Second World War. This therefore is the appropriate moment to record a response particularly to my dossier, from Alia Arasooghly, a diasporic Palestinian. Earlier in this piece, I remarked that, at first glance, it seemed that the stake in Khomeini's agency was islamism in the regulation of migrancy. Arasooghly points out persuasively how the production of the Ayatollah Khomeini as the punisher was also a *mise-en-scène* of the claiming of proper agency in Islam's own house, "as though God's death were but a play."[49] This is, paradoxically, not a realist reading of magical realism, but the reverse move: here scripture, the ground of the real, is performed as representation, a script. Arasooghly cites a counter-claim by the Iraqi film *al-Qadissiya* . . .

which recreates the early Arab/Muslim battle and defeat of the Persian/ Zoroastrians at Qadissiyah which opened Persia to Islam and to the Arab Empire (at the time of the Ummayad dynasty the defeaters of the Shiites!), a most significant and crucial battle for the Arabs, against claims to leave the Persians alone.

By her reading,

the main audience the Iranian Islamic Republic has addressed itself to since its inception, after its own people has been the "real Muslims"— the Arabs, *Khomeini could not speak in the name of Islam if he did not also speak for the Arabs.* The Quran [and the Prophet] were sent to the Arabs in Arabic, other Muslims either have to learn Arabic, or have access to a second hand interpretation via a translation . . . the largest . . . Islamic Empire/State was during Arab rule. Ottoman rule brought stagnation and decay. Islam's three Holy cities, Mecca, Medina, and Jerusalem are in Arab lands.

The *mise-en-scène,* "the main audience," and now the substance of the performance: "the Ayatollah declared/showed Muslims how to be powerful against the Great Satan, the U.S.A. and denounced its client satan, Israel."

An interesting conclusion arises from Arasooghly's reading. Khomeini's "antidemocratic, anti-Enlightenment" behavior was not only not direct and unmediated evidence of the immutable essence of Islam, but it was a deliberate cultural-political self-representation as an unmediated testifier for the immutable essence of Islam. Thus Arasooghly suggests that "Khomeini as Salahdin," the countercrusader, "baffled the 'international' sensibility [by] not playing by the rules put out by Europe": the hostage syndrome, the death threat against Salman Rushdie.

III

I promised in the final section to provide an element of intellectual history. I will make no more than a few cryptic suggestions, remaining within the story of what Michel de Certeau has defined as a shift in the *Lebenswelt*—the formal praxis of life—"from religious systems to the ethics of the Enlightenment."[50] De Certeau must be read against the grain because, like most European intellectuals writing on the history of European consciousness, he does not take imperialism into account.

In section 4 of *The Writing of History,* de Certeau lays out a story that is not altogether unknown, although in the telling of it, a Derrida would emphasize Kant and Hegel, an Abrams the poets.[51] With his brilliant historian's eye, de Certeau tells us how "the practical organization of Christianity is 'socialized' in being stripped of its beliefs" (MDC, 179), how in the seventeenth and eighteenth centuries Christianity is recoded, laundered, and sublated into philosophy and ethics.

> *De-Christianization reveals in its formality the Christian practice,* but hereafter that practice is thrown out of the orbit of the *Logos* which had verified it. . . . It "betrays" Christianity in both senses of the term: it abandons it, and it unveils it. A social reinterpretation of Christianity is thus inaugurated, which will flow back over Christian milieus: in them it will develop missionary practices turned toward the "other" . . . in them it will later provoke the reproduction of the ethics of progress in the form of a theology of history. . . . (MDC, 179)

Such a sublation/graduation of a monotheism into secularism as such at the end of the seventeenth and eighteenth centuries in a certain place has something like a relationship with the ideological requirements of the release of the abstractions of monopoly capitalist (rather than pre-capitalist) imperialism. To repeat that move with the other great monotheism, Islam, is not possible again precisely because the seventeenth and eighteenth centuries have taken place. The ethical has to entail the universal, although it must always also be accessible to a singular or a collective case. The attempt to fashion an ethical universal out of a religious base, which is subsequently not called Christian but simply secular, then goes out of joint with the conjuncture, especially with a (national) subject not of the monopoly-capitalist dominant. "Conjuncture" is a word that would give its antonym in plain English as being "out of joint."

Thus it is futile (if not reactionary) to look for parallels between the seventeenth- and eighteenth-century Euro-Atlantic and contemporary West Asia/North Africa/South Asia. One glimpses asymmetrical reflections, as in a cracked mirror, only to put them aside:

> these movements are symptoms of *an order that is being undone* . . . religious structures begin to "turn" quite differently, as if they were taken up en masse into the political element. . . . Traditional "heresy," a social form modeled on a theological truth, becomes less and less possible. The orthodoxy in terms of which this form was determined will now be more of a civil than religious nature. . . . The choice between Christianities is effected in terms of practices (MDC, 154, 158, 168, 162).

The residual appearances in contemporary global Islam are not "atheism, sorcery, mysticism." Paradoxically, because the effort at globalizing

240 / Outside in the Teaching Machine

Islam is wounded and incapacitated by the detritus of an imperialist formation already in place, we have to locate them on a much larger scale: the Khilafat movement, dismantled by Kamal Ataturk's modernization of Turkey; the Muslim contingency in the making of the Indian Constitution; and varieties of "fundamentalism," a repetition and a rupture, and a reaction to the U.S.-Israel combination.

"One of the tasks of history consists of measuring the distance or the relations between the formality of practices and their representations" (MDC, 158). There is indeed a distance between the formality of historians' practices and their self-representation in the matter of imperialism. The invocation of "missionary practices" cannot cover the distance altogether. And, where the descriptions are almost on target, the fact that colonialism/imperialism remains conspicuous by its absence makes the distance intractable: "State policy already turns the country into a mercantilist and capitalist enterprise," for example, or, worse, "a dominant *political* ethics is born of the enormous effort that allowed the eighteenth century to create nations and pass from Christianity to modern Europe" (MDC, 155, 176).

Given that the story of Christianity to secularism is the only story around, we tend to feel quite justified when we claim, in praise or dispraise of reason, that reason is European. The peculiarity of historical narratives such as the one I have loosely put together in this section is that it is made up of contingencies which can also be read as Laws of Motion. I would like to suggest that it is the reading of one of those contingencies—the fit between monopoly capitalist imperialism and monotheist Christianity-into-secularism—as a Law of Motion that makes us presuppose that Reason itself is European. It might be better to recode the gift of contingency rather than construct a fantasmatic present or future in the name of that presupposition. In aid of what? A competition about monotheisms? How about polytheisms or animisms? How far must discord be taken? Rather than lament reason, put it in a useful place, precisely to avoid these contingencies. Accept the limits of the contingency of history.

In place of mere secularism, the Southall Black Sisters might propose an instrumental universalism, always under the fire of doubt and transgression.

IV

As I have indicated, this chapter reconstructs the beginnings of the Rushdie case. In it, I have first offered a literary critical plot summary of the book because I think one must be a schoolteacher in the classroom when it becomes impossible. I have done it almost as an act of disciplinary piety towards what is, after all, a novel. Next I have presented a dossier trying to focus on what people who are diversely connected to this event are saying. I have paused for a moment upon the uses to which the spectacular rational abstractions of democracy can sometimes be put. I have gone on to sketch the possibility of questioning what we often take as given, that the idea of reason—since I see reason itself as a *pharmakon*, rather than an unquestioned good or an unquestioned evil—is *necessarily* Eurocentric.

Finally, then, an exhortation: whenever they bring out the Ayatollah, remember the face that does not come together on the screen, remember Shahbano. She is quite discontinuous with Salman Rushdie's fate as it is being organized on many levels. The Rani of Sirmur emerged in the East India Company records only when she was needed to make "History" march.[52] Shahbano's emergence is structurally comparable. When the very well-known face is brought out, remember the face that you have not seen, the face that has disappeared from view, remember Shahbano. Woman in difference, outside in the machine.

12

Sammy and Rosie Get Laid

I have been trying to make the point, over and over again, that migrant and postcolonial mixtures and (mis)appropriations—catachreses—are different in degree within their two different spheres but also different in kind one from the other. Sometimes "hybridity"—like the old "androgyny" theory of feminism—can make us forget these differences.[1] By play of chance, Rushdie's novel hyphenated the two spheres. It must be said that the novel attempted to recognize these differences as well. In his *My Beautiful Laundrette* (directed by Stephen Frears, as is *Sammie and Rosie Get Laid*), Hanif Kureishi tries to mark the gap in the character of the postcolonial subject who is the father of the hero. I have tried elsewhere to place Kureishi's *The Buddha of Suburbia* squarely within a taxonomy of degrees and kinds.[2] In this chapter I comment on his second novel/film *Sammy and Rosie Get Laid*. The chapter is based on a conversation with Colin MacCabe. I have made little attempt to change its tenor.

My task is made easier in that Frears/Kureishi's technique is resolutely allegorical: the Oedipal parricide succeeds by way of the mismatch between the migrant son in Thatcherite Britain and the postcolonial father from Bhutto's Pakistsan, the latter nostalgic for the colonial metropolis as the source of imperialist culture.

I'd like to preface my remarks by saying that I don't know how to talk about films. At the same time I want to talk about *My Beautiful Laundrette* and *Sammy and Rosie Get Laid* and especially the movement from one to the other because of my special interest in the difficulty of making clear to people, particularly in the United States, that the questions of race and postcoloniality are neither identical nor opposed.

This is, of course, different yet again from the difference between migrancy and postcoloniality. The difference in *kind* is that the first difference can be bridged with less immense systemic efforts than the second. This is why the second sometimes seems jaded with irony. I no longer have the feeling that looking at these films in Britain is not as difficult as it is for the United States general cultural worker. With the global reterritorializing in the New World Order, migrant reality and globality are taking all the attention of the radical cultural worker in the metropolis, as the terrain of decolonization is becoming standardized through the neoliberal policies of the International Monetary Fund and the World Bank. It is almost as if a delinking is operating in the sphere of cultural/cognitive mapping even as, in the economic sphere, the North-South divide is being "equalized" (*gleichgesetzt*), and, as a result of this removal of barriers between the national economies of the South and the international economic system, the capacity of the state to organize its affairs for just redistribution becomes progressively reduced, so that, in the political sphere, orthodox constraints appear. It is as if, once again, the workings of radical metropolitan culture, separated from what I have elsewhere called "transnational literacy," operate to give support to the transparent and abstract mechanics of the economic text as it imbricates and constitutes the political as palimpsest. Strictly speaking, *Sammy and Rosie* is premonitory of this separation, staging it in the break between father and son, and the general crisis of the legacy of heterosexism. Maybe a New York audience is different. But in the universities, our colleagues and our students don't quite have the wherewithal to read these films. I am using "read" quite deliberately. I am a literary–philosophical critic, and, as is clear from my treatment of *Genesis*, that's the only way I know how to talk about film. I see them as didactic pieces. And I'm interested in the fact that there is a lot to read there.

From this specialized perspective then, let me say that Channel 4 [of British Independent Television] is interested in something like what Gramsci calls the formation of the intellectual, the preparation of viewership. Thus the role of these television channels is also didactic. If part of this role is to educate the so-called minorities, part is to educate the so-called dominant viewership about the minorities as well. Stephen Frears's films fit this latter role more persuasively, I think. As such, they renegotiate the relationship between aesthetics and politics.

Perhaps *My Beautiful Launderette* was too lyrical. Is this a pattern? A Mahasweta Devi, or a Ngugi wa Thiong'o—and others can be named— often begin from political-*personal* concerns, a privatized confrontation with what Jameson might call the cognitive mapping—a concern with where this individual, this minority individual, fits into broader structuring of politics. And then in authors like Devi and Ngugi, and now with Kureishi as well, one can see a growing boredom with that project and a subsequent interest in a more collective representation.

With *The Buddha of Suburbia* I am not at all sure that Kureishi's work has sustained this pattern, if indeed it is one. But it can certainly be sensed in the movement from *Laundrette* to *Sammy*. One of the features of this move from the personal to the collective may be the loss in importance of a "central" character. Indeed you may not even know who the central character is. From that point of view what I liked about *Sammy and Rosie* was the representation of Rosie. It seemed to me, again following a didactic reading, that the old British ideological subject of radicalism has become very indeterminate and that Rosie was that subject in the film. She was white, deliberately downwardly class-mobile, a social worker, heterosexual. She seemed almost to embody the inherent orthodoxy of that position which Raymond Williams describes at the end of his wonderful essay entitled "The Bloomsbury Fraction":

> The early confidence of the position [of the civilized individual], in the period before 1914 has, in its long encounter with all these other and actual social forces, gone, in Leonard Woolf's title, downhill all the way. For all its continuing general orthodoxy, it appears now much more often as a beleagured rather than as an expanding position.[3]

Given our general unpreparedness for knowing what is and is not radical, that beleaguered position is today the white ideological subject-position of reactive welfare-state radicalism. You cannot really be against Rosie, but she has no final determination. She loves all the right people. She's a white heterosexual woman who loves lesbians, loves blacks, is in an interracial marriage, etc., etc. And you have in a very unemphatic way the real representative of the old Bloomsbury fraction in the general culture which is the character played by Claire Bloom. I choose to speak about these two people rather than the Pakistanis first because this is the closest Frears gets to a critique of the genre. What are we to make of the fact that the only white men of any focus in the film are the police, Colin MacCabe, and Alice's friend who allows her to find Rafi? The only possible moment of racial self-criticism would be the police. I do agree with bell hooks that making the police shoot the black woman in self-defense puts the film's race-perspective in some doubt right from the start.[4]

In the first version of this essay, I wrote that I taught *Sammy and Rosie* to introduce my students to the British social text and its difference from the American one. Here in parenthesis I add that that distinction, between the maps of migrancy and diaspora in the U.S.A. and the E.E.C. now occupies a rather large part of my work.[5] What I say in the paragraph below, then, is rather a partial reflection of my current agenda.

In particular I teach this piece to give to my students a sense that the agenda of the sixties was not the same in Britain and the United States. When Andrew Milner, writing about Christopher Hill on Milton, accuses Christopher Hill of being too sixties, he's got it wrong, I think.[6] Hill's position is not a sixties one, it is part of this whole mindset which was already established as a class producing its own radicalism from within. A critique of imperialism which in itself was class-marked. (This is the ideological cusp of displacement between the Old Left and the New Left in Britain, perhaps.) *A Passage to India* comes out of that critique and there is nothing which corresponds to it in the United States because of the fact that the United States has no history of nineteenth-century territorial imperialism quite in that way. If you want to understand the difference between Britain and the United States in the sixties you have to go much further back. (There is hardly a trace of continuity between the thirties Left and the New Left in the United States.) And those differences persist in a lot of academic political positions in the two countries.

Today I realize that that uneven fracture has something like a relationship with the difference between the New Europe and the "multiculturalist" U.S.A., and is not unrelated to the disappearance of practical postcoloniality in postmodernity, a disappearance or emptying-out unwittingly allegorized by Rafi's suicide. This fracture, paradoxically, sustains us, not only in our academic games, playing as if outside, in the teaching machine, but also, and incidentally, the global social relations that some of us soldier to undermine. I cannot call this merely ideological. Working with Derrida and Foucault, I have long been uneasy with "ideology" as a tool. I found some ease with Stuart Hall's thought of ideology as inadequate explanation.[7] Worrying about this generally sustaining fracture, I realized that when I thought "sustained"—held up—I was literally and idiosyncratically translating the word *dharma.*

Dharma means what holds you up, what supports you. It is also the loose calculus that allows you to implement ethical convictions as well as the systemic doctrine that you inherit or espouse as the semiotic for social justice or salvation. And *Dharma* as Law of Motion operates in spite of the subject. Thus it is also the religious name by which an ethnic community is interpellated. Ideology relates to dharma, which is rather a more robust as well as a more elusive concept.

What makes a dharma elusive is its utterly situational irruption, which yet effects a change, however infinitesimal, in its entire systematicity. (Although I remain out of patience with a style of film criticism which analogizes screen-work with the relationship between philosophical categories, I should mention here that this situationality/systematicity is what

Gilles Deleuze notices in Henri Bergson's third thesis in the former's book *Cinema 1*.[8] Rosie's elusiveness in *Sammy and Rosie* may have a metonymic relationship with dharmic elusiveness.

(I am using "dharma" here as a handy instrument for analyzing, as a name for something rather larger and more adventurous in terrain than ideology. I am in no way suggesting that Rosie's representation has Indic attributes rubbed off on Frears because of Kureishi's cultural difference. No doubt the paleonymy of "dharma" will interfere. But then "ideology," or any other word I might have chosen, would have paleonymic associations as well.) Rosie's elusiveness may be rather specific to Britain and may have to be taught in the U.S. One way is to go by the way the camera holds on close-ups of Rosie's face. One of the most important moments in the film is when Rafi and Rosie are having their row in the restaurant. Rafi's line is that she doesn't know what it is like in decolonized countries and she's giving the line about there being no excuses for torture. They're screaming at each other and everybody in the restaurant forms a sort of audience so that it becomes a public performance. At a certain moment the camera holds on a close-up of Rosie so that it almost looks like a still. Rosie has very sharp weapon-like earrings, and the profile is frozen in such a way that it looks as though a caged beast has been cornered: the beleaguered position of the civilized conscience for whom torture is bad under any circumstances. In *Analyzing Marx* Richard Miller takes up the question of why Marx repudiates the merely moral position.[9] It might be interesting to compare the two positions.

The elusiveness of Rosie's presentation, her aporetic quality—we can neither disagree nor agree with her and are uneasy in every way—is the predicament of a dharmic elusiveness in a rational analytic world that understands morality in systems. Rosie the character *is* not this, but Rosie the bit of filmic text shows this up. Paradoxically, the same aporetic character pervades the decolonized justification of torture as the system that cures the inconvenience of mere moral systems. We cannot just dismiss Rafi without dismissing what produces him. The world of the London Asian is hung between the two.

The comprehensive and elusive dharmic aporia of Rosie's representation involves not only the difference between the heritage of imperialism (postcoloniality) and of British bourgeois antiimperialism or the Bloomsbury fraction with the London Asian hung in-between. It also involves the difference between genders and the confusion between sexual difference and gender difference. Rosie, often available in close-ups, is didactically useful, because her representation stages the stalling of programs of reading. Rosie dramatizes this confrontation between radicalism and an old-fashioned simple Enlightenment morality based on rather simple ethics which is opaque to the unenlightened. And that is the great unreadable at the moment in terms of genders.

Should homosexuality accept ethical heterosexuality as a model or what? *My Beautiful Laundrette* answered the question simply. But it comes open again in *Sammy*. And the film shows that in those close-ups where you can't really read Rosie as a character. Now of course many critics might object to this inability to read characterologically but it doesn't upset a reader like me because those moments of bafflement are the moments which make the film didactically useful and that's how a deconstructionist reads. It is the stalling of a program of reading that is dramatized here, just as much as the *différend* is staged in that moment in Quentin Crisp's *Resident Alien* when Crisp literally "confronts" a group of New York male homosexuals. Let us look, then, at the portrayal of lesbians in the film.

To grasp this portrayal let us make use of the meaning of the word "dharma" as "nature." What is the dharma of being-man and being-woman? One can dismiss ideology-as-nature as ideology-given-out-as-nature. But a nominalist use of dharma (as in Foucault "power," in Marx "value," in Derrida you choose) would alert us to the seriousness of nominalism. For the word "dharma" also *means* nature. The seriousness of nominalism is marked in this basically straight film by the relationship between lesbians and the use of language. Nothing is advanced about the "nature" of lesbianism. But if "nature" is trapped in the history and usage of a definitive word, lesbians are shown to be the custodians and manipulators of a considerable range of the geography of language. In other words, one can read the representation of lesbians in this film as indicating (the structural elusiveness entailed by one kind of) range by (the structural control over another kind of) range. Diachronic range by synchronic range, if you like. The focused difference here is not specifically between postcolonial and migrant, but between same-sex and same-gender.

This is indeed richer than *My Beautiful Laundrette* where interraciality was presented in a lyrical way, between the Pakistani boy and Daniel Day-Lewis, as a gay love with all the erotic furniture of romantic heterosexuality. It reminded one of nothing more than the liberal intellectual notion of the sweet and philosophical erotic permissiveness of classical Greece, when Greek boys could be boys and still become men. Having argued some years ago that Derrida writes as if the only position for a male feminist is to begin to understand the gay male rather than to begin to patronize women, I am obliged to acknowledge the element of daring in the idea of a gay male lead among London Asians.[10] But in *Sammy and Rosie,* the stake seems more serious. I am aware that the actual choice of black lesbians might have been in response to a more or less derisive p.c. challenge. The point is, surely, what came in response? It remains noticeable that in this film, interraciality is predominantly lesbian, and that the other side of white is a variety of blackness. And the indication of the historical range of the understanding of human sexual dharma (nature) by the spatial range of the dharma of language is didactically usable in the lesbians' control of the entire spectrum of language use. They move from an expository fact-finding use of English, in the scene in the office where the woman who speaks with a fairly heavy accent is Chinese–British, to hurling abuse in Urdu. This is boldly different from modeling gay male love on straight romance or the boys of Greece. It is not simply that their comments about heterosexuality are always funny. It is more important that they are never confined to one place, whereas in the earlier film the two boys had been kept in one place: the development of the solution to interracial problems. Although lyrical it was much more overtly didactic. The protagonist in *Launderette* says he doesn't want to fight and gets beaten up. In the end you have all the splashing-water ablution with the music welling up as the dirt is erased, so they are cleansed. The lesbians in *Sammy and Rosie,* by contrast, have a role that you cannot specify as a model in the same way because the didactic focus is blurred. From one perspective the central issue is Rafi and his son Sammy: the postcolonial and the migrant. On the other hand, the lesbians are not a subplot, their function is crucial to the film. It is because of their fact-finding that the film can utilize somewhat old-fashioned nonrealistic techniques, montage, the ghost figure, etc. The film justifies its move away from realism, its stylistic transformation, in terms of the two lesbians. In a certain sense one can say that the lesbian scenario operates the other.

The range of language includes the use of music. Kureishi uses Indy Pop in *Sammy and Rosie* but he didn't use it in *My Beautiful Laundrette.* An American audience has to be taught to appreciate that the social positioning of Indy Pop or Punjabi New Wave, is, for historical reasons, completely different from Ravi Shankar, Ali Akbar, Allen Ginsberg, sutras, the "hippie" India of the American sixties, descended from the collaboration between high European enthusiasm and one offshoot of high nationalist culturalism, and now being reterritorialized by Indian-Americans, demographically different from London Asians.[11] When Kureishi uses Indy Pop you do not have to understand the language of the lyrics. This is the predicament of the underclass postcolonial. That loss, the real cut-off from the so-called native language of the mainland, was in the case of the elite postcolonial, or the native bourgeoisie, a deliberate loss which has to be undone. In the case of the disenfranchised, one has to recognize that language has lost its properness in that situation. So the music in fact never interferes, is never explained, and needn't be. It's not verbally understood, it's always just under the threshold. What is understood is the American Motown stuff that the Blacks do. It is understood because there is a historical antecedent which is accessible, an antecedent established upon the remoter forgetfulness of the languages of Africa and the Greater Caribbean.

Over against both on the scale of intelligibility is the postcolonial's claim, an ugly yet comic self-separation from the less advantaged of the former colony, tragedy as well as farce: "London for me is tea and toast, and cunty fingers." Other examples of this genre would be Raju's use of English against Sanskrit in the film version of R.K. Narayan's *The Guide*, and the benign culturalist approval bestowed by Surendra Jain upon *Magiciens de la terre* that I touched upon in Chapter Ten. The only way out of this is self-conscious migrant race-mobility ("hybridity"-talk). Its seemingly political intellectual reification in "theory" is an extreme manifestation, useful for us, because it creates disturbance within the teaching machine. Kureishi's bitterly ironic comment on this is the deliberately pedantic subtitling of the lesbians' violently obscene abuse in Urdu.

Kureishi-Frears probably doesn't have a clue how to romanticize the two lesbian figures. The result comes out as convincing within its limits and funny. Whereas the two boys in *My Beautiful Laundrette* are landed with all the problems of being used in an erotic text which has long been established by Greek erotico-muscularism, used also by the fringes of that earlier wave of British antiimperialism of which Rosie and Alice are late blooms. It's the same problem in a minor key which gives us the cover chosen for the English version of volume 2 of Foucault's *History of Sexuality*.

Some have read the end of the film as a reassertion of the values of the heterosexual couple. That may certainly still be true. Yet some of its last-ditch precariousness is surely lodged in Sammy's statement, "We are not British, we are Londoners." In that difference of status or identification or label (and none of those words are adequate) we can grasp all the overdetermination of the migrant diaspora rather than the diasporic post-colonial. In that overdetermination we can begin to grasp what dominant-subordinate interraciality might mean: It's quite often understood as a sort of chromatic issue, as a question of skin color. It is of course very much more complicated, not a cultural exchange, but a moving target based on the city—*civitas* (for civil-ity rather than civilization), *polis* (for street politics rather than the political system). The cultural base is firm, compromised and defensive, and quite differently gendered; producing self-evidence out of synch with the politico-civil base of the *polis/civitas*. Inhabitants of the "inner city," the target of Thatcher's voice, which opens the film; yet also disengaged, part of a lyrical pseudoculture that feeds upon it. Sammy who attended the trendy University of Sussex, regularly visits the Institute of Contemporary Art, etc., is also completely into a version of "Oedipalism" with his Dad while at the same time talking a good game about all that 1960s stuff. On the other hand, Rosie does not commit to those narratives quite in the same way because of her cultural antecedents. Rosie's relationship to the family romance is not the same at all. Her chat about her father is on a different terrain. And so the whole texture of the social and the cultural-political differences within it become part of the heterosexual couple's coupleship. The heterosexual relationship is redefined—as Deleuze and Guattari would want to redefine it—in the context of a much broader network of relationships. Now I think Kureishi is less good in handling the heterosexuals than he is in handling the lesbians because with the lesbians he lets his good sense take over. Nonetheless I think there is a real attempt to see that a heterosexual relationship is not just Papa/Mama but a much larger network. And this comes through as an accessible allegory. Is it simply a way of declaring for the strength of heterosexual love? I don't want to let myself be troubled by it. Now that I have repeated my formula I hope I will be understood— yet what is it to understand or be understood?—when I say that I use that formulation for definite reasons. I think there are ways of reading texts which are more useful. I'm not excusing Kureishi. He may indeed have this problem. But for me that is not the important issue. For me the important issue is that I can quite happily read the end not as a declaration for the act of heterosexual love but rather as a premonition that the idea of such a courtship is defunct.

In this book I have repeatedly emphasized the formula of the new politics of reading: not to excuse, not to accuse, establish critical intimacy, use (or ab-use) the seeming weak moments for scrupulous ends. It is by way of that formula that I approach the question of *Sammy and Rosie*'s end. I read the end that way in terms of the debate on the relationship between crisis and the everyday. We've seen enough of whatever is called the everyday in Sammy and Rosie's life to doubt the solidarity that only a moment of crisis can bring. One can think of it in terms of the relation between revolution and postrevolution, the strongest statements of this from feminists in Algeria. They became comrades during the revolution. Once the dust had settled and the transitionality of the crisis is over, they go back to the old sexist ways of coping with the everyday. Let us read the comradeship of the couple in crisis with this lesson in mind.

"We are not British, we are Londoners."
In this book and elsewhere, I have discussed challenges to the idea of the nation, not from elite postnationalism, but from the historical dharma of varieties of the subordinant. Women carry internalized the lesson of the exchangeability of the home, the basis of identity. The superexploited women in Export Processing Zones are set adrift from "cultures" that are, in context, not necessarily "national." Homeworkers across the world are a systemic challenge to the notion of nation. The gendered tribal subaltern shares this lesson with the subaltern's distancing from both the culture of imperialism and anticolonial and postcolonial nationalism (Chapter Four). That quiet challenge to the nation-state comes both from the social inscription of bonded labor and the nominal identity of the tribal village: "This country is India. No, no, Madhpura" is to be compared with "We are not British, we are Londoners" in ways that *The Buddha of Suburbia* cannot fathom. The two points of view, the postcolonial subaltern (not Rafi, the postcolonial elite) and the migrant male assimilating by marriage, cannot possibly understand each other. In many ways, one is based on a refusal of the other. It is to Rushdie's credit that he attempts to mark this with his "I left home"; yet *Satanic Verses* falls back on magic realism for the laying out of village India. I will merely touch upon the migrant refusal of postcoloniality in my last chapter. I am developing this in my current work in terms of the negotiable nationality of the economic migrant in the context of transnational literacy.

"We are not British, we are Londoners." This is also a challenge to the refusal of entry into the nation that is the lot of the migrant. If it can be said that in cities is the sublation of the nomadic and communal living of forest and village, we have guarded that anthropological fiction in words like politics and citizenship. I can read Sammy with his uprooted roots as a discontinuous displacement of Douloti on her way home. Yet Britain and India are still nations—a fragile rational fiction that serves well in wars, border disputes, daily suspicion, and prejudice. If in the urban public culture of the migrant these hostilities are provisionally suspended, should we declare the world in its model and predict a world-peace telos, banal as any other, in the utopian nonrecognition that the hybridization of "national" cultures—through imperialism and development—does not resemble migrancy?

The final scene shows us Sammy and Rosie simply weeping in response to a crisis, as the group at the table depart. It is possible to use this scene in the classroom transactionally with students to talk about the relation of the crisis and the everyday. This is how solidarities are fabricated, manufactured directly in response to crisis and such alliances are very fragile. The rest of the film has prepared us to see this fragility and we should pay attention to the rest of the film.

In the wake of the Los Angeles clash between African-Americans and Asian migrants in the Rodney King Protest of 1992, it would be idle to deny that one of the facts of the migrant's or marginal's everyday that all must combat in crisis and after is the hostility between inner-city Blacks of Afro-Caribbean, African, and Asian origin. I am not sure if Kureishi, himself belonging the latter group, has been able to pull it off by constructing a figure who is totally outside of crisis yet reaching out, a figure of radical innocence, a cross-dressing would-be androgyne, a sweet fake drag queen, the other side of the savvy lesbians, the nicest all-around hybrid you could wish for: Danny-Victoria. But it must be admitted that he tries. A measure of his attempt is marked by Danny-Victoria's misreading of India. Danny-Victoria says to Rafi (and in the process he confuses India with Pakistan): "after all your way is just to sit down and be nonviolent and that's what we really ought to learn." And, of course, Rafi rises to the bait and is benevolent about Gandhi, a typical example of a postcolonial indigenous elite falling into a Ministry of Culture patter. But *we* know his standard defense of torture. And indeed Kureishi, a London Asian of Pakistani origin, is explicitly critical of the postcolonial Pakistani here, an attitude rather different from the usual ethnic-partisan root-searching. We might also remember that, although the moment is comic, it is this sort of misreading that produces great mobilizing signifiers of political action.

I am no longer sure that Kureishi succeeds in this. But in the name of the new politics of reading, as an Asian economic migrant in the United States, I pull at the possible faults and produce new uses: radical innocence, not stupidity; interracial solidarity in crisis, not romantic love. Have I read right? Will you grasp me? I cannot know. All I can be sure of is that to construct an ever-narrowing circle of politically acceptable texts spells danger, makes us forget our common enemy.

I would rather read the white American woman's ass with the two Ws, shown immediately after the death of the black woman, as a bitter comment on the roving American journalist—a common enough topos after Graham Greene's inauguration of it in *The Quiet American*—than Asian anti-Africanism yet once again. I would rather consider how much our own revolutionary tourism—I remember a renowned militant showing me her $400 Neiman-Marcus shoes minutes before entering a lecture room to electrify an audience with accounts of her racist exploitation— is complicit with those obscene buttocks.

If Rosie's radicalism misses the responsibility for the failure of decoloni- zation, Danny's innocence knows nothing of it. She is an official social worker, he unofficial. His educated accent, and his appreciation of her "downward mobility"—his words—make them best lovers. But they are not a couple. Danny is on the move, he has trouble with institutionality. The easy allegory of the film shows him struggling to get off an under- ground train as the main action opens. It must, however, be said that if Rushdie's limits were made visible in his choice of magic realism to depict village India, Kureishi's limits are marked by this ghostly figure, who locates the sins of indigenous capital in the South only in crimes against labor unions. But I must stop here. *Feminism in Decolonization* is another book.

A word in closing about the use of montage. It is in keeping with the film's juxtaposition of a whole range of fact-finding, social engineering activities. The film gives us a spectrum of the social text. There is Rosie the social worker and the American woman doing her photographs and articles and there are the two lesbian women finding out facts. A whole chain of displacements in terms of which you are shown how a quick fix or a quick judgment or a quick read is productively resisted by the film. I like the film better than *My Beautiful Laundrette,* which in some ways did give you that quick fix. In the article wrongly titled in English as "Commitment" Adorno says of Brecht that his use of montage in *The Resistible Rise of Arturo Ui* simply turns a political problem into a joke.[12] One hopes that Kureishi's montage technique would have satisfied Adorno. It is much more concerned with negotiating a certain kind of unease, a laughter tinged with unease and bafflement. That comes through in the montage particularly well as the film moves away from realism and the ghostly figure of the torture victim becomes more prominent. This ghost doesn't quite qualify as the guardian at the margin. That may be the price of privileging migrancy—history as an open wound, inside the machine.

13

Scattered Speculations on the Question of Culture Studies

Introduction

If in these last sections I have drawn upon theoretical work by Marx, Neitzsche, Beauvoir, Foucault, Derrida, Cixous, Irigaray, for reasons that I have tried always to keep up front, my substantive concern has been largely with the difference between the postcolonial and the migrant, although I have, of course, touched upon other issues as well. The practical imperative has been the use or ab-use of theory in the teaching of these diversified matters in U.S. postsecondary education. And, finally, with the limits of teaching.

In this essay I turn to the United States. My current work concerns itself much more intensely with the U.S. scene and transnationality. To provide a transition to the final section as well as to work that goes beyond the covers of this book, a few words might be in order. In the process, I will also tie together some lines of argument already laid out in these pages.

In Chapter Three, I have remarked on the new problems that arise when a word like "marginality" enters academic discourse. In Chapter Four, I attempt to point at the rural subaltern scene that is paying the price of (the failure of) decolonization. You will remember the role played by contractors in Devi's story—the lowest level of "development" activity in a developing country.

It is through a critique of "development" ideology that we can locate the migrant in the First World in a transnational frame shared by the obscure and oppressed rural subaltern. Otherwise, in our enthusiasm for migrant hybridity, Third World urban radicalism, First World marginality, and varieties of ethnographically retrieved ventriloquism, the subaltern is once again silent for us. By the Foucauldian logic laid out in Chapter Three, it is no surprise therefore that this critical avenue is now being occupied by techniques of knowledge. It is here that we track the appropriation of ecology. I turn briefly to the work of Vandana Shiva, a powerful figure in feminist-subalternist-ecology, to attend to her cautions:

> "Environmentalism" has finally become part of the dominant discourse. "Development" has given way to "sustainable development," and "growth" has given way to "green growth." Yet the ruling paradigm about environmental issues continues to be biased in favor of the North, and the elites of the South.[1]

It is the remoteness of the connections that allow the elite of the South to ignore their importance. Thus rural ecological problems, when noticed, are perceived as peripheral and precapitalist, and concern for their solution considered nonprogressive in other quarters; as sentimental, or subjective. And, as Shiva points out, we see each cluster of issues, if we see them at all, as individual "sets," "antisystemic movements," rather than operative moments in the functioning system of transnational capitalism determining itself through development, as in a prior dispensation through imperialism. As I have indicated throughout these chapters, that other, largely urban or metropolitan, subaltern, the homeworker, remains invisible for comparable reasons. Both our support of culture and/or race identity *and* our distrust of general narratives, stand in the way of this holistic perception. We will not understand that these movements, although local, are fully nonlocal in their impact, in order that transnational money-lending can be dissimulated as interest for the poor. Here the Derridean isolation of commercial capital as the object of criticism can perhaps be utilized; but even so the homeworker's relationship to women's waged and unwaged labor will skew our thought towards the surplus value of the human body, not only revenue and profit on the body of the earth. Be that as it may, if we dismiss general systemic critical perception as necessarily totalizing or centralizing, we merely prove once again that the subject of Capital can *in*habit its ostensible critique as well.

This expansion of the subjectship of Capital, as its post-Marxist, or feminist, or culturalist critique, is so pervasive that we might stop to think about it whenever spurious binaries arise: Third World Issues Must Be Kept Separate from Multiculturalism (director of a Women's Studies Institute in the E.E.D.); the Study of Postcoloniality Is Not Feminist (white feminist professor in the U.S.). There is interest, often unperceived by us, in not allowing transnational complicities to be perceived. There Capital is not the narrative of reference (Jameson) or *sub*individual (Foucault). If anything, it can be compared to Foucault's imagining of the field of force: "these then form a general line of force that traverses the local oppositions and links them together; to be sure, they also bring about redistributions, realignments, homogenizations, serial arrangements, and convergences of the false relations" (*HS*, 94). Shiva's call for "lip-service" (from radical intellectuals) to make this thinking "fashionable" shows us that careful cognitive mapping (Jameson) with the deconstructive awareness of complicity can have its uses for the internationalist activist, even if, in the intellectual's own circuit, it leads merely to self-perpetuating discourse at the mercy of the forces of reaction.[2]

At best I can write as one such intellectual. In that spirit, writing these words in the offices of an Alternative Development Research Collective in Dhaka (Bangladesh), let me tell a few stories before we enter the next section. I will let the reader draw her own conclusions, knowing the risks on both sides.

In a series of videos made by Christian Aid, John Marshall, an activist priest working in Hackney, a poor multiethnic area of London, makes the point that although their absolute standard of living is higher, the rehabilitation of these disenfranchized migrants would help forge links with the bottom layers of society in postcolonial countries. As one who constantly shuttles on the cheap flights favored by migrants on visits home (rather unlike the sensationalism of migrant-woman thrillers), I would, with respect, differ. The trajectories of the Eurocentric migrant poor and the postcolonial rural poor are not only discontinuous but may be, through the chain-linkage that we are encouraged to ignore, opposed. This is not an accusation. The migrant poor are certainly victims of racism. But, in a non-Eurocentric frame, disavowal of their hope of insertion into a developed economy is of no use; although this hope is only a discolored, rejected, and broken fragment of the materials that build the edifice of development.

I came upon the video by chance in a rural health center in Bangladesh and watched it in the house of a resident woman doctor. In another context, and in a rather inaccessible interior village, I was chatting with another woman (an officeholder in the government's program of Women's Development) about the Bangladeshis of London's East End and the white Londoner's racist contempt. My friend, speaking from the perspective of an educated provincial middle-class woman government worker, exclaimed, of these London Bangladeshis, "But they're rich!" And indeed, the "although their absolute standard of living is higher. . . ." of John Marshall shows once again a set-perception, not a systemic one. On the other hand, the fact that these migrants might send money home is not their critique of development. With the lapse of time, even this connection becomes tenuous.

Both separations and false continuity are therefore part of the problem. In the name of transnationality, let us enter the United States.

I

I wrote the first part of this paper in response to a hundred-odd manuscript pages of Bruce Ackerman's book *Discovering the Constitution*.[3] Fleshing it out, I have come to sense that the paper shares some of the occupational weaknesses of the new and somewhat beleaguered discipline of a transnational study of culture, especially if that study steps back from what is perceived as contemporary. Conceptual schemes and extent of scholarship cannot be made to balance. Once again, then, the following pages must be offered as possible directions for future work. I hope this will satisfy those friendly critics who have remarked that my point is that one needs to know nothing in order to do Culture Studies!

Here is a summary of my understanding of what I read in Ackerman's manuscript pages:

A dualist view of U.S. political practice is true to American political philosophy and history. Legitimizing it in terms of foreign (read European) models is incorrect. The dualism is between normal everyday politics where We the People are not much involved. Contrasted to this are the great changes in political practice—constitutional politics—where We the People are mobilized and involved in the process of change through higher lawmaking. Professor Ackerman is aware that by thus naming the letter and the spirit of the law, so to speak, as *normal* and constitutional, he is taking the view that the role of We the People in the American polity is activated in "exceptional" cases.

Ackerman's historical account discloses that these revolutions in the law are also managements of crisis. Although We the People were mobilized at the time of Reconstruction, it was the crisis of a possible impeachment of the president that brought the Constitutional amendments. Similarly, in spite of the electoral mobilization of We the People, it was the crisis of a possible court-packing that brought in the welfare state of the New Deal. Thus the changes from a federalist division of powers through a nationalist separation of powers to the consolidation of presidential power can be inserted into a continuation of *normal* political practice. Indeed, if I understand right, Ackerman comes close to suggesting that, in the modern context at least, the electoral mobilization of We the People provides an alibi for domestic crisis-management among the powers by allowing the party to claim "A People's Mandate."

We are, in other words, hearing the story of the gradual constitution (small c), normalization, and regularization of something called the People (capital P) as a collective subject (We) in the interest of crisis-management. Ackerman acknowledges that "the Constitution presupposes a citizenry," and calls this process the "popular cultivation of the arts of liberal citizenship." And if you will forgive a slightly tendentious phrase, "the ideological state apparatus" does work to this end.

Here, for trouble-free normal politics, is the making of a collective "We the People" in the high school classroom:

> Mr. Bower's American Government class has been studying the U.S. Constitution. He has designed a rich multiple-ability groupwork task to help his students understand the relationship among the three branches of the federal government. To reach his objectives, he wants to challenge the students to think metaphorically and to produce insights that allow students to use their critical thinking skills. . . . The task will require many different abilities. Some students will have to be good conceptual thinkers; some will need to be good artists; at least one person will have to be able to quickly find the relevant passages in the Constitution; and someone will need to have strong presentation skills. . . . [This] example . . . demonstrate[s] the advantage of groupwork that may be gained with the proper preparation and structure necessary for success.[4]

In fact, if not in intent, Mr. Bower is preparing a General Will where the signifier "People," seemingly remaining constant as a referent, is being charged with a more and more distanced and mediated signification, as actual agency passes from the popularly elected House of Commons model to today's electoral securing of the noun implicit in the adjective "Popular" in "Popular Mandate." I do not question the astuteness of Ackerman's analysis or the efficiency of the gradual reconstitution of the signifying phrase "We the People." I do however question the conviction that this reading gives America back to the people in the American way. I dare to say this because such an unexamined view of the academic's social task (that would in fact be dormant and uncritical in everyday politics) is currently laying waste our own field of humanistic education— the proper field of the production of something called a "People."[5]

If we move from the techniques of knowledge production to the techniques of the electoral securing of the Popular Mandate, this becomes even clearer. Editorials in all major newspapers have commented extensively on the fact that, under media management, candidates at all levels are becoming detached from local or popular constituencies. Jean Baudrillard

260 / Outside in the Teaching Machine

has called this the electronic production of the "hyper-real," which is simulated by agencies of power as the way things really are. "Simulation" here means declaring the existence of something that does not exist. Derrida has pointed at the ceaseless effort to construct the simulacrum of a committed and participatory public through talk show and poll, thus apparently (but only apparently) freezing the irregular daily pulse of democracy (see Chapter Five). Attention to the details of meaning-making might describe the mechanisms of securing a higher law as a spectacular and seamless exercise in simulation.[6]

I have taken a dualist, exceptionalist, and crisis-management reading of the Constitution as instrument of higher lawmaking through Popular Mandate to its logically rather unsettling consequences to highlight an obvious point: A constitutional victory operates within a calculus that does not correspond to the possibility or even the guarantee of justice in the name of any personalized picture of a collection of subjects called "We the People." In fact, as I will insist later in this paper, a constitution can operate only when the person has been coded into rational abstractions manipulable according to the principle of reason. The presupposed collective *constitutional* agent is apart from either the subject, or the universal-in-singular ethical agent.

Yet the narrative guarantee of justice in the name of a collection of subjects is perennially offered as legitimation to the people who will secure the "Popular Mandate." And the authority behind this narrative legitimation—the Constitution as the expression of the general will to justice exercised in time of crisis—is itself secured with reference to an origin-story: the original documents left by the Founding Federalists, Reconstruction Republicans, New Deal Democrats.

It seems to me that an innovative and flexible text for use such as the U.S. Constitution can only be given what Jean-François Lyotard has called a paralogical legitimation.[7] In other words, it provides occasion for morphogenetic innovation—innovations leading to new forms.

Strictly speaking, *para*logical legitimation is not *teleo*logical. Yet the legitimizing debates at times of crisis impose closure by claiming faithfulness to original intent, even if only the intent to keep the document historically flexible, and thus restoring its origin by gaining its end. The more "accurate" guarantee, not of justice as the expression of a general will of We the People, but of a persistent critique of originary legitimations, by the very people who supply the Popular Mandate for the electoral machinery, can be precariously fabricated if the paralogical is kept in mind.

One of the counternarratives that can help as a reminder of the paralogical is that of the contingency of origins. Let us consider an example. Ackerman correctly states that the American origin was not simply "an escape from old Feudalism," as de Tocqueville would have it, but a new start. Is it banal to remind ourselves that this new start or origin could be secured because the colonists encountered a sparsely populated, thoroughly precapitalist social formation that could be managed by prepolitical maneuvers? Robin Blackburn's recent compendious book *The Overthrow of Colonial Slavery* has argued that the manipulation of chattel slavery as an item of political economy was also effective in securing a seemingly uninscribed slate in a space effectively cleared of political significance in the indigenous population.[8] No discussion of the historical development of the mode of operation of the Constitution can afford altogether to ignore this rusing at the origin:

> The key slogan in the struggle against the British had been "no taxation without representation." . . . The acceptance that slaves as wealth should entitle Southern voters to extra representation built an acknowledgement of slavery into the heart of the Constitution. . . . The text of the Constitution resorted to shamefaced circumlocution rather than use the dreaded words "slave" and "slavery": "Representatives and direct Taxes shall be apportioned among the several states which may be included within this Union, according to their respective Numbers, which shall be determined by adding to the whole Number of free Persons, including those bound to Service for a Term of Years, and excluding Indians not taxed, three fifths of all other persons."[*]

Later in this essay I will present Derrida's discussion of the originary ruse that produces all signatories: the politics of the proper name. Here the origin of the "Good People" of these colonies guaranteeing as they are guaranteed by the signatories is secured by staging the ruse in a theater of violence.

Since I am an Indian citizen, let me offer you a counternarrative of what, in Ackerman's vocabulary, may be called a "failed originary moment." "After much hesitation . . . Elizabeth [I] . . . granted a charter of incorporation on December 31st 1600" to the East India Company. As is well known, there was increasing conflict between the British government and the Company until, by Pitt's India Act of 1784, "the control of the Company was brought under the House of Commons."[9] Of course it is absurd to offer a fable as fact, or attempt to rewrite history counterfactually. But let us remember that Ackerman has the integrity to admit that he too is retelling a story. Let us also remember that in the eighteenth century, economists such as Adam Smith, functionaries of the East India Company, as well as the British popular press, were exercised by the failed parallel between the American and Indian examples.[10] Let me therefore ask you to imagine that, because the East India Company was incorporated, and because India was not a sparsely populated, thoroughly precapitalist social formation easily handled through pre-political maneuvers and the manipulation of chattel slavery, in other words because it was not possible for a group of British merchants to establish a settlement colony there, no apparent origin could be secured and no Founding Fathers could establish the United States of India, no "Indian Revolution" against Britain could be organized by foreign settlers.

I admire the United States greatly, so much so that I have made it my second home, lived and worked here over half my life. Speaking as a not-quite-not-citizen, then, I would submit to you that Euramerican origins and foundations are *also* secured by the places where an "origin" is violently instituted. In the current conjuncture, when so much of the identity of the American nation-state is secured by global economic and political manipulation, and when the imminent prospect of large-scale fence-mending beckons and recedes into a New World Order, it is not disrespectful of the energy of We the American People to insist that domestic accounts that emphasize American as a self-made giant illegally wrenching the origin of freedom from merely a moribund Europe has its own political agenda.

II

Constitutional talk is normally a tale of transactions between Europe and America. Transnational Culture Studies must put this transaction in an international frame. If, for example, the project of recovering or discovering the true structure of the national discourse from ideas of foreign manufacture is taken as a general principle of the study of constitutions, the enterprise would become productively problematic as soon as we move outside Euramerica. One cannot substitute "native" for "national" in that undertaking. A transnational study of culture will not neutralize or disciplinarize the problem by defining it away as "comparative" work, assimilate it by considering the last great wave of imperialism as basically a part of metropolitan history, or yet, however implicitly, bestow upon colonialism what Bernard Williams has called "moral luck" in the context of ethical philosophy. (See Chapter Three.)

Turkey is a most interesting case in point. If we take the Conquest of Istanbul (1453) as a dividing line, we can see parallel but highly differentiated formations developing in Mediterranean and Western Europe on the one hand and the Ottoman Empire on the other.[11] What characterizes the latter is the extraordinarily active and vastly heterogeneous diasporic activity that is constantly afoot on its terrain.

There is still an unfortunate tendency, in the "comparativist" arena, to represent the Ottoman Empire as governed by the static laws of something like "the Asiatic Mode of Production," with its change-inhibiting bureaucratic hierarchy and absence of private property in land.[12] If, however, Western Europe is not taken as a necessary norm, the successes and vicissitudes of the Ottoman Empire can be seen as an extraordinary series of experiments to negotiate questions of ethnicity, religion, and "national" identity upon a model rather different from the story of the emergence of nationalism in the former space. How much of the events of the nineties in Eastern Europe retain the lineaments of the nonteleological (tactical) nature of those ceaseless negotiations, suppressed for almost a century under the ferocious teleology of the Bolshevik experiment, and now emerging into a completely different field of strategy? The conflict over Nogorny-Karabakh had seemed an interesting example in 1988, when Chapter Three was first put together. Four years later, at the time of revision, that plot of land has become the issue around which Turkey is rethinking its role, as the Russia-based conglomerate formation in the area has come apart.

The staging of the fragments of Islam in that region is today under question once again. By citing an inter- or multinationality whose control was Islamic, I am of course not interested in legitimizing the Eurocentric model by endorsing an "Islamic Revival," where an "Islam" contained in diversified nation-states, in postcoloniality and migrancy, is demonized or sacralized as a monolith. It has been argued by contemporary scholars that the economic formations of late eighteenth-century Western Europe began to shift the balance within the Ottoman Empire so that its Muslim component began increasingly to slip or remain contained in a precapitalist mode. Kemal Kerpat has argued that what was a curiosity about the West was gradually recoded as the necessity to imitate.[13] Religious nationalism began to grow as "the ideal of impartiality which insulated the bureaucracy" began to break down.

The Ottoman trade monopoly on the Black Sea came to an end in 1774. The Mediterranean trade had been dominated by the West. Now "for the common good of the two Empires," Russia stepped into the Black Sea trade. In 1798 Napoleon invaded Egypt, threatening the British trade route to India. "The Ottoman economy gradually entered a period of total submission to the industrial giants of Europe." In this transforming society, religious difference gradually gets politically recoded as majorities and minorities, until, in a century's time, "the Ottoman government [is] increasingly called 'Turkish,' and 'Turkish' [now] means a dominant Muslim majority."

This is not merely a demographic change imposed from without. It is a discursive shift making possible certain kinds of statements, ultimately making possible a Turkish nationalist who "finds it 'in vain to offer resistance' to European civilization," the "visionary mimic man as father of the nation," Mustafa Kemal Ataturk.[14]

We are speaking of the same period—1774, 1798—as in the cases of the U.S. and India. But the narrative is different again. In the case of the United States, an originary claim is secured. In the case of India, colony and empire step forth as place-holders for "a failed originary moment." Here the question of origin is settled differently.

Let us consider secularism without the moralistic fervor with which we contemplate its "organic development" in the West (as we tried at the end of Chapter Eleven) just as we thought of "nation"s a moment ago without necessarily checking them against the story of the rise of nationalism in the West.[15] In a practically multinational empire like the Ottoman, the separation of Church and State was practically effective in the interest of the overarching State. This secularism was not the name of the socializing of Western Christianity which has something like a relationship with the rise of industrial monopoly capitalist imperialism. It was rather a precapitalist practical (not philosophical) secularism which was given loose ideological support by a communitarianist universalism taken to be present in the Islamic *umma*. (Any suggestion that this can be suddenly injected into "Islamic" politics today is to work in the "naive conviction that the Muslim masses are still living in the religious atmosphere of the Middle Ages.")[16]

The impact of a shift in world trade begins to reconstitute the *habitus* (Pierre Bourdieu's term) of the region into the Western European discursive formation at the end of the eighteenth century. In other words, things begin to "make sense" in Western European terms. The Ottoman example is now a "deviation." And now, in a reconstituted Muslim-majority Turkish State, it is possible for Western Europe to *offer* an *originary* model. Turkey begins to constitute itself as a nation-state. The Constitution of 1876 is its first inscription, the general "balkanization" of the empire after the First World War its necessary military-political consolidation.[17]

I have argued in Chapter Eleven that the peculiar play of contingency in the narrativization of history should not be construed as the Laws of Motion of History. My argument has been developed in the context of presenting a contrast between the circumstances contingent upon two great monotheisms—Christianity and Islam—in the possibility of their reinscription as secularism as such. Here I offer an example from recent Indian history.

The Khilafat movement (1918–1925) in India, launched in the name of a multinational unitarian universalist Islam supporting the Ottoman Caliphate, was out of joint with the times.[18] It was in fact an anti-imperialist nationalist attempt at the consolidation of the minority rights of Islam in India. Here too, the reconstitution of the Imperial Mughal State and the independent principalities of India through (more direct) contact with industrial monopoly capitalist imperialism had established a new habitus: majority-minority. In the sphere of decolonization it was European-style nationalism that was on the agenda. (In fact, that was the subtext of the Khilafat movement.) Thus, although the Khilafat movement lent support to the rise of Mustafa Kemal, the creator of "modern Turkey," it was by Kemal's Constitution, in early 1924, that the actual Khilafat or Caliphate was abolished. For the Indians, after a negotiated Independence, in 1947, Western European codes and English Common Law offered models of origin. The constitution of the secular state of India was launched under the auspices of Lord Mountbatten, although the voice of Islam and a semitized Hinduism as alternatives to the European Enlightenment were still heard.[19]

Let us look now at the question of origin in the Turkish case. A simulated alien origin or source, from which to draw "modernization" and constitutionality appears, politically and philosophically cognizable, facing a terrain reterritorialized in response to the global release of industrial capital. The teleological vision of a Turkish "nation" now effaces the incessantly negotiated multinationality that was the Ottoman Empire because that can no longer be recognized as multi-"nation"-ality. The gap can be measured by the distance between Midhat Pasha's Constitution of 1876 and Mustafa Kamal's Constitution of 1924.

> 1876: Art. 1. The Ottoman Empire comprises present countries and possessions and semi-dependent provinces. It forms an indivisible whole from which no portion can be detached under any pretext whatever. . . . Art. 8. All subjects of the Empire are called Ottomans, without distinction, whatever faith they profess; the *status* of an Ottoman is acquired and lost, according to conditions specified by law.[20]

1924: Art. 2. The Turkish State is republican, nationalist, populist, etatist, secular and reformist. . . . Art. 68. Every Turk is born free, and free he lives.[21]

Whatever the discrepancy, in the U.S. or in Turkey, "between constitutional norms and political realities," between empire and nation, by 1924 "the free Turk" is coded into constitutional rationality as a person, as opposed to the Ottoman.[22] "The free American," comparably coded, can disavow the contingent securing of his origin, and present his felicitous connection with world trade at the moment of origin (compounded by domestic simple commodity production with "organic" links to industrial capitalism) as *only* a bold rupture.[23] "The free Turk" is obliged to a perennial acknowledgment of European debt.

As for the Republic of India, which is now attempting to consolidate central power in the place of a loose federalist model, the most horrifying dissension is arising there from the lack of fit between the constitutional presupposition of a "People" and a heterogeneous electorate not "organically" deduced from it, blindly seeking other channels to national agency. The national agency of "foreign" provenance still remains the shaky alibi for federal policy. (Under the New World Order, the protected economy of the Nehru-Mountbatten Constitution has at last been effectively undone. Has the constitutional status of the Indian subject been affected? That question now waits upon the emergence of "Hindu India" as a deterrent to "Islamic Fundamentalism," a violent regression that will still use the alibis of constitutionality.)[24]

The Japanese constitutions from 1889 to 1947, the latter (though this is at issue at the moment) drafted by staff members of General Douglas MacArthur, would provide another, quite different, set of manipulations of narratives of origin and end. In the interest of balance, I will not proliferate examples here.

I should, however, like to look at the "free Turk" in a sharper focus.

In the brief first section, entitled "Declarations of Independence," of *Otobiographies,* Derrida points out that "the good People of these Colonies" in whose name the representatives sign the American Declaration of Independence do not, strictly speaking, exist.[25] As such they do not yet have the name and authority before the Declaration. At the same time, they are required to produce the authority for a Declaration which gives them being.

"This unheard-of thing [is] an everyday occurrence." That fact does not, however, authorize us to ignore it as trivial.

This undecidability between, let's say, a performative structure and a constative structure is *required* in order to produce the sought-after effect. . . . The signature [on the Declaration] invents the signer [the name and authority of "the good People"] . . . in a sort of fabulous retroactivity. . . . [T]his fabulous event is only possible in truth thanks to [*par*] the inadequation to itself of a present. . . . The constitution . . . guarantee[s] . . . your passport . . . marriages . . . checks . . . [by] the signature of each American citizen [which] depends, in fact and by right, on this indispensable confusion. . . . [The "good People"] sign in the name of the laws of nature and in the name of God, creator of nature . . . and present performative utterances *as* constative utterances.[26]

This confusion guarantees the identity of the national agent—passport, marriage, check. But this originary "hypocrisy," entailing the involvement of the laws of nature, guarantees/produces the national agent *as such,* who is also the guarantor of the guarantee. The first is seen in the constative/ performative in "every Turk is *born* free" (1924). The second is seen in the guarantor/guaranteed in the self-inadequate present of "the system *is* based on the principle that the people personally and effectively *direct* their own destinies" (1921).

If the series of Turkish constitutions are read with Derrida's extraordinary attention to detail, we would, again and again, trace this disclosure/ effacement of the trace, at the origin of the founding of modern constitutions. Undecidability secures the agent's ability to decide as a free national agent.

Why do we need to remember this? So that the possibility of agency is not taken to guarantee the self-proximity of the subject, and national or ethnic *identity* do not become fetishized. Nationalism in the context of metropolitan countries can then become the justification for the founding racist ideology of imperialism and neocolonialism, "the end of history," declaring "the triumph of the West," predicated upon being "turned off by [the] nihilistic idea of what literature was all about [taught by] Roland Barthes and Jacques Derrida."[27] In the context of the Third World, if the undecidable and slippery founding of agency is seen to be the birth of a new man/woman, the act of the founding, celebrating *political* independence, comes to be seen as an end in itself. We have seen in Chapter Four that some remain outside this constative/performative ruse. By contrast, the transplanting of nationalities in migrancy shows up the negotiability of the Constitutional subject.

Responding to the U.S. reception of his *Islam and Capitalism,* so staunch a Marxist as Maxime Rodinson is obliged to renounce both economics as the last instance and access to scientific truth:

> I merely hold that the translation of the popular will into political decisions requires something else than free parliamentary elections, quite other arrangements differing according to the social condition of the population under consideration. . . . My struggle [is] precisely against faith in the panacea of political independence. That does not mean that I scorn political independence, that I renounce my support of the struggle for decolonization. . . . Just as it is important to perceive, behind the scenes in the representative institutions, the reality of the forces of economic pressure, so too is it necessary to understand that a world of independent political units, each with an equal voice at the U.N., even endowed with representative institutions, does not, in itself, make a "free world." That is undoubtedly obvious to the most naïve observer of the international political game, but the ideology that sacralizes political institutions impedes acknowledgement of all the consequences. . . . The whole truth is no more accessible to man than full freedom or complete harmony of social relations.[28]

In the midsixties, writing for a French rather than U.S. audience, Rodinson had told his readers that "there remain[ed] a very large area of the field of learning that can and must be explored with . . . philosophical presuppositions provisionally suspended . . . and the positivist procedure is the one to follow."[29] The American Preface, quoted above, shows the suspension of assurances of positivism as well. Activist thinkers of the third or any world, not merely anxious "to shine in some salon, lecture-theatre or meeting-hall," repeatedly come up against the call to suspension when questions of originary justification for labels of identity confront them.[30]

Having acknowledged that basing collective practice on the ground of identity begs the question in the very house of self-evidence, how do we reopen the distinction between the U.S. and Turkish cases? It is in the area of the origin from which the new nation separates itself, an issue, as we have noticed in Ackerman's discussion, that is not without a certain importance: "In this case, another state signature had to be effaced in 'dissolving' the links of colonial paternity or maternity."[31] As the Declaration states: "it becomes necessary for one people to dissolve the political bands which have connected them with another." It is here that the laws of God and Nature provide the necessary last instance that can accommodate "the hypocrisy indispensable to a politico-military-economic, etc. coup de force."[32] And stand behind the Constitution as pretext. The difference between this confident dissolution of origin and the cultural confusion and disavowal attendant upon migrancy is the difference between colonialism and migrancy. Here we are discussing a historical version of the precursor of modernization which will not fit the colonial discourse model too easily.

Like the U.S. Declaration, what the Turkish Constitution separates itself from is its own past or rather it secures a separation already inaugurated by the Ottoman Constitution of 1876. In terms of the access to agency, the earlier constitution had not yet fully coded a *coup* (blow) as a *coupure* (cut). The irreducible performative/constative confusion sustaining Art. 3 (1924): "sovereignty belongs *unconditionally* to the nation," depends on the abolition of the Caliphate.

And this is not declared in the name of the Good People of Turkey; merely in the unwritten name of Europe. The "national" is already catachrestic, "wrested from its proper meaning." I have discussed this in its current context in Chapter Three.

It might therefore be politically useful to consider whether Euro-American origins are also not catachrestic, secured by *other* places; to consider, in Derrida's words, "the politics of the proper name used as the last instance." God/Nature in the case of the United States, Europe in the case of Turkey. The two must be read side by side. Turkey is especially interesting because it is not a case of decolonization, but rather an obligatory self-de-imperialization. For a transnational study of culture, the "comparative" gesture cannot be docketed in a comfortable academic subdivision of labor; but rather, the inexhaustible taxonomy of catachreses—*how* a constitution begs the question of origin—must at least be invoked at every step.[33] Culture Studies must therefore constantly risk (though not flaunt) a loss of specialism.

III

It is perhaps unrealistic to expect transnational literacy in the high school classroom. Indeed, I have argued elsewhere that even the undergraduate classroom might be too early to broach true transnational literacy.[34] It was, however, interesting to find that, although "Constitutional Convention," "constitutional monarchy," and "Constitution of the United States" were three items listed under "What literate Americans know" in E.D. Hirsch's provocative book *Cultural Literacy*, the Constitution was not an index entry. In other words, constitutional matters did not form part of Hirsch's own thinking in the making of his argument. There is nothing in his index between "Conservatism" and "Constructive

Hypothesis."[35] In Sections I and II, I have tried to build toward the argument that, if one is going to speak for or plan for that complicated thing, an "American," one must think of his or her relationship to the Constitution.

If the high school social sciences class gives America to the people in the American way, and if the American way is divided into the *normal* and the constitutional, and the high school humanities class is restructuring itself by way of books such as *Cultural Literacy,* humanities teachers on the tertiary level ought perhaps to ask what the cultural politics of the production of the "American Way" might be.

Like E.D. Hirsch, Jr., I am a teacher of English. I must take into account that English is in the world, not just in Britain and the United States. Yet, English is the medium and the message through which, in education, Americans are most intimately made. And, (1) the history of higher law-making, the reality of normal politics, and changes in electoral mechanics show us that the connection between "We the People" and a General Will is constantly negotiable; (2) a making of Americans that would be faithful to American origins is not just a transaction with Europe; (3) as teachers in the humanities, and as teachers of English, our role in training citizens should not ignore this.

I entered a department of English as a junior in 1957 in another world, in Presidency College at the University of Calcutta. Yet, such is the power of epochs or eras that I did not come to the slow thinking of *other* worlds choreographing the march of English until about eighteen years ago, when I had already been teaching in the United States for about a decade. Thus here too my perspective is of the not-quite-not-citizen, an economic migrant with a toehold in postcoloniality.

As such, I must speak from within the debate over the teaching of the canon.

There can be no general theory of canons. Canons are the condition of institutions and the effect of institutions. Canons secure institutions as institutions secure canons. The canon as such—those books of the Bible accepted as authentic by the Church—provides a clear-cut example. It is within this constraint, then, that some of us in the profession are trying to expand the canon.

Since it is indubitably the case that there is no expansion without contraction, we *must* remove the single author courses from the English major curriculum. We must make room for the coordinated teaching of the new entries into the canon. When I bring this up, I hear stories of how undergraduates have told their teachers that a whole semester of Shakespeare, or Milton, or Chaucer, changed their lives. I do not doubt these stories, but we have to do a quality/quantity shift if we are going to canonize the new entries. I have given something like a general rationale for this expansion in the first part of my paper. And, to be consistent with this resolve, even the feminist approaches to Shakespeare, the Marxist approaches to Milton, and the antiimperialist approaches to Chaucer (are there those?) will have to relinquish the full semester allowed on the coattails of the Old Masters of the Canon. The undergraduates will have their lives changed perhaps by a sense of the diversity of the new canon and the unacknowledged power-play involved in securing the old. The world has changed too much. The least we can do to accept it is to make the small move to push the single author courses up into the terminal M.A.

The matter of the literary canon is in fact a political matter: securing authority. In order to secure authority we sometimes have to engage in some scrupulous versions of "doctrinaire gesture politics."[36] But, in the double-take that the daily administering of that authority entails comes the sense

> that there can be no "knowledge" in political practice. . . . Political practice involves the calculation of effect, of the possiblities and results of political action, and that calculation rests on political relations [in this case within the institutional network of United States tertiary education] which condition the degrees of certainty of calculation and the range of the calculable.[37]

A well-known paragraph in Capital, III, stages this double-take impressively. First the tremendous gestures toward the Realm of Freedom and the Realm of Necessity, the entire span of the human being in Nature and in social action; finally, the brief concluding sentence of the range of the calculable: "The reduction of the working day is the founding condition [Grundbedingung]."[38] A model for emulation: a lot of gesture politics, talk of other worlds. But the reduction of the space and time spent on the old canon is the founding condition.

What comes to fill the released space and time? Even the most cursory look at the publishers' catalogues that cross our desks, and the ever-proliferating journals concerned with the matter of the countercanon convinces us that there is no shortage of material. What I will say will seem to leave out many subtleties of approach. But please bear with me, for that is the hazard of all overviews. Let me then tabulate the "others," at least keeping in mind that the lines cross, under and over one item to another: Women; women of color; gays, lesbians; Afro-America; immigrant literature; literature of ethnicity; working-class literature; working-class women; non-Western literature; and, in peculiar companionship, something called "theory."[39]

I am not the only feminist who thinks that the situation of women's literature as such is rather particular here. Some women had made it into the general canon. "A gentleman's library," wrote H.P. Marquand, a thoroughly sexist genteel American novelist writing in 1958 in his particularly sexist novel *Women and Thomas Harrow*, "as the [small-town, New England, nineteenth-century] Judge very well understod, comprised the British poets, the works of Bulwer Lytton, the Waverly Novels, Dickens and Thackeray, Austen and the Brontë sisters and Trollope."[40] We can update this list by at least Virginia Woolf, Toni Morrison, and perhaps Edith Wharton.

With regard to these writers, even more than with the old masters, it is a question of restoration to a feminist perspective. But outside of this sphere, there were all the certainly-as-good-as-the-men women writers who did not get into the canon, as critics like Jane Tompkins and Elaine Showalter have shown and inspired other scholars and critics to work at showing, because the larger grid of social production would not let them in.[41] (I am naming recent critics, but of course there are hundreds of people to name. The choice is dictated by range, time, the limits of my knowledge, and the circle of my friends.)

In this broad sweep, and speaking only from the angle of bursting into the canon, how can the institution be obliged to calculate the literature of gender-differentiated homosexuality? Only with the assumption that, since sexuality-and-sexual-difference is one of the main themes and motors of literary production, this literature, in its historical determinations, continues to complicate and supplement that network, not only by giving us the diverse scoring of "the uses of pleasure," but also by showing us how, by the divisive logic of normalizing the production of reproductive heterosexuality, we work at the continued securing of even the enlarged canon.

Two such different scholars and critics as bell hooks and Hazel Carby have shown that the moment the color black is injected into these calculations, the structures of exclusion that have to be encountered appear much less accessible, much more durable.[42] We need an approach here that is more than an awareness of the contemporary culture of white supremacy, of the fetishization of the black body, of the histories of black heroism in the nineteenth century that complete the list. The work on slave narratives done by women like Mary Helen Washington and others begins to give us a sense of what has been called *"the reverse side"* of the mere "trac[ing] back from images to . . . structure," a tracing that constituted the self-representation of the American literary canon since its inception.[43] By comparison, the restoration and insertion of the white-majority feminist canon is a matter of correcting and altering the established image-structure line of representation as if it restrained the garment of the body politic. With the able editorship of Henry Louis Gates, Jr., and others, explosive quantities of material for study are being made available. Gates's own work, tracing figurations of Africa, takes us out of the strictly English canon into the area of culture studies.[44]

This literature, the literature of slavery, struggle, freedom, social production, is different from the narratives of migrant ethnicity inscribed on the body of something called "America." There cannot be a general concept of the other that can produce and secure both. In the interest of solidarity and gesture politics, we must forget these differences. For the painstaking task of training students and teachers within the institutional obligation to certify a canon, however, we must remember them.

It seems right that the literature of the working class should form a part of disciplinary preparation. Yet in this parade of abstract figures on the grid of canonical calculation—woman, gay, lesbian, black, ethnic—the class-subject is aggressively more abstract as a concept. And on that level of abstraction, there may be a contradiction between embattled class consciousness and the American Dream. Perhaps in Britain the situation is different; both because of its *earlier* entry into the organized left and its *later* entry into something resembling the American Dream, through Thatcher's brilliant maneuvers.[45] One cannot not commend the study of the writing of the exploited in struggle. Yet is there something particularly disqualifying about "working-class" becoming a canonical descriptive rather than an oppositional transformative? Certainly the basic argument of Jonathan Rée's *Proletarian Philosophers* would seem to suggest so.[46]

This could in fact be the problem with all noncanonical teaching in the humanities, an implicit confusion between *descriptive* canonical practices within an institution and *transformative* practices relating to some "real" world. It is this area of confusion that can be depolemicized and made productive, through deconstructive strategies of teaching. With this in mind, I will soon touch upon the need for deconstructive, power/knowledge-based, generally poststructuralist, preparation for our *faculty*. My cautions about the *undergraduate* teaching of poststructuralism relates to the breeding of recuperative analogies or preprogrammed hostility toward poststructuralism within the institutional calculus.

Let us, for the moment, avoid this problem and go back to our English major, strung tight with the excitement of learning to read the diversity of the new canon: a bit of the old masters in new perspectives, women's literature, black women's literature, a glimpse of Afro-America, the literature of gendered homosexuality, of migrant ethnicity, of the exploited in struggle.

We are taking good teaching for granted, a teaching that can make the student grasp that this *is* a canon, that this *is* the proper object of study of the new English major. Teaching is a different matter from our list of ingredients.[47] The proof of the pudding is in the classroom. And, as I will say again, pedagogy talk is different from conference talk. Let us then return to our well-taught undergraduate and look at the last two items on our list: theory, and the literature of the rest of the world.

Theory in the United States institution of the profession of English is often shorthand for the general critique of humanism undertaken in France in the wake of the Second World War and then, in a double-take, further radicalized in the midsixties in the work of the so-called poststructuralists. I believe this material has no claim to a *separate* enclave in our undergraduate major.[48]

(This remark is not as dire as it sounds. It is because I am confident of the *practical* possibilities of the critique of humanism that I am cautious about using it too soon as more than a pedagogic method, or as a pervasive and foregrounded structural topic of discussion. I am *not* discouraging theoretical teaching, or even an integration of theory into the general approach, on the undergraduate level. And I insist that the critical moment be included in teaching the great masters of European criticism, a practice that is all-too-often ignored even in graduate teaching.)

The critique of humanism in France was related to the perceived failure of the European ethical subject after the War. The second wave in the midsixties, coming in the wake of the Algerian revolution, sharpened this in terms of disciplinary practice in the humanities and social sciences because, as historians, philosophers, sociologists, and psychologists, the participants felt that their practice was not merely a disinterested pursuit of knowledge, but productive in the making of human beings. It was because of this that they did not accept unexamined human experience as the source of meaning and the making of meaning as an unproblematic thing. And each one of them offered a method that would challenge the outlines of a discipline: archaeology, genealogy, power/knowledge reading, schizo-analysis, rhizo-analysis, nonsubjective psychoanalysis, affirmative deconstruction, paralogic legitimation. At the end of the Second World War, the self-representation of the United States, on the other hand, was that of a savior, both militarily and, as the architect of the

Marshall Plan, in the economic and therefore sociocultural sphere. (This self-staging is being played out again as the New World Order After Communism, even as what has been called the "Third World War"—the inroads of the World Bank and the International Monetary Fund in the name of "sustainable development"—proliferates unchecked.) In fact, given the nature of United States society, the phrase "failure of the ethical subject felt by humanist intellectuals" has almost no meaning. And, given the ego-based pragmatism in the fields of history, philosophy, sociology, psychology, and, indeed, literary criticism in the United States, the majority of United States teachers in the humanities saw and see the relevant French intellectuals as merely being *anti*humanists who believe that there is no human subject and no truth. As Pierre Bourdieu makes clear in his *Homo Academicus,* this group of intellectuals did not have an impact on the protocols of institutional pedagogy in France either.[49] I think therefore it is absurd to expect our undergraduate majors to clue into this package called "theory" as part of the canon. There is often a required History of Criticism course for them. I suppose the impact of "theory" in literary criticism can find a corner there.[50] If they can understand Plato against the poets, or Coleridge on the Imagination, and Freud on Hoffmann, they can understand Barbara Johnson on Poe. And the critique of the subject that they *can* learn from the countercanonical new material is that the old canon conspired, only sometimes unwittingly, to make the straight white Christian man of property the ethical universal.

Because the use of what is called "theory" is in "educating the educators," it is the doctoral student—the future teacher—who can be carefully inserted into it. And although I see no harm in introductory courses in theory on this level, I feel its real arena is an elected sequence, where interested students are prepared to resonate with something so much outside their own thoroughly pragmatic national tradition. By "preparation" I do not mean just chunks of Marx, Nietzsche, Freud, Heidegger. I mean practice in analyzing critical prose. I have limited experience in long-term teaching at elite institutions. In my experience doctoral students in English are generally encouraged to judge without preparation. This is lethal in the critique of the canon, and doubly so in the study of so-called "theory," for the practitioners there are writers of historical, sociological, philosophical, psychological prose who rely on rhetoric to help them. These students must also take seriously their foreign language requirement, which is generally a scandal. The intellectual-historical difference between Western Europe and the Anglo-United States in the postwar and Cold War years and indeed the difference in the fate of liberal humanism in these spaces is such that the most conscientious translators have often destroyed and trivialized the delicacy as well as the power of the critique, not knowing what to preserve.

These students must learn that it is possible to be "wrong" on a certain restrictive level and take that as an incentive for further inquiry. I know the bumper sticker says "Kids need praise everyday," but doctoral students, who are going to reproduce cognitive authority soon, might be encouraged to recognize that acknowledgment of error before texts from another tradition need not be disabling or paralyzing. I emphasize this because here we are attempting not merely to enlarge the canon with a countercanon but to dethrone canonical *method:* not only in literary criticism but in social production; the axiom that something called concrete experience is the last instance. The canon is, after all, not merely the authentic books of the Bible, it is also, the *OED* tells us, "a fundamental principle . . . or axiom governing the systematic or scientific treatment of a subject." Why is it necessary to gut the canon in this way? I hope to touch upon it in my last section. But I also hope that those students in the doctoral stream who choose to follow this counterintuitive route will acquire some notion of its usefulness.

I have kept the rest of the world till the end. I think a general acquaintance with the landmarks of world literature outside of Euramerica should be part of the general undergraduate requirement. On the level of the English major, especially if we keep the single-author courses, a survey course is an insult to world literature. I would propose a one-semester senior seminar, shared with the terminal M.A., utilizing the resources of the Asian, Latin American, Pacific, and African studies, in conjunction with the creative writing programs, where the student is made to share the difficulties and triumphs of translation. There is nothing that would fill out an English major better than a sense of the limits of this exquisite and supple language.

The division between substantive expansion of the canon and a critique of canonical method is most rigorously to be kept in mind in world literature studies on the graduate level: colonial and postcolonial discourse, studies in a critique of imperialism. As long as this line of work is critical of the canon it can remain conscientiously researched straight English: Laura Brown's work with Swift and Gauri Viswanathan's on T.S. Eliot come to mind. One can think of the role of the navy in Jane Austen's *Mansfield Park,* or of Christianity in *Othello,* and so on.[51] But as soon as it becomes a substantive insertion *into* the canon, we should call a halt.

(Of late this argument has been meretriciously used against the expansion of the canon in English departments. Nothing could be further from my intentions. My argument is *against* being fully satisfied with little gains, not *for* being satisfied with nothing.)

There has been a recent spate of jobs opening up in the anglophone literature of the Third World. This is to be applauded. But the doctoral study of colonial and postcolonial discourse and the critique of imperialism as a substantive undertaking cannot be contained fully within English, although the first initiative might well come from there. In my thinking, this study should yoke itself with other disciplines, including the social sciences, so that we have degrees in English *and* History. English *and* Asian Studies, English *and* Anthropology, English *and* African Studies, where the English half of it will allow the student to read critically the production of knowledge in the other discipline, as well as her own all-too-easy conclusions. *Mutatis mutandis,* metropolitan national literature departments can also serve as bases.

I think this specialty should carry a rigorous language requirement in at least one colonized vernacular. What I am describing is the core of a transnational study of culture, a revision of the old vision of Comparative Literature. Otherwise:

Colonial and postcolonial discourse studies can, at worst, allow the indigenous elite from other countries to claim marginality without *any developed* doctoral-level sense of the problematic of decolonized space and without any method of proper verification within the discipline. (The broad-range implications of this have been presented by way of Vandana Shiva's work in the introductory pages to this chapter.)

If this study is forever contained within English (or other metropolitan literatures), without expansion into fully developed transnational culture studies, colonial and postcolonial discourse studies can also construct a canon of "Third World Literature (in translation)" that may lead to a "new orientalism." I have written about this phenomenon in Chapter Three and at length elsewhere. It can fix Eurocentric paradigms, taking "magical realism" to be the trademark of third world literary production, for example. It can begin to define "the rest of the world" simply by checking out if it is feeling sufficiently "marginal" with regard to the West or not.

We cannot fight imperialism by perpetrating a "new orientalism." My argument is not a guilt and shame trip. It is a warning. Indeed, the institutional imperatives for breaching the very *imperium* of English, even with its revised canon, cannot be fully developed from within English departments, for in its highly sophisticated vocabulary for cultural descriptions, the knowledge of English can sometimes sanction a kind of global ignorance.

Here is a rationalist empiricist historian's warning, sounded nearly two decades ago, against what we might be doing if we stopped with revising the English canon.

> Any serious theoretical explanation of the historical field outside of feudal Europe will have to supersede traditional and generic contrasts with it, and proceed to a concrete and accurate typology of social formations and State systems in their own right, which respects their very great differences of structure and development. It is merely in the night of our ignorance [and we sanction this ignorance by canonizing it within English] that all alien shapes take on the same hue.[52]

IV

Arrived here, it seems to me that institutes and curricula for a historically sophisticated transnational study of culture have become an item on the agenda. They can help us undo disciplinary boundaries and clear a space for study in a constructive way. They can provide the field for the new approach.

The point is to negotiate between the national, the global, and the historical as well as the contemporary diasporic. We must both anthropologize the West, and study the various cultural systems of Africa, Asia, Asia-Pacific, and the Americas as if peopled by historical agents. Only then can we begin to put together the story of the development of a cosmopolitanism that is global, gendered, and dynamic. In our telematic or microelectronic world, such work can get quite technical: consideration of the broader strategies of information control, productive of satisfactory and efficient cultural explanations; consideration of the systems of representation for the generated explanations; mapping out the techniques of their validation and deployment. This can disclose an inexhaustible field of connections. A discipline must constrain the inexhaustible. Yet the awareness of the potential inexhaustibility works against the conviction of cultural supremacy, a poor starting point for new research and teaching.

This last paragraph is grant proposal talk. How does that type of prose translate to teaching talk? Let us move from high tech to humanism. Let us learn and teach how to distinguish between "*internal* colonization"— the patterns of exploitation and domination of disenfranchised groups *within* the United States—and the various different heritages or operations of colonization in the rest of the world.[53] The United States is certainly a multiracial culture, but its parochial multicultural debates, however animated, are not a picture of globality. Thus we must negotiate between nationalism (uni- or multicultural) and globality.

Let us take seriously the idea that systems of representation come to hand when we secure our own culture—our own cultural explanations. Think upon the following set:

1. The making of an American must be defined by at least a desire to enter the "We the People" of the Constitution. There is no way that the "radical" or the "ethnicist" can take a position against civil rights, the Equal Rights Amendment, or great transformative opinions such as *Roe v. Wade*. One way or another, we cannot not want to inhabit this great rational abstraction.

2. Traditionally, this desire for the abstract American "we" has been recoded by the fabrication of ethnic enclaves, artificial and affectively supportive subsocieties that, claiming to preserve the ethnos or culture of origin, move further and further away from the vicissitudes and transformations of the nation or group of origin. If a constitution establishes at least the legal possibility of an abstract collectivity, these enclaves provide a countercollectivity that seems reassuringly "concrete."

3. *Our* inclination to obliterate the difference between United States internal colonization and the dynamics of decolonized space makes use of this already established American ethnocultural agenda. At worst, it secures the "they" of development or aggression against the constitutional "we." At best, it suits our institutional convenience and brings the rest of the world home. A certain double standard, a certain sanctioned ignorance, can now begin to operate in the areas of the study of central and so-called marginal cultures.

There is a lot of name-calling on both sides of the West-and-the-rest debate in the United States. In my estimation, although the politics of the only-the-West supporters is generally worth questioning, in effect the two sides legitimize each other. In a Foucauldian language, one could call them an opposition within the same discursive formation. The new culture studies must displace this opposition by keeping nation and globe distinct as it studies their relationship, and by taking a moratorium on cultural supremacy as an unquestioned springboard.

I am not speaking against the tendency to conflate ethnos of origin and the historical space left behind with the astonishing construction of a multicultural and multiracial identity for the United States. What I am suggesting is that if, as academics in the humanities, we take this as the founding principle for a study of globality, then we are off base. In the most practical terms, we are allowing a parochial decanonization debate to stand in for a study of the world.

A slightly different point needs to be made here. I am not arguing for an unexamined nativism as an alibi for culture studies. To keep the rest of the world obliged to remain confined within a mere ethnic pride and an acting out of a basically static ethnicity is to confuse political gestures with an awareness of history. That confinement was rather astutely practiced by the traditionally defined disciplinary subdivision of labor within history, anthropology, and comparative literature. Cultural studies must set up an active give-and-take with them so that it gains in substance what it provides in method. And, the educators must educate themselves in effective interdisciplinary (postdisciplinary?) teaching. As a practical academic, one must be thinking about released time for faculty and curricular development in the newly instituted programs. These endeavors must ask: How can models of reasoning be taken as culture-free? How can help and explanation be both culture specific and "objective"? If there are answers to these questions, how can they remain relevant across disciplines?

V

In conclusion, I will try to indicate how deconstruction, Marxism, and feminism might make a change in the teaching of transnational culture studies. I will deal with the three positions in different ways. The deconstructive position, as it operates postcoloniality and marginality, has been rather extensively dealt with in this book. I will therefore simply recite here a passage from Chapter Four where the argument has been summarized. The rethinking of Marxism in the New World Order has perforce become extremely important in my current work. I will therefore point forward in my brief consideration of Marxism in these concluding pages. Feminism remains a consistent and often dislocating theme within these meditations, of course. Yet, because the relationship of feminism to constitutionality is so crucial, I have written somewhat more extensively on our role here. In doing so, I have drawn forward certain considerations made in Chapter Seven.

Deconstruction: Postcoloniality—the heritage of imperialism in the rest of the globe—is a deconstructive case. As follows: Those of us from formerly colonized countries are able to communicate with each other and with the metropolis, to exchange and to establish sociality and transnationality, because we have had access to the culture of imperialism. Shall we then assign to that culture, in the words of the ethical philosopher

Bernard Williams, a measure of "moral luck?" I think there can be no doubt that the answer is "no." This impossible "no" to a structure which one critiques, yet inhabits intimately, is the deconstructive philosophical position, and the everyday here and now of "postcoloniality" is a case of it. Further, the political claims that are most urgent in decolonized space are tacitly recognized as coded within the legacy of imperialism: nation-hood, constitutionality, citizenship, democracy, socialism, even cultural-ism. Within the historial frame of exploration, colonization, and decolonization, what is being *effectively* reclaimed is a series of regulative political concepts, the supposedly authoritative narrative of whose pro-duction was written elsewhere, in the social formations of Western Europe. They are thus being reclaimed, indeed claimed, as concept meta-phors for which no *historically* adequate referent may be advanced from postcolonial space. That does not make the claims less urgent. A concept metaphor without an adequate referent may be called a catachresis by the definitions of classical rhetoric. These claims to catachreses as foundations also make postcoloniality a deconstructive case. Deconstruction, para-doxically, is the most useful position in the study of a globality not confused with ethnicity. As for the reification of ethnicity in the constitu-tion-transplanting operation of migrancy, I have already hinted how it lays bare the founding performative-constative ruse of the supposedly primordial constitution of subject.

Marxism: By Marx's own estimation, the most original thing that he stumbled upon was that the human being produced not objects but a "contentless and simple" thing which got coded as soon as produced.(*C1,* 19) This contentless thing, misleading and conveniently called the "value-form," is not pure form, but just a general description of being human that subsumes "consciousness" *and* "materiality." The coding of value makes all exchange possible. In the European nineteenth century and for Marx, the most important arena of value-coding for study and action was economic. But if one considers one of Marx's most important premises, one can see that this idea of value-producing/value-coding/code-exchang-ing as being-human has many areas of operation. To "name" a few: affective value, cognitive value, indeed "cultural" value. To see this allows us to negotiate escapes from fairly static notions of cultural identity ready to be investigated and reported on. It allows us to use and transform some of the best suggestions of poststructuralism and feminism. It allows us to transform what is most fragile in Marx—and indeed now crumbled in its most familiar form—the predictive Eurocentric scenario, buttressed only by a spectacular *scaffolding* of crisis theory and the theory of a world market far in the future.

Marx's fully developed economic analysis is situated within this more inclusive approach. It would be out of place—and time—here to present a full-dress account of the responsible displacement of the "economic in the last instance" to the "economic as the most abstract instance" in the complex network of value codings. The massive ongoing new work of the supplementing of Marx's rational "social" with the feminist ecological "social" can only be mentioned here. Let me rather end with a heavily coded sentence: As the apparatuses of higher education in the humanities incessantly recode, through fully developed techniques of knowledge, the web woven by the rational (dynamic) abstractions of the constitutionality of the world's nation-states on the one hand and the electronic (mathematical) abstractions of the economic as such on the other; a responsible study of culture can help us chart the production of versions of reality.

Such heavily coded sentences are properly unpacked in books, practically reassembled in teaching. Indeed, the hoped-for future of everything written in the name of culture studies today must, I think, be the classroom staged as intervention, always moving outside in the teaching machine.

Feminism: In Chapter Seven, I have discussed the implications, for feminism in decolonization, of Hélène Cixous's statement that "as subject *for* history, woman always occurs simultaneously in several places." To summarize here, Cixous is not speaking of woman as world-historical subject, or as subject *of* history. In her view and mine all historizing is narrativizing—putting in the form of a story. (This view does not assert that truth is fiction in the narrow sense.) Cixous is speaking, I think, of how woman must be presupposed so that she would be appropriate for a new story—a new narrativizing. Cixous is fortunate that the history of the French language offers her this double sense in the ordinary use of the word *histoire*. "Herstory," billed as tendentious, has not caught on.

Let us hold on to the idea of an alternative history/story *for* which woman must be newly imagined as pluralized subject. The new story will make visible what, in the old figurations of the pluralized woman (as mother, wife, sister, daughter, widow, female chattel, whore, exceptional stateswoman or public woman with femininity recoded, and so on) was excluded as historical narratives were shored up, in many different ways, with the representative man as its subject. (The Turkish or Indian accounts given above, for example, would have to be broken up if women were the subject *for* history.)[54]

In this context, we *are* speaking of a subject, broader than the intending person, with outlines that are overdetermined by the many networks (psychosexual, familial, political, legal—to *name* a few) in which it puts itself together.

The notion of "woman's history" as one of the levers for deconstructing the discipline of history, is one of immense theoretical and practical interest. The scope of the venture is far-reaching, and can be surmised through the more empirical work of, say, the History Workshop in Britain, *Signs* in the U.S., and the feminist contingent of the Subaltern Studies Collective in India. In this paper I am concerned with the legitimation of the normative and privative idiom of constitutions. I must therefore restrain my interest in plurality and recall my earlier remark: "the constitutional agent is apart from either the subject or from the universal-in-singular ethical agent."

What I am now going to write can easily be misread as "postmodern modesties replac[ing] Marxist certitudes," as antilibertarian antifeminist irresponsible dream talk.[55] This is the risk that one must run in order to understand how much more complicated it is to realize the responsibility of playing with or working with fire than to pretend that what gives light and warmth does not also destroy.

U.S. women must of course use the Constitution to guarantee the possibility of securing the paralogical legitimation of what is defined as "women's rights," because "abortion in the U.S. hovers tenuously in a repressive political climate and a dominant antifeminist culture."[56] Yet, as I have pointed out in Chapter Seven, Rosalind Petchesky rightly insists,

> to deny that there will always be a residual conflict between . . . the idea of concrete individuality, or subjective reality—and that of a social and socially imposed morality of reproduction seems not only naive but dismissive of an important value.

I am pointing at the confusion underlying the conflict and suggesting that, *residually*, we must remember while we are in struggle that, just as a computer codes language production into rationally manipulable bits on the model of artificial intelligence(s), so also must constitutional law code the woman's presupposed self-proximity to her body into abstractions manipulable on the model of simulated person(s). What is compromised or effaced by this is the affective-cognitive-political-social-historical plurality (to *name* a few strands) of "woman" seized as a springboard for a critique of homogenizing reason. Woman's involvement with the Constitution is thus not an unquestioned teleological good but a negotiation with enabling violence. Perhaps this will make clear the structural import of the postcolonial negotiation with the originary discourses of constitutionality.

If we present the urgency of the negotiation as an unquestioned teleological good, we disavow the fact that the best and the worst in the history of the feminist movement also entail capitalism and imperialism, often presupposing *woman* as unified representative subject. In this divided terrain, as woman is normalized into the discursive constitution (both small *and* large C) of "We the People," through struggle over both the instruments that Ackerman helps us to understand anew, *both,* that is to say, "transformative opinions" *and* "constitutional amendments," both *Roe v. Wade and* the ERA, how are we to deal with this defining of ourselves into part of a General Will by way of articles of "foreign"— that is to say gender-alienated—manufacture? The negotiative precarious- ness of the enterprise comes particularly clear if we notice that the issue of reproductive rights is edging into constitutional rationality by way of the most public (constitutional) framing of the area marked "private." This is indeed a precious simulation of "privacy" in the narrow sense that can never be adequate to the area where the very notion of privacy is contested in the most general sense. To identify the two is to confuse the subject with the agent by way of a pragmatic notion of the person. As if, after a constitutional victory, there is nothing left to do but to protect the right and train more lawyers. The present of the subject is not adequate to itself. The agent in its constitution both effaces and discloses it.

By contrast, I am suggesting that U.S. women, if they are attentive to the importance of frame-narratives, are in a unique and privileged position to continue a *persistent* critique of mere apologists for their Constitution, even as they use its instruments to secure entry into its liberating purview. Favorite sons and daughters who refuse to sanctify their father's house have their uses. Persistently to critique a structure that one cannot not (wish to) inhabit is the deconstructive stance. Transnational feminism is neither revolutionary tourism, nor mere celebration of testimony. It is rather through the route of feminism that economic theories of social choice and philosophical theories of ethical preference can be complicated by cultural material.

I have given equal time to Ackerman's new telling of the U.S. constitu- tional narrative on the one hand, and, to two noncanonical issues on the other. I say this in conclusion because I have become accustomed to the usual benevolent universalist dodge: the third world (odious phrase) and women are of course very important issues, but they are not relevant to the topic at hand, and would distract from the seriousness of the debates intrinsic to it. A Transnational Culture Studies would persistently ask: Why? and provide reasons why not.

Notes

Foreword

1 "Criticism, Feminism and the Institution," in Bruce Robbins, ed., *Intellectuals: Aesthetics, Politics, Academics* (Minneapolis: University of Minnesota Press, 1990), pp. 153–171.

2 Janet Todd, *Feminist Literary History* (Cambridge: Polity, 1988), pp. 127–128.

3 Deborah Mitchell, "Doodles," *New York Observer* (October 28, 1991).

4 Russell Berman, "Troping to Pretoria: The Rise and Fall of Deconstruction," *Telos* 85 (Fall 1990): p. 16.

5 Jacques Derrida, "The Force of Law: 'The Mystical Foundation of Authority,' " in *Deconstruction and the Possibility of Justice, Cardozo Law Review,* 11:5–6 (July–August 1990): p. 1035.

Chapter 1: In a Word: *Interview*

This interview was held in Pittsburgh on December 9, 1988. The questions were crafted in consultation with Naomi Schor and Elizabeth Weed. We thank Erika Rundle for her heroic work of transcription and Nicole Cunningham for producing the final text.

1 Frances Ferguson, "Rape and the Rise of the Novel," *Representations,* 20 (Fall 1987): pp. 88–112. Elizabeth V. Spelman, *Inessential Woman: Problems of Exclusion in Feminist Thought* (Boston: Beacon, 1988). Denise Riley, *"Am I That Name?" Feminism and the Category of "Women" in History* (Minneapolis: University of Minnesota Press, 1988). Donna J. Haraway, *Simians, Cyborgs, and Women: the Reinvention of Nature* (London: Free Association Books, 1991), pp. 109, 95, 91, 94.

Space doesn't permit me to do justice to Ferguson's extraordinarily interesting and intricate essay. Her analysis reveals that the legal system's preference for addressing "stipulated states" enabled it to evade the systemic problem of the contempt for women's testimony on rape. Ferguson points out that it also makes it extremely difficult for women who are attacked by men they know to convince district attorneys even to press charges. (Ferguson cites Susan Estrich's discussion of "simple rape.") At the same time, in her analysis of *Clarissa,* Ferguson stresses that stipulation *can* be used, in particular cases, to combat phallocentric constructions of sexuality and sexual violence.

2 Denise Riley, *"Am I That Name?" Feminism and the Category of 'Women' in History* (Minneapolis: U of Minnesota P, 1988), pp. 103, 92.

3   Donna Haraway, "A Manifesto for Cyborgs: Science, Technology and Socialist Feminism in the 1980s," *Socialist Review* 80 (1985) in *Coming to Terms: Feminism, Theory and Politics,* ed. Elizabeth Weed (New York: Routledge, 1989), p. 173.

4   Alice Jardine, "Men in Feminism: Odor di Uomo or Compagnons de Route?" *Men in Feminism,* Ed. Jardine and Paul Smith, (London: Methuen, 1987), p. 58.

5   Bruce Robbins, "American Intellectuals and Middle East Politics: Interview with Edward Said," *Social Text* 19/20 (1988), p. 51.

6   Kathy E. Ferguson has recently remarked: "Spivak's excessive self-referencing suggests . . . a claim to authority. . . . While simpler considerations of vanity or convenience might also be at work, the politics of the gesture should not be overlooked" (Kathy E. Ferguson, *The Man Question: Visions of Subjectivity in Feminist Theory,* Berkeley: University of California Press, 1993, p. 201). This helpful analysis came too late for me to make serious changes to the footnote practice in this book. Indeed, beginning with an interview might itself be a sign of the sort of politics Ferguson exposes. I acknowledge my intention to be responsive to this warning in the future by attaching this codicil to my first self-reference, which comes, in this case, from Ellen Rooney. See Gayatri Chakravorty Spivak, *In Other Worlds: Essays in Cultural Politics* (New York: Methuen, 1987).

We must of course remind ourselves, our positivist feminist colleagues in charge of creating the discipline of women's studies and our anxious students, that essentialism is a trap. It seems more important to learn to understand that the world's women do not relate to the privileging of essence, especially through "fiction," or "literature," in the same way (p. 89). Reading the work of Subaltern Studies from within but against the grain, I would suggest that elements in their text would warrant a reading of the project to retrieve the subaltern consciousness as the attempt to undo a massive historiographic metalepsis and "situate" the effect of the subject as subaltern. I would read it, then, as a *strategic* use of positivistic essentialism in a scrupulously visible political interest. This would put them in line with the Marx who locates fetishization, the ideological determination of the "concrete," and spins the narrative of the development of the money-form; with the Nietzsche who offers us genealogy in place of historiography; the Foucault who plots the construction of "counter-money"; the Barthes of semitropy; and the Derrida of "affirmative deconstruction." This would allow them to use the critical force of antihumanism, in other words, even as they share its constituting paradox: that the essentializing moment, the object of their criticism, is irreducible (p. 205).

7   See Spivak and Ranajit Guha, eds., *Selected Subaltern Studies* (New York: Oxford University Press, 1988).

8   Louis Althusser, "Marxism and Humanism," in *For Marx,* trans. Ben Brewster (London: Verso, 1985), p. 230.

9   Gayatri Chakravorty Spivak, *In Other Worlds: Essays in Cultural Politics,* (New York: Methuen, 1987), p. 201.

10 Gilles Deleuze and Felix Guattari, *Anti-Oedipus: Capitalism and Schizophrenia,* trans. Robert Hurley, Mark Seem, and Helen R. Lane (Minneapolis: University of Minnesota Press, 1983).

11 Spivak, *Worlds,* pp. 253–54.

12 Jamaica Kincaid, *Lucy* (New York: Penguin, 1990), pp. 39–41.

13 Here is Derrida on the topic of the decentered subject: "one can doubtless decenter the subject, as is easily said, without challenging anew the bond between, on the one hand, responsibility, and, on the other, freedom of subjective consciousness or purity of intentionality. This happens all the time, and is not altogether interesting, since nothing in the prior axiomatics is changed: one denies the axiomatics *en bloc* and keeps it going as a survivor, with minor adjustments *de rigueur,* and daily compromises lacking in rigor. Thus coping, thus operating at top speed, one accounts, and becomes accountable, for nothing: not for what happens, not for the 'why' of assuming responsibilities when lacking a concept" (Derrida, "The Conflict of the Faculties," in Richard Rand, ed., *The Conflict of the Faculties in America* [Lincoln, University of Nebraska Press, forthcoming]; "Mochlos ou le conflit des facultes," in Derrida, *Du droit a la philosophie* [Paris: Galilee, 1990], p. 408).

14 Ruth Salvaggio, *Enlightened Absence: Neo-Classical Configurations of the Feminine* (Urbana: University of Illinois Press, 1988).

15 Karl Marx, *Capital,* trans. David Fernbach (New York: Vintage, 1981), vol. 3, pp. 953–970. Hereafter included in text as C3, followed by page number.

16 Marx, *Karl Marx Friedrich Engels Werke* (Berlin: Dietz, 1977), vol. 23, pp. 11–12; Karl Marx, *Capital,* trans. Ben Fowkes (New York: Vintage, 1977), vol. 1, pp. 89–90. Hereafter cited in text as C1, followed by page number.

17 Frobel Folker, Jürgen Heinrichs, and Otto Kreve, *The New International Division of Labour: Structural Unemployment in Industrialized Countries and Industrialization in Developing Countries,* trans. Pete Burgess (Cambridge: Cambridge University Press, 1980), and Nigel Harris, *The End of the Third World: Newly Industrializing Countries and the Decline of Ideology* (London: Penguin, 1987).

18 Chakravarthi Raghavan, *Recolonization: GATT, The Uruguay Round and The Third World* (London: Zed Books, 1990).

19 I refer my readers to Jean Franco, *Border Trouble* (Harvard University Press, forthcoming), for a detailed study of this problematic.

20 Gayle Rubin, "The Traffic in Women: Notes on the 'Political Economy' of Sex," in *Toward an Anthropology of Women,* ed. Rayna Reiter (New York: Monthly Review, 1975), pp. 157–210.

21 Richard Rorty, "Philosophy As a Kind of Writing: An Essay on Derrida," in *Consequences of Pragmatism Essays: 1972–1980* (Minneapolis: University of Minnesota Press, 1982), pp. 90–109.

22 Jean Grimshaw, " 'Pure Lust': The Elemental Feminist Philosophy of Mary Daly," *Radical Philosophy,* 49 (1988): pp. 24–30.

23 Kalpana Bardhan, "Women's Work, Welfare and Status: Forces of Tradition and Change in India," *South Asia Bulletin,* 6:1 (1986): pp. 3–16.

24 Paul de Man, *The Rhetoric of Romanticism* (New York: Columbia University Press, 1984), p. xi.

25 For the idea of two sessions, general and narrow, see Jacques Derrida, "The Double Session," in *Dissemination,* trans. Barbara Johnson (Chicago: University of Chicago Press, 1981).

Chapter 2: More on Power/Knowledge

1   Michel Foucault, *The History of Sexuality,* trans. Robert Hurley (New York: Vintage, 1980), vol. 1. The particular title of this volume in French is *The Will to Knowledge.* I will occasionally refer to the book by that title. All translations, from this and other French texts, have been modified when necessary.

2   Ernesto Laclau and Chantal Mouffe's provocative and influential *Hegemony and Socialist Strategy: Towards a Radical Democratic Politics,* trans. Winston Moore and Paul Cammack (London: Verso, 1985) must be counted among these.

3   For the academic circumstances, see Didier Eribon, *Michel Foucault* (Paris: Flammarion, 1989), pp. 144–147. Roy Boyne, *Foucault and Derrida: The Other Side of Reason* (London: Unwin Hyman, 1990) sees Foucault's entire subsequent project as a considered response to Derrida's early critique, going beyond the published reply, which was confined to "the sociological phenomenon of academic disputations" (p. 88).

4   Irene Diamond and Lee Quinby, eds., *Feminism and Foucault: Reflections on Resistance* (Boston: Northeastern University Press, 1988).

5   Zillah R. Eisenstein, *The Female Body and the Law* (Berkeley: University of California Press, 1988), pp. 6–41.

6   Edward W. Said, "Michel Foucault, 1926–1984," in Jonathan Arac, ed., *After Foucault: Humanistic Knowledge, Postmodern Challenges* (New Brunswick: Rutgers University Press, 1988), pp. 1–2.

7   Foucault, *History of Sexuality,* p. 93. The two following passages are also on this page. I have related this to "woman" as masterword in Chapter One.

8   Said's work acknowledges Foucault's influence too frequently for a single reference. I am referring specifically to Edward W. Said, "Foucault and the Imagination of Power," in David Cozens Hoy, ed., *Foucault: A Critical Reader* (London: Blackwell, 1987), pp. 149–155. Sheldon Wolin, "On the Theory and Practice of Power," in *After Foucault,* pp. 179–201.

9   Hoy, *Reader,* p. 135. The following passage is on the same page.

10   Hoy, *Reader,* pp. 128, 136. Emphasis mine.

11   For a different and most interesting sense of nominalism, see Etienne Balibar, "Foucault et Marx. L'enjeu du nominalisme," in George Canguilhem, ed., *Michel Foucault: philosophe* (Paris: Seuil, 1989), pp. 74–75.

12   To compile a responsible balance sheet of the two bodies of thought, to bring about articulation, is a somewhat different enterprise. For a consideration of Foucault's politics from a deconstructive point of view, see Tom Keenan, "The 'Paradox' of Knowledge and Power: Reading Foucault on a Bias," *Political Theory,* 15:1 (February 1987): pp. 5–32. For a broader articulation, see Boyne, *Foucault and Derrida.* This book came to my attention after I had completed the initial draft of this essay. Although I cannot agree with many of the details of interpretation in it, I am in general sympathy with Boyne's careful attempt at articulation. By contrast, my essay does not offer a survey but rather moves out in irregular circles from one sentence in Foucault.

13   Jacques Derrida, *Of Grammatology,* trans. Gayatri Chakravorty Spivak (Baltimore: The Johns Hopkins University Press, 1976), p. 47. Hereafter cited as *OG* in the text

followed by page reference. The rest of the citations in this paragraph are from the same passage.

14 Boyne's sense of "reason-in-general" in Derrida is much more localized than my own reading of the general and the narrow.

15 Richard Rorty, "Moral Identity and Private Autonomy," *Foucault: philosophe*, p. 388.

16 Jürgen Habermas, *The Philosophical Discourse of Modernity*, trans. Frederick Lawrence (Cambridge: MIT Press, 1987), pp. 185–210.

17 Rorty, "Moral Identity," p. 390.

18 Although Habermas is more respectful towards Foucault, he puts him with Derrida in his insistence that Foucault is too "literary," *Modernity*, p. 238.

19 Richard Rorty, "Habermas and Lyotard on Postmodernity," in Richard J. Bernstein, ed., *Habermas and Modernity* (Cambridge: MIT Press, 1985), p. 173.

20 For a discussion of the Heideggerian swerve see Jacques Derrida, "The Ends of Man," in *Margins of Philosophy*, trans. Alan Bass (Chicago: University of Chicago Press, 1982) and the magesterial *Of Spirit: Heidegger and the Question*, tr. Geoffrey Bennington and Rachel Bowlby (Chicago: University of Chicago Press, 1989). The Foucault passage on Heidegger is from "Final Interview," trans. Thomas Levin and Isabelle Lorenz, in *Raritan*, 5:1 (Summer 1985): p. 8. It is characteristic of Habermas's strong misreading of Foucault that he sees the connection with Heidegger, articulates it as yet another French failure to use German material, contrasts Foucault yet once again to Adorno who did so much better along this line, and finally diagnoses the Heidegger connection as an irritating affinity for Foucault to acknowledge (Habermas, *Modernity*, pp. 256–257)! It is beyond the scope of this essay to engage with Pierre Bourdieu's account of the Heideggerian trajectory itself in Pierre Bourdieu, *The Political Ontology of Heidegger*, trans. Peter Collier (Oxford: Polity Press, 1991).

21 Jacques Derrida, *"Comment Donner Raison? 'How to Concede, With Reasons?,'"* *Diacritics*, 19:3–4 (Fall–Winter 1989): p. 8. This is no place for undertaking a commentary on Derrida's turning of Heidegger. As of this writing, Herman Rappaport, *Heidegger and Derrida: Reflections of Time and Language* (Lincoln: University of Nebraska Press, 1989) is perhaps the most recent extended publication on this subject.

22 Martin Heidegger, *Being and Time*, trans. John Macquarrie and Edward Robinson (New York: Harper and Row, 1962), p. 39; emphasis mine.

23 Michel Foucault, *La volonté de savoir* (Paris: Gallimard, 1976), p. 122.

24 This pervasive suggestion in Derrida begins to appear as early as "Structure, Sign, and Play in the Science of Man," in Richard Macksey and Eugenio Donato, eds., *The Structuralist Controversy: the Languages of Criticism and the Sciences of Man* (Baltimore: The Johns Hopkins University Press, 1972).

25 Jean Baudrillard is excited by the electrical metaphor and understands the need for catachresis in his *Forget Foucault*, Eng. trans. (New York: Semiotext(e), 1987), p. 33f. But he is so intent on proving the superiority of his own idea that the real is forgettable, that he seeks to demolish Foucault's notion of power by complaining that there *is* no such example of power to be found in reality!

26 Walter J. Ong, *Orality and Literacy: The Technology of the Word* (New York: Methuen, 1982).

27 Rorty, "Moral Identity," p. 388.

28   *The Common Good: Social Welfare and the American Future* (New York: Ford Foundation, 1989), p. 2.

29   Hoy, "Power, Repression," pp. 142–143.

30   Hoy, "Power, Repression," p. 139.

31   Michel Foucault, "The Subject and Power," in Hubert L. Dreyfus and Paul Rabinow, *Michel Foucault: Beyond Structuralism and Hermeneutics* (Chicago: University of Chicago Press, 1983), 2nd ed., p. 225.

32   Jana Sawicki, "Feminism and the Power of Foucaldian Discourse," in *After Foucault*, p. 166.

33   For a detailed discussion of these aggregative apparatuses, see Gilles Deleuze, "Qu'est-ce qu'un dispositif?," in *Foucault: philosophe*, pp. 185–193.

34   Habermas's casual inattention is nowhere more marked than in his bulldozing of this passage, with no reference:

> In his later studies Foucault will . . . comprehend power as the interaction of warring parties, as the decentered network of bodily, face-to-face confrontations, and ultimately as the productive penetration and subjectivizing subjugation of a bodily opponent (*Modernity*, p. 255).

35   François Ewald (of Richard Rorty), "Compte rendu des discussions," *Foucault: philosophe*, p. 39f.

36   Jacques Derrida, "Cogito and the History of Madness," in *Writing and Difference*, trans. Alan Bass (Chicago: University of Chicago Press, 1978), p. 49; word-order rearranged for coherent citation.

37   Although Hegel is not mentioned in Derrida's essay, this extinction may be dramatized in the break between the Absolute Necessity of Being and the beginning of Determinate Being in Hegel's *Science of Logic*, trans. A.V. Miller (New York: Humanities Press, 1969), pp. 108–109.

38   Derrida, "Cogito," pp. 57–58, 61.

39   Derrida, "Cogito," p. 60. Was Foucault "right or wrong" in rapping Derrida on the knuckles in his well-known response, "My Body, This Paper, This Fire," trans. Geoff Bennington, *Oxford Literary Review*, 4:1 (Autumn 1979)? Let the more mature Foucault provide the answer: "There are the sterilizing effects: Has anyone ever seen a new idea come out of a polemic? And how could it be otherwise, given that here the interlocuters are incited, not to advance, not to take more and more risks in what they say . . ." ("Polemics, Politics, and Problemizations," in Paul Rabinow, ed., *The Foucault Reader* [New York: Pantheon, 1984]). Derrida's point is not really about dreams and madness. But Foucault has a lot at stake in dreams. For the reader of the exchange, it remains interesting that Foucault's avowed origin is in the decipherment of dreams (Michel Foucault and Ludwig Binswanger, *Dream and Existence*, trans. Forrest Williams and Jacob Needleman, a special issue from *Review of Existential Psychology and Psychiatry*, 19:1 [1984–85]), and the end is also with a book of dreams: *The Care of the Self* opens with Artemidorus's *Interpretation of Dreams*.

40   I believe this to be so much an ordinary-language aspect of the doublet that most French interpretations simply take it for granted. See for example *Foucault: philosophe*, pp.

61, 65, 95–96, 207. Deleuze's book on *Foucault* [trans. Sean Hand [Minneapolis: University of Minnesota Press, 1988]) comes alive if this is kept in the mind. I have hyphenated *pouvoir-savoir* whenever I have wanted to emphasize this aspect.

41 For relevant discussions in the later Foucault, see "The Ethic of Care for the Self As a Practice of Freedom," in James Bernauer and David Rasmussen, eds., *The Final Foucault* (Cambridge: MIT Press, 1988), pp. 114, 122–123, 130. At this point the onticoontological *différance* has been rewritten as an entry way: "I have tried to know [savoir] how the human subject entered into games of truth"; *pouvoir-savoir* rendered into "how games of truth can put themselves in place and be linked relationships of burden of paleonymy": "The word 'game' can lead you into error: when I say 'game,' I say an ensemble of rules for truth-production [*je dis un ensemble de règles de production de la vérité*]."

42 This fits the U.S. case. Looking forward to my last section, let me simply remind the reader that the possibilities within a feminist pedagogy of the oppressed in decolonized areas are of course much more complicated.

43 Michel Foucault, *The Archaeology of Knowledge and the Discourse on Language,* trans. A.M. Sheridan Smith (New York: Pantheon, 1973), p. 15f. The next passage is on p. 119.

44 Foucault, *Archaeology of Knowledge,* pp. 79–80.

45 Jacques Derrida, *Of Spirit,* p. 32. Heidegger, *Being and Time,* p. 423.

46 For a staging of this see Jacques Derrida, "My Chances/*Mes Chances:* A Rendezvous with Some Epicurean Stereophonics," in Joseph H. Smith and William Kerrigan, eds., *Taking Chances: Derrida, Psychoanalysis, and Literature* (Baltimore: The Johns Hopkins University Press, 1984).

47 Foucault and Binswanger, *Dream and Existence.* "To study forms of experience in this way—in their history—is an idea that originated with an earlier project, in which I made use of the methods of existential analysis in the field of psychiatry and in the domain of 'mental illness' " (Preface to the *History of Sexuality,* vol. 2, in Rabinow, *Reader,* p. 334). At that earlier stage, Foucault conceived of his project in Husserlian terms. But the lineaments of the thematic—of making the constitutive rupture workable—that I have been at pains to disclose are straining through. "Phenomenology has managed to make images speak; but it has given no one the possibility of understanding their language. . . . The dream is situated in the ultimate moment in which existence is still its world; once beyond, at the dawn of wakefulness, already it is no longer its world. . . . Analysis of a dream starting from the images supplied by waking consciousness must precisely have the goal of bridging that distance between image and imagination. . . . Thus is the passage from anthropology to ontology, which seems to us from the outset the major problem of the analysis of Dasein, actually accomplished" (Foucault and Binswanger, pp. 42, 59, 73). With benefit of hindsight, one can see the way clear from the rarefied *énoncé* of the *Archaeology* to the ethical self-constitution of the final phase: "The dream is not meaningful only to the extent that psychological motivations and physiological determinations interact and cross-index in a thousand ways; on the contrary, it is rich by reason of the poverty of its objective context [English translation unaccountably has 'content' here]. . . . Cultural history had carefully presented this theme of the ethical value of the dream" (Derrida, "My Chances/Mes Chances: A Rendezvous with Some Epicurean Stereophonics," pp. 44, 52).

48 Quoted in Eribon, *Foucault*, p. 94.

49 Foucault, *Archaeology*, p. 16.

50 Boyne, *Foucault and Derrida*, p. 32; the next passages are from pp. 35, 70. I have quoted these three passages from Boyne to demonstrate Boyne's feeling for the readings, though not necessarily for their philosophical moorings and undermoorings.

51 Jacques Derrida, *Glas*, trans. John P. Leavey, Jr. and Richard Rand (Lincoln: University of Nebraska Press, 1986).

52 Michel Foucault, *Folie et déraison: Histoire de la folie à l'âge classique* (Paris: Plon, 1961).

53 "I did not want to make history of that language; rather the archaeology of that silence" (Foucault, *Folie et déraison: Histoire de la folie à l'âge classique*, p. v).

54 Dreyfus and Rabinow, *Foucault*, p. 209.

55 See Derrida, "The Ends of Man." Dreyfus can make the case for a substantive affinity between Heidegger's "Being" and Foucault's "power" by rendering Heidegger into what I shall call the Anglo-U.S. episteme later in this essay, and by refusing to "read" all the passages from Foucault that he cites, in "De la mise en ordre des choses," in *Foucault: philosophe*.

56 This point of view is to be found in Rorty, "Moral Identity."

57 André Glucksmann, "Le nihilisme de Michel Foucault," in *Foucault: philosophe*, p. 389.

58 Jacques Derrida, "The Politics of Friendship," *Journal of Philosophy*, 85:11 (November 1988): pp. 632–644. This is an abridged version of a longer unpublished paper, "Of Friendship and Democracy."

59 Jacques Derrida, "Violence and Metaphysics," in *Writing and Difference*, pp. 79–153.

60 In view of Derrida's intense concern for "the sign 'man' " since "The Ends of Man," Boyne's note 18 in *Foucault and Derrida*, p. 89 is surprising. Major Derrida texts mobilized by this concern are *Glas* and *The Post Card*, trans. Alan Bass (Chicago: University of Chicago Press, 1986). On the latter I feel constrained to cite Gayatri Chakravorty Spivak, "Love Me, Love My Ombre, Elle," in *Diacritics*, 14:4 (Winter 1984), because it is a feminist discussion.

61 James Joyce, *Finnegans Wake* (New York: Viking, 1969), p. 51.

62 Dreyfus and Rabinow, *Foucault*, p. 240. The earlier passage is from Foucault, "An Aesthetics of Existence," in John Johnston, trans., *Foucault Live: Interviews, 1966–84* (New York: Semiotext(e), 1989), p. 312, 310–311.

63 Foucault, "Preface to the *History of Sexuality*," vol. 2, p. 339.

64 Foucault, "Ethic of Care," p. 118.

65 Foucault, "Ethic of Care," p. 256.

66 Rabinow, *Reader*, p. 389.

67 Habermas, *Modernity*, p. 256. Thus I must read Thomas Flynn's account of the change in Foucault's last lectures as, strictly speaking a displacement upon the constituted subject where it is the agent of truth-telling rather than simply a changeover to "the subject as the 'agent' of truth-telling" (Thomas Flynn, "Foucault as Parrhesiast: His Last Course at the Collège de France," in Bernauer and Rasmussen, *The Final Foucault*,

p. 106). Flynn's lovely essay can take this reading on board. As he writes: "It is clear that Foucault continued to respect these 'structuralist' concepts as he insisted that we 'rethink the question of the subject'. . . . He was not growing soft on subjectivism" (Flynn, "Parrhesiast," p. 225).

68 Foucault, "Final Interview," p. 12. Emphasis mine.

69 Foucault, "Polemics," *Reader*, p. 389.

70 Foucault, "Ethic of Care," p. 115.

71 For my use of (im)possibility, see Gayatri Chakravorty Spivak, *In Other Worlds: Essays in Cultural Politics* (New York: Methuen, 1987), pp. 263, 308 n. 81. Flynn signals the final shift as follows: "What is at issue is not a 'testing' of one's life once and for all but an on-going practice, a certain style of life" (Flynn, "Parrhesiast," p. 219). In the model I derive from Derrida, it is the testing itself that is an askew on-going practical counterpoint, employing all the subterfuges of any serious technē.

72 Gary Gutting, *Michel Foucault's Archaeology of Scientific Reason* (Cambridge: Cambridge University Press, 1989).

73 Gutting, *Foucault's Archaeology*, p. 261. Michael Donnelly wants "to reformulate some of Foucault's concepts, to make them at once more analytically adequate and more accessible to historians and social science researchers" ("Des divers usages de la notion de biopouvoir," *Foucault: philosophe*, p. 231). Manfred Frank throws down the gauntlet for Foucault's critique of ethics by suggesting that the writing of books like *The Birth of the Clinic* and *Discipline and Punish* presupposed an ethical decision (*Foucault: philosophe*, p. 259). And Frank Lentricchia, finding Foucault a champion of the individual, writes: "Foucault is not sanguine about the survival of the individual. Discipline insidiously invades the ground of individuality in order to master it" (Lentricchia, *Ariel and the Police: Michel Foucault, William James, Wallace Stevens* [Madison: University of Wisconsin Press, 1988], p. 26).

74 Dreyfus and Rabinow, *Foucault*, p. 231.

75 Paul Bové, "The Foucault Phenomenon: The Problematics of Style," in Deleuze, *Foucault*, trans. Sean Hand (Minneapolis: University of Minnesota Press, 1988), p. ixf.

76 Boyne, *Foucault and Derrida*, p. 158; subsequent passages in this paragraph are from pp. 130, 131, 143.

77 For the relevant passage in Derrida, see "Of Grammatology As a Positive Science" (OG, 74–93).

78 The passages in this paragraph are from Boyne, *Foucault and Derrida*, pp. 79, 90, 170.

79 Against Habermas's feeling that, for Foucault, "the politics that has stood under the sign for the revolution since 1789 has come to an end" (*Modernity*, p. 282); or Rorty's that Foucault's "remoteness . . . reminds one of the conservative who pours cold water on hopes for reform, who affects to look at the problems of his fellow-citizens with the eye of the future historian" (Rorty, "Habermas and Lyotard," p. 172) is the final Foucault's counterpointed distance: "We have a subject who was endowed with rights or who was not and who, by the institution of a political society, has received or has lost rights. . . . On the other hand, the notion of governmentality allows one, I believe, to set off the freedom of the subject and the relationship to others, i.e., that which constitutes the very matter of ethics" ("Ethic of Care," p. 131).

80 Alessandro Pizzorno, "Foucault et la conception libérale de l'individu," *Foucault: philosophe*, p. 238.

81 Flynn, "Parrhesiast," p. 227.

82 Foucault, "Ethic of Care," pp. 113–114.

83 Bhikhu Parekh, "Identities on Parade," in *Marxism Today* (June 1989): p. 27.

84 I cannot go here into the considerable difference in historicopolitical inscription of our two philosophers. Suffice it to say that as a Sephardic Jew growing up in North Africa, Derrida is not exactly a participating member in the colonial enterprise.

85 Rorty, "Moral Identity" p. 387.

86 The rejection of Melanie Klein by official North Atlantic feminism can resonate with this.

87 Mahasweta Devi, "Draupadi," "Breast-Giver," in Spivak, *In Other Worlds*. A discussion of "The Hunt" is to be found in Spivak, "Who Claims Alterity?," in Barbara Kruger and Phil Mariani, eds., *Remaking History* (Seattle: Bay Press, 1989).

88 Michel Serre, "Literature and the Exact Sciences," *Sub-Stance*, 18:2 (1989): p. 4. The subsequent passages are from pp. 6, 23.

89 Forthcoming in Mahasweta Devi, *Imaginary Maps*, trans. Gayatri Chakravorty Spivak (Routledge). For more on this story, see Chapter Five. "Pterodactyl" is also included in this volume.

Chapter 3: Marginality in the Teaching Machine

1 In terms laid out in the previous chapter, it is perhaps a confusion between the critical and dogmatic that makes Dipesh Chakrabarty side (unwittingly?) with Richard Rorty and perceive the institutional situation as leading to a counsel of despair: " . . . since 'Europe' cannot after all be provincialized within the institutional site of the university whose knowledge protocols will always take us back to the terrain where all contours follow that of my hyperreal Europe—the project of provincializing Europe must realize within itself its own impossibility. It therefore looks to a history that embodies this politics of despair" (Chakrabarty, "Postcoloniality and the Artifice of History: Who Speaks for the 'Indian' Pasts?," *Representations*, 37 [Winter 1992]: pp. 22–23. Since our writings usually resonate, I am hoping that future discussion will persuade Dr. Chakrabarty to consider the alternative. Is one obliged to mark the historiality of epistemes, even when institutionally historicized, with conflicting geographical proper names: "Europe," "India"? That question is in fact the substance of this chapter.

2 It is my conviction of the power of collectivities that will not allow me to ignore that the realization of the "potential" is an incessantly betrayed struggle undermined by the longing for upward class mobility in those among the nonrevolutionary underclass who feel they might have the possibility of a foothold in the ladder. In the rest of this first section I try to argue that radical teachers at universities—an important apparatus of upward class mobility—should attend to the nature of the institution that is their contractual space—and not ignore their obligation by claiming a spurious marginality, and declare the desire for revolution as its accomplishment. I believe the teacher, *while operating within the institution,* can foster the emergence of a committed collectivity by not making her institutional commitment invisible: outside in the teaching-machine.

3   See Ranajit Guha, *A Rule of Property for Bengal: An Essay on the Idea of Permanent Settlement* (New Delhi: Orient Longman, 1981); and Victor Kiernan, *Marxism and Imperialism* (London: Edward Arnold, 1974), p. 206f. I hope the reader will not consider this mention of the name "Bengali" a proof of "high flying Bengali cultural revanchism." There seems to be no way around the fact that the speaker's native language is Bengali.

4   In "Representing the Colonized: Anthropology's Interlocutors," Edward Said is quite correct in reminding us that "We should first take note of how . . . the United States has replaced the great earlier empires as *the* dominant outside force" (*Critical Inquiry*, 15 [Winter 1989]: p. 215). It seems to me that the displacements entailed by this shift in conjuncture must also be kept in mind. "The West" is not monolithic.

5   See Carl Pletsch, "The Three Worlds, or the Division of Social Scientific Labor, circa 1950–1975," *Comparative Studies in Society and History,* 23:4 (October 1981).

6   See Chapter One, note 11 (p. 000). The situation has changed even further with the displacement of the East-West divide by the North-South.

7   Michel Foucault, *Language, Counter-Memory, Practice: Selected Essays and Interviews,* trans. Donald F. Bouchard and Sherry Simon (Ithaca: Cornell University Press, 1977), p. 145. Hereafter cited in the text as *LCP*.

8   Experts in the mainstream are not charitable to this impulse: "Many acts of revenge have been and are still taken against citizens of the former colonial powers, whose sole personal crime is that of belonging to the nation in question . . . That Europe should in her turn be colonized by the peoples of Africa, of Asia, of Latin America (we are far from this, I know) would be a sweet revenge, but cannot be considered my ideal . . . This extraordinary success [that the colonized peoples have adopted our customs and put on clothes] is chiefly due to one specific feature of Western civilization which for a long time was regarded as a feature of man himself, its development and prosperity among Europeans thereby becoming proof of their superiority: it is, paradoxically, Europeans' capacity to understand the other" (Tzvetan Todorov, *The Conquest of America: The Question of the Other,* trans. Richard Howard [New York: Harper and Row, 1984], pp. 256, 258). Or to give only two examples, this comment on "Sartre's creative use of terrorism. The true precursor of Sartre was not so much Marx as Sorel, whose belief in the efficacy of violence as a purgative anticipated his own. Curiously Sartre's apologia for 'terrorism-fraternity' found its real home not on French soil, but in the underdeveloped countries of the third world, where terror was recommended, as a cure-all for colonial-induced psychopathologies" (Steven B. Smith, *Reading Althusser: An Essay on Structural Marxism* [Ithaca: Cornell University Press, 1984], p. 67).

9   Said, *Orientalism* (New York: Pantheon Books, 1978).

10 Chapter Thirteen considers the attendant pedagogical situation in greater detail. For a brief checklist of required reading, see Chinua Achebe, "Colonialist Criticism," *Morning Yet on Creation Day: Essays* (Garden City: Anchor Press, 1975); Ngugi Wa Thiong'o, *Writers in Politics* (London: Heinemann, 1981); Ashis Nandy, *The Intimate Enemy: Loss and Recovery of Self Under Colonialism* (New York: Oxford University Press, 1983); Ranajit Guha and Gayatri Spivak, eds., *Selected Subaltern Studies* (New York: Oxford University Press, 1988); Stuart Hall and James Donald, *Politics and Ideology* (London: Open University Press, 1985); Hazel Carby, *Reconstructing Womanhood: The Emergence of Afro-American Women Novelists* (New York: Oxford University Press, 1987); Sneja Gunew (with Uyen Loewald), "The Mother Tongue and

Migration," *Australian Feminist Studies,* 1 (Summer 1985); Trinh T. Minh-ha and Jean-Paul Bourdier, *African Spaces: Designs for Living in Upper Volta* (New York: Africana Press, 1985); Paulin J. Hountindji, *African Philosophy: Myth and Reality,* trans. Henri Evans (Bloomington: Indiana University Press, 1983); Henry Louis Gates, Jr., *Figures in Black: Worlds, Signs, and the "Racial" Self* (New York: Oxford University Press, 1986); Lata Mani, "Contentious Traditions: The Debate on SATI in Colonial India," *Cultural Critique* (Autumn 1987); Mick Taussig, *Shamanism, Colonialism, and the Wild Man: A Study in Terror and Healing* (Chicago: University of Chicago Press, 1987); Mary Louise Pratt, "Scratches on the Face of the Country; or What Mr. Barrow Saw in the Land of the Bushmen," *Critical Inquiry,* 12:1 (Autumn 1985). Of the numerous journals coming out in the field, one might name *Cultural Critique, New Formations, Criticism, Heresy, Inscription, Third Text.* (So much good work has appeared since the first publication of this text that it seemed impractical to update this footnote.)

11   For a superb analysis of this fantasm in the context of the United States, see Barbara Hernstein Smith, "Cult-Lit: Hirsch, Literacy, and 'The National Culture,' " *South Atlantic Quarterly* (Winter 1990).

12   Michel Foucault, *The History of Sexuality,* vol. 1, p. 99. Hereafter cited in the text as HS.

13   The virulent attacks against "political correctness" have made my argument somewhat dated. The dynamics of the cultural apparatus outstrip the old-fashioned pace of academic publication.

14   Fredric Jameson, "On Magic Realism in Film," *Critical Inquiry,* 12:2 (Winter 1986). Most noticeable texts are, of course, V.S. Naipaul, *Guerrillas* (New York: Alfred A. Knopf, 1975) and Salman Rushdie, *Midnight's Children* (New York: Alfred A. Knopf, 1981).

15   The Freudian term *"Besetzung,"* translated as "cathexis" in *The Standard Edition,* is translated *"investissement"* [lit. investment] in French. The Freudian term means, roughly, "to occupy with desire." Since Foucault did not use Freudian terms in their strict sense, "cathecting" or "occupying with desire" might be inadvisable here. On the other hand "invest" has only an economic meaning in English and the psychoanalytic usage is never far below the surface in poststructuralist French writers. I decided on the somewhat odd "switch it on."

16   Benita Parry, "Problems in Current Theories of Colonial Discourse," *Oxford Literary Review,* 9:1–2 (1987).

17   J.M. Coetzee, *Foe* (New York: Viking Penguin, 1987).

18   For interesting speculations on "moral luck," see Bernard Williams, *Moral Luck: Philosophical Papers 1973–1980* (Cambridge: Cambridge University Press, 1981), pp. 20–39. But moral luck is an after-the-fact assignment. "The justification, if there is to be one, will be essentially retrospective" (p. 24). The impossible and intimate "no" might thus involve our consideration of the historical production of our cultural exchangeability. Why does it involve the long haul toward a future? I attempt to answer this in the text. (I am also aware that the delicacy of Williams's concern with the individual moral agent is travestied when transferred to something like "the culture of imperialism." It would be interesting to "apply" Williams's brilliantly inconclusive speculations to individual imperialist reformists.)

19   Spivak, "Theory in the Margin: Coetzee's *Foe* reading Defoe's *Crusoe/Roxana,*" in Jonathan Arac and Barbara Johnson, eds., *Consequences of Theory* (Baltimore: The Johns Hopkins University Press, 1990, p. 172.)

20   Spivak, "Theory in the Margin," pp. 172–173.

21   Most thoughtfully for example, in Richard Rorty, "Solidarity and Objectivity?" in John Rajchman and Cornel West, eds., *Post-Analytic Philosophy* (New York: Columbia University Press, 1985).

22   Whenever someone attempts to put together a "theory of practice" where the intending subject as absolute ground is put into question, catachrestical master-words become necessary, because language can never fully bypass the presupposition of such a ground. "Value," and consequently "value-form," are such words for Marx. The particular word is, in such a case, the best that will serve but also, and necessarily, a misfit. (There can, of course, be no doubt that the Marxian theory of ideology put into question the intending subject as absolute ground.) The choice of these master-words obliges the taking on of the burden of the history of the meanings of the word in the language (paleonymy). Thus "value" (as "writing" in Derrida, "power" in Foucault, or yet "desire" in Deleuze and Guattari) must necessarily also mean its "ordinary" language meanings, material worth as well as idealist values, and create the productive confusion that can, alone, give rise to practice. It must be said, however, that these master-words are misfits only if the ordinary use of language is presupposed to have fully fitting cases. Thus "to fit" is itself a catachresis and points to a general theory of language as catachrestical that must be actively marginalized in all its uses.

23   Marx, *Capital,* vol. 1, p. 90. According to Marx, in capital value sublates its own definition by becoming content rather than form (of measurement), through the commodifications of labor-power (Karl Marx, *Grundrisse: Foundations of the Critique of Political Economy,* trans. Martin Nicolaus [New York: Vintage, 1973], p. 469). It is no doubt a futile gesture to speculate that both in Marx and in the tradition of critique it is the investigation of value, in one form or another, that becomes content; if only because it may lead to the despairing politics of "the text deconstructs itself" rather than persistent critique/affirmative deconstruction.

24   Karl Marx, *Selected Correspondence* (Moscow: Progress Publishers, 1975), p. 228.

25   Indeed, this is Marx's firm point about workers' "identity" as individuals producing use-values and working-class solidarity based on the value-coding of the "social." The social sphere is where work is measured in value rather than use. Harry Cleaver's *Reading Capital Politically* (Austin: University of Texas Press, 1979), p. 19, suffers from a misunderstanding of this ambivalent relationship between capital(ism) and (the) social(ism). Bernard Williams's use of "currency" has something like a relationship with our use of "value" (*Moral Luck,* p. 35). Yet because he can only see value-coding as singular and rational, rather than heterogeneous and coherent, he dismisses it as impossible in the moral sphere, and indeed is skeptical about the possibility of moral philosophy on related grounds. I am in basic sympathy with his position though I cannot accept his presuppositions and conclusions about "currency." Here perhaps attending to the metaphoricity of a concept would help. For the metaphoricity of the concept of currency, as for concepts and metaphors in general, see Jacques Derrida, "White Mythology: Metaphor in the Text of Philosophy," in *Margins of Philosophy,* trans. Alan Bass (Chicago: University of Chicago Press, 1982), pp. 207–271.

26   I have discussed this in "Scattered Speculations on the Question of Value," in Gayatri

Chakravorty Spivak, *In Other Worlds: Essays in Cultural Politics* (New York: Methuen, 1987).

27 See especially Melanie Klein, "Envy and Gratitude," in Klein, *Envy and Gratitude and Other Works* (New York: Free Press, 1984), pp. 176–235; and "Love, Guilt, and Reparation," in Klein, *Love, Hate, and Reparation, and Other Works* (New York: Free Press, pp. 306–343).

28 Tim Mitchell, "The World as Exhibition," *Comparative Studies in Society and History*, 31:2 (April 1989).

29 The *intellectual* kinship between Africa and African-Americans is an example of such international cultural exchange. This is rather different from the issue of the heterogeneity of the metropolitan proletariat and subproletariat. I should of course also mention the cultural and political solidarity between Arab-Americans and the Palestine Liberation struggle as an example of two-way exchange. My general point about academic practice in defining marginality and postcoloniality remains generally unaffected by this.

30 The *OED* defines "catachresis" as "abuse or perversion of a trope or metaphor." It should by now be clear that we appropriate this to indicate the originary "abuse" constitutive of language-production, where both concept and metaphor are "wrested from their proper meaning." Thus, it is only in the narrow sense, a word for which there is no adequate referent to be found. We have resolutely kept ourselves to this narrow sense rather than enter the general philosophical position that all language is catachrestic, where the notion of catachresis might itself be catachrestic.

31 Some of us have been intoning this larger sense, with not too much effect, against what Geoff Bennington calls "the beginner's error of conflating 'text' in Derrida's sense with 'discourse' " ("L'arroseur arrosé(e)," *New Formations*, 7 [Spring 1989]: p. 36). See also Gayatri Chakravorty Spivak, "Speculation on Reading Marx: After Reading Derrida," in Derek Attridge, et al., eds., *Post-Structuralism and the Question of History* (Cambridge: Cambridge University Press, 1987), p. 30.

32 Jean-François Lyotard, *The Postmodern Condition: A Report on Knowledge*, trans. Geoff Bennington and Brian Massumi (Minneapolis: University of Minnesota Press, 1984).

33 Jacques Derrida, "Signature Event Context," in *Glyph*, 1 (1977), p. 94.

34 J.B. van Bruitenen, trans., *The Bhagavadgita in the Mahabharata* (Chicago: University of Chicago Press, 1981), p. 87.

35 Karl Marx, "Economic and Philosophical Manuscripts," in Rodney Livingstone and Gregor Benton, trans., *Early Writings* (Harmondsworth: Penguin, 1975), p. 20.

36 Antonio Gramsci, "The Study of Philosophy," in Quentin Hoare and Geoffrey Nowell-Smith, trans., *Selections from the Prison Notebooks* (New York: International Publishers, 1971), p. 324.

37 I take this distinction from Foucault, *Archaeology of Knowledge*, pp. 88–105.

38 The *OED* defines "parabasis" as "going aside," "address to the audience in the poet's name, unconnected with the action of the drama." We appropriate this as a transaction between postcolonial subject-positions, persistently going aside from seeming allegorical continuity.

39 For a treatment of the Armenian case from the point of view of catachrestical claims

to nationhood, see David Kazanjian and Anahid Kassabian, "Naming the Armenian Genocide: The Quest for Truth and a Search for Possibilities," *New Formations,* 8 (Summer 1989): pp. 81–98; Boris Kagarlitsky, *The Thinking Reed: Intellectuals and the Soviet State: 1917 to the Present,* trans. Brian Pearce (London: Verso, 1988), fast becoming the text on the new U.S.S.R., does not yet take into account the breaking open of the available value-coding of ethnicity and nationalism. These words have become even more pertinent in 1992, as of last writing. And in 1993, the Serbo-Croatian "War in *Europe!*"—a lamentation widely heard in the European Economic Community—has further dislocated our stereotyped staging of Islam.

40   I hope it is not out of place to point out that I have tried to assess the implications of these events for multiculturalist teaching in the United States in Spivak, "Teaching for the Times," *MMLA Quarterly* (Spring 1992).

41   Umberto Melotti unwittingly exposes this in *Marx and the Third World,* trans. Pat Ransford (London: Macmillan, 1977), pp. 28–29.

42   Derrida, "Conflict" ("Mochlos," p. 401). For "truth" as one case of general iterability, see Jacques Derrida, *Limited Inc.* ed. Gerald Graff (Evanston: Northwestern University Press, 2d. ed, 1988). Hereafter cited in text as *LI.*

43   (*OG*) p. 47. It is time to admit that I am naturalizing Derrida's general description. Derrida's next sentence makes clear that his concern is in another place from language acquisition.

44   Marcel Proust, *Cities of the Plains,* trans. C.K. Scott Moncrieff (New York: Vintage Books, 1970), p. 99. Professor Jessie Hornsby's extraordinary knowledge of Proust helped me locate a merely remembered passage.

45   Star: "This *Ursprache* as German scholars termed it . . . which we might term Proto-Indo-European . . . could be reconstructed . . . The asterisk being used by convention to indicate reconstructed parent words which were not directly attested by any language known . . ." (Colin Renfrew, *Archaeology and Language: The Puzzle of the Indo-European Origins* [New York: Cambridge University Press, 1987], p. 14). Caught between two translations: "Indeed it was not until 1947 that a good bilingual inscription was found at the site of Karatepe, written in Phoenician (a well-known Semitic language) as well as in hieroglyphic Hittite, so that real progress could be made with it" (Renfrew, *Archaeology and Language,* p. 51). Japhetic: "the story in the book of Genesis of the three sons of Noah, Ham, Shem, and Japheth was taken as a perfectly acceptable explanation of the divergence of early languages. The languages of Africa were thus termed Hamitic, those of the Levant Semitic, and those to the land of the north Japhetic" (*Ibid.,* p. 13). Since "Semitic" is still in use, I am using "Japhetic" within the allegorical frame of the authority still given to the Biblical myth in certain situations of global politics. See V.N. Volosinov's underscoring of a differentiated origin for "Japhetic languages" in his discussion of N. Ja Marr in *Marxism and the Philosophy of Language,* trans. Ladislav Mateika and I.R. Titunik (New York: Seminar Press, 1973), pp. 72, 76, 101.

46   Friedrich Engels, *The Origin of the Family, Private Property, and the State* (New York: Pathfinder Press, 1972). Gayle Rubin's sympathetic critique of Engels in "Traffic" is exemplary.

47   This is in striking contrast to the story's "source," Samaresh Basu's "Uratiya," a poignant semifantastic staging of patriarchal conflict. Another case of the narrativiza-

tion of an alternative history that will not allow the verification of a possible world by the actual world is brilliantly telescoped in the tribal half-caste woman's utterance in Mahasweta Devi's "The Hunt": "If my mother had killed her white daughter at birth . . . I would not have been" ("The Hunt," forthcoming in *Imaginary Maps*).

48 I started to develop this argument in *In Other Worlds*, pp. 241–247; for a dismissal where concept and rhetoric are resolutely identified with the disciplines of "philosophy" and "literary criticism" (aesthetics), see Habermas, *Modernity*, pp. 161–210.

49 Engels, *Origin*, pp. 74–75.

50 Engels, *Origin*, pp. 68–69.

51 For a taxonomy of possible diversity here, see for example the articles in *Cultural Critique*, 6 and 7 (Spring and Autumn 1987).

52 For a detailed study of Marx and Foucault, see Barry Smart, *Foucault, Marxism and Critique* (London: Routledge, 1983).

Chapter 4: Woman in Difference

1 Marie-Aimeé Hélie-Lucas, "Bound and Gagged by the Family Code," in *Third World— Second Sex: Women's Struggles and National Liberation*, Miranda Davies, ed. (London: Zed Books, 1987), vol. 2, p. 14.

2 Devi, "Douloti the Bountiful," is forthcoming in *Imaginary Maps*. Douloti is the daughter of a tribal bonded worker. India has an aboriginal tribal population of over seventy million. A bonded worker offers free work as "repayment" of a small loan, at extortionate rates of interest, often over more than one generation. Douloti is abducted by an upper-caste (nontribal) Indian from her home with a false promise of marriage. She is sold into bonded prostitution, ostensibly to repay her father's loan. She descends down the hierarchy of "favor" in the house of prostitution. Devastated by venereal disease, she accomplishes a journey to a hospital, only to be directed to another hospital, much further away. She decides to walk home instead and dies on the way. The rhetorical and narrative details are filled out in my reading of the story in this chapter.

3 "Invested" is used here as an alternative for "cathected," or "occupied in desire." Mapping one's terrain is certainly a matter of "investment." In a whole spectrum of the senses in that this meaning of the word can take on board. Preliminarily one can say that Mahasweta wants to occupy with a desire for sociality the area of "India," the general principle of whose cartography is quite different from bonded labor. In cartography "proper," by contrast, "physical geography" or "politics" do not need the effort of social investment as does "bonded labor."

4 The notion of cuts (*découpages*, not "circumscription," as in the English translation) is borrowed from Jacques Derrida, "My Chance/*Mes Chances:* A Rendezvous with Some Epicurean Stereophonics," in *Taking Chances: Derrida, Psychoanalysis, and Literature*, ed. William Kerrigan and Joseph H. Smith (Baltimore: The Johns Hopkins University Press, 1984), p. 27.

5 Jean-François Lyotard, *The Différend: Phrases in Dispute*, trans. Georges van den Abbeele (Minneapolis: University of Minnesota Press, 1988).

6 Bardhan, "Women's Work, Welfare and Status," p. 10.

7 This is an enormous network of arguments. Let me just cite the Engels-Gayle Rubin

circuit, on the one hand and the Britain-India circuit, on the other (Anna Davin, "Imperialism and Motherhood," *History Workshop*, 5 [Spring 1978]: pp. 9–65 and *ReCasting Women: Essays in Colonial History*, ed. Kum kum Sangari and Sudesh Vaid [New Delhi: Kali for Women, 1989]).

8   For an analysis of the historical construction of the bond-laborer from precapitalist hierarchical social relations to colonial/postcolonial capitalist exploitative social relations, see Gyan Prakash, *Bonded Histories: Genealogies of Labor Servitude in Colonial India* (New York: Cambridge University Press, 1990). Prakash theorizes the resistance to "betterment" on the part of *kamiya* groups in terms of this discursive redefinition from above. This is a helpful model for understanding Devi's depiction of Douloti's and the majority of the bond-laborers' acceptance of bondslavery as "natural" on the part of the *kamiyas*. When the dominant mode in the country is capitalist, however, the activist must, as I will suggest in the case of Shahbano (Chapter Twelve) and consistently in this book, proceed on a different register, that of the more "aggregative" (see Chapter Two) level of agency, rather than the subindividual level of *pouvoir-savoir* or "grasp." On that register, the more workaday assumption that this residual discursive production is "internalized constraint seen as choice," however asymmetrical and interested, must serve. Yet "literature" can stage it with sympathy because "literature" is allowed to straddle the gap between "theory" and its setting-to-work outside the book. Prakash is right in pointing out that "interestingly, like resistance in the colonial period, these post-colonial structures neither stem from nor are confined by the official projects of reform. The continuity that the kamias have maintained in their refusal to participate in the official project, and in mounting struggles against domination experienced at the point of power's exercise, far from indicating passivity, ought to be seen as their recognition of power concealed by the juridical guise of rights. It represents their critique of the discourse of freedom, their pronouncement that there is 'bondage' in freedom" (p. 225). "Douloti the Bountiful," if read with attention, can resonate here.

9   Let us remember that the "schizo" marks the spot where the papa-mama-baby explanations, consolidating the romance in the nuclear family, find their limit. This is somewhat different from noticing a similar structure more aggressively foregrounded in *The Satanic Verses*, a novel of identity-formation in culture/ideology/religion/nation. (See Chapter Eleven.)

10   Spivak, *In Other Worlds*, pp. 187–196.

11   The continuity between Empire and Nation can be seen in this sphere. Imperialism has regulated land—creating private property in land. See Ranajit Guha, *A Rule of Property for Bengal: An Essay on the Idea of Permanent Settlement* (New Delhi: Orient, Longman, 1981). Now postcoloniality is building a new agricapitalism on that base. For a mere sampling of the spectrum of debate around local rural self-government (Panchayati Raj), see Arun Ghosh, "The Panchayati Raj Bill, " *Economic and Political Weekly*, 24:26 (July 1, 1989) and Indira Hirway, "Panchayat Raj at Crossroads," *Economic and Political Weekly*, 24:29 (July 22, 1989).

12   Judging from reactions to Spivak's "Can the Subaltern Speak?," in *Marxism and the Interpretation of Culture*, ed. Larry Grossberg and Cary Nelson (Urbana: University of Illinois Press, 1988) and to Spivak's "Three Women's Texts and a Critique of Imperialism," in *Race, Writing and Difference*, ed. Henry Louis Gates, Jr. (Chicago: University of Chicago Press, 1986), pp. 262–280, it seems necessary to say that such

a narrative representation of breaking-off does not mean a bad mark for the author. One might describe these break-offs as the opposite kind of *découpage* to the ones that "arise in the place where, between the movement of science—notably when it is concerned with the random structures—and that of philosophy or the arts—literary or not—the limits cannot be actual or static or *solid* but rather only the effects of contextual *découpage*" (Derrida, "My Chances," p. 27).

13 This is particularly true of the "Re-Thinking Marxism" group at the University of Massachusetts-Amherst, with whose general positions I am broadly in sympathy.

14 Bardhan, "Women, Work, Welfare and Status," p. 5.

15 Since this piece was first written, the use of the rational abstractions of "democracy" as "alibis" has become so abundant that this point is either not worth making or has been disproved if placed against the rational abstractions of communism.

16 Bardhan, "Women, Work, Welfare and Status," p. 12.

17 Simone de Beauvoir, *The Second Sex*, trans. H.M. Parshley (New York: Vintage, 1952), pp. 541–588.

18 For a study of international feminist theory that stands the test of decolonization, it is useful to see which bits of metropolitan theory can retain their plausibility "outside." This is not ahistorical theorizing about universals "from above" but contact with a space so intimate that it is both random and inaccessible "below." This is more fully discussed in Chapter Seven.

19 Beauvoir, *The Second Sex*, p. 583.

20 "Breast-Giver" by Mahasweta Devi, is included in *In Other Worlds*, pp. 222–240.

21 Teresa de Lauretis, "Sexual Indifference and Lesbian Representation," *Theatre Journal*, 40:2 (May 1988): pp. 155–177.

22 Teresa de Lauretis, "Sexual Indifference," pp. 175–177. "Third world feminism" seems to mean here the specific feminist movement among women of non-Atlantic origin in the U.S. & U.K., perhaps also Canada.

23 See Jacques Derrida, "Geschlecht: différence sexuelle, différence ontologique," in *Psyche: Inventions de l'autre* (Paris: Galilée, 1987), pp. 395–414.

24 This is an illegitimate thematization of (*OG*, 47).

25 Sigmund Freud, "Analysis Terminable and Interminable," in vol. 23 of *The Standard Edition of the Complete Psychological Writings*, trans. James Strachey, et al. (London: Hogarth Press, 1961), pp. 210–253.

26 On the other hand, if we see this move toward literature and culture precisely as marking a substitute-wish for "the dramatic character that one has so often wished to have lie down on the couch," we can say "literature [or culture] perhaps need not resist this clinic" (Derrida, "My Chances," p. 28). To this wish the nationalist backlash to expatriates writing about postcoloniality is an unacknowledged accomplice rather than an adversary.

27 Anika Lemaire, *Jacques Lacan*, trans. David Macey (London: Routledge, 1977), p. vii.

28 Karl Marx, *Early Writings*, trans. Rodney Livingstone and Gregor Benton (Harmondsworth: Penguin, 1975), p. 324.

29 Jacques Derrida, *Glas*, trans. John P. Leavey, Jr. and Richard Rand (Lincoln: University of Nebraska Press, 1986), p. 236ff.

30 Guy Brett, *Through Our Own Eyes: Popular Art and Modern History* (London: GMP Publishers, 1986), pp. 7–8. The next pasage is also on p. 8.

Chapter 5: Limits and Openings of Marx in Derrida

1 This paper was given at the symposium on Derrida's work organized at the Centre Culturel International de Cerisy-la-Salle in 1980. The proceedings of the colloque are collected in Philippe Lacoue-Labarthe and Jean-Luc Nancy, eds., *Les fins de l'homme: à partir du travail de Jacques Derrida* (Paris: Galilée, 1981). Hereafter cited in text as *FH*. The presence of Derrida's essay, "Les fins de l'homme," collected in *Marges de la philosophie* (Paris: Minuit, 1972) was strongly felt throughout the symposium. My immediate reference is to the English translation of that essay, "The Ends of Man," included in *Margins of Philosophy*, trans. Alan Bass (Chicago: University of Chicago Press, 1982), p. 114. Hereafter cited in text as *EM*. I have modified all quotations from translated texts, whenever I have felt that the wording of the original required it.

2 Here Kathy Ferguson has been constructive. In her critique of my self-referencing she writes: "For the convenience of the reader, particular arguments are developed more fully. But in that case a few broadly sketched references to other texts would suffice" (*Man Question*, p. 201). I hope this headnote is such a "broadly sketched reference."

3 I need not remind the reader that the "we" in this part of the essay is a group of largely French Derridians, with a sprinkling of French-influence international academics. I realize in the revision that the constituency of the first person plural in the essay changes imperceptibly. The vicissitudes of traveling theory, of inhabiting various worlds in the interest of cultural-political fieldwork!

4 In colloquial French, *le politique* is the political person and *la politique* the field of politics. The nature of the distinction as developed at the symposium is discussed in this chapter. My position with respect to this distinction is elaborated chiefly in reaction to Lacoue-Labarthe's paper (*FH*, pp. 493–497), presented the previous day.

5 See the discussion after Jean-Luc Nancy's paper ("La voix libre de l'homme") in *FH*, pp. 183–184. In the actual discussion, which was considerably longer than what is transcribed in the book, the contrast between preserving the question and calling to the wholly-other was sharper.

6 An inkling of this pervasive obsession with "purity" is to be found in the privileging of philosophy as point of departure and destiny in Lacoue-Labarthe's opening program-statement (*FH*, p. 12 and passim).

7 Jacques Derrida, "The Double Session," in *Dissemination*, trans. Barbara Johnson (Chicago: University of Chicago Press, 1981), p. 207.

8 Spivak, *In Other Worlds*, p. 76.

9 Jacques Derrida, "Economimesis," trans. Richard Klein, *Diacritics*, 2:2 (Summer 1981): p. 3. Hereafter cited in text as *E*.

10 Jacques Derrida, "Restitutions of the *Truth in Pointing* [pointure]," in *Truth in Painting*, trans. Geoff Bennington and Ian McLeod (Chicago: University of Chicago Press, 1987), pp. 260, 261, 271. Hereafter cited in text as *RTP*.

11 An exception may be made for "White Mythology: Metaphor in the Text of Philosophy," in *Margins of Philosophy*, where the footnotes contain some extended references to a selective group of texts.

12 Jacques Derrida, "The Age of Hegel," in *Glyph Textual Studies I* (Minneapolis: University of Minnesota Press), p. 35.

13 Jacques Derrida, "Où Commence et comment finit un corps enseignant," in *Politiques de la philosophie,* Dominique Grisoni, ed. (Paris: Grasset, 1976), p. 67. I have substituted the phrase "political economy" for "phallogocentric ontotheology." Hereafter cited in text as *CE.*

14 "A Cold Eye at the Discount Window," *Business Week,* 2645 (July 14, 1980): p. 82. I have not collected here the innumerable journalistic examples that I could have found in the intervening years.

15 Silviu Brucan, "War and Peace Today," *Marxist Perspectives,* 2:4 (1979–1980): p. 13. In the wake of the dissolution of the U.S.S.R., this problem is ever more acute today.

16 The development of the E.C.U., and the interchangeability of national currencies in the E.E.C. make the import of these remarks far stronger than could have been imagined in 1980.

17 Sigmund Freud, *The Standard Edition of the Complete Psychological Writings,* trans. James Strachey, et al. (London: Hogarth Press, 1953), vol. 4, pp. 283, 284, 292.

18 This word must be rigorously distinguished from *Beziehung* (more important in Heidegger), also translated as "relationship." Marx's Hegelian habit of thinking led him to look for a structural relationship as the irreducible law of the real: "the truth of Appearance is the essential relation [*Verhältnis*]" (Hegel, *Science of Logic,* trans. A.V. Miller [New York: Humanities Press, 1969], p. 512).

19 Karl Marx, *Grundrisse: Foundations of the Critique of Political Economy,* trans. Martin Nicolaus (New York: Vintage, 1973), p. 269. Hereafter cited in text as *GR.*

20 Jacques Derrida, "Force of Law."

21 Jacques Derrida, "The Purveyor of Truth," in *The Post Card* and "Call It a Day for Democracy," in Derrida, *The Other Heading: Reflections on Today's Europe,* trans. Pascale-Anne Brault and Michael B. Naas (Bloomington: Indiana University Press, 1992). Hereafter cited in text as *OH.*

22 Jacques Derrida, *Of Spirit.*

23 "Usurer's capital has capital's mode of exploitation without its mode of production. . . . What distinguishes interest-bearing capital in so far as it forms an essential element of the capitalist mode of production, from usurer's capital is in no way the nature or character of this capital itself. It is simply the changed conditions under which it functions" (*C* 3:732, 735). "Usurers' capital . . . [is] incompatible with the nature of money and therefore inexplicable from the standpoint of the exchange of commodities" (C1, 266–267).

24 Jacques Derrida, "The Force of Law," p. 991.

25 Jacques Derrida, "The Principle of Reason: The University in the Eyes of Its Pupils," trans. Catherine Porter and Edward P. Morris, *Diacritics,* 3:20 (Fall 1983): pp. 18–19; emphases author's. I have substituted the rather awkward translations for *au-delà* and *mise-en-oeuvre* for the more sensible choices made by Porter and Morris because in both cases the English is obliged to produce a more substantial substantive effect, introducing a "what is beyond" to the more indefinite *au-delà* and putting a completed action in the place of the process implied in *mise-en-oeuvre.* The idea of the "setting-into-work of truth" in art is to be found in Heidegger's "The Origin of the Work of

Art" and elsewhere. Derrida's meticulously detailed critique of the itinerary of "the setting-into-work-of-truth" can be drawn from *Of Spirit.* I contrast it to Gianni Vattimo's superficial and literalist account of this notion so that Derrida's elaboration of responsibility to the outside is not mistaken for a version of this particular Heideggerian enterprise (Vattimo, *The End of Modernity: Nihilism and Hermeneutics in Postmodern Culture,* trans. Jon R. Snyder [Baltimore: the Johns Hopkins University Press, 1991], pp. 51–109). Incidentally, this yearning of "a certain deconstruction" towards "the polis" is quite overlooked in the system-bound arguments found in pieces like Simon Critchley, "The Chiasmus: Levinas, Derrida and the Ethical Demand for Deconstruction," *Textual Practice,* 3:1 (Spring 1989): pp. 91–106. (The Derridean phrases in the previous sentence are from "Force of Law," pp. 931–933).

26 Jacques Derrida, "Différance," in Alan Bass, trans., *Margins of Philosophy* (Chicago: University of Chicago Press, 1982), p. 17. The following quoted sentence is *ibid.,* p. 12.

27 The world "invisible" is used repeatedly by social scientists and activists to describe the global phenomenon of sweated female pieceworkers who work at home. This phenomenon ranges from precapitalist cottage work (long absorbed into capitalism) to work created by contemporary high technology. For a discussion of these women's "invisibility" from analysis, statistics, and organization, see, for example, Sheila Allen and Carol Wolkowitz, *Homeworking: Myths and Realities* (London: Macmillan, 1987).

28 In Chapter One of *An Unfashionable Grammatology,* forthcoming from Harvard University. I like this analysis, and I cannot control the urge to self-cite.

29 Derrida, "The *Retrait* of Metaphor," trans. the editors, *Enclitic* (1978). Hereafter cited in text as *RM.*

Chapter 6: Feminism and Deconstruction, Again: Negotiations

1 Alice Jardine, *Gynesis: Configurations of Woman and Modernity* (Ithaca: Cornell University Press, 1985); Linda Nicholson, ed., *Feminism/Postmodernism* (New York: Routledge, 1990). There is a whole literature now on this topic. Some particularly interesting examples are Meaghan Morris, *The Pirate's Fiancée: Feminism, Reading, Postmodernism* (London: Verso, 1988); Andrew Ross, ed., *Universal Abandon?: The Politics of Postmodernism* (Minneapolis: University of Minnesota Press, 1988); and Joanna Hodge, "Feminism and Postmodernism: Misleading Divisions Imposed by the Opposition between Modernism and Postmodernism," in Andrew Benjamin, ed., *The Problems of Modernity: Adorno and Benjamin* (London: Routledge, 1989).

2 With reference to this complaint, see Derrida's spirited defense of the Nambikwara against the charge that peoples without a recognizably phono- or ideo-graphic writing were "without writing," (*OG,* 101–140).

3 For two different approaches to this question, see Ashis Nandy, *The Intimate Enemy: Loss and Recovery of Self Under Colonialism* (Oxford: Oxford University Press, 1983) and Dipesh Chakrabarty, "Postcoloniality and the Artifice of History: Who Speaks for 'Indian' Pasts?," *Representations,* 37 (Winter 1992): pp. 1–26.

4 Thomas Nagel, *Mortal Questions* (Cambridge: Cambridge University Press, 1979), p. xii.

5   Edward A. Gargan, "India Flirts with Hope, Despite Disasters," *New York Times* (March 1, 1992).

6   Jacqueline Rose, *Sexuality in the Field of Vision* (London: Verso, 1986).

7   Margaret Homan, "Feminist Criticism and Theory: The Ghost of Creusa," *Yale Journal of Criticism* 1:1 (Fall 1987), pp. 153–182. Showalter quoted by Elizabeth Skolbert, "Literary Feminism Comes of Age," *New York Times Sunday Magazine* (December 6, 1987): p. 112.

8   *See* Partha Chatterjee, *Nationalist Thought and the Colonial World: A Derivative Discourse?* (London: Zed, 1986).

9   Rose, *Sexuality*, p. 23.

10   Rose, *Sexuality*, p. 15.

11   The difference between the desire for an impasse and negotiating with an enabling double bind seems important if we wish to acknowledge that we are "free agents" produced by and written in history. Ignoring of the double bind in nonfoundationalist philosophy is now affecting Euroamerican Marxism as well: "a justification of Marxian theory on the grounds of its social context and consequences amounts to warranting a theory by the means of the self-same theory . . . we are not bothered by the nature of [the alternative antiessentialist] infinite regress that is independent of these 'independent terms' and can serve as an ultimate ground of truth for these meanings." (Stephen A. Resnick and Richard D. Wolff, *Knowledge and Class: A Marxian Critique of Political Economy* [Chicago: University of Chicago Press, 1987], p. 28.)

12   Rose, *Sexuality*, p. 5.

13   It would be to belabor the obvious to point out that there is rather a straight and self-conscious line here between Kant and Freud. See, for example, Freud, *Standard Edition*, vol. 22, pp. 61, 163. The relationship between the knowing and acting subject is a rupture rather than a continuous progression. It is surely one of the gifts of structuralist and poststructuralist psychoanalysis to make us productively uneasy about that relationship. (I use "productive" where I should perhaps say "potentially productive." I mean that the unease can be less intransigent than a mere privileging of either theory or practice, or the assumption of achievable continuity between them.)

14   Again, this is rather a prominent cornerstone of the critique of humanism. The lines here fall unevenly between Nietzsche, Heidegger, Foucault, and Derrida. Foucault, having decided to name the problem itself the empirico-transcendental-discursive mark of the modern, went off in other interesting directions. Derrida has kept patiently producing its implications. He stated the problem simply in 1963 (in a sentence that I often quote) with special reference to the anthropologizing of philosophy, a project in which the later Rose as a feminist (Derrida is speaking of Sartre as a humanist) is perhaps also engaged: "Everything occurs as if the sign(man) has no origin, no historical, cultural, linguistic limit" (*Margins of Philosophy*, p. 116).

15   Jacques Derrida, *Spurs*, trans. Barbara Harlow (Chicago: University of Chicago Press, 1978).

16   Derrida, *Spurs*, p. 109. The essay "Geschlecht: différence sexuelle, différence ontologique," in *Psyche: Inventions de l'autre* (Paris: Galilée, 1987) should be considered if one wants to engage Derrida specifically on the issue of the place of sexual duality in Heidegger's thought. It has little to do with the argument here.

17 Derrida, *Spurs,* p. 109.

18 Louis Althusser, "Ideology and Ideological State Apparatuses (Notes Towards an Investigation)," in *Lenin and Philosophy and Other Essays,* trans. Ben Brewster (New York: Monthly Review Press, 1971), p. 159. Theodor Adorno, "Subject and Object," in *The Essential Frankfurt School Reader,* trans. Andrew Arato and Eike Gebhardt (New York: Urizen, 1978), p. 508.

19 Althusser, "Ideology," p. 176.

20 Derrida, *Spurs,* p. 110.

21 Derrida, *Spurs,* p. 111.

22 Derrida, *Spurs,* p. 110.

23 Gayatri Chakravorty Spivak, "Displacement and the Discourse of Woman," in Mark Krupnick, ed., *Displacement: Derrida and After* (Bloomington: Indiana University Press, 1983). I do mention the fact of the "name," but do not seem to grasp its import.

24 Derrida, *Spurs,* p. 51.

25 Derrida, *Spurs,* p. 51.

26 Rose, *Sexuality,* p. 21 n.38.

27 This phase in Derrida begins as early as his deconstructive reading of the philosophy of Emmanual Levinas in "Violence and Metaphysics," published in 1964 (and in *Writing and Difference,* trans. Alan Bass [Chicago: University of Chicago Press, 1978]). Levinas argues there that Husserl and Heidegger, both within the Greek tradition, ultimately write philosophies of oppression. Neutralizing the other, fundamental ontology and phenomenology perform the same structural operation as philosophies of knowledge, appropriating the other as object. By contrast, Levinas suggests, the gaze toward the other must always be open, an open question, the possibility of the ethical. "Before the ontological level, the ethical level" (p. 98). Derrida reads Levinas critically, suggesting that he too is complicit with philosophy in the Greek. But about the openness of the question, the prior claim of responsibility to the trace of the other (which will be for him the possibility of "the non-ethical opening of ethics": *Of Grammatology,* p. 140), he is in agreement.

28 Jacques Derrida, *The Ear of the Other: Otobiography, Transference, Translation,* trans. Peggy Kamuf (New York: Schocken, 1985).

29 The paleonymic burden of the word "love" for a feminist is to be distinguished rigorously from the gentlemanly or belle-lettristic attitude of "love for the text."

30 "Structure, Sign, and Play in the Discourse of the Human Sciences," in *Writing and Difference.*

31 Part of the idea behind spelling "différance" with an "a" was that it would be a neographism, be visible, not audible. To keep the word in English and to pronounce it in the French way has foiled that project. Since another part of the idea was to include both "differ" and "defer" and indicate that this was the spacing/time structure of the inevitable break between, among other things, theory and method (epistemo/ontology and axiology, too, of course), I propose "difering" in English. I will do nothing to give this translation currency.

32 "The Supplement of Copula: Philosophy Before Linguistics" in *Margins of Philosophy.*

The "supplement"—both adding to a preexisting whole and filling a preexisting hole—is something like the "difering" that every "is" pretends or professes it isn't doing.

33 As I have pointed out earlier in this book, the "(im)" in such a formulation marks the enabling double bind at the inauguration of practice that, literalizing a catachresis, allows the possibility of practice as craft. I believe there is no particular virtue in making it sound less abstract in its formulation, and thus taking away precision. If the reader wants the "concrete," she will have to check it out in doing, not grasping easily.

34 I add this parenthesis because, when I gave a version of this paper at the University of Virginia, so clear a thinker as Richard Rorty thought that my message was that feminism must "ignore" deconstruction altogether in order to act. To spell it out this way sounds bizarre. In the doing it is something like a reflex, the "faith" (habit?) that Gramsci refers to in "The Formation of Intellectuals" (Antonio Gramsci, *Selections from the Prison Notebooks,* trans. Quintin Hoare and Geoffrey Nowell-Smith [New York: International Publishers, 1971], p. 339). I think, although it does not matter to me very much, that Derrida himself is aware of this at all times, and that it is because of this that in the introduction to his 1987 collection *Psyche,* he calls the unifying themes of his writings of the last decade a *théorie distraite*—the best English translation of which would be, in my judgment, "an inattentive theory" (*Psyche,* p. 9). I have claimed this myself in the introduction to this book. Such "inattention"—pointing toward the constancy of a habit—has interesting connections with the Freudian notion of hypercathexis.

35 Allen and Wolkowitz, *Homeworking,* p. 73.

36 Derrida, *The Ear of the Other,* pp. 16–17, 38.

37 It is interesting to see that Derrida falls back on the most "orthodox" model of deconstructive method-reversal and displacement—when he makes a somewhat similar point and does not, of course, refer to his own position within patriarchal presuppositions: Derrida, "Women in the Beehive," in Paul Smith and Alice Jardine, eds., *Men in Feminism* (New York: Methuen, 1987), pp. 194–195. It is these presuppositions of the name "woman," rather than the morphology of "différance," that will not allow for the acknowledgment of class and race specifically in women—racial heterogeneity in another guise—that I go on to discuss in my text.

38 Foucault fabulates this anxiety poignantly in the adult male Greek's anxiety about the loss of the boyhood of the boy as erotic object in *The Use of Pleasure: The History of Sexuality,* trans. Robert Hurley (New York: Vintage, 1986), vol. 2.

39 Jacques Lacan, "God and the Jouissance of Woman, A Love Letter," in *Feminine Sexuality,* trans. Jacqueline Rose (London: Macmillan, 1982), p. 155f.

40 An interested insistence of this sort, not absolutely justified by theory, is, of course, pervasively crucial to deconstructive method. The two articulations that I still find most useful are *OG,* 62, and "The Double Session," in *Dissemination,* trans. Barbara Johnson (Chicago: University of Chicago Press, 1981), p. 235.

42 Foucault, *Archaeology,* p. 96.

43 For this particular bonding, see Richard Rorty, "Solidarity or Objectivity?," in Cornel West and John Rajchman, eds., *Post-Analytical Philosophy* (New York: Columbia University Press, 1985).

44 Nagel, *Mortal Questions,* p. xiii.

45 I thank Jacques Derrida for sharing unpublished material with me. The revised published version might be somewhat different, of course.

Chapter 7: French Feminism Revisited

1 Chafika Marouf, "Etat de la recherche sur le monde féminin et la famille en Algérie et au Maghreb," in *Femme, famille et société* (Oran: URASC, 1988), p. 5; translation mine.

2 In Joseph H. Smith and William Kerrigan, eds., *Taking Chances: Derrida, Psychoanalysis, and Literature* (Baltimore: The Johns Hopkins University Press, 1984).

3 Patricia J. Williams, *The Alchemy of Race and Rights* (Cambridge, Mass.: Harvard University Press, 1991), p. 8; emphasis mine.

4 Pierre Bourdieu defines it as a risk, in somewhat more aggressive language: "It is on condition that they take what it indeed the greatest possible risk, namely that of bringing into question and into danger the philosophical game itself, the game to which their own *existence* as philosophers, or their own participation in the game, is linked, that philosophers can assure for themselves the privilege that they almost always forget to claim, that is to say their freedom in relation that authorizes and justifies them in calling themselves and thinking of themselves as philosophers." "The Philosophical Institution," in Alan Montefiore, ed., *Philosophy in France Today* (Cambridge: Cambridge University Press, 1983), p. 8. I quote this passage in full so that my position is not identified with the position stated in it. For me the line between freedom and uncertainty is itself uncertain.

5 These three self-references are in the interest of offering past work for verification and evaluation of learning, not for claiming authority.

6 Gayatri Chakravorty Spivak, "French Feminism in an International Frame," in *In Other Worlds*, pp. 134–153.

7 Richard Rorty attempts to recode these traits of historicoeconomic chance for the North Atlantic as grounds for rewriting universalism (objectivity as solidarity in, for example "Solidarity." I have called this "bonding" in the previous essay. It is this historical advantage that allows contemporary U.S. imperialism its attempt to consolidate itself in spite of relative economic decline.

8 Marie-Aimée Hélie-Lucas, "Bound and Gagged by the Family Code," in *Third World: Second Sex: Women's Struggles and National Liberation,* Miranda Davies, ed., (London: Zed Books, 1983), vol. 2, pp. 3–15. Hereafter cited in text as *BG.*

9 Jacques Derrida, "My Chances," pp. 3, 4.

10 Simone de Beauvoir, *The Second Sex*, pp. 540–588. Hereafter cited in text as *SS.*

11 Quoted in Toril Moi, unpublished manuscript. I am grateful to Professor Moi for letting me see this work. See also Anne Tristan and Annie de Pisan, "Tales from the Women's Movement," and Michèle Le Doeuff, "Women and Philosophy," in Toril Moi, ed., *French Feminist Thought: A Reader* (New York: Basil Blackwell, 1987), pp. 197–221.

12 Jean-Paul Sartre, *Being and Nothingness,* trans. Hazel E. Barnes (New York: Pocket Books, 1966). Hereafter cited in text as *BN.* Derrida's critique is in *EM.*

13 Karl Marx, *Early Writings*, Rodney Livingstone and Gregor Benton, trans. (Harmondsworth: Penguin, 1975), pp. 327–330.

14 Marx, *Early Writings*, p. 328.

15 We have read criticially, in the previous chapter, Derrida's version of Nietzsche's distinction between the scenes of the father and the mother, in "The Ear of the Other."

16 I must here record that my own birth-mother, Sivani Chakravorty, liberated me from any arranged marriage in 1957 (at her own peril, how much I could not then know), understanding responsibility beyond cultural norms, "giving the mother to the other woman" that I would be, using almost the same words, which I reproduce here in translation: "I cannot imagine your future good, because it exceeds me." She had not then and has not now read *The Second Sex*. And Melanie Klein has at last made me understand the power of gratitude as productive of social force.

17 Margaret Atwood, "Giving Birth," in *Dancing Girls* (New York: Simon and Schuster, 1977), pp. 225–240.

18 Elaine Marks, "Feminism's Wake," in *Boundary 2*, 12:2 (Winter 1984): pp. 99–110.

19 See Derrida, *Psyche*, p. 41, for the formal argument.

20 Richard Rorty, "Private Irony and Liberal Hope," in *Contingency*, pp. 73–95.

21 Zillah R. Eisenstein, *The Female Body*, pp. 6–41.

22 Rosalind Pollack Petchesky, *Abortion and Woman's Choice: The State, Sexuality, and Reproductive Freedom* (London: Verso, 1986), pp. 241–276.

23 Petchesky, *Abortion and Woman's Choice: The State, Sexuality, and Reproductive Freedom*, p. 395.

24 This last sentence is by now either familiar to the reader via Derrida's notorious text *Limited, Inc.*, ed. Gerald Graff, 2nd ed. (Evanston: Northwestern University Press, 1988), p. 96, or it would take too lengthy an exposition. The operative sentence in the Derrida text is, of course, "the possibility of fiction cannot be derived."

25 Hélène Cixous, "The Laugh of the Medusa," in Elaine Marks and Isabelle de Courtivron, eds., *New French Feminisms: An Anthology* (New York: Schocken Books, 1981), pp. 245–264. Hereafter cited in text as LM. As Verena Conley and others point out, this piece is not representative of the current Cixous (Verena Andermatt Conley, *Hélène Cixous: Writing the Feminine*, expanded ed. [Lincoln: University of Nebraska Press, 1991], pp. xi–xxiii). It is, however, representative of that moment in "French" feminism which has become a flashpoint for feminist intellectuals.

26 Heidegger, *Being and Time*, p. 25.

27 *"Coming to Writing" and Other Essays*, Hélène Cixous, with a foreword by Susan Rubin Suleiman, ed. Deborah Jensen, trans. Sarah Cornell, et al. (Cambridge, Mass.: Harvard University Press, 1991).

28 The word "lent" comes from Foucault's powerful remark that one must be a nominalist when thinking power. In such nominalism, names are "lent" to networks. The word is quite correctly translated "attributed" in HS, 93. But I think the literal translation for *prêter* is more apposite here.

29 There is a peculiar relevancy to this because, in the French that has been dehegemonized by the underclass or rural Algerian, the vous ("you" as opposed to "thou") hardly exists, all exchange is in the "thou" or *tu*. It is only half fanciful to say that the language

of imperialism loses its power to achieve the ethical distinction outside of the culture of imperialism, in subalternity.

30 It is a mistake, I think, to call Cixous, simply, an "Algerian," as does Conley in her otherwise interesting book (*Cixous*, p. 4); in the interest of fleshing out this argument, I refer to Spivak, "Imperialism and Sexual Difference," in Robert Con Davis and Ronald Schleifer, eds., *Contemporary Literary Criticism: Literary and Cultural Studies* (New York: Longman, 1989).

31 Hélène Cixous and Catherine Clément, *The Newly Born Woman*, trans. Betsy Wing (Minneapolis: University of Minnesota Press, 1986).

32 These mysterious and regular references to Melanie Klein reflect the excitement of new work. I understand that Jacqueline Rose will soon be publishing a new study of Melanie Klein. I look forward to its publication, for I expect to learn from it and resonate with it. This also gives me the opportunity to say that, having reread Rose's "Dora— Fragment of an Analysis" in *Sexuality in the Field of Vision*, I recognize that my critique of Derrida in the previous chapter resonates with her critique of Freud in that essay. Namely, that since Derrida is written in the narrative of his own understanding of femininity, he undermines his own best insights of deconstruction and "naturalizes" it in woman's case. As Rose pleads to sister-feminists, do not repeat Freud's mistake but *use* the best of psychoanalysis, so do I for Derrida and deconstruction.

33 For a discussion of the significance of the French "corps," see Jacques Derrida, "Où commence et comment finit," pp. 55–97.

34 For the French intellectuals of 1968, this conviction found strict theoretical focus in the useful idea of Capital as the abstract as such, one of the operative presuppositions of Gilles Deleuze and Félix Guattari, *Anti-Oedipus.*

35 *L'Histoire terrible mais inachevée de Norodom Sihanouk roi de Cambodge* (1985) and *L'Indiade où l'Inde de leurs rêves* (1988), both published by Paris: Théâtre du soleil.

36 The complex and contrastive relationships between Benedict Anderson, *Imagined Communities*, rev. ed. (London: Verso, 1991), Partha Chatterjee, *Nationalist Thought and the Colonial World: A Derivative Discourse?* (London: Zed Books, 1986), and Andrew Parker, ed., *Nationalisms and Sexuality* (New York: Routledge, 1991) are instructive here.

37 This is the ground level of conscientization necessary for any internationalist vision. Marx's Economics and Philosophical Manuscripts concern themselves with producing a critique of "*national* economy." *Capital* is a critique of *political* economy. The transition is worked out (or is it?) in "Forms Which Precede Capitalist Production" in the *Grundrisse*, pp. 471–479. What is the mysterious bond that seems to tie blood and land? That a sufficiently critical answer to this question was not produced by Marx is too obvious to argue. In this connection, Crystal Bartolovitch's forthcoming book *Making Space* will be useful.

38 For a report on the organization, see Hélie-Lucas, "Women Living Under Muslim Laws," in *South Asia Bulletin*, 10:1 (1990): p. 73.

39 For *antre*, see Jacques Derrida, "Dissemination," p. 212. I am obliged to report an unverifiable anecdote here, as part of the social textiling of feminism. On a panel on the Gulf War at the 1990 Socialist Scholars' conference in New York, I had suggested that although secularism was absolutely to be supported in the legal sphere, and the consolidation of theocracies to be opposed in every way, it must also be acknowledged

that it is, in former colonies, a class-internalized position, belonging to the very class that had had "free" access to the culture of imperialism; that it was not a moral position; and finally that, for precisely these reasons, it could not be effectively used as ethical persuasion against religious violence. In the corridor after the session, a secularist Muslim academic woman based in the U.S. bitterly rebuked me and remarked, "Islam is against women like me!" That is precisely the aporia of secularism that I was and am pointing to.

40 Rather: "if the style were (just as the penis would be according to Freud 'the normal prototype of the fetish') the man, writing would be the woman" (Jacques Derrida, *Spurs*, p. 57, translation modified).

41 Luce Irigaray, "Plato's *Hystera*," in *Speculum of the Other Woman*, trans. Gillian C. Gill (Ithaca: Cornell University Press, 1985), pp. 243–264.

42 Irigaray, "Plato's *Hysteria*," p. 358. Melanie Klein can be supplemented with this.

43 Luce Irigaray, "The Fecundity of the Caress: A Reading of Levinas, *Totality and Infinity* section IV, B, 'The Phenomenology of Eros,'" in *Face to Face with Levinas*, trans. Carolyn Burke, ed. Richard Cohen (Albany: SUNY Press, 1986), pp. 231–256. Hereafter cited in text as *FC*.

44 Luce Irigaray, "Sexual Difference," in *French Feminist Thought*, ed. Toril Moi, p. 122. Hereafter cited as *SD*. See also the mother and the veil in Assia Djebar, "Forbidden Gaze, Severed Sound," in *Women of Algiers in Their Apartments*, trans. Marjolijn de Jager (Charlottesville: University of Virginia Press, 1992), pp. 133–154.

45 Emmanuel Levinas, *Totality and Infinity: An Essay on Exteriority*, trans. Alphonso Lingis (Pittsburgh: Duquesne University Press, 1969), pp. 256, 264, 261. Hereafter cited in text as *TI*.

46 See Derrida's treatment of Hegel on the fetish in *Glas*, pp. 207ai–211ai and passim. The importance of coming interminably to terms with Heidegger's involvement with National Socialism and Paul de Man's wartime journalism is also important in this context (See Jacques Derrida, *Of Spirit: Heidegger and the Question*, trans. Geoffrey Bennington and Rachel Bowlby [Chicago: University of Chicago Press, 1989], and ("Like the Sound of a Deep Sea Within a Shell: Paul de Man's War," in Werner Hamacher, et al., eds., *Responses: On Paul de Man's Wartime Journalism* [Lincoln: University of Nebraska Press, 1989], pp. 127–164). The position is stated more forcibly in "The Ear of the Other," p. 25f.

47 For "people of the book," see Mark Shell, "Marranos (Pigs), or from Coexistence to Toleration," *Critical Inquiry*, 17:2 (Winter 1991): pp. 306–355. For the effort to transcribe psychoanalysis into Islam, see *Cahiers Intersignes*, I (Spring 1990).

48 Martine Medejel, "L'exil d'un prénom étranger," *Intersignes* I, pp. 63–70.

49 Remarks made at a conference on "Decolonizing the Imagination: The New Europe and Its Others," Amsterdam, May 6, 1991.

Chapter 8: Not Virgin Enough to Say That [S]he Occupies the Place of the Other

1 Conference on Deconstruction and the Call to the Ethical, Cardozo Law School, Fall 1990.

2 "Polytheism" is a word generated by monotheist space. Since we have not left that stage, I will use this word uneasily.

3 Letter from Jean-Luc Nancy (January 18, 1991), available at Cardozo Law Library.

4 See L. Dumont, *Homo Hierarchicus: The Caste System and Its Implications*, trans. M. Sainsbury (Chicago: University of Chicago Press, 1980). Kristeva somewhat tediously takes this book as authority in her fantasies about the abject in Hinduism; Julia Kristeva, "Approaching Abjection," in *Powers of Horror: An Essay on Abjection*, trans. Leon S. Roudiez (New York: Columbia University Press, 1982), pp. 75–77.

5 Bimal Krishna Matilal and Gayatri Chakravorty Spivak, "Epic and Ethic in Indian Examples" (New York: Routledge, forthcoming).

6 Geoffrey Bennington and Jacques Derrida, *Jacques Derrida* (Paris: Seuil, 1991). *The Other Heading* appeared since this writing. I have discussed it in Chapter Five.

7 I use "desist" in the way in which Derrida wants us not to use it, I think: " . . . the word désistance, in French, a word that Lacoue-Labarthe never uses and that moreover does not yet exist, could prove useful. On the condition that it not be simply transcribed in English, without further precautions, as 'desistance!' " Jacques Derrida, "Introduction: Désistance," in P. Lacoue-Labarthe, *Typography: Mimesis, Philosophy, Politics* 4, C. Fynsk, ed. (Cambridge: Harvard University Press, 1989). To measure my faithfulness in transgression, the reader must go to Derrida's text.

8 "The Trinity Formula" is the title of a chapter in C3. Here Marx suggests that to assume that all societies are class structured as under industrial capitalism is to mistake a historical moment for a general social law. The very last paragraph suggests that on the other side of that particular situational class analysis the category of class fades into the indefinite.

9 Drucilla Cornell, "Civil Disobedience and Deconstruction," *Cardozo Law Review*, 13 (1991): pp. 1309, 1314.

10 The following excerpts are from Matilal and Spivak, "Epic and Ethic." The references are to Draupadi, but they will remain obscure without consulting the Sanskrit text of the Critical Edition of the *Mahābhārata* ed. Vishnu S. Sukthankar, et al. (Poona: Bhandarkar Oriental Research Institute, 1927–66). My intransigence reflects an impatience with the intense concentration of the Western religious narratives at the conference—as if that was the only one that instantiated the Call to the Ethical—and the absurdity of five minutes in its face. I refer the reader to "Epic and Ethic" for a full discussion.

Chapter 9: The Politics of Translation

1 The first part of this essay is based on a conversation with Michèle Barrett in the summer of 1990.

2 Forthcoming from Seagull Press, Calcutta.

3 "Facilitation" is the English translation of the Freudian term *Bahnung* (pathing) which is translated *frayage* in French. The dictionary meaning is:

> Term used by Freud at a time when he was putting forward a neurological model of the functioning of the psychical apparatus (1895): the excitation, in passing from one neurone to another, runs into a certain resistance; where its

passage results in a permanent reduction in this resistance, there is said to be facilitation; excitation will opt for a facilitated pathway in preference to one where no facilitation has occurred (J.B. Pontalis, *The Language of Psychoanalysis* [London: Hogarth Press, 1973], p. 157).

4   Jacques Derrida, "The Force of Law," p. 923.

5   "The Wet-Nurse," in Kali for Women, eds., *Truth Tales: Stories by Indian Women* (London: The Women's Press, 1987), pp. 1–50 (first published by Kali for Women, Delhi, 1986), and "Breast-Giver," in Spivak, *In Other Worlds*, pp. 222–240.

6   Sudhir Kakar, *The Inner World: A Psycho-Analytic Study of Childhood and Society in India*, 2nd ed. (Delhi: Oxford University Press, 1981), p. 171ff. Part of this discussion in a slightly different form is included in my "Psychoanalysis in Left Field; and Field-working" (London: Routledge, forthcoming).

7   For a feminist attempt at understanding such figures, see Kumari Jayawardena, *The White Woman's Other Burden* (forthcoming).

8   See Partha Chatterjee, "Nationalism and the Woman Question," in *ReCasting Women*, ed. Kumkum Sangari and Sudesh Vaid (New Brunswick: Rutgers University Press, 1990), pp. 233–253, for a detailed discussion of this gendering in Indian nationalism.

9   I mention these details because Ram Proshad's dates and his rural situation make his pattern of recognition of the outsider on the landscape significantly different from that of the colonially educated, urban, ex-Communist, deeply nationalist/internationalist Vivekananda. Indeed, the latter's mediation into a text such as Ram Proshad's through the rural-origin urban-bound visionary Rama Krishna, his *guru*, makes his use precisely a "citation," in the most robust sense—"translation" into a displaced discursive formation. The first version of this essay was written at speed in Cambridge and reproduces a "life-history" of Ram Proshad firmly entrenched in the Bengali imaginary. I have corrected the details in this version.

10 Max Weber, *The Religion of India: The Sociology of Hinduism and Buddhism*, trans. Hans. H. Gerth and Don Martindale (Glencoe, Ill.: Free Press, 1958).

11 Ifi Amadiume, *Male Daughters Female Husbands* (London: Zed Books, 1987).

12 For background on Akhter, already somewhat dated for this interventionist in the history of the present, see Yayori Matsui, ed., *Women's Asia* (London: Zed Books, 1989), chap. 1. See also her *Depopulating Bangladesh: Essays on the Politics of Fertility* (Dhaka: Narigrantha, 1992).

13 I have given an account of this in Spivak, "Acting Bits/Identity Talk," *Critical Inquiry* 18:4 (Summer 1992).

14 Spivak, "Can the Subaltern Speak?," in *Marxism and the Interpretation of Culture*, ed. Larry Grossberg and Cary Nelson (Urbana: University of Illinois Press, 1988), pp. 271–313.

15 Toni Morrison, *Beloved* (New York: Plume Books, 1987). Hereafter cited in text as *B* with page numbers included.

16 Wilson Harris, *The Guyana Quartet* (London: Faber, 1975). These quotations are from Wilson Harris, "Cross-Cultural Crisis: Imagery, Language, and the Intuitive Imagination," Commonwealth Lectures: University of Cambridge, Lecture no. 2 (October 31, 1990).

17 Derrida traces the trajectory of the Hegelian and pre-Hegelian discourse of the fetish in *Glas*. The worshipper of the fetish eats human flesh. The worshipper of God feasts on the Eucharist. Harris transverses the fetish here through the native imagination.

18 Slavoj Žižek, *The Sublime Object of Ideology*, trans. Jon Barnes (London: Verso, 1989), pp. 203, 208, 212.

19 Peter de Bolla, *The Discourse of the Sublime: Readings in History, Aesthetics, and the Subject* (Oxford: Blackwell, 1989). Page numbers are given in my text.

20 References and discussion of "The Begums of Oudh," and "The Impeachment of Warren Hastings" are to be found in *The Writings and Speeches of Edmund Burke*, ed. P.J. Marshall (Oxford: Clarendon Press, 1981), vol. 5, *India: Madras and Bengal*, pp. 410–412, 465–466, 470; and in vol. 6, *India: Launching of the Hastings Impeachment*, respectively.

21 See my "Reading the Archives: The Rani of Sirmur," in Francis Barker, ed., *Europe and Its Others* (Colchester: University of Essex, 1985), vol. 1, pp. 128–151.

22 De Bolla, *Discourse*, p. 182.

23 De Bolla, *Discourse*, p. 324.

24 Paul de Man, "The Purloined Ribbon," reprinted as "Excuses (*Confessions*)," in de Man, *Allegories of Reading* (New Haven: Yale University Press, 1979), pp. 278–301.

Chapter 10: Inscriptions: of Truth to Size

1 Monika Gagnon has given a lovely reading of this piece in "Al Fannanah'l Rassamah: The Work of Jamelie Hassan," *Third Text*, 7 (Summer 1989).

2 Foucault, "The Ethic of Care," pp. 113–114.

3 Jacques Derrida, "Restitution of the Truth in Painting (*pointure*)," p. 314. The following two passages are from pp. 255, 292–293.

4 "Size" was the word chosen for *pointure* in the first translation of "Restitution de la vérité en pointure," by John P. Leavey, Jr. published in *Research in Phenomenology*, 8 (1978). In the later translation, included in *The Truth in Painting*, Geoffrey Bennington and Ian McLeod chose the equally appropriate "pointing." For my purposes, I have retained "size" here.

5 Interview with Diane Nemiroff, in catalogue essay for "Songs of Experience," National Gallery of Canada, Ottawa, May 2–September 1, 1986, p. 101.

6 For a brilliant account of the manipulation of "truthspeak" in museum space, see Mieke Bal, "Showing, Telling, Showing Off," *Critical Inquiry*, 18:3 (Spring 1992): pp. 568, 579.

7 Michel Foucault and Ludwig Binswanger, *Dream and Existence*, p. 44.

8 Most of the phrases quoted here were spoken by the participants in the Symposium.

9 For the Hegelian epistemograph, see Spivak, "Time and Timing: Law and History," in John Bender and David Wellbery, eds., *Chronotypes: The Construction of Time* (Stanford: Stanford University Press, 1991), p. 100.

10 Martin Heidegger, "The Origin of the Work of Art," in *Poetry, Language, and Thought*, trans. Albert Hofstadter (New York: Harper, 1975), pp. 17–87.

11 Emmanuel Levinas, *Time and the Other*, trans. Richard A. Cohen (Pittsburgh:

Duquesne University Press, 1987), and Johannes Fabian, *Time and the Other* (New York: Columbia University Press, 1983).

12 See Spivak, "Imagining Academic Freedom in Gendered Post-Coloniality" (Cape Town: University of Cape Town Press, 1992).

13 For the museal manipulation of racism among humans by deploying racial difference (and sameness) between human and animal see Bal, "Showing, Telling," p. 565f.

Chapter 11: Reading *The Satanic Verses*

1 Salman Rushdie, *The Satanic Verses* (New York: Viking, 1989). Page references have been included in the text after the initial letters *SV*.

2 Peter Bürger, *Theory of the Avant-Garde,* trans. Michael Shaw (Minneapolis: University of Minnesota Press, 1984), pp. 25–27.

3 James Atlas, "What is Fukuyama Saying? (Francis Fukuyama on the End of History)," *New York Times Magazine* (October 22, 1989).

4 Roland Barthes, "The Death of the Author," trans. Stephen Heath, *Image-Music-Text* (New York: Hill and Wang, 1977), p. 148. The following quotation is from the same page.

5 Barthes, "The Death of the Author," pp. 145–146.

6 Michel Foucault, "What is an Author?," in *Language, Counter-Memory, Practice: Selected Essays and Interviews,* trans. Donald F. Bouchard and Sherry Simon (Ithaca: Cornell University Press, 1977).

7 Barbara Johnson, *The Critical Difference: Essays in the Contemporary Rhetoric of Reading* (Baltimore: The Johns Hopkins University Press, 1981).

8 Jacques Derrida, "Otobiographies: The Teaching of Nietzsche and the Politics of the Proper Name," in *The Ear of the Other.*

9 Derrida, "Otobiographies," p. 10.

10 Salman Rushdie, " . . ." *Granta,* 28, Birthday Issue (Autumn 1989): p. 29. For reasons of security, I presume, this poem is irreproducible.

11 Derrida, "Otobiographies," p. 11.

12 For a somewhat tendentious but intriguing genealogy of "magical realism," see Jeffrey Hart, *Reactionary Modernism: Technology, Culture, and Politics in Weimar and the Third Reich* (Cambridge: Cambridge University Press, 1984).

13 Timothy Bennan, *Salman Rushdie and the Third World: Myths of the Nation* (London: Macmillan, 1989). Perhaps because of his clear-cut position on the nation, Mr. Brennan is weak in the representation of the place of the novel in the Indian literary traditions (pp. 18, 79–80). Incidentally, Arjuna and Bhima are completely human characters in an epic, not "figures in the Hindu pantheon" (p. 109). Rushdie's use of Hindu material gives us a sense of the nonsanctimonious "secularism" which is a fact of the subcontinental everyday. It does matter in that context that we distinguish between Achilles and Zeus, and not call both gods. Mr. Brennan's sense that *Midnight's Children* put "the Indo-English imagination on the map" (p. 80) is a step ahead of Alan Yentob's inspired polarization of India/Pakistan and the West as "oral tradition" and the "modern novel"! (Lisa Appignanesi and Sara Maitland, eds., *The Rushdie File* [London:

Fourth Estate, 1989], p. 197.) In Macaulay's day, Arabic and Sanskrit writing at least filled a school library shelf. With friends like these!

14 Rushdie, "Interview with Sean French," *File*, p. 9.

15 I feel solidarity with men who let women in. But I cannot see this gesture as the performance of feminism. On this particular point, I must take exception even from my friend Srinivas Aravamudan's outstanding essay, a full-dress scholarly treatment of the novel. To create women as "strong characters" is not necessarily to "pursue . . . [t]he issue of *feminism* and Islam" (" 'Being God's Postman Is No Fun, Yaar': Salman Rushdie's *The Satanic Verses*," *Diacritics*, 19:ii [Summer 1989]: p. 13; emphasis mine). And it is here that I must also split from Rukmini Bhaya Nair's impressive "Text and Pre-Text: History as Gossip in Rushdie's Novels": "The Prophet's own intellectual, moral, and practical dilemmas are brought closer to use through his wives, Khadijah and Ayesha, who implicitly believed in him, and the (un)common whores of Jahilia who imitated every move of the women proximate to the Prophet. Through the gossip of women, we come to a truer understanding of the 'sinuous complexities of history.' Public facts alone are insufficient and unconvincing" (*Economic and Political Weekly*, 24:13 [May 6, 1989]: p. 997). That private-public divide is old gender-coding. We must set these things on the move.

I repeat, I support men who make the effort. And it is in that spirit that I quote here my translation of a poem, just in from Bangladesh, by Farhad Mazhar, a secularist Muslim poet, where a desire is recorded and the possibility of an alternative history is glimpsed in a counterfactual complement. I have commented at greater length on such counterfactual moves in Chapter 3. I quote Mazhar's poem in full because I doubt the reader of this book would otherwise have access to the work of this considerable poet-activist:

I write these verse in Mistress Khadija's name:
I'll not say bismillah, just take her name.
Lord, permit me. No anger, please, just once.
In her name, I'll write my poem, Lord of Praise.

Dear Prophet's name? No, his name neither, boss.
Just'n Khadija's name—in exquisite Khadija's name
For once I'll forget all other names on earth
Forget you too, forget my Prophet.

Only she, Lord, only in her wage work
Was my dear Prophet ensconced, rapt with camel and trade.
Don't show off—he was your beloved,
But for her, a salaried worker—
All women know you are puny here
But don't show it abroad for respect's sake.

16 This is the productive unease in Fredric Jameson, "Third World Literature in the Era of Multinational Capitalism," *Social Text* 15 (1986).

17 Deleuze and Guattari, *Anti-Oedipus*, pp. 5, 36. See also p. 12.

18 For the notion of biography—the staging of the author is part of this—see Derrida, "Otobiographies," cited at the opening of this chapter. For Schreber, see Sigmund

Freud, "Psychoanalytic Notes on an Autobiographical Account of a Case of Paranoia (*Dementia Paranoides*)," *Standard Edition*, vol. 12.

19 David Erdman, *Blake, Prophet Against Empire: A Poet's Interpretation of the History of His Own Times*, 3rd ed. (Princeton: Princeton University Press, 1977).

20 J.L. Austin, *How to Do Things With Words* (Oxford: Oxford University Press, 1965), pp. 22–22; quoted in Derrida, "Signature Event Context," in *Limited, Inc.*, p. 16.

21 Nair, "Text and Pre-Text," p. 995.

22 *Ibid.*, p. 1000.

23 Spivak, "Subaltern Studies: Deconstructing Historiography," in *In Other Worlds*.

24 The phrase "criticism by hearsay," used in an academic context, comes from Paul de Man, "The Resistance to Theory," in *The Resistance to Theory* (Minneapolis: University of Minnesota Press, 1986), p. 15.

25 Aziz Al-Azmeh, "More on *The Satanic Verses*," *Frontier*, 21:25 (February 4, 1989): p. 6.

26 Appignanesi, *File*, is, of course, now a much more extensive source.

27 Gita Sahgal, "Transgression Comes of Age," *Interlink*, 12 (May–June 1989): p. 19. I am grateful to Peter Osborne and John Kraniauskas for help in assembling this dossier.

28 "Dubious Defenders," *Economic and Political Weekly*, 24:17 (April 29, 1989): p. 894. Ali A. Mazrui strikes a similar chord in "The Moral Dilemma of Salman Rushdie's *Satanic Verses*," in Appignanesi, ed., *File*.

29 Wole Soyinka, "Jihad for Freedom," *Index on Censorship*, 18:5 (May–June, 1989): p. 20. All references to *Index* are to this issue.

30 "Identities on Parade: A Conversation," *Marxism Today* (June 1989): p. 27.

31 "Open Letter to Rajiv Gandhi," *New York Times* (October 19, 1988). Since then, Rushdie's relationship to declarations of faith have taken many situational turns.

32 Rajewari Sunder Rajan and Zakia Pathak, " 'Shahbano,' " *Signs*, 14:3 (Spring 1989): pp. 558–559, 572.

33 Sunder Rajan and Pathak, " 'Shahbano,' " p. 573. Emphasis mine.

34 Sunder Rajan and Pathak, " 'Shahbano,' " pp. 576–577.

35 For *pharmakon*, see Jacques Derrida, "Plato's Pharmacy," in *Dissemination*.

36 Sahgal, "Transgression," p. 19.

37 Albert Memmi, "For Secularism," *Index*, p. 18.

38 Farzaneh Asari, "Iran in the British Media," *Index*, p. 11.

39 Mehmet Ali Dikerdem, "Rushdie, Islam and 'Islam,' " *End*, 37 (June 1989): p. 4.

40 For another view see Afsaneh Najmabadi, "Interview with Gayatri Spivak," *Social Text*, 9:3 (1991): p. 122–134.

41 The first quotation is from Donna Haraway, "The Biopolitics of Postmodern Bodies: Determination of the Self in Immune System Discourse," *differences*, 1:1 (Winter 1989): p. 10. All quotations from Asari are from "Iran in the British Media."

42 The most astute discussion of the inaccessibility of the absolutely other is still Jacques Derrida, "Violence and Metaphysics." For a powerful feminist reading, see Luce Irigaray, "The Fecundity of the Caress," discussed in Chapter Seven.

43 Sahgal, "Transgression," p. 19.

44 For an extended discussion of this, see my forthcoming study of Peter Dickinson's *The Poison Oracle*.

45 For an astute practical account of this coding, see Barbara Epstein, "The Reagan Doctrine and Right-Wing Democracy," *Socialist Review*, 19:1 (January–March 1989). The dynamics of this coding has gone into many global moves since this writing.

46 Emily Prayer, "Rushdie Judgment," *Village Voice*, 34:10 (March 7, 1987): p. 23. The conduct of the Anglo-U.S. publishing world is undoubtedly an important matter. But to reduce the Rushdie affair to nothing but an assessment of that conduct is typically ethnocentric.

47 As I have argued in Najmabadi, "Interview," the British dossier shows that in Britain, as opposed to the U.S., this critical recoding is strongly present. It is significant that Peter Porter, can write as follows in so establishment an organ as the *Times Literary Supplement*:

> . . . sincerity proves to be not enough. . . . Everything is Westernized so that the differences between the Christian and Imperial bigotry faced by Molière and Voltaire, and the underdog upsurge of today's Islamic crowd are ignored. . . . It cannot have been [Tony] Harrison's intention, but some of the scenes and part of the commentary [in *The Blasphemer's Banquet* on BBC1's *Byline*] took on a racist tone—our Christian heritage, it seemed to say, is falling to the Crescent of Islam (August 11–17, 1989).

51 The classic analysis of the representation of Islam is, of course, Edward W. Said, *Covering Islam: How the Media and the Experts Determine How We See the Rest of the World* (New York: Pantheon, 1981).

49 W.B. Yeats, "Two Songs from a Play." Arasooghly, who is a filmmaker and teacher of Film Studies at Northeastern University, gives a much more detailed account than I have been able to quote. Where I summarize, the interpretation is necessarily my own. "The Fatwa" section of Appignanesi, ed., *File*, supports her point of view. See especially pp. 95, 106. The *Observer*, Bombay, had this to say two days after the Bombay killings: "It has not only helped [the Ayatollah] upstage his opponents in Iran who are harking for change, but also in realizing an impossible dream—through his kill Rushdie fatwa, he has succeeded in some extent to cutting across the Shia-Sunni divide and assuming the posture of the tallest leader within the global community of Muslim fraternity, forcing more level-headed Islamic leaders to stand up and be counted" (p. 132). Interestingly, Iqbal Wahhab, a more "level-headed Muslim," writing from Britain one day *before* the riot, had questioned that authority: "A negligible proportion of the Muslim population in Britain is Shia, and the Ayatollah's call had, by and large, fallen on deaf ears in this country. To Sunnis, he has no authority to make such a threat" (p. 129). See also Engineer, et al., "Dubious Defenders," *Economic and Political Weekly*, 894.

50 Michel de Certeau, "The Formality of Practices: From Religious Systems to the Ethics of the Enlightenment (the Seventeenth and Eighteenth Centuries)," in *The Writing of History* (New York: Columbia University Press, 1988). All passages from de Certeau are from this chapter. Page references have been included in the text following the initials MDC.

51 See especially Jacques Derrida, *Glas,* the left-hand column; and M.H. Abrams, *Natural Supernaturalism* (New York: Norton, 1971).

52 I have tried to tell her story in "Reading the Archives: The Rani of Sirmur."

Chapter 12: *Sammy and Rosie Get Laid*

1 I am grateful for Professor Jean Franco for this insight.

2 Spivak, "The Burden of English," in Rajeswari Sunder Rajan, ed., *The Lie of the Land: English Literary Studies in India* (Delhi: Oxford University Press, 1991).

3 Raymond Williams, "The Bloomsbury Fraction," *Problems in Materialism and Culture* (London: Verso, 1980), p. 165.

4 bell hooks, *Yearning: Race, Gender, and Cultural Politics* (Boston: South End, 1990), p. 158.

5 Reflected for the moment in Spivak, "Teaching for the Times," *MMLA Quarterly* (Spring 1992).

6 Andrew Milner, *John Milton and the English Revolution: A Study in the Sociology of Literature* (Basingstoke: Macmillan, 1981).

7 Stuart Hall, "The Rediscovery of 'Ideology': The Return of the Repressed in Media Studies," in M. Gurevitch, T. Bennett, J. Curran, and J. Woollacott, eds., *Culture, Society and the Media* (London: Methuen, 1982).

8 Gilles Deleuze, *Cinema 1: Movement-Image,* trans. Hugh Tomlinson and Barbara Habberjam (Minneapolis: University of Minnesota Press, 1986), pp. 8–11.

9 Richard Miller, *Analyzing Marx* (Ithaca: Cornell University Press, 1984), pp. 15–97.

10 Spivak, "*Glas*-piece: A Compte-rendu," *Diacritics,* 7:3 (Fall 1977).

11 See the "Hinduism" issue of the Indian journal *Seminar* (September 1985).

12 Theodor Adorno, "Commitment," in *The Essential Frankfurt School Reader,* pp. 300–318.

Chapter 13: Scattered Speculations on the Question of Culture Studies

1 Vandana Shiva, *Ecology and the Politics of Survival: Conflicts over Natural Resources in India* (London: Sage, 1991), p. 10.

2 Shiva, *Ecology,* p. 327.

3 I am grateful to Professor Ackerman for allowing me to refer to then unpublished work, now published as *We the People* (Cambridge: Harvard University Press, 1991). My references are to the manuscript.

4 Elizabeth G. Cohen and Joan Benton, "Making Groupwork Work," *American Educator,* 12:3 (Fall 1988): pp. 11–12.

5 E.D. Hirsch, Jr., *Cultural Literacy: What Every American Needs to Know* (New York: Vintage Books, 1987), and the recent directive for a 50-hour curriculum by Lynn Cheney, the director of the National Endowment for the Humanities are two tremendously influential examples.

6 Jean Baudrillard, "The Precession of Simulacra," in *Simulations,* trans. Paul Foss, et al. (New York: Semiotext(e), 1983).

7   Jean-François Lyotard, *The Postmodern Condition: A Report on Knowledge,* trans. Geoff Bennington and Brian-Massumi (Minneapolis: University of Minnesota Press, 1984).

8   Robin Blackburn, *The Overthrow of Colonial Slavery 1776–1848* (London: Verso, 1988). The quoted passage is from pp. 123–124.

9   Arthur Berridale Keith, *A Constitutional History of India: 1600–1935,* 2nd ed. (London: Methuen, 1937), p. 1.

10   Adam Smith, *An Inquiry into the Nature and Causes of the Wealth of Nations* (Chicago: University of Chicago Press, 1976), vol. 2, pp. 150–151. Ranajit Guha, *A Rule of Property for Bengal,* pp. 62n.2, 45, 75, 76.

11   This section relies on Maxime Rodinson, *Islam and Capitalism,* trans. Brian Pearce (Austin: University of Texas Press, 1978) and Kemal H. Kerpat, *An Inquiry into the Social Foundations of Nationalism in the Ottoman State: From Social Estates to Classes, from Millets to Nations* (Princeton: Princeton University Research Monograph No. 39, 1973). I have followed through their English-language documentation as far as possible. I am also grateful to Dr. Aysegul Baykan and Dr. Mehmet Ali Dikerdem.

12   Two impassioned exhortations against such tendencies are Perry Anderson, "Appendix," *Lineages of the Absolutist State* (London: Verso, 1974) and Edward W. Said, *Covering Islam.*

13   Kerpat, *Inquiry,* p. 52. See also 57f. Quotations in the following paragraph are from pp. 55, 92.

14   Extract from a speech by Atatruk, quoted in Rodinson, *Islam,* p. 127.

15   That moral fervor itself has often served as alibi, "It [the pursuit of happiness] was developed into a supra-natural secular ideology first in the form of the 'liberal-humanitarian' ideology (to use Mannheim's terminology), with mobilizing forms such as French Jacobinism, in a number of countries (including the East) and in a variety of periods. . . . But the use made of this ideology to provide cover for domination by the powers of money, and especially by American 'Big Business,' and also to disguise domination by Europe, has done it a very great deal of harm," Rodinson, *Islam,* p. 234. This is of course rather an obvious point. I am always surprised to note how often it bears repeating. My source here is Rodinson because I am using him as one of my main secondary texts.

16   Rodinson, *Islam,* p. 231.

17   At this writing the *New York Times* for Sunday, November 12, 1989, offered a series of rough maps of the area around East Germany in order to clue the reader into the nationalist-political movements after *glasnost.* It is interesting to watch the emergence and the disappearance of the word "Ottoman" between the explanatory material of the second and third frames (1933 to 1943!). If at all noticed, it stands in for a barely noticed prehistory for the U.S. reader careful enough to notice.

18   See Gail Minault, *The Khilafat Movement: Religious Symbolism and Political Mobilization in India* (New York: Columbia University Press, 1982).

19   See Maurice Gwyer and A. Appadorai, eds., *Speeches and Documents on the Indian Constitution* (New York: Oxford University Press, 1957). See also Granville Austin, *The Indian Constitution: Cornerstone of a Nation* (Bombay: Oxford University Press, 1972).

20   *Turkey*, No. 2 (1877): *Correspondence Respecting the Conference at Constantinople and the Affairs of Turkey, 1876–1877* (London: Harrison and Sons, 1877).

21   Helen Miller Davis, *Constitutions, Electoral Laws, Treaties of States in the Near and Middle East* (Durham: Duke University Press, 1953).

22   Bert P. Blaustein and Gisbert H. Flanz, eds., *Constitutions of the Countries of the World* (New York: Oceana, 1976), p. 4.

23   For a discussion of the paired modes of production, see Samir Amin, *Unequal Development*, trans. Brian Pearce (New York: Monthly Review Press, 1976), p. 21. The link is also between Virginia and New England.

24   For a study of communalism in India, see Bipan Chandra, *Communalism in Modern India* (New Dehli: Vikas, 1984). The following remark appeared in "The Week in Review," *New York Times,* (October 15, 1989): "Many Indians say the legislature's importance has been declining for two decades, first under Prime Minister Indira Ghandhi and now under her son Rajiv. . . . A leading social scientist, Rajni Kothari, said in a recent interview that the five years of Mr. Gandhi's Government 'have been, institutionally, the worst in Indian history.' " The *New York Times* is not a scholarly organ, but it does reflect ideological trends. And Mr. Kothari is indeed a social scientist of stature. (The massive changes in the Indian polity in the last four years cannot be indicated by updating a footnote.)

25   Jacques Derrida, "Declarations of Independence," trans. Tom Keenan and Tom Pepper, New Political Science 15 (Summer 1986). The first quoted sentence is on p. 10.

26   Derrida, "Declarations of Independence," pp. 9–11. I have rearranged the word order slightly in order to make coherent extrapolations.

27   Atlas, "What is Fukuyama Saying?"

28   Rodinson, *Islam,* pp. xxiii, xxv, xxvi.

29   Rodinson, *Islam,* p. xv.

30   Rodinson, *Islam,* p. 2.

31   Derrida, "Declarations," p. 11.

32   Derrida, "Declarations," p. 12.

33   For a somewhat schematic view on this from the disciplinary perspective of history, see Charles Bright and Michael Gyer, "For a Unified History of the World in the Twentieth Century," *Radical History Review,* 39 (1987): pp. 69–91.

34   See Spivak, "Teaching for the Times."

35   Hirsch, *Cultural Literacy,* p. 164.

36   Barry Hindess and Paul Q. Hirst, *An Auto-Critique of the Pre-Capitalist Modes of Production* (Atlantic Highlands, N.J.: 1987), p. 58.

37   *Ibid.,* p. 59. I should add that my practical conclusions from the positions shared with these two authors are very different from those drawn by them.

38   C3, p. 959. For a sense of how important the calculation is, see David R. Roediger and Philip S. Foner, *Our Own Time: A History of American Labor and the Working Day* (New York: Greenwood Press, 1989).

39   This is a somewhat parochial United States list. Any consideration of global postcoloniality will have to include diasporas.

40 H.P. Marquand, *Women and Thomas Harrow* (Boston: Little, Brown, 1958), p. 92.

41 Elaine Showalter, *A Literature of Their Own: British Women Novelists from Brontë to Lessing* (Princeton: Princeton University Press, 1976); Jane P. Tompkins, *Sensational Designs: The Cultural Work of American Fiction, 1790–1860* (New York: Oxford University Press, 1985).

42 bell hooks, *Ain't I a Woman? Black Women and Feminism* (Boston: South End Press, 1984), and *Talking Black: Thinking Feminist, Thinking Black* (Boston: South End Press, 1989); Hazel V. Carby, *Reconstructing Womanhood: The Emergence of the Afro-American Novelist* (New York: Oxford University Press, 1987).

43 Mary Helen Washington, *Black-Eyed Susans—Midnight Birds* (New York: Anchor Books, 1990). The quoted passage is from Deleuze and Guattari, *Anti-Oedipus*, pp. 308–309.

44 Henry Louis Gates, Jr., *The Signifying Monkey: A Theory of Afro-American Literary Criticism* (New York: Oxford University Press, 1988); as ed., *Black Literature and Literary Theory* (New York: Methuen, 1984) and *The Schomburg Library of Nineteenth-Century Black Women Writers* (New York: Oxford University Press, 1988).

45 Stuart Hall, *The Hard Road to Renewal: Thatcherism and the Crisis of the Left* (New York: Verso, 1988).

46 Jonathan Rée, *Proletarian Philosophers: Problems in Socialist Culture in Britain, 1900–1940* (Oxford: Oxford University Press, 1984).

47 Nancy Fraser's important article, "Solidarity or Singularity? Richard Rorty Behind Romanticism and Technocracy," *Praxis International*, 8:3 (October 1988): pp. 256–283, still remains a list of ingredients, not, as it claims to be, a "recipe."

48 Edward Said makes this point in a general way in "Traveling Theory," in his *The World, the Text, and the Critic* (Cambridge, Mass.: Harvard University Press, 1983), pp. 226–247. I would extend "theory" to include general instruction in the great European watershed theorists like Marx and Freud outside of the context of intellectual history.

49 Pierre Bourdieu, *Homo Academicus*, trans. Peter Collier (Oxford: Oxford University Press, 1988).

50 For the relationship between "theory" and literary criticism, see the introductory chapter of Rodolphe Gasché, *The Tain of the Mirror: Derrida and the Philosophy of Reflection* (Cambridge, Mass.: Harvard University Press, 1986).

51 We need no longer merely think of this but read Edward Said's study of this novel in *Culture and Imperialism* (New York: Knopf, 1993).

52 Perry Anderson, *Lineages of the Absolutist State*, p. 549.

53 Samir Amin, *Unequal Development: An Essay on the Social Formations of Peripheral Capitalism*, trans. Brian Pearce (New York: Monthly Review Press, 1976), p. 369.

54 See Aysegul Baykan, "Modernism, Fundamentalism, and the Women in Between" (paper presented at the 1989 ASA Conference).

55 Jeffrey C. Goldfarb, "The Age of Dissent: Democracy Crashes Party," *Village Voice Literary Supplement* (October 1989).

56 Petchesky, *Abortion and Woman's Choice*, p. vii.

Index

334 / Outside in the Teaching Machine

Shame (Rushdie), 2
Shiites, 238
Shiva, Vandana, 256, 277
Showalter, Elaine, 140, 272
Signs, 283
Siva, 184
Slavery: and political economy, 261–62; and Constitution, 262; literature of, 273
Smart, Barry, on Marx and Foucalt, 299n
Smith, Adam, 262
Smith, Barbara H., 295n
Smith, Steven B., 295n
Souleymane, Cisse, 64
Southall Black Sisters, 228, 240
Soyinka, Wole: on the Salman Rusdie death sentence, 229, 235, 236
Speech and Phenomena (Derrida), 103
Spurs (Derrida), 125–26
Sri Lankan Civil War, 122
Storra, Benjamin, 212
Subaltern, the: literature of, 8–9; in postcolonialism, 63; and colonialism, 78; space of ,78; heterogeneity of, 79; relation to historiographic metalepsis and the effect of the subject, 286n
Subaltern Studies Group, 3, 4, 14
Supreme Court of India, 230–31
Sussex, University of, 251

Talmud, The, 173
Tagore, Rabindrath, 223
Tanner, Alain, 64
Taylor, Charles, 43
Teaching: and marginality, 53–76; and revolutionary practices, 53; and cultural identity, 54; of cultural studies, 255–284
Teheran, demonstrations in, 233
Thatcher, Margaret, 251, 273
Thé au harem d'Archemide (Charif), 64
Theories of Surplus Value (Marx), 62
Theory in literary criitcism, teaching of, 275–76

Thinking Reed, The (Kagarlitsky), 298n
Third World: and essentialism, 12–13; paradigmatic literary styles of, 57–58; teaching literature of, 277
Thomas, Dylan, 182
Thompson, Robert Farris, 211, 215
Through Our Own Eyes (Brett), 94
Times Literary Supplement, 318–19n
Todorov, Tzvetan, 295n
Tompkins, Jane, 272
"Traffic in Women, The" (Rubin), 16
Translation: and the agent, 179; as reading, 180–194; as surrender to the text, 183; of Bengali, 185–87; and women, 186–94; and the migrant, 192–97; and postcolonialism, 197–200
Transnational Culture Studies, 262, 284
Truth in Painting (Bennington/McLeod), 315n
Turkey: Ottoman empire, 238, 263–65; trade on Black Sea, 263; compared to U. S. in 1798, 264; Constitution of 1876, 264–65; of 1924, 265–66; compared with U.S. Constitution, 267

Umma, the, 264
Ummayad dynasty, 238
Une flame dans le couer (Tanner), 64
United States: Constitution of, 258–60, 261; compared with Turkish Constitutions, 266–67; Reconstruction period, 258; *Roe v. Wade* and Equal rights Amendment, 279, 284; morphology of "We the People", 258–261, 284; mainstream feminism in, 4; as the Great Satan, 238
Use of Pleasure, The (Foucalt), 308n

Valéry, Paul, 111–13
Value, 61–64
Vattimo, Gianni, 304n
Visual art, 201–216
Viswanathan, Gauri, 276